MAGISTER AMORIS

FOR MALCOLM
maistre, enseigneur et famillier

Magister amoris

The *Roman de la Rose* and Vernacular Hermeneutics

ALASTAIR MINNIS

OXFORD
UNIVERSITY PRESS

OXFORD
UNIVERSITY PRESS

Great Clarendon Street, Oxford OX2 6DP

Oxford University Press is a department of the University of Oxford.
It furthers the University's objective of excellence in research, scholarship,
and education by publishing worldwide in

Oxford New York

Athens Auckland Bangkok Bogotá Buenos Aires Cape Town
Chennai Dar es Salaam Delhi Florence Hong Kong Istanbul Karachi
Kolkata Kuala Lumpur Madrid Melbourne Mexico City Mumbai
Nairobi Paris São Paulo Shanghai Singapore Taipei Tokyo Toronto Warsaw

and associated companies in Berlin Ibadan

Oxford is a registered trade mark of Oxford University Press
in the UK and in certain other countries

Published in the United States
by Oxford University Press Inc., New York

British Library Cataloguing in Publication Data

Data available

Library of Congress Cataloging in Publication Data
Minnis, A. J. (Alastair J.)
Magister amoris: the Roman de la rose and vernacular hermeneutics/Alastair J. Minnis.
p. cm.
Includes bibliographical references and index.
1. Guillaume, de Lorris, fl. 1230. Roman de la Rose. 2. Jean, de Meun, d.
1305?—Criticism and interpretation. 3. Sex in literature. 4. Love in literature. I. Title.
PQ1528.M56 2001 841′.1—dc21 00-065228

ISBN 0-19-818754-8

1 3 5 7 9 10 8 6 4 2

Typeset in Sabon by
Cambrian Typesetters, Frimley, Surrey
Printed in Great Britain
on acid-free paper by
Biddles Ltd, Guildford and King's Lynn

100306191 1

Preface

'Tu . . . mervilleusement interpretes ce qui est dit clerement et a
la lectre,' exclaims an exasperated Christine de Pizan at one
point to Pierre Col. Her opponent is interpreting in a marvellous
and incredible way a part of the *Roman de la Rose* which to her
is perfectly obvious and literally clear. Many of the *Rose*'s readers, both ancient and modern, have shared those feelings of
exasperation and conviction, in the face of yet another interpretation of that most challenging and elusive of medieval texts.

This study seeks to elucidate the intellectual purchase of
different medieval understandings of the *Rose*, my fundamental
assumption being that the poem admits of various and varied
reading, indeed invites them. A further assumption is that these
readings made sense within medieval culture: and I have sought
the various senses which were made. Medieval literary theory,
as channelled by the glosses and commentaries on the authoritative Latin texts, or *auctores*, which were studied in medieval
classrooms, was a major resource upon which the *Rose*'s interpreters drew, whether they proffered commendation or condemnation. And some of its characteristic discourses had played a
major part in the writing of the poem itself. In sum, I believe
that such theory was of crucial importance in the formation and
reception of the *Rose*.

At the centre of this inquiry is, inevitably, Ovidius Publius
Naso—an *auctor* of pre-eminent significance for vernacular
poetics. Exegesis of his poetry by generations of medieval
'masters' of grammar (and indeed of higher-status disciplines)
effected the fabrication of a *magisterium amoris*, the office or
profession of teacher about love, a vocation which was viewed
with considerable irony and had great potential for both earnest
and game. It could also provoke extreme hostility. This mock-
magisterium was appropriated by vernacular writers—among
whom, I believe, Jean de Meun ranks as the most outstanding—
who found in the old master an almost inexhaustible source and
stimulus for ideas not only about sexuality but also about a

wide range of human activities and aspirations. Being a medieval *magister amoris* might mean, for example, enlisting the Roman *praeceptor* in the ranks of the satirists, reworking and reinterpreting his rich mythology, exhibiting his character creations either *in bono* or *in malo*, amplifying or diminishing his most misogynistic statements, or containing his powerful evocation of human desire within an affirmation of the natural valence and economic advantages of marriage as an essential part of the 'active life'.

Interpretation of Ovid's text and gloss by Jean de Meun *cum suis* will be placed within the wider context of European vernacular hermeneutics. The movement of the discourses of literary theory from Latin into the emergent vernaculars resulted in a rich array of continuities and beginnings, contiguities and transformations. Sometimes exegesis in Italian, French and Spanish seemed to be carrying on the business of Latin commentary; on other occasions it posed and faced fresh challenges. Furthermore, on the one hand the relationship between text and gloss was perceived as disjunctive, dichotomous: even when writers provided commentary on their own poems they tended to construct themselves as anonymous scholars living in the margins of their own texts (for the very good reason that this impersonal display of sound doctrine intimated that the object of commentary deserved a place within the canon of authoritative literature). On the other, the relationship could be perceived as interactive, particularly when translation (of the original Latin text into the vernacular) was concerned: translation was described as the exposition of meaning in another language.

Then again, vernacular hermeneutics operated within and around texts. Within, inasmuch as glosses both text-specific and theoretical served the very dynamic of the vernacular work, supplying everything from cursory explanations of obscure materials to generic parameters and didactic purposes. Our primary example of this is, of course, Jean de Meun's part of the *Rose*. Around, in the sense that Latin commentary provided both models and materials for 'new' and vernacular commentary: exceptional scholars set about providing glosses on contemporary writers and indeed on their own productions, affording those *moderni* attention and respect of a kind hitherto reserved for the *antiqui*. The quarrel over the *Rose* was heavily indebted to conventions of Latin commentary on grammatical *auctores*, particularly Ovid, and indeed (to a lesser extent) to biblical commentary, two parallel traditions which in medieval Tuscany first Dante and subsequently Petrarch and Boccaccio were to bring together to such transformative effect. However, no scholar attempted a formal, blow-by-blow commentary on the *Rose* itself. Sporadic glossing may indeed be found in certain manuscripts of the *Rose*, but no systematic exposition was produced. The earlier reception of the poem is marked rather by extensive textual revision, ranging from small-scale—but often highly significant—*abbreviatio* and *amplificatio* to the more ambitious interventions of writers who present themselves as its new authors. (By contrast, the trecento Dante–commentators regarded the *Comedy* as a 'hermeneutically sealed' text, to be commented upon rather than entered into.) It was the distinction of a later poem, a composition which had attempted to prune many of the *Rose*'s excesses, to become the first original French text to have a full-scale French commentary written on it. Evrart de Conty's sophisticated commentary on the *Eschez amoureux* is a major monument of vernacular hermeneutics, and a fitting testimony to the spirit of the age of Charles V, even though it actually saw the light of day after the king's death.

The many disappointments of the reign of Charles VI, including a decline in state-sponsored hermeneutics, are a salutary reminder of just how important the right political conditions were for the promotion of the vernacular literatures and of the literary criticism which accompanied them. Neither should 'humanism' be regarded as the inevitable friend and fellow-traveller of those developing literatures. Jakob Burckhardt believed that the imitation of classical Latin and the development of the vernacular languages were defining features of the Renaissance, a claim recently echoed by a distinguished scholar of fifteenth-century French humanism, Gilbert Ouy. This is no doubt true at the level of general principle, but in practice those two developments could contest and challenge each other—as in fifteenth-century Italy, when new expositions of that most important of all the 'new authors', Dante, were few and far between, in marked contrast to the fourteenth century, when Dante

commentary enjoyed its golden age. The trajectory of vernacular hermeneutics from Middle Ages to Renaissance was neither
direct nor unimpeded.

Here, then, is the context of vernacular hermeneutics within
which I wish to locate the *Rose* and its reception. In pursuing
this research, I have benefited enormously from the intellectual
stimulus of the University of York's Centre for Medieval
Studies, and a special word of thanks is due to Dr Andy Tudor
of the Department of Sociology. A particular debt is owed to
Professor Simon Gaunt (of King's College, London) who read
the entire manuscript in penultimate form and made many
astute suggestions for improvement, as an official reader for
Oxford University Press. (I also wish to thank the anonymous
readers who reviewed the project for OUP at the initial stage,
for their support and constructive suggestions.) Helpful
comments were also provided by Dr Rosalind Brown-Grant
(Leeds) and Dr Ian Johnson (St Andrews). During my time as
Distinguished Visiting Professor in Medieval Studies at the
University of California at Berkeley, Professors David Hult,
Ralph Hexter, and Albert Ascoli also read my typescript—I am
most grateful for their warm encouragement and good counsel.

Earlier versions of some of the discussions included in this
book have previously appeared in published papers, and so I
must acknowledge with gratitude the reprinting permissions as
obtained from the following publishers: Boydell and Brewer Ltd
(Woodbridge), E. J. Brill (Leiden), Yushodo Press Co., Ltd
(Tokyo), and the Centre for Late Antique and Medieval Studies
of King's College, London. Chapter 4 contains materials—heavily revised and amplified—originally published in: 'A Rose by
Many Names: Jean de Meun's Competition of Genres', in
Barbara Frank, Thomas Haye, and Doris Tophinke (eds.),
Gattungen mittelalterlichen Schiftlichkeit. Tübingen: Narr
1997. © 1997 Gunter Narr Verlag Tübingen. Pp. 183–99. The
photograph incorporated into the jacket design is used with the
permission of the Bibliothèque Nationale, Paris.

*

This book is dedicated to Dr Malcolm Parkes, who did so much
to inspire and assist me in my days as a postgraduate student at

Oxford University (where I studied as a 'Migrant Graduate' in pursuit of a doctoral degree from the Queen's University of Belfast, an institution which—to my enduring gratitude—sanctioned my faith in the existence and importance of medieval literary theory). After Malcolm had gone to work on it, my prose style was never the same again, though he is certainly not to blame for any blemishes in the present book. Fortunately, in the early 1970s we shared a relish (and had the stamina) for intellectual engagements which would begin around midnight and continue into the small hours of the morning. In this atmosphere of intellectual excitement and sleep deprivation my ambition to be a medievalist was consolidated, the lure of Anglo-Irish literature being resisted (albeit with many regrets). To borrow words from Pierre Col's eulogy of Jean de Meun: thank you, Malcolm, *maistre, enseigneur et famillier.*

Contents

ABBREVIATIONS   xiii

INTRODUCTION: MAISTRE JEHAN DE MEUN
AND THE *MAGISTERIUM AMORIS*   1

1. ACADEMIC PROLOGUES TO OVID AND THE
   VERNACULAR ART OF LOVE   35
   Textual transformations: Jacques d'Amiens,
      the *Confort d'amour*, Guiart   39
   Scholia secularized: *L'Art d'amours*   44
   Sex and the sermon-prologue: Juan Ruiz and
      Richard de Fournival   62

2. LIFTING THE VEIL: SEXUAL/TEXTUAL
   NAKEDNESS IN THE *ROMAN DE LA ROSE*   82
   Competing theoretical discourses: allegorical
      covering *versus* satiric stripping   87
   Ovid among the satirists   99
   Ovid unveiled   104
   Integumanz at last: the garments of Genius   108

3. *PARLER PROPREMENT*: WORDS, DEEDS, AND
   PROPER SPEECH IN THE *ROSE*   119
   Vulgar talk and vernacular revaluation   122
   Improper speech and the politics of   131
      interpretation
   Reasonable shame and the human institution of
      speech   140
   From Latin to vernacular: broadening the
      discourse   158

4. *SIGNE D'ESTRE MALLES*: GENRE, GENDER,
   AND THE END OF THE *ROSE*   164
   Phallocentric exegesis: the emasculation of Orpheus   165
   Rewriting nature: insular values and their revision   174
   Sis homo semper: being male in the Latin *comediae*   179
   Imaging clerical potency: cocks and other creatures   185
   Comic climax and performance of masculinity   192

5. THEORIZING THE *ROSE*: CRISES OF TEXTUAL
   AUTHORITY IN THE *QUERELLE DE LA ROSE*   209
   Debat gracieux, campus duelli? The terms of
      engagement   211
   In propria persona, in persona aliorum: author
      versus character   219
   Jean de Meun as Medieval Ovidian   234
   Beyond Ovid: the precedent of biblical lovers   247

6. PRUNING THE *ROSE*: EVRART DE CONTY
   AND EUROPEAN VERNACULAR
   COMMENTARY   257
   State hermeneutics: Charles V's commentary-
      translations   266
   Quasi comento: Latin traditions, vernacular texts   272
   Speaking *par figure et fabuleusement*: Evrart de
      Conty's theory of poetic fiction   282
   From academe to lay audience: the chequered
      reception of vernacular commentary   296
   Translatio studii, translatio auctoritatis?   312

BIBLIOGRAPHY   320

INDEX   345

Abbreviations

Accessūs ad auctores, ed.
Huygens

AHDLMA

Badel, *Rose au XIVe siècle*

BHS
Brown-Grant, *Moral Defence*

Brownlee and Huot (eds.),
Rethinking the Rose

CCCM

Copeland, *Rhetoric,
Hermeneutics*

Coulson, 'Unedited Lives of
Ovid'

Le Débat, ed. Hicks; trans.
Baird and Kane

EETS, ES

*Accessus ad auctores; Bernard
d'Utrecht; Conrad d'Hirsau*, ed.
R. B. C. Huygens (Leiden, 1970)
*Archives d'histoire doctrinale et
littéraire du moyen âge*
P.-Y. Badel, *Le 'Roman de la Rose' au
XIVe siècle: Étude de la réception de
l'œuvre* (Geneva, 1980)
Bulletin of Hispanic Studies
Rosalind Brown-Grant, *Christine de
Pizan and the Moral Defence of
Women* (Cambridge, 1999)
Kevin Brownlee and Sylvia Huot
(eds.), *Rethinking the 'Romance of
the Rose': Text, Image, Reception*
(Philadelphia, 1992)
Corpus christianorum, continuatio
medievalis
Rita Copeland, *Rhetoric,
Hermeneutics, and Translation in the
Middle Ages: Academic Traditions and
Vernacular Texts* (Cambridge, 1991)
Frank T. Coulson, 'Hitherto
Unedited Medieval and Renaissance
Lives of Ovid (1)', *MS* 49 (1987),
152–207
*Le Débat sur le 'Roman de
la Rose'*, ed. Eric Hicks (Paris, 1977).
Trans. Joseph L. Baird and John R.
Kane, *La Querelle de la Rose: Letters
and Documents*, North Carolina
Studies in the Romance Languages
and Literatures 199 (Chapel Hill,
1978)
Early English Text Society, Extra
Series

Eschez amour. moral., ed. Guichard-Tesson and Roy	Evrart de Conty, *Le Livre des Eschez amoureux moralisés*, ed. Françoise Guichard-Tesson and Bruno Roy, Bibliothèque du moyen français 2 (Montreal, 1993)
Ghisalberti, 'Arnolfo d'Orléans'	F. Ghisalberti, 'Arnolfo d'Orléans, un cultore di Ovidio nel secolo XII', *Memorie del Reale Istituto Lombardo di Scienze e Lettere*, 24.4 (1932), 157–234
Ghisalberti, 'Mediaeval Biographies of Ovid'	F. Ghisalberti, 'Mediaeval Biographies of Ovid', *Journal of the Warburg and Courtauld Institutes*, 9 (1946), 10–59
Hexter, *Ovid and Medieval Schooling*	Ralph J. Hexter, *Ovid and Medieval Schooling: Studies in Medieval School Commentaries on Ovid's 'Ars Amatoria', 'Epistulae ex Ponto', and 'Epistulae Heroidum'* (Munich, 1986)
Hout, *Rose and Its Readers*	Sylvia Huot, *The 'Romance of the Rose' and Its Medieval Readers* (Cambridge, 1993)
Minnis, *Authorship*	A. J. Minnis, *Medieval Theory of Authorship: Scholastic Literary Attitudes in the Later Middle Ages*, 2nd edn. (Aldershot, 1988)
Minnis, *Chaucer: Shorter Poems*	A. J. Minnis, *Oxford Guides to Chaucer: The Shorter Poems* (Oxford, 1995)
Minnis and Scott, *Medieval Literary Theory*	A. J. Minnis and A. B. Scott, with the assistance of David Wallace (eds.), *Medieval Literary Theory and Criticism, c.1100–c.1375: The Commentary Tradition*. Rev. edn (Oxford, 1991)
MLN	*Modern Language Notes*
MS	*Mediaeval Studies*
PL	*Patrologia Latina*, ed. J.-P. Migne
RTAM	*Recherches de théologie ancienne et médiévale*
SATF	Société des anciens textes français
Vulgate Commentary, ed. Coulson	*The 'Vulgate' Commentary on Ovid's 'Metamorphoses': The Creation Myth and the Story of Orpheus*,

	ed. Frank T. Coulson (Toronto, 1991)
Ziolkowski (ed.), *Obscenity*	Jan M. Ziolkowski (ed.), *Obscenity: Social Control and Artistic Creation in the European Middle Ages* (Leiden, 1998)

I have used the edition of the *Roman de la Rose* by Félix Lecoy (Paris, 1965–70), and drawn on the translations—though with some alterations, the most important of which are specified in my notes—by Charles Dahlberg (Hanover, NH, 1971, repr. 1983) and Frances Horgan (Oxford, 1994).

Introduction: *Maistre Jehan de Meun*
and the magisterium amoris

Provoked by Christine de Pizan's attack on the *Roman de la Rose* for its alleged obscenity and antifeminism, Gontier Col launched into a fulsome panegyric upon his beloved

maistre, enseigneur et famillier, feu maistre Jehan de Meun—vray catholique, solempnel maistre et docteur en son temps en saincte theologie, philosophe tres parfont et excellent sachant tout ce qui a entendement humain est scible, duquel la glorie et rennommee vit et vivra es aages avenir entre les entendemens par ses merites levéz, par grace de Dieu et euvre de nature.

[master, teacher, and friend, the lamented Master Jean de Meun, true Catholic, worthy master, and, in his time, doctor of holy theology, a most profound and excellent philosopher, knowing all that to human understanding is knowable, whose glory and fame lives and will live in the ages to come among understanding men, elevated by his merits, by the grace of God, and by the work of Nature.][1]

Elsewhere Gontier praises 'that very excellent and irreproach-able doctor of holy divine Scripture, high philosopher, and most learned clerk in all the seven liberal arts'.[2] There is no external evidence to confirm that 'maistre Jehan de Meun' had indeed received the degrees of master of arts and doctor of theology. However, Gontier was writing in 1401, by which time the 'cult' of Jean de Meun as a celebrated 'learned doctor' (as David Hult

---

[1] *Le Débat*, ed. Hicks, pp. 9–10; trans. Baird and Kane, p. 57. Both Gontier and Pierre Col are titled in the debate as 'secretaries of the King our Lord' (Hicks, pp. 11, 24, 115; Baird and Kane, pp. 59, 62, 117). A. Coville's study *Gontier et Pierre Col et l'humanisme en France au temps de Charles VI* (Paris, 1934) is highly specu-lative and hampered by many unfortunate (not to say dated) assumptions about the origins of French humanism. A useful critique has been provided by Franco Simone, *The French Renaissance: Medieval Traditions and Italian Influence in Shaping the Renaissance in France*, trans. H. Gaston Hall (London, 1969), pp. 134–6.

[2] *Le Débat*, ed. Hicks, p. 23; trans. Baird and Kane, p. 60. Similarly, Gontier's brother Pierre described Jean de Meun as 'ce tres devolt catholique et tres eslevey theologien, ce tres divin orateur et poete et tres parfait philozophe' (*Le Débat*, ed. Hicks, p. 89; cf. trans. Baird and Kane, p. 92).

has termed it)[3] was well established. In 1398 Honoré Bouvet's allegorical poem *L'apparition de maître Jean de Meun* had afforded him star billing as an outspoken critic of contemporary society. Given this exceptional reputation, along with the popularity of the *Rose*, Christine's attack was a high-risk strategy.
  She was not alone, however. Jean Gerson (1363–1429), Chancellor of the University of Paris, declared that Jean 'is damned if he did not repent'[4] those sins which are writ large in his *Rose*, and accused him of having squandered his talents: 'dommage fu que fole jeunesse ou aultre mauvaise inclinacion deseu ung tel clerc a tourner nicement et trop volgarement a tele legiereté reprouvee son subtil engin, sa grande estude et fervent, et son beau parler en rimes et proses: voulsist Dieu que meulx en eust usé!' ['it is regrettable that youthful folly or some other evil inclination should have seduced such a clerk to apply so irresponsibly his fine mind, vast knowledge, erudition, and talent in rime and prose to such frivolity. Would to God that he had used them better'].[5] The reasons why, and how, the *Rose* could induce such conflicting responses will be at the centre of the present study.
  Jean de Meun was residing in Paris at the time of his death in 1305, and there can be no doubt that he was familiar with many of the intellectual debates of its university. Most obviously, he has his character Faus Semblant support William of Saint-Amour, who had preached against certain mendicant claims of powers and privileges, and names the Joachite *Introductorius ad evangelium aeternum*—a work published in 1255, according to Jean (the actual date seems to have been 1254; the author was Gerard of Borgo San Donnino).[6] Faus Semblant complains

---

  [3] 'Jean de Meun's Continuation of *Le Roman de la Rose*', in Denis Hollier et al., *A New History of French Literature* (Cambridge, Mass., 1989), p. 102.
  [4] In a sermon preached on 17 Dec. 1402; in *Le Débat*, ed. Hicks, p. 180; trans. Baird and Kane, p. 159.
  [5] *Traité contre le Roman de la Rose* (completed 18 May 1402), in *Le Débat*, ed. Hicks, p. 66; trans. Baird and Kane, p. 76. Another translation of the *Traité* is included in *Jean Gerson: Early Works*, trans. and introd. Brian Patrick McGuire (New York, 1998), pp. 378–98.
  [6] It could be objected that this controversy was some time away from 1275, the date at which Jean de Meun's part of the *Rose* is generally believed to have been written, and therefore Jean was hardly *au fait* with contemporary concerns. However, the controversy to which William of Saint-Amour had contributed so substantially rumbled on for a long time, and bitter memories lingered. It had deeply

that any man or woman in Paris could get the book to copy, there in the square in front of Notre-Dame, and accuses the university of having been asleep when this 'book written by the devil' had appeared.

Here Maistre Jehan de Meun may well be seen as a 'vray catholique', but any attempt to identify at this point Gontier Col's 'solempnel maistre et docteur en son temps en saincte theologie' must be disturbed by the fact that we are dealing with the discourse of a highly dubious figure, 'False Seeming'. And here we confront one of the most pressing of all the interpretative problems of the *Rose*: how to cope with the cacophony of voices of *personae* which drowns out any views for which the author might be held responsible—this being a major source of irony, ambivalence, and downright confusion.

We are on more secure ground in considering Gontier Col's claim that Jean was a 'most learned clerk in all the seven liberal arts'. Many of the *Rose*'s sources—including Ovid, Boethius, Terence, Juvenal, Martianus Capella, and Alan of Lille—were staple reading in medieval faculties of arts; some were taught in the grammar schools. The 'opera plurima' which Jean lists in the preface to his translation of the *Consolatio philosophiae* of Boethius (generally believed to have been written near the end of his life) bespeak similar interests. Following the dedication to King Philippe le Bel (reigned 1285–1314) and a perfunctory plot summary of the *Rose*, Jean names four texts which already he has translated 'de latin en françois': 'le livre Vegece de Chevalerie et le livre des Merveilles de Hyrlande et la Vie et les Epistres Pierres Abaelart et Heloys sa fame et le livre Aered de Esperituelle Amitié'.[7] Vegetius' *De re militari* was deemed a

---

divided the Parisian scholarly community; indeed, at one point the university was effectively dissolved by the secular masters, in response to the new pope Alexander IV's restoration of the friars' privileges (as removed by his predecessor, who had supported William's line). Moreover, William's chief polemical tract, *De periculis novissorum temporum* (condemned by Alexander IV in 1256), became 'the most important antifraternal work of the next two centuries'. See Penn R. Szittya, *The Antifraternal Tradition in Medieval Literature* (Princeton, NJ, 1986), pp. 15–17.

[7] *Li Livres de confort de philosophie*, ed. V. L. Dedeck-Héry, *MS* 14 (1952), p. 168. Christine de Pizan, rather huffily, remarked that in the 'prologue de Boece que il translata' Jean had enumerated the translations and the various writings which he had made; 'I don't believe that he forgot a single one' (*Le débat*, ed. Hicks, p. 121; trans. Baird and Kane, p. 121). Christine's point (made for specific polemical purposes) is that if Jean had written other works he would have named them here. Given that Jean was introducing a translation, however, it made sense for him to

major reference book on warfare, much esteemed by knightly practitioners of the art and translated into many European vernaculars.[8] Gerald of Wales's *Topographia Hibernica* offered natural science with many a marvel besides, whilst Aelred of Rievaulx's *De spirituali amicitia*, though ostensibly a theological work, offered discussion of love and friendship which appealed to an audience far wider than one consisting of professional theologians, as its use in Andreas's *De amore* and Jean's *Rose* illustrates.[9] This is not, of course, to rule out the possibility that in the works mentioned above we have a *docteur en saincte theologie* at play; my argument is simply that the vast majority of Jean's texts and intellectual pursuits are of kinds which were common in the thirteenth-century Parisian Faculty of Arts.

Several of the intricate philosophical issues raised by the *Rose*

focus on his earlier translating activities. Other works have been attributed to him, with varying degrees of confidence and credibility. The *Testament* seems definitely to be Jean's (not even Christine doubted that); see the edition by Silvia Buzzetti Gallarati, *Le testament maistre Jehan de Meun: un caso letterario* (Turin, 1989). Jean's translation of the letters of Abelard and Heloise has also survived, thanks to the autograph manuscript of Gontier Col (the only surviving copy). Editions have been published by Fabrizio Beggiato, *Le lettere di Abelardo ed Eloisa nella traduzione di Jean de Meun*, Studi, testi e manuali, Istituto di filologia romanza dell'Università di Roma, 5 (Modena, 1977); and by Eric Hicks, *La vie et les epistres Pierres Abaelart et Heloys sa fame: traduction du XIIIe siècle attribuée a Jean de Meun*, Nouvelle bibliothèque du moyen âge 16 (Paris, 1991). For other works which may or may not be Jean's (the *Codicille* and *Trésor*) see Huot, *Rose and Its Readers*, pp. 33, 76. It is depressing that we are so far away from a modern scholarly edition of Jean's entire œuvre.

   [8] Jean's version has been edited by Ulysse Robert, *L'art de chevalerie: Traduction du 'De re militari' de Vegèce par Jean de Meun*, SATF (Paris, 1897); this publication includes the verse abbreviation of Jean's prose translation which was made by Jean Priorat de Besançon. For a comparison of Jean's translation with the later rendering by Jean de Vignay, see Claude Buridant, 'Jean de Meun et Jean de Vignay; traducteurs de l'*Epitoma rei militaris* de Végèce: Contribution à l'histoire de la traduction au Moyen Âge', in *Études de langue et de littérature française offertes à André Lanly* (Nancy, 1980), pp. 51–69. See further C. R. Shrader, 'The Ownership and Distribution of Manuscripts of the *De re militari* of Flavius Vegetius Renatus before 1300' (Ph.D. diss., Columbia University, 1976), and, as an introduction to the English versions, H. N. McCracken, 'Vegetius in English: Notes on the Early Translations', in *Anniversary Papers by Colleagues and Pupils of G. L. Kittredge* (Boston, 1913), pp. 398–403.
   [9] Neither of these translations has survived. The French rendering of the letters of Abelard and Heloise is a complete surprise; Jean's mention of them in the *Rose* is the first known reference to this corpus. Indeed, the suggestion has been made that Jean himself invented them. See below, p. 172, n.22.

had certainly been debated by Parisian *artistae*. Jean's references to light, optics, and the properties of mirrors, which form part of Nature's confession to Genius (17983–8030, 18123–256), reveal what has been termed 'an astonishing familiarity with the details of optical studies during the period'.[10] That may be to overstate the matter somewhat, but Jean is definitely aware of the importance of Alhazen as an authority on refraction (rainbows) and reflection (mirrors). Aristotle and Ptolemy are also cited, and Jean displays familiarity with ideas which may be found in, for example, Robert Grosseteste's *De iride et speculo* and treatises *de perspectiva* by Roger Bacon and John Pecham.

Paris was also *the* centre for the study of semantic theory and 'speculative' or 'modistic' grammar, the so-called *modi significandi*;[11] most of the key thinkers taught or had been taught there. We shall be drawing on such doctrine in Chapter 3, in an attempt to throw light on Jean de Meun's infamous justification of 'dirty talk' with reference to the relationship between words and deeds. Then there were the debates on predestination, providence, and the freedom of the will, no doubt of great interest to the poet who had reprised Dame Fortune from the *Consolatio philosophiae* in his part of the *Rose*, and chronicled therein the falls from prosperity to adversity of Seneca, Nero, and Croesus (to which the more contemporary figure of King Manfred was added, within the Boethian framework).

As befits a poet who contributed so substantially to the poetic form of dream-vision, Jean de Meun shows himself to be extremely knowledgeable about the theories of sleep and dreaming which had been prompted by the Parisian reception of several of the recently recovered works of Aristotle, particularly

---

[10] Bonnie P. Baig, 'Vision and Visualization: Optics and Light Metaphysics in the Imagery and Poetic Form of Twelfth- and Thirteenth-Century Secular Allegory, with Special Reference to the *Roman de la Rose*' (Ph.D. diss., Berkeley, Calif., 1982), p. 137; cf. p. 170. See further Patricia Eberle's substantial article, 'The Lovers' Glass: Nature's Discourse on Optics and the Optical Design of the *Romance of the Rose*', *University of Toronto Quarterly*, 46 (1977), 241–61.

[11] In this area of inquiry grammar was not 'studied as a key to knowledge of classical literature and the Bible', but 'became a branch of speculative philosophy, and grammar was now studied, not by illustration from classical literature, but by systems of logic and metaphysical theories of reality': G. L. Bursill-Hall, *Speculative Grammars of the Middle Ages* (The Hague, 1971), p. 27. Of course, basic 'pedagogical grammar' (with its *auctores* like Ovid) continued to be taught, but there was an 'increasing rift' between it and 'philosophical treatises on grammatical theory'.

the *De somniis* and *De divinatione per somnium*.[12] Taking a far
more sceptical line than Plato's, Aristotle was concerned about
the imagination's potential for deception when it is not
controlled by the reason, as when someone is gripped by some
powerful emotion, or is asleep.[13] What, then, of those dream-
images which seem to refer to future events—are they to be
regarded as prophetic? This is not incredible, says Aristotle, but
it is highly unlikely.[14] The idea that dreams have a divine origin
is absurd, pronounces Aristotle, because, in addition to the
obvious irrationality of this idea, one observes that they do not
come to the best and wisest, but to commonplace persons, all
sorts of men. He then suggests a rational explanation for such
phenomena, concluding that most allegedly prophetic dreams
are to be classed as mere coincidences.[15] This doctrine is picked
up, for example, by the 'Latin Averroist' Boethius of Dacia, a
major figure in the Parisian Arts Faculty in the early 1270s, that
being the decade in which Jean de Meun composed his continuation of Guillaume de Lorris's *Rose*. Some of our dreams have
no connection whatever with future events, Boethius argues, but
are matters of coincidence: 'the event would have happened
even if there had been no appearance similar to it in a dream'.[16]
Dreams can be caused not by external but by internal forces,
from the body or from the soul. Bodily causes include the
motions and combinations of fumes and vapours; hence, black
and earthly vapours may cause someone to dream of flames and
fires, and certain foolish people, on 'being awakened, swear that
they have seen devils when they were asleep'.[17] On the other
hand, clear vapours may move the imagination so that sleepers
'dream that they are seeing brilliant places and angels singing
and dancing. And when they have awakened they swear that
they were carried away (*raptos*) and have in truth seen angels.
And they are deceived because they are ignorant of the causes of
things.' Illness may produce similar effects. Then Boethius
moves to discuss dreams produced in us from the soul. Clearly

[12] For a fuller discussion see Minnis, *Chaucer: Shorter Poems*, pp. 36–55, on
which the following account is based.   [13] *De somniis*, iii (460b–1a).
[14] *De divinatione per somnium*, i.   [15] *De divinatione*, 462b, 463a–b.
[16] Boethius of Dacia, *On the Supreme Good; On the Eternity of the World; On
Dreams*, trans. John F. Wippel (Toronto, 1987), p. 71.
[17] Ibid. 75.

influenced by Aristotle, he notes that 'when a sleeper is subject to a strong passion of fear or love, his imaginative power forms images which correspond to those passions such as a phantasm of an enemy or of his beloved'.[18]

The extent to which Boethius of Dacia strives to arrive at a scientific explanation for dreams in terms of their causes is remarkable. A similar interest is evinced by Jean de Meun, who is uneasy about the human powers of eyesight and imagination, and inclined to seek natural causes for unusual phenomena. His Dame Nature remarks that many people are so deceived by their dreams that they suffer extreme forms of sleepwalking, getting up and preparing themselves for work, even travelling considerable distances on horseback. Then, when they awake, they are lost in wonder and amazement, and tell people that devils took them from their homes and brought them there (18274–96). Sometimes sickness, or an excess of melancholy or fear, acting on the imagination can cause extraordinary effects. Then again, some contemplatives 'font apparair en leur pansees / les choses qu'il ont porpansees' [cause 'the objects of their meditations to appear in their thoughts'], and 'les cuident tout proprement / voir defors apertement; et ce n'est for trufle et mançonge' ['truly believe that they see them clearly and objectively. But these are merely lies and deceits'] (18327–33). Such a person, Nature declares with heavy irony, has experiences similar to Scipio's, seeing 'ciel et air et mer et terre / et tout quan que l'an i peut querre' ['hell and heaven, the sky and the air, the sea and the land, and all that you might find there'] (18337–40). Alternatively, he may dream of wars and tournaments, balls (*baleries*) and dances, or indeed of feeling his sweetheart in his arms although she is not really there (18351–8).

> ... cil qui fins amanz se claiment,
> don mout ont travauz et enuiz,
> quant se sunt endormi de nuiz
> en leur liz ou mout ont pansé ...
> si songent les choses amees
> que tant ont par jour reclamees ...
> (18365–72)

[18] Ibid. 76–7.

[Those who claim to be true lovers love one another with burning devotion and endure great toil and trouble as a result, then when they fall asleep at night in their beds, . . . they dream of their beloved, whom they have so often longed for by day.]

Similarly, those who are in a state of deadly hatred dream of anger and battles, and so forth. These remarks place the opening statement of the *Rose* in a fascinating light. There Guillaume de Lorris had cited Macrobius' commentary on the dream of Scipio as proof that dream-visions can be true and authentic, *pace* those who say there is nothing in dreams but lies and fables (*fables non et mençonges*: 1–10). Jean de Meun seems to be agreeing with those doubters, holding that most dreams are indeed nothing but *fables* and *mençonges*. This undermines the authority—or at least brings out the ambivalence—of the foundational literary form in which the *Rose* is composed. And he is leaving open the possibility that the entire poem may be read as a passion-induced fancy on the part of the lover-narrator Amant, hardly one of 'the best and wisest' of men, who vividly illustrates that overthrow of rational judgement which commonly occurs during sleep.

The sceptical approach of Boethius of Dacia, as illustrated above, was far too naturalistic for some. The thirty-third article on the list of propositions condemned at Paris by Bishop Stephen Tempier in 1277, 'that raptures and visions do not take place except through nature', seems to refer to his *De somniis* (read in a biased manner, to be sure). The bishop, prompted by a papal mandate, was seeking to root out philosophical errors in the Parisian arts faculty. It has been suggested that some of the other propositions on his list are similar to opinions which can be found in, or inferred from, the *Rose*.[19] Examples include the doctrines 'that simple fornication, namely, that of an unmarried man with an unmarried woman, is not a sin'; and 'that continence is not essentially a virtue'.[20] However, the very same

---

[19] Hult, 'Jean de Meun's Continuation', pp. 97–8. See further Badel's important discussion of the *Rose*'s 'milieu culturel': *Rose au XIVe siècle*, pp. 32–8.

[20] For discussion of the condemnations and their intellectual context, see R. Hissette, *Enquête sur les 219 articles condamnés à Paris le 7 Mars 1277* (Louvain, 1977); and John F. Wippel, 'The Condemnations of 1270 and 1277 at Paris', *Journal of Medieval and Renaissance Studies*, 7 (1977), 169–201.

ideas can be found in the *De amore* of Andreas Capellanus, a text far more likely to have been Tempier's specific target in view of the fact that it is named in the introduction to the condemnations and indisputably identified by its *incipit* and *explicit*.[21] For long the *De amore* has been dated to the 1180s and located in Marie de Champagne's milieu. However, Alfred Karnein believes it originated in the chancellery of Philip II Augustus, king of France, being intended for the entertainment of a learned and Latinate coterie which would have viewed the supposed goings-on at the court of Champagne with superior scorn.[22] More radically still, given that the first reference to *De amore* is not until 1238, and in view of its appearance in the 1277 condemnations (which addressed pressingly topical issues), Peter Dronke has argued that it was composed in the 1230s at Paris.[23] But even if this later date is accepted and *De amore* is consigned to thirteenth-century Paris, we are left with a puzzling absence of precise verbal parallels between the Latin treatise and the French poem, *pace* those critics who confidently assert that Andreas was a source on which Jean de Meun drew. The closest parallel concerns the definition of love itself. For Andreas love is a *passio* (here meaning a mental suffering rather than 'passion' in the modern sense of the term) 'which results from the sight of, and uncontrolled thinking about, the beauty of the other sex. This feeling makes a man desire before all else the embraces of the other sex, and to achieve the utter fulfilment of the commands of love in the other's embrace by their common desire'.[24] According to Jean's Raison, love is a mental illness (*maladie de pensee*)

[21] The two propositions here quoted, among others, have been identified with passages in *De amore* by A. J. Denomy, 'The *De amore* of Andreas Capellanus and the Condemnation of 1277', *MS* 8 (1946), 107–49. See further Alfred Karnein, *De amore in volkssprachlicher Literatur, Untersuchungen zur Andreas-Capellanus-Rezeption in Mittelalter und Renaissance* (Heidelberg, 1985), pp. 168–75.

[22] Ibid. 21–39. For a lively critique of aspects of this view, see Don A. Monson, 'Andreas Capellanus and the Problem of Irony', *Speculum*, 63 (1988), 547–8, 550–4.

[23] 'Andreas Capellanus', *Journal of Medieval Latin*, 4 (1994), 51–63.

[24] Andreas Capellanus, *De Amore (on Love)*, ed. and trans. P. G. Walsh (London, 1982), p. 33.

> autre .II. persones annexe,
> franches entr'els, de divers sexe,
> venanz a genz par ardeur nee
> de vision desordenee,
> pour acoler et pour besier
> pour els charnelment aesier.
>
> (4347–54)

[afflicting two persons of opposite sex in close proximity who are both free agents. It comes upon people through a burning desire, born of disordered perception, to embrace and to kiss and to seek carnal gratification.]

Even Karnein, who is convinced that direct influence occurred here, admits that 'the translation is not entirely accurate' and uses Drouart la Vache's considerably later French version of *De amore* (1290) to help make the case that there is 'little room for doubt that Jean de Meun used the *De amore* treatise'.[25]

Here I am not seeking to rule out the possibility that Jean had read Andreas, but simply suggesting that the common supposition concerning *De amore* as a source of the *Rose* has less textual support than some of its proponents may realize. It is perfectly possible to argue that most if not all of the similarities between the two texts are due to their authors' shared 'mastership' of the medieval art of love rather than to direct and deliberate borrowing. They may be traced back, through many medieval overlays, to the old master himself, Publius Ovidius Naso.

> Siquis in hoc artem populo non novit amandi,
> Hoc legat et lecto carmine doctus amet.
> ... ego sum praeceptor amoris.
>
> (*Ars amatoria*, I. 1–2, 17)

---

[25] Karnein, *De amore*, pp. 190–3; also his paper '*Amor est Passio*: A Definition of Courtly Love?', in *Court and Poet: Selected Proceedings of the Third Congress of the International Courtly Literature Society*, ed. G. S. Burgess (Liverpool, 1980), pp. 215–21 (p. 218). Despite his assumption that Jean de Meun knew the *De amore*, Douglas Kelly points to major differences between the definitions of love which function in the two works: *Internal Difference and Meanings in the 'Roman de la Rose'* (Madison, 1995), pp. 37–8, 40, 56–61. It is indubitable that Evrart de Conty used *De amore* in the commentary on the *Eschez amoureux* which he composed between 1398 and 1405 (see Ch. 6 below), but Evrart seems to have been ignorant of its authorship and period of composition—the work is cited as that of 'un saiges anciens'. It is probably over-ingenious to suggest that, because of the controversy and condemnation surrounding *De amore*, Evrart sought to conceal its origins, since many other fifteenth-century writers used it without any apparent uneasiness.

[If anyone among this people knows not the art of loving, let him read my poem, and having read be skilled in love. . . . I am Love's teacher.][26]

Ovid's love poetry was composed to entertain a sophisticated audience of young Roman aristocrats, who would find in the *Ars amatoria* at once sexual comedy, seduction techniques, and worldly cynicism—an unstable mixture of the serious and the scurrilous, the elevated and the obscene. Yet, by a curious twist of fate, in the Middle Ages this poetry formed part of the staple fare of grammar school teaching. In their glosses, generations of medieval *magistri* sought to impose some sort of order on its riotous profusion of reference by claiming that Ovid's work 'pertained to ethics' (*ethice supponitur*) or some superior branch of knowledge. Any problems raised by the youthfully improper *Ars amatoria* were defused by reference to the supposedly apologetic *Remedia amoris,* read as a product of the poet's repentance. Ovid's exile was (on one theory at least) reassuringly deemed a fitting punishment for his immoral verse, from which experience he emerged a sadder and wiser man. Thus the *praeceptor amoris* became 'the clerk Ovid',[27] a figure on whom had been thrust a distinctively medieval *magisterium.*Then there was the tradition of the allegorized Ovid, largely featuring the *Metamorphoses,* wherein classical myths were made to bear the weight of a wide range of moral, and sometimes specifically Christian, meanings. By such means the Roman poet's writing was accommodated to what Judson B. Allen has called the medieval 'ethical poetic'.[28] But of course the *Ars* and the *Remedia* could not be circumscribed by the masters' totalizing glosses; there is no reason to doubt that many readers noticed that the former said many negative things about love while the latter could be just as erotic as the poem which it was supposed to be recanting. It was admitted that the authorial intention of

[26] *The Art of Love and Other Poems,* ed. with an English translation by J. H. Mozley (Cambridge, Mass., 1969), pp. 12–13.

[27] As the late fourteenth-century English poet John Gower terms him in his *Confessio amantis,* i. 2274; ed. G. C. Macaulay, *The English Works of John Gower,* EETS, ES 81 and 82 (London, 1900), i. 97.

[28] See Allen's two monographs, foundational for the modern study of medieval literary theory, *The Friar as Critic* (Nashville, 1971) and *The Ethical Poetic of the Later Middle Ages* (Toronto, 1982).

the *Amores* (usually referred to as Ovid's 'book without a title') was 'to give pleasure', and while in theory the *Heroides* offered patterned *exempla* of commendable and reprehensible behaviour in love, in practice it empowered medieval writers to explore, however stumblingly, female passion and emotional psychology.[29] For its part, the *Metamorphoses* remained a vital index to pagan sex and science, ever-resistant to allegorical *reductio*.

An *œuvre* which is marked by inherent instability of meaning was interpreted and augmented by medieval scholars and writers in ways which often accentuated that instability. Little wonder, then, that most if not all of the 'Medieval Ovids' considered below (with Jean de Meun having the greatest claim to the *magisterium amoris*) produced works which are remarkable, if not notorious, for their irreducible ambiguities of tone and significance, slipperiness of authorial viewpoint, and apparent inconsistencies of discourse and purpose. Stabilizing structures were imposed, of course; explicitly Christian statements set in place to shore up edifices of dubious ethical import. But such measures often achieved little success, as fissures widened into gulfs under the pressure of medieval expansion and adaptation. Ovidian poetics remained obstinately resistant to closure, refused to be reducible to neat critical aphorism. This was, of course, a wonderfully creative space for a writer to inhabit. And the best of the writers treated below made the most of it.

Ovid's ambiguous textual authority will be addressed in the following chapters. The initial discussion will concentrate on several French translations of his Latin love poetry, specifically the work of Jacques d'Amiens, Guiart, and the anonymous writer of *L'Art d'amours*. All of these renderings mark the move from classroom concerns to secular interests and fashions; all

---

[29] See the representative *accessūs* to the *Amores* and the *Heroides* trans. in Minnis and Scott, *Medieval Literary Theory*, pp. 20–4, 27–8. It is explained that Ovid left the former untitled to obscure the fact that he had written yet another book about love, which, following the outrage caused by his *Ars amatoria*, would have offended Augustus and other Romans even more. On the *Heroides* as a major determining influence on the construction of female characters in medieval romance and 'epic' tradition, see Barbara Nolan, *Chaucer and the Tradition of the 'Roman Antique'* (Cambridge, 1991), and the relevant discussion in Götz Schmitz, *The Fall of Women in Early English Narrative Verse* (Cambridge, 1990).

are aware (though to varying extents) of the conventions of *fine amor* or 'courtly love', which sometimes conflict with Ovid's aggressive rhetoric of seduction. The *L'Art d'amours* displays its academic origins most obviously, given that gloss as well as text is rendered into French. It draws on materials from some school commentary, and makes sophisticated (and secularizing) use of information traditionally found in the *accessūs* or academic prologues to Ovid commentaries.[30] But the anonymous author is not willing to settle for mere translation; for instance, he makes use of medical discourse, which counterbalances (or perhaps challenges) the moralizing discourse which he inherited from Latin literary theory.

We may then move on to consider more elaborate manifestations of medieval Ovidianism, in works by Richard de Fournival and Juan Ruiz. The *Libro de buen amor* of Juan Ruiz seems to have been written in the early fourteenth century; a prose preface, which is the main concern of our analysis, appears in the Salamanca manuscript of this work, which is dated 1343. We turn to this Spanish '*accessus*' because it illustrates superbly well the highly innovative uses to which the forms and contents of academic prolegomena, especially the *accessūs Ovidiani*, can be put; I know of no other short text which so challengingly presents the competing impulses (ethical and erotic, sacred and profane, didactic and destabilizing) that result when Ovid is subjected to medieval *amplificatio* and (attempted) assimilation to larger value systems. Juan Ruiz's artistry needs no defence; that of Richard de Fournival (1201–60) perhaps still does, since

---

[30] I am using '*accessus*' in the general sense which it has acquired in much modern scholarship, as a term of convenience to designate certain types of schematic introductions to 'set texts' in the medieval schools. The term had a far more limited circulation in the Middle Ages than this scholarship may imply. My term 'academic prologue' includes both the *accessus ad auctorem* and the broader type of introduction to an art or science in general, the type which in its various manifestations has been called the 'extrinsic' prologue (on which see below) and the 'type D' prologue. For the latter term see R. W. Hunt's seminal article 'The Introductions to the *Artes* in the Twelfth Century', in *Studia medievalia in honorem R. M. Martin, O.P.* (Bruges, 1948), pp. 85–115; repr. in Hunt, *The History of Grammar in the Middle Ages: Collected Papers*, ed. G. L. Bursill-Hall (Amsterdam, 1980), pp. 117–44. Two earlier studies are still of importance, since neither has been superseded fully: G. Przychocki, 'Accessus Ovidiani', *Rozprawy Akademii Umiejetnosci*, wydzial filologiczny, serya 3, tom. iv (1911), 65–126, and E. A. Quain, 'The Medieval *Accessus ad auctores*', *Traditio*, 3 (1945), 228–42.

he has sometimes suffered from incomprehension or underestimation.[31] One of the greatest bibliophiles of the time, Richard was successively canon, deacon, and chancellor of the Chapter of Notre Dame, Amiens, and in addition held the ecclesiastic appointments of a canonric in Rouen and a chaplaincy to Cardinal Robert de Sommercote. Richard may have been responsible for the Pseudo-Ovidian *De Vetula* (in Latin, but there is a French version by Jean Le Fèvre). Here is a *remedium amoris* with a vengeance, for the text (allegedly found in Ovid's tomb!) narrates how its poet, sickened by his experience with a deceitful old woman and subsequently disillusioned by the ravages which age has inflicted on his young beloved, becomes a Christian.[32] The progression of this work, as it shifts from the art of love to its rejection and thence to the affirmation of superior Christian doctrine, traces a pattern which we will find in many a medieval Ovidian poem. Richard achieved unusual success, however, in convincing many readers that his creation was actually the work of Ovid himself. Several amatory works in French have also been attributed to Richard; there seems to be no doubt, however, that he was responsible for a love treatise of a highly unusual kind, this being the *Bestiaires d'amours*, in which, so to speak, Ovid finds himself thrust into the medieval beast-fable tradition. We will turn to Richard's work on several occasions throughout this book, and certainly not as a mere foil to Jean de Meun's Ovidian achievements.

But those achievements are, of course, quite remarkable, and the following three chapters are devoted to them. Fom the point of view of the *Roman de la Rose* the Ovid translation (and transformation) treated in the first chapter may be seen as a prelude to the part Jean de Meun played in the enclosure of 'l'art d'Amors' (cf. *Rose*, 37) within a textual framework far more ambitious than any of those discussed previously, and as a

[31] See e.g. Thomas J. Daly, 'The Dialectical Crisis of the Thirteenth Century and Its Reflection in Richard de Fournival' (Ph.D. diss., Tufts University, 1975), who treats Richard patronizingly as one who 'in his own minor way ... emerges as a "watershed" figure for many medieval currents and fancies', 'a bookish dilettante who serves to confirm what is demonstrated far more remarkably by others' (pp. 2, 3). In particular, the subtle wit of the *Bestiaires d'amours* is lost on Daly.

[32] On the *De Vetula*, see below, pp. 58–9, 71, 184–5, 202 n.101, 207.

means of placing in a wider cultural context the way in which his vernacularization (a far from passive process) of Latin literary theory contributed to the poem's hermeneutic and generic experimentation. Chancellor Gerson accused Jean of having forced together diverse and ill-fitting source materials so that, by seeming to have experienced and studied many things, 'il fut mieulx creu et de plus grande auctoritey' ['he would be the better believed and have greater authority'].[33] If that was indeed Jean's aim, then he cannot be credited with having achieved it.

There is no single and consistent authority claim in this poem: Jean draws on several literary-theoretical rationales from Latin tradition which had the potential for such development, but does not settle for any one of them. Chapter 2 considers two major discourses which compete in the *Rose*, relating to 'integumental' covering and satiric stripping respectively. The former seeks to valorize meaning through decorous concealment; the latter affirms the virtues of blatant (sometimes aggressive and indeed 'vulgar') revelation of truths which can be harsh in the extreme. Since this terminology is of crucial importance throughout the following book, it must be introduced here in some detail.

A clear definition of *integumentum* is provided in the prologue to an *Aeneid* commentary which has been attributed to Bernard Silvester (*c.*1100–*c.*1160), who taught in the cathedral school at Tours.[34] There it is explained that the 'integument is a kind of teaching which wraps up the true meaning inside a fictitious narrative (*narratio fabulosa*), and so it is also called "a veil" (*involucrum*)'.[35] In another commentary which may be the work of Bernard, this time on Martianus Capella's *De nuptiis philologiae et mercurii*, a distinction is made between *integumentum*, which is a feature of philosophical writing, and *allegoria*, which pertains to Holy Scripture: 'Allegory is a mode of discourse (*oratio*) which covers under a historical narrative a true meaning which is different from its surface meaning, as in the case of Job wrestling with an angel. An *integumentum*, however, is a mode of discourse which covers a true meaning

---

33 *Traité*, in *Le Débat*, ed. Hicks, p. 63; trans. Baird and Kane, p. 73.
34 For the controversy concerning the authorship of this work see the references on p. 83, n.4 below.
35 Minnis and Scott, *Medieval Literary Theory*, p. 152.

under a fictitious narrative, as in the case of Orpheus.'[36] Both poets and philosophers made good use of *integumenta*, the Martianus commentator explains: Virgil used fictional coverings to describe 'the temporal life of the human spirit within the body'[37] whereas Plato, 'when he came to speak of the soul, said figuratively that its matter is number' (an allusion to the doctrine which medieval scholars extracted from the *Timaeus*). Furthermore, '*integumenta* have double and even multiple meanings'; for example, Juno can signify both the 'lower air' or, in the case of the judgement of Paris, the 'practical life', in contrast with the theoretical and voluptuous lives (Pallas and Venus respectively). This is, the commentator freely admits, 'the greatest source of confusion for readers' of *De nuptiis*, and he illustrates the phenomenon with a further example: 'when the name of Mercury has been used figuratively in connection with speech, suddenly a transition takes place and the same name refers to the planet'.[38] The question may now be asked, does this same sort of confusion occur in the *Rose*? And is correct reading of fluctuating, polysemous integumental discourse the key to its interpretation?

Several modern scholars have thought along those lines,

[36] *The Commentary on Martianus Capella's 'De nuptiis Philologiae et Mercurii'* attributed to *Bernardus Silvestris*, ed. H. J. Westra (Toronto, 1986), p. 24. A later echo of this distinction may be found in John of Garland's *Parisiana Poetria*, wherein *integumentum* is described as 'truth cloaked in the outward form of a story (*veritas in specie fabule palliata*) whereas *allegoria* 'means truth cloaked in the words of history (*veritas in verbis hystorie palliata*)'. *The 'Parisiana Poetria' of John of Garland*, ed. and trans. Traugott Lawler (New Haven, Conn., 1974), pp. 104–5. On the development of the two discrete allegory systems, see Minnis and Scott, *Medieval Literary Theory*, pp. 120–2, 324, particularly Dante's distinction between the 'allegory of the poets' and the 'allegory of the theologians', pp. 382–3, 396.

[37] Here the commentator alludes to the tradition of reading the *Aeneid* integumentally in terms of the ages of man and the stages of virtue, as undertaken by Fulgentius and developed in the 'Bernard Silvester' *Aeneid* commentary. See Christopher Baswell, *Virgil in Medieval England: Figuring the 'Aeneid' from the Twelfth Century to Chaucer* (Cambridge, 1995), pp. 96–8, 106, etc.; cf. Minnis and Scott, *Medieval Literary Theory*, p. 153, n. 159.

[38] *Commentary on Martianus Capella*, ed. Westra, p. 25. Similarly, in his *Aeneid* commentary 'Bernard Silvester' explains that 'the possibility of the integuments relating to different things, and of multiple signification in all mystical material, must be taken into account if the truth cannot stand supported on one interpretation'. For instance, Saturn 'you understand sometimes as a star, and again, immediately after, as representing time'. Minnis and Scott, *Medieval Literary Theory*, p. 154.

given the complex use made of classical 'fictitious narratives' in the *Rose* and particularly in view of Jean de Meun's clear reference to integumental discourse at a critical juncture in his text (when the significance of the mythic castration of Saturn is addressed). To put their learned and forcefully presented argument at its most basic, D. W. Robertson and John V. Fleming believe that figurative veils or clothes of style play a major part in achieving what they regard as its highly moral and rigorously Christian purpose.[39] On this reading the poem is determinately indebted to the genre and techniques of moral mythography, treated as a work which may (in large measure) be bracketed with the relevant writings of Fulgentius, the Vatican Mythographers, Alberic of London, and (to go beyond the age of Jean de Meun), John Ridevall and Pierre Bersuire. While I would warmly endorse the view that both Guillaume de Lorris and Jean de Meun brilliantly deployed an impressive array of pagan fables, and to that extent can be regarded as having written within the mythographic tradition, in my opinion an all-controlling integumental programme is not to be found in the *Rose*. The *Rose* poets, particularly Jean de Meun, make their own, often highly original and indeed eccentric, use of classical narratives. In his foundational *Aeneid* commentary, Servius had remarked that 'the poets frequently vary fables' (*frequenter . . . variant fabulas poetae*).[40] There may be a distant echo of this in the statement of Jean's first-person narrator to the effect that he

---

[39] Here I refer primarily to the work of D. W. Robertson, *A Preface to Chaucer: Studies in Medieval Perspectives* (Princeton, NJ, 1962), pp. 91–104, 196–207, 361–5, etc., and to John V. Fleming's two books, *The 'Roman de la Rose': A Study in Allegory and Iconography* (Princeton, NJ, 1969) and *Reason and the Lover* (Princeton, NJ, 1984). The *Rose* is, on Fleming's reading, charged with 'considerable moral seriousness'; Jean de Meun set about 'pillorying, mocking and condemning his "hero" [i.e. Amant], mercilessly and without sympathy, through thousands of lines of mordant verse' (*Allegory and Iconography*, pp. 237, 247). An important critique of Fleming's position is provided by Badel, *Rose au XIVe siècle*, pp. 9–13. See further Per Nykrog, 'Obscene or Not Obscene: Lady Reason, Jean de Meun, and the Fisherman from Pont-sur-Seine', in Ziolkowski (ed.), *Obscenity*, pp. 319–31 (esp. pp. 322–6).

[40] Comment on *Aeneid* vi.617, in Servius, *In Vergilii carmina commentarii*, ed. G. Thilo and H. Hagen (Leipzig, 1881–7), ii.87. Cf. Nicolette Zeeman, who argues that 'integrally associated with poetic license' is a kind of choice which commentators often offer their readers, of choosing one among different possible interpretations of a given myth: 'The Schools Give a License to Poets', in Rita Copeland (ed.), *Criticism and Dissent in the Middle Ages* (Cambridge, 1996), pp. 162, 171.

is making some additions to what his authorities say about women, 'on his own account'—and this 'costs you little', for poets do this sort of thing among themselves: 'quelque parole n'i ajoute, / si con font antr'eus li poete' (15205–7). Whatever the truth of that may be, it is certain that Jean varies the *fabulae poetarum* for his own ends and in line with his own stylistic strategies. Sometimes he treats them in a quite literalizing way, and prefers the direct signification of *exempla* to the hidden meanings of integumental discourse. In any case, there are few if any sudden transitions from one significance to the other in the poem's deployment of pagan mythology. The kind of 'confusion' which 'Bernard Silvester' found in *De nuptiis* does not seem to be present in the *Rose*: other forces are at work in the making of this text's multivalence.

Furthermore, on occasion Jean engaged in that blatant outspokenness deemed by medieval theorists to be characteristic of satire, which was supposed to have a methodology that was diametrically opposed to that of *integumentum*. A quintessentially literalistic form, it sought to strip away all the veils of social and textual subterfuge to expose the naked truth. Hence a representative *accessus* to Persius can declare that 'satire is nude. It reprehends not through involutions and ambiguities but nakedly and openly, and it strips naked and lays open vices.'[41] Here is an unusual clerical inscription of the naked female body—its frequent function was rather to image lust and debauchery, or some other reprehensible activity, as when the 'Bernard Silvester' commentary on Martianus Capella explains that Venus is 'depicted nude, either because the criminality of desire is barely concealed, or because desire strips one of good counsel'.[42] But nakedness is undeniably positive in medieval theory of satire, in recognition of the fact that desperate measures—sharp outspokenness, stark clarity of expression—

---

[41] See Suzanne Reynolds, *Medieval Reading: Grammar, Rhetoric and the Classical Text* (Cambridge, 1996), p. 204, n. 56.

[42] *Commentary on Martianus Capella*, ed. Westra, p. 57; cf. Sarah Kay, 'Venus in the *Roman de la Rose*', *Exemplaria*, 9.1 (1997), 35. According to Fulgentius, the ancients depict Venus naked 'either because she sends out her devotees naked or because the sin of lust is never cloaked or because it only suits the naked'. *Mitologiarum libri tres*, ii. 1, trans. Leslie George Whitbread, *Fulgentius the Mythographer* (Columbus, Oh., 1971), p. 66.

were needed to eradicate desperate vices. Moreover, satire was rude as well as nude. As John of Garland put it in his *Parisiana Poetria* (*c.*1220, revised 1231–5),

> Indignans satyra deridet, nuda operta,
> Voce salit, viciis fetet, agreste sapit.
>
> (v. 363–4)
>
> [Indignant satire mocks, lays bare secrets,
> skips around, stinks of vices, smacks of coarseness.]⁴³

All of these features are writ large in the *Rose*, and I believe that in at least parts of his poem Jean de Meun was writing under the influence of the medieval literary theory and practice of satire. The literal status of satire is further indicated by its classification, alongside tragedy, as a type of 'historical narrative'.⁴⁴ In the 'Bernard Silvester' commentary on Martianus Capella, satire and tragedy are seen as subdivisions of *historia*. 'That type of *historia* which is satire, wholly consists in fighting against the vices and praising the virtues', it is argued, 'while tragedy is about the endurance of hardship (*labor*).'⁴⁵ *Historia* was deemed to be the literally true record of actual happenings (*gestae res, res factae*) which were removed in time from the recollection of our age, whereas *fabula* comprised untrue events, fictitious things (*res fictae*) which neither happened nor could have happened. However, in the commonplace view of medieval clerics, history was as much concerned with moral as with

---

⁴³ *Parisiana Poetria*, ed. Lawler, pp. 102–3. Similar verses occur in the longer version of Geoffrey of Vinsauf's *Documentum*; in *Parisiana Poetria*, ed. Lawler, p. 332. Cf. Lawler's note to *Parisiana Poetria*, v. 363–4, on pp. 255–6.

⁴⁴ See esp. the important discussion of Päivi Mehtonen, who suggests that satire must 'belong to the "historical" genres since it censures vices "nakedly" or openly, and employs the resources of literal meaning rather than the more overtly fictional and veiled realms of *argumentum* or *fabula*'. *Old Concepts and New Poetics: Historia, Argumentum, and Fabula in the Twelfth- and Early Thirteenth-Century Latin Poetics of Fiction* (Helsinki, 1996), p. 78 n.

⁴⁵ *Commentary on Martianus Capella*, ed. Westra, p. 81. Bernard, if indeed this is his work, then moves immediately into an account of how Ulysses encourages us to regard fortune with contempt, as it shows him, as one who once prospered (*florebat*), being cast down. Clearly, this is intended as an instance of tragic writing. Generally, he continues, a poem offers *exempla* of good and bad behaviour, whence *poeseos*, rightly understood, means the 'eradication of vices and the introduction of virtues'. This definition is obviously respectful of the specific work of satire, and seeks to find a common denominator between it and tragedy.

factual truth; it offered lucid examples of good and bad behaviour to its audience—as did satire and tragedy. Hence Arnulf of Orléans (*fl.* 1175), commenting on Lucan's *Pharsalia*, can declare that it pertains to ethics (*ethice supponitur*), because Lucan encourages us to practise the four virtues of courage, wisdom, self-control, and justice 'by means of appropriate figures (*personae*), showing us good morality as in the case of Cato and other citizens who strive after those virtues in the state which pertain to ethics'.[46] Here historical personages are read as having an exemplary function, the writing being literal and not requiring interpretation of the type usually afforded to *fabulae*.[47] Ralph of Longchamps, commenting on the *Anticlaudianus* of Alan of Lille (*c.*1116–1202/3), could affirm that 'sub historia continetur satira et tragedia' and set these genres in opposition to *fabula* since it employs fictional narrative.[48] In conclusion, on the definitions here offered, it seems perfectly obvious that satire should belong with history, as didactic forms of writing which presented their ethical illustrations and teachings on the literal surface of the text. And, as I will argue in Chapter 2, much of the meaning of the *Rose* is to be found on the literal surface of its text.

My discussion there should not be taken as implying that Jean has enlisted the power of satire against Amant as the poem's key and thematically unifying target; that sort of argument could well deliver the conclusions of the panallegorists by a different route, and I do not believe that such a methodical trajectory is operating in the *Rose*. No precedent may be found in the commentators' typical definitions of satiric intention: it is described in the most general terms as 'to rescue the erring from their vices' and 'to lead them to a better way of life',[49] with the several objects of satiric reprehension being identified as they

---

[46] Minnis and Scott, *Medieval Literary Theory*, p. 155.

[47] Of course, historical writing could on occasion quote or allude to particular *fabulae*, a fact fully accepted by Arnulf in his *Pharsalia* commentary. This text, indeed, presented a special case, given that Lucan was seen as 'a poet and historiographer combined'. See Minnis and Scott, *Medieval Literary Theory*, p. 115.

[48] 'Satira vero tota est in extirpandis vitiis et informandis virtutibus; tragedia tota est in contemptu fortunae'. *In Anticlaudianum Alani commentum*, ed. Jan Sulowski (Wrocław, 1972), p. 44. Ralph flourished in the second half of the twelfth century and the first two decades of the thirteenth.

[49] Minnis and Scott, *Medieval Literary Theory*, p. 61; cf. p. 135.

appear in the text. Moreover, it is notable that female vice—as illustrated in the speeches of Ami and La Vielle—is the presenting cause of Jean's *apologia,* wherein (as will be argued below) many of the constitutive idioms of satiric theory are echoed: Amant's situation is not at issue there. Above all else, I am not suggesting that literalistic satire is the dominant literary-theoretical discourse of Jean's *Rose:* such a single, authoritative discourse does not operate, in my view, and I certainly would not wish to propose the replacement of one totalizing discourse (i.e. allegoresis, in the version urged by Robertson and Fleming) with another. My opinion is rather that both these discourses function powerfully in the *Rose,* and just as the terms 'naked' and 'clothed' are relative to and presuppose each other, so too do integumental and satiric versions of narrative—or, more accurately, Jean de Meun has made them function thus. That is the fundamental point of Chapter 2, wherein considerable use will be made of the *accessūs* to Juvenal, Perseus, and Horace, alongside materials from the opposing tradition of moralization of pagan fables, for which the *Metamorphoses* was a major source; there, declared Pierre Bersuire, 'all the fables truly seem to be collected together as it were in the manner of a register (*tabula*)'.[50]

Following up on this chapter's initial treatment of Raison's use of such words as *coillon* and *viz* or *vit* (*Rose,* 6936, 7087), Chapter 3 moves into different hermeneutic territory to consider Jean de Meun's pronouncements on speech which is 'proper' or directly significative of its referents, with special reference to Raison's infamous claim that she has the right to name the male genitalia in the plainest of terms. 'There should be at times an uncouthness of style to conform to the ugliness of the subject-matter,'[51] conceded Alan of Lille, though he himself was disinclined to enter those vulgar regions, at least in *De planctu naturae* and the *Anticlaudianus.* However, uncouth

---

[50] Ibid. 369. This statement occurs in the prologue to the *Ovidius moralizatus* which constitutes the fifteenth book of the monumental *Reductorium morale.* Bersuire, a Benedictine monk, seems to have completed the first redaction of this moralization of the *Metamorphoses* by 1340, at Avignon. Dissatisfied with it, he produced a second redaction whilst living in Paris between *c.*1350 and 1362 (the year of his death). His influence on the *Eschez amoureux* commentary is discussed in Ch. 6.

[51] *De planctu naturae,* viii, pr. iv, trans. J. J. Sheridan (Toronto, 1980), p. 144.

style and ugly subject-matter are at the very centre of textual attention for Jean de Meun (and Geoffrey Chaucer after him), and value judgements like 'uncouth' and 'ugly' are implicitly called into question. In the search for answers, or at least for better appreciation of the questions, we will draw on language theory, current at the University of Paris of Jean's day, relating to the human institution of language and the characteristics of figurative or 'improper' speech, meaning speech which is not to be understood in terms of the 'proper' (i.e. the normal, immediately obvious and primary) senses of the words in question. The fact that Jean was knowledgeable about such matters should not, it will be argued, prompt us to confuse earnest with game. But major issues are at stake. Is 'dirty talk' to be justified with reference to theory of linguistic *impositio* and *institutio*, or attacked on grounds of the social embarrassment or 'shame' which it causes? Furthermore, what exactly is 'vulgar' or inappropriate material for literature written *in vulgari*?

Chapter 4 examines the semantic cross-currents which complicate the ending of the *Rose*, rendering closure impossible and consequently undermining the text's occasional aspirations towards historical, moral, or metaphysical truth. Ovidian comedy conflicts with the moral affirmation of 'natural' sexuality which Jean inherited from *De planctu naturae*, as Jean has his lover-figure put on a richly problematic performance of normative masculinity. This is not to deny, however, that the earlier narrative offers hints of homoeroticism. In particular, the male gender of Bel Acueil (representing the lady's 'Fair Welcome') is tantalizing and troubling. J. A. Hoeppner Moran has gone so far as to claim that Jean 'gradually weans his lover from homosexual to heterosexual intercourse' as he shifts his attentions from Bel Acueil to the Rose herself.[52] In a more comprehensive study, which seeks to accommodate a wide range of possible readings (including a 'queer' interpretation) of Bel Acueil, Simon Gaunt claims that 'a model of sexuality (and subjectivity) that functions through the opposition of heterosexual to homosexual desire' is in fact subverted in the *Rose*. According to Gaunt's argument, the poem 'may condemn

---

[52] 'Literature and the Medieval Historian', *Medieval Perspectives*, 10 (1995), 49–66.

homosexual activity, but its allegorical love plot is articulated through the love story of two masculine figures [i.e. Amant and Bel Acueil] while its erotic metaphors are susceptible to a reading that renders them potentially homoerotic rather than heteronormative'.[53] My own argument is that the 'exuberant exploratory play and indeterminacy' which pervades the *Rose* does not extend that far. There are indeed, as I have acknowledged above, homoerotic hints—and certain readers of the *Rose* did respond to them, as Gaunt's splendid study brings out. But there was a strong impulse in the early reception of the *Rose* to normalize the poem, to remove the thorns of its most radically experimental erotic language, as I suggest at the beginning of Chapter 6 (with reference to Jean's heterosexual 'dirty talk'). In any case, many aspects of the relationship between Amant and Bel Acueil can be considered in terms of homosociability rather than homoeroticism. Furthermore, Amant's handsomeness, kissable mouth, and sweet breath are indeed praised to encourage Bel Acueil's receptiveness to his advances,[54] but it is a female figure (Venus) who is doing the praising here, from a female subject-position and ultimately for a female recipient, the Rose herself; similarly with La Vielle's recommendation of Amant to Bel Acueil. The gendering of personifications in this allegory of love is certainly confusing but is not necessarily subversive of sexual norms.

Chancellor Gerson would doubtless have been horrified by any suggestion of homosexual valence in the *Rose*; its manner of heterosexual pronouncement was quite bad enough. He was incensed by the ending of the *Rose*. Affirming the proverb 'En la fin gist le venin' (which may be rendered as 'The sting lies in the tail'), he exclaims: 'Las! Quelle ordure y est la mise et assemblee! quelz blasphemes y sont dis! quelle dyablie y est semee!' ['Alas, how much impurity is set down and accumulated in the tail of this book! What blasphemies! What diabolical wickedness is sown therein!'][55] De Meun's oblique account of Amant's sexual spectacular provoked further anger. It is the height of evil, the chancellor declares, to say 'teles choses estre sactuaires

[53] 'Bel Acueil and the Improper Allegory of the *Romance of the Rose*', *New Medieval Literatures*, 2 (1998), 91–2.   [54] Ibid. 69–70.
[55] *Traité*, in *Le Débat*, ed. Hicks, p. 78; trans. Baird and Kane, p. 84.

et euvres sacrees et adourees' ['such things are sanctuaries, sacred and estimable acts']. In thus speaking of God and mixing (*entouillier*) the vilest things with divine and holy words, he committed as much irreverence as if he had thrown 'le precieux corps Nostre Seigneur entre les piés de pourceaulx ou sur ung fiens' ['the precious body of Our Lord Jesus Christ under the feet of swine or upon a heap of dung'].[56] Admittedly, Jean had abstracted materials from the great Alan's book—but *corrumpuement* ('corruptly'), Gerson insisted.[57] De Meun's arch-defender Jean de Montreuil saw the matter very differently.[58] For him the 'end' (*finis*) of the *Rose* is the continuation of the human race—and that, of course, is very much the purpose of *De planctu naturae*.[59] Here de Montreuil is employing *finis libri* to designate the 'end' in the sense of the aim or objective of a text, this usage deriving from the term's usual signification in the *accessūs ad auctores*.[60] But this ingenious defence fails to take account of the poem's very marked genre-shift from complaint (in the sense of Alan's *planctus*) to comedy. The *finis* and/or *utilitas* of the *Pamphilus*—to cite the best-known representative of medieval Latin comedy—were generally described as 'showing how to find beautiful girls' or 'the knowledge of those things contained in this book', while its claim to be an ethical work supposedly rested on the fact that it 'spoke about behaviour'.[61] Such vague and totalizing categorizations will simply not work for either the 'end' or the ending of the *Rose*. Far more sophisticated—and contested—sites of value are involved, as I argue in Chapter 4.

---

[56] *Traité*, in *Le Débat*, ed. Hicks, p. 79; trans. Baird and Kane, p. 85.

[57] *Traité*, in *Le Débat*, ed. Hicks, p. 80; trans. Baird and Kane, p. 86.

[58] De Montreuil is described by Christine as 'secretary (*secretaire*) of the King our Lord and Provost of Lille'; *Le Débat*, ed. Hicks, p. 11; trans. Baird and Kane, p. 46. Still useful is A. Combes's forceful study *Jean de Montreuil et le chancelier Gerson*, (Paris, 1942).

[59] *Le Débat*, ed. Hicks, p. 44; trans. Baird and Kane, p. 154. See further below, pp. 174–6.

[60] De Montreuil may have had in mind the actual sexual climax of the poem as well, however, including its (albeit brief) declaration of the Rose's impregnation, since here he seems to be taunting the celibate Gerson with the suggestion that his religious vocation led him to think ill of the *Rose*—or perhaps he is the kind of man who is unable to play any part in the propagation of the species! See below, pp. 194–5. On the two senses of *fin* cf. the discussion by Brown-Grant, *Moral Defence*, p. 35.

[61] See e.g. the *accessus* to the *Pamphilus* ed. Huygens, *Accessūs ad auctores*, p. 53.

In any case, neither Gerson nor de Pizan was prepared to laugh off an ending which they found deeply offensive. One can imagine de Montreuil asking them, 'But surely you know that the satirist has a special poetic license, a recognized office, which allows him to do things which are prohibited to other writers?[62] Don't you realize that the laughter which de Meun is provoking is that righteous risibility which is one of satire's most powerful weapons, as it seeks to strip away hypocrisy and expose vice in its true colours?'[63] To which Gerson would have no doubt replied that, by de Montreuil's leave, he did know Juvenal very well,[64] and Jean de Meun's humour was of a very different kind, quite debased and scurrilous. Gerson put it clearly on record that he regarded the *Rose* as no laughing matter: 'ce n'est point jeu: et n'est plus perilleuse chose que de semer mauvaise doctrine es cuers des gens' ['it is not a jest, neither is anything more dangerous than to disseminate a perverse doctrine in the hearts of men'].[65] Christine de Pizan heartily agreed. Had de Meun told us something about bears or lions or birds or other strange creatures, this would have been matter for laughing (*matiere de rire*) on account of the fable. But instead he had maligned the female sex in a work which can neither be read nor quoted at the table of queens, princesses, and worthy women.[66]

The great problem for friend and foe alike of the *Rose* is, of course, its sheer excess—it mixes together so many different *matiere*s, so many different genres (with all their various formulae, manoeuvres and expectations), that no clear route through the text is visible or perhaps even possible. P.-Y. Badel speaks of how the poem 'fait jouer les structures les unes dans et contre les autres';[67] Douglas Kelly has written a substantial monograph

---

[62] On what de Montreuil actually said about the *satirici officium* see *Le Débat*, ed. Hicks, p. 42; trans. Baird and Kane, p. 154, and also the discussion on p. 92 below.

[63] On satire's righteous risibility see below, Ch. 2. Moreover, Ovid's *Ars amatoria* was sometimes described in *accessūs* as a jocular work (see below, p. 207), but of course Jean's opponents in the *querelle* refused to see the joke.

[64] On Gerson's irritation at what he took to be the implication that he was ignorant of the sources of the *Rose*, see *Responsio ad scripta cuiusdam* (apparently to Pierre Col), in *Le Débat*, ed. Hicks, p. 172; trans. Baird and Kane, p. 151.

[65] *Traité*, in *Le Débat*, ed. Hicks, p. 69; trans. Baird and Kane, p. 78.

[66] *Le Débat*, ed. Hicks, p. 20; trans. Baird and Kane, p. 54.

[67] Badel, *Rose au XIVe siècle*, p. 54.

with the pellucid title *Internal Difference and Meanings in the
'Roman de la Rose'*;[68] Sarah Kay finds it full of 'play in the
sense of space for movement: instability; uncertainty';[69] while
Simon Gaunt suggests that its openness to the various 'interpretative agendas' of different readers is due to a deliberate 'multi-
valency' which 'is enabled by the allegorical play that ultimately
prohibits the determination of fixed meaning'.[70] Jean Gerson
confronted the issue more caustically: 'that work is rightly
called a formless chaos, a Babylonian confusion, and a German
broth, like Proteus changing into all his shapes'.[71] Little wonder,
then, that so many of the *Rose*'s readers have tried to prune its
superabundance of meaning, to pluck individual petals rather
than the entire flower. Chapters 5 and 6 describe several such
attempts by medieval interpreters and imitators of the poem, the
fundamental thesis being that medieval literary theory, as channelled by commentary-tradition and its beneficiaries, helped to
shape the reception of the *Rose*, just as it had contributed to the
formation of the poem itself.

Our discussion begins with an account of how, in the
querelle, the Col brothers and Jean de Montreuil sought to
affirm its textual authority while its opponents directly challenged that very claim. It is highly revealing to note the site on
which the disputants chose to fight. In the first instance, the
defenders did not indulge in integumental analysis of the *Rose*,
promote hermeneutics of a kind which allegorized the text's
troublesome indeterminacies and subversions out of existence.
Neither did they exploit the 'satire justification', by arguing
comprehensively that de Meun's outspokenness, and indeed his
occasional obscenity, were justified by the *satirici officium* which
entitled that type of poet to boldly go where others were forbidden. True, on two occasions Jean de Montreuil did briefly touch
on this method of rationalization. But he failed to develop it—
thereby ignoring what was, in my own view, the best opportunity on offer from Latin literary theory. But could de Montreuil
have indeed presented Master Jean de Meun in this way in his

---

[68] For full reference see n. 25 above.
[69] Sarah Kay, *The Romance of the Rose* (London, 1995), p. 52. Cf. the conclusion to her article 'Venus in the *Rose*', p. 28.
[70] 'Bel Acueil and Improper Allegory', p. 91.
[71] *Le Débat*, ed. Hicks, p. 166; trans. Baird and Kane, p. 147.

non-extant French treatise in defence of the *Rose*,[72] thereby providing what would have been a sort of theoretical companion piece to Honoré Bouvet's *L'Apparition de maître Jean de Meun*, where the poet appears as a mordant social critic? On the face of it, this seems unlikely: otherwise Christine de Pizan or Jean Gerson would have felt obliged to call into question de Meun's satiric credentials and credibility.

The main battle was waged, in fact, over the status of the *Rose* as a poem about love (which conveyed its doctrine in a manner that no one had to dig deep to understand). De Meun was perceived as a 'Medieval Ovid' by his lovers and loathers alike. For his defenders the comparison with Ovid was a crucial means of authorizing the *Rose*; for his attackers it was a means of destroying any claim to authority which the poem might conceivably have. Hence both camps drew many of their crucial critical terms and categories from the standard medieval commentary on Ovid (particularly the ideas of literary 'utility' or moral usefulness, and of the general, good authorial intent which ultimately reconciles apparent differences and discrepancies). For Christine de Pizan and Jean Gerson the *Rose* was a despicable *ars amatoria*, even worse than Ovid's original treatise. For his part, Pierre Col mounted an ingenious defence of the poem as a more comprehensive and accessible *remedium amoris* than the one Ovid had provided (in particular, the *Rose*'s vernacular doctrine was easily available to women, who could now learn how to defend themselves against male assault).[73] Theory of *personae* was also brought to bear, as when de Meun's defenders argued that as a moral writer he is to be regarded as quite distinct from those characters in the poem who express opinions which are dubious or simply wrong. But Gerson and Christine de Pizan refused to accept this distinction, arguing that a writer is responsible for all the views expressed in his work, immoral characters indicating an immoral writer.

The level of Christine's Latinity, and the extent of her learning, is a matter of some controversy in modern scholarship. She

---

[72] This lost work is referred to in de Montreuil's letter *Cum, ut dant*, in *Le Débat*, ed. Hicks, p. 28; trans. Baird and Kane, p. 40: 'in the French language (*gallica scriptione*) I described the genius [*ingenium*—more prudently translated as 'ingenuity'] of the author . . .'. A reconstruction has been attempted by Peter Potansky, *Der Streit um den Rosenroman* (Munich, 1972). [73] See below, pp. 76–8.

may well have learnt Latin (or improved on her existing knowledge of the language) at the court of Charles V. Inevitably that would have entailed some study of the traditional 'set texts', the *auctores* (including Ovid), together with the *accessūs* which accompany them in manuscript and which represent the standard introductory teaching on those texts.[74] *Accessus* vocabulary passed into their vernacular translations and imitations, and no doubt Christine knew some of them. Her contributions to the *querelle de la Rose* reveal that she was quite conversant with many of the crucial discourses of academic literary theory. For instance, when Christine accused the *Rose* of being 'lacking in utility', she was apparently mindful of the technical sense which the Latin form *utilitas* bears (in the *accessūs* and beyond) as designating the didactic effect and moral worth which the commentator had to identify in order to confirm the authority of the text he was describing. In the *accessūs,* moreover, discussion of *utilitas* involved, or was related to, assignment of the text to the branch of knowledge (or *pars philosophiae*) to which it rightfully belonged. By denying the *Rose* any utility, Christine was in effect refusing the poem entry into the canon of authoritative texts and denying it any function as a scientific work.[75] Her knowledge of the academic methodology of establishing *auctoritas* is evident, as is the skill with which she uses this knowledge for her own polemical purpose.

Christine definitely had a clear sense of the crucial position of Ovid within the school curriculum; in her view, it was as if poison had entered literate society particularly through the reading of this syllabus *auctor*.[76] Hence in her *Epistre au dieu*

---

[74] On the issue of Christine's education, see below, pp. 215–17.

[75] See below, pp. 235–9.

[76] Christine was by no means unique in her antipathy towards Ovid as *magister amoris*. Guibert of Nogent (1064?–*c.*1125) lamented how, in reading 'Ovid and the pastoral poets', his 'mind' had been 'led away by the enticements of a poisonous license': see John F. Benton, *Self and Society in Medieval France: The Memoirs of Abbot Guibert of Nogent* (New York, 1970), p. 87 n. Other twelfth-century monastic writers, particularly Bernard of Clairvaux and William of St Thierry, sought to establish a religious art of love in opposition to Ovid's secular one, as is argued by Jean Leclercq, *Monks and Love in Twelfth-Century France* (Oxford, 1979). An anonymous fourteenth-century poem, the *Antiovidianus*, 'attacks Ovid for using the beauty of his art to hide his foul and dangerous matter', as Michael A. Calabrese puts it in his monograph *Chaucer's Ovidian Arts of Love* (Gainesville, Fla., 1994), p. 24. On this work see also Hexter, *Ovid and Medieval Schooling*, pp. 96–9.

d'Amours she has the God of Love condemn the early teaching of the *Remedia amoris*, wherein Ovid attributes to women many nasty ways, 'repulsive, sordid, filled with wickedness' (281–5). This text engenders in clerics a prejudice against the entire female sex which they, in turn, pass on to their pupils.

'Si ont les clercs appris trés leur enfance
Cellui livret en premiere scïence
De gramairë, et aux autres l'apprennent
A celle fin qu'a femme amer n'emprennent'.

(291–4)

['Now since their childhood days the clerks have read
That book in grammar class, the subject that
One studies first. They'll teach it to the rest
In hopes they'll not seek out a woman's love'.][77]

The point is made even more trenchantly in George Sewell's eighteenth-century translation of Thomas Hoccleve's Middle English version of Christine's poem:

These wicked Clerks, averse to honest Truth,
Debauch the tender Principles of Youth;
Teach them, by idle Books, and foolish Rhymes,
To shun their [i.e. women's] Charms, and hate the Sex betimes;
Of guilty Maids, and Lovers lost, enroll
A canting, lying, lamentable Scroll.
Thus ev'ry Boy of some false Nymph can tell,
And curses Woman, as he learns to spell.

(249–56)[78]

Christine took her revenge by, *inter alia*, providing an alternative *vita Ovidii* to the type which those 'wicked Clerks' would have read in grammar class and which is preserved in the *accessūs*. In the *Cité des dames*[79] she recounts how Ovid had affairs with lots of women, since he had no sense of moderation and showed no loyalty to any particular one. Because of

---

[77] *Poems of Cupid, God of Love. Christine de Pizan's 'Epistre au dieu d'Amours' and 'Dit de la Rose'; Thomas Hoccleve's 'The Letter of Cupid'*, ed. T. S. Fenster and M. C. Erler (Leiden, 1990), pp. 48–9.

[78] *The Proclamation of Cupid*, in Fenster and Erler, *Poems of Cupid*, p. 230.

[79] On the *Cité* as 'the most powerful profeminine work of the Middle Ages' see Alcuin Blamires, *The Case for Women in Medieval Culture* (Oxford, 1997), pp. 219–30.

his licentiousness, he was sent into exile. Thanks to his influential friends, however, the poet was allowed to return to Rome. But he could not help falling back into his wicked old ways, and finally, because of his immorality, he was castrated.[80] This is particularly ironic, given the *Rose*'s obsession with castration as a threat to manliness, and Jean de Meun's counter-affirmation of the integrity of the male body and its natural assertion in heterosexual activity (as discussed in Chapter 4). One wonders if Christine ever wished castration on de Meun as well.

'Tu . . . mervilleusement interpretes ce qui est dit clerement et a la lectre' ['you interpret marvellously what is said clearly and literally'], exclaims an exasperated Christine de Pizan at one point to Pierre Col.[81] Our inquiry into the different ways, marvellous and otherwise, in which medieval readers interpreted and exploited the *Rose* continues in the final chapter, which concentrates on the text and gloss of the *Eschez amoureux*, a work profoundly influenced by the earlier poem but which seeks to diminish its subversive potential by compartmentalizing its love interest and affirming the superiority of Pallas (=Wisdom) over Venus. The *Eschez* is a much more orderly enterprise, and seems certain of its target audience in a way that the *Rose* never was. Obviously designed for the entertainment and sociopolitical education of young courtiers, it moves methodically from love to wisdom, ending (in the fullest text we have) with advice on the proper conduct of a marriage, how to bring up children and manage servants, the best location and plan for a house, and, finally, ways of making money. This process of integration, of reconciliation of at least some (for selectivity is crucial) of those elements which Jean de Meun had 'brought together and drawn in by force',[82] continues in an extensive mythographic commentary on the *Eschez* which dates

[80] *The Book of the City of Ladies*, i. 9; trans. Rosalind Brown-Grant (Harmondsworth, 1999), pp. 20–1. The tale of Ovid's dismemberment also appears in Jean Le Fèvre's *Livre de leesce* and at the beginning of his French translation of the pseudo-Ovidian *De Vetula*: see below, p. 167, n.12. Here Christine is, in effect, opposing Ovid's 'official' Latin life (which in itself is subject to considerable variation) with one which derives from vernacular elaborations and reworkings of it.

[81] *Le Débat*, ed. Hicks, p. 127; trans. Baird and Kane, p. 125.

[82] To quote Gerson's negative assessment ('assemblés et tirés come a violance'); *Traité*, in *Le Débat*, ed. Hicks, p. 76; trans. Baird and Kane, p. 83.

from the late fourteenth century. Recently this has been attributed, on convincing grounds, to Evrart de Conty (*c.*1330–1405), physician to Charles V of France and one of the group of translators who contributed to the extensive translation programme promoted by the king. Evrart's treatise draws on a major early medieval commentary, Macrobius' exposition of Cicero's *Somnium Scipionis*, as well as having been influenced by the *accessūs Ovidiani* (from which Evrart derives many of his critical terms) and indeed by scriptural exegesis (particularly commentary on the Song of Songs and the Apocalypse). By developing the medieval literary theory of *persona* (as transmitted by commentary tradition), Evrart asserts the ethical credentials of the *Eschez* and paves the way for the point at which the poem itself becomes blatantly moral—as it does in its final (extant) section, when the superiority of the love of wisdom is proclaimed.

This sixth and final chapter seeks to do two things. First, to bring out the way in which, for Evrart de Conty, taking on the mantle of the *magister amoris* meant a socioeconomic valorization of married love within the 'active life', *pace* Andreas Capellanus's misogamistic statements, which Evrart carefully ignores whilst drawing on the doctrine of love as passion expounded in *De amore*. Secondly, to locate Evrart's commentary on the *Eschez amoureux* within the history of vernacular hermeneutics. Here is the first full-scale commentary on a work written originally in French. In order to understand better the cultural significance of this fact, we must relate Evrart's work to the wider context of the European 'vernacular commentary tradition'—this term being deliberately ambiguous, to encompass both vernacular and Latin commentary on vernacular works, the essential point being that it is vernacular text which is the object of exegesis. My concern is with the processes of 'authorization', and I take it as axiomatic that *auctoritas* and canonicity are culturally conferred (for all kinds of reasons, including the political and socioeconomic) rather than the inevitable external reaction to literary merits which are inherent in the text, whether seen as quasi-mystical functions of textuality or as the sediments of authorial genius. Rather than asking if a writer's originality and inscribed selfhood were recognized and respected by his admiring public, I would ask, with

Foucault, such questions as 'where does [this discourse] come from, how is it circulated; who controls it?'[83]

Hence a brief review of parallel developments in Italy and Spain during the same period will be offered for purposes of comparison, and the question posed why there should have been a dearth of vernacular hermeneutics in late medieval England, a period which saw a remarkable flowering of original poetry in Middle English. The answer will help us to understand better the nature of French literary-cultural achievements in the age of Charles V, however short-term their effects may have been. Furthermore, without wishing for a moment to deny the significance of such instances of vernacular commentary tradition as have come down to us, it is important to acknowledge the relatively limited and local impact of many of them. Late medieval vernacular commentary was, with some distinguished exceptions, a coterie practice and interest, which failed to achieve deep penetration of the respective national cultures. Given that there was rarely any large-scale medieval copying of the most important documents, their survival was a matter of the merest chance. Dino del Garbo's scholarly (Latin) commentary on *Donna mi prega*, the *canzone d'amore* of Guido Cavalcanti (*c.*1259–1300), was preserved thanks to the copy which Giovanni Boccaccio made by his own hand. While commentaries on Dante Alighieri (1265–1321) flourished in the fourteenth century, only two appeared in the fifteenth and three in the sixteenth century—in some measure a consequence of humanistic disrespect for anything in the vernacular, even the mould-breaking *Comedy*, though it must be added that Dante's controversial political and theological views failed to win him friends in certain high places. Turning to Spain, it is sobering to note that the quite stunning commentary on the first three books of the *Aeneid* by Enrique de Villena (1384–1434) survives in a unique manuscript. Returning to France, the case may be cited of the Latin glosses in the single surviving manuscript fragment of the *Eschez amoureux* poem. This is not to be confused with Evrart de Conty's extensive commentary; what

---

[83] Michel Foucault, 'What Is an Author?', in *Language, Counter-Memory, Practice*, ed. and trans. D. F. Bouchard and S. Simon (Ithaca, NY, 1977), pp. 113–38 (p. 138).

we are dealing with here is a set of brief and very specific textual glosses written either by the author himself or someone close to him.

All of this is, I believe, quite true, and perfectly fair comment. And yet—counter-statements can be made to balance all of those remarks. At the outset, we should recall that a large number of what are nowadays deemed to be masterpieces of medieval poetry survive in unique or few copies; hence the dangers of a merely quantitative measure should be recognized. However, if one wishes to maintain that quantitative measure, it may be noted that the decline in Dante's hermeneutic fortunes coincided with a rise in Petrarch's: ten major commentaries on *Il Petrarcha* appeared during the fifteenth and sixteenth centuries. Furthermore, and somewhat ironically perhaps, the manuscripts of Evrart de Conty's commentary on the *Eschez amoureux* far outnumber those of the poem itself: six complete copies plus a fragment as opposed to a single copy. (Another manuscript of the *Eschez amoureux* did survive into the twentieth century, but the text is now illegible, due to damage sustained during the Allied bombing of Dresden in 1945.) Most important of all for our purposes, the *Roman de la Rose*, a work within which medieval literary theory figures so crucially, enjoyed a quite extraordinary reception. This medieval best-seller is extant in over 300 manuscripts, was translated into English, Dutch, and Italian,[84] and continued to be read well into the Renaissance. Gontier Col was right, then, to predict that Jean de Meun's 'glory and fame . . . will live in the ages to come', to return to the quotation which opened this Introduction. He was wrong about the reasons for this, however. The *Rose* flourished not because Jean de Meun was successful in formulating coherent doctrine in 'saincte theologie' or 'philosophie' but rather on account of his disinterest in doing so—or, better, his interest in a far wider range of textual engagements. One of the poem's most discerning recent commentators has suggested that the secret of the *Rose*'s long success lies in the

[84] The most radical 'translation' of the *Rose* must surely be the Italian *Fiore*, where the basic narrative has metamorphosed into a sonnet sequence. For recent scholarship see the proceedings volume of the 1995 Cambridge conference on this work, ed. Z. G. Barański and Patrick Boyde as *The 'Fiore' in Context: Dante, France, Tuscany* (Notre Dame, Ind., 1997).

'possibilities' its allegory offers for 'exhuberant exploratory play and indeterminacy'; 'the *Rose* was popular not despite this apparent incoherence, but because of it'.[85] And here is the very quality which perplexed Jean de Meun's medieval opponents: for them, such incoherence resulted in the *Rose*'s failure to provide clear moral direction. Hence Chancellor Gerson's characterization of the poem as a 'formless chaos' and 'Babylonian confusion'.[86]

In my view, what contributed most to that 'play' or 'confusion' was Jean de Meun's ambitious attempt to overgo Ovid and succeed to the mastership of love, with all the intellectual instability, challenge and contestation which that office involved. By concentrating on the medieval literary theory within and around the protean *Rose*, the following chapters will, it may be hoped, demonstrate that any 'chaos' which it presents is due not to a lack of form but rather to a surfeit of competing forms, a true embarrassment of riches.

[85] Gaunt, 'Bel Acueil and Improper Allegory', p. 91.
[86] Cf. p. 26 above.

CHAPTER I

Academic Prologues to Ovid and the Vernacular Art of Love

Ovid was the most ambivalent of all the grammatical *auctores*—the expert on both the art of love and its rejection, an apparent misogynist (who could criticize women in the most brutal of terms) yet also a champion of legal, married love, an acclaimed mythographer (witness the *Metamorphoses*, regarded as a sort of 'Pagan Bible') as well as the ancient 'master of love'. These paradoxes afforded at once a challenge and an opportunity to medieval scholars, translators and imitators of the ancient poet, as they twisted the waxen nose of Publius Ovidius Naso in different directions,[1] quoting him as an expert on physics or medicine here, using him as a source and model for fashionable love poetry there. Moreover, he proved invaluable to vernacular poetics, since his text and gloss provided the means and the method for bestowing value on contemporary poetry in a way which would affirm its moral credentials while accommodating its interest in human desire.[2]

Then there is the all-important but exceptionally difficult matter of the intended and actual audiences of the several Medieval Ovids.While some of the works which we will touch on seem to fall within the genre of the clerical *jeu d'esprit*— being products of a world without women, texts written by *cognoscenti* for the recreation of their fellows—at least some of them seem to mark a point of transition. Ovid has left the medieval schoolroom and joined the secular society of medieval

---

[1] For Alan of Lille's remark about the 'waxen nose' of authority see below, p. 138.

[2] See A. J. Minnis, 'Authors in Love: The Self-Exegesis of Medieval Love Poets', in C. Morse, P. Doob, and M. C. Woods (eds.), *The Uses of Manuscripts in Literary Studies: Essays in Honor of Judson B. Allen* (Kalamazoo, Mich., 1992), pp. 161–91.

aristocrats. Consequently the scholarly apparatus of *accessūs*[3] and glosses which accompanied his work in manuscript, and above all else the scholastic literary attitudes which permeated those hermeneutic procedures, have been adapted to suit the needs of this larger, and more heterogeneous, interpretative community.

Thanks to recent research it is now known that 'the age of Ovid' occurred rather later than once supposed.[4] It was not until the time of Arnulf of Orléans that the *Metamorphoses* received full exegetical treatment, a set of largely philological glosses being complemented with an allegorical exposition.[5] Arnulf was a major influence on three thirteenth-century works of Ovid scholarship, William of Orléans's *Bursarii Ovidianorum*, John of Garland's *Integumenta Ovidii* (*c*.1230), and the anonymous 'Vulgate' commentary on the *Metamorphoses* (composed *c*.1250, possibly at Orléans).[6] According to Arnulf's *vita Ovidii*, which was adapted by the 'Vulgate' commentator,[7] both the *Remedia amoris* and the

---

[3] For a definition of the term as used here see p. 13, n.30, above.

[4] See e.g. Birgen Munk Olson, 'Ovide au moyen âge (du IXe au XIIe siècle)', in G. Cavallo (ed.), *Le Strade del testo* (Bari, 1987), pp. 67–96, together with the relevant material in his book *I classici nel canone scolastico altomedievale* (Spoleto, 1991), pp. 23–55, 120; also Frank T. Coulson's introduction to his edition of the 'Vulgate' Commentary on Ovid's *Metamorphoses: Vulgate Commentary*, pp. 2–7. See further Coulson, 'Unedited Lives of Ovid', pp. 152–207, and Coulson and U. Molyviati-Toptsis, 'Vaticanus latinus 2877: A Hitherto Unedited Allegorization of Ovid's *Metamorphoses*', *Journal of Medieval Latin*, 2 (1992), 134–202.

[5] The main study of Arnulf as Ovid commentator remains Ghisalberti, 'Arnolfo d'Orléans'. See further Frank T. Coulson, 'New Manuscript Evidence for Sources of the *Accessus* of Arnoul d'Orléans to the *Metamorphoses* of Ovid', *Manuscripta*, 30 (1986), 103–7, and Ralph Hexter, 'Medieval Articulations of Ovid's *Metamorphoses*: From Lactantian Segmentation to Arnulfian Allegory', *Mediaevalia*, 13 (1987), 63–82. Hexter notes that 'medieval Ovid commentaries were not by nature allegorizing and moralizing', and so 'we must see Arnulf's inclusion of allegorical interpretation . . . as an innovation' (p. 77).

[6] On William of Orléans see Hugues-V. Shooner, 'Les *Bursarii Ovidianorum* de Guillaume d'Orléans', *MS* 43 (1981), 405–24. For the John of Garland poem see the edition by F. Ghisalberti, *Integumenta Ovidii: Poemetto inedito del secolo XIII* (Messina, 1933). On the 'Vulgate' commentary see Coulson's partial edn. (n. 4 above) and also his article 'The "Vulgate" Commentary on Ovid's *Metamorphoses*', *Mediaevalia*, 13 (1987), 29–61.

[7] For Arnulf's *vita*, see Ghisalberti, 'Arnolfo d'Orléans', pp. 180–1, repr. in A. G. Elliott, '*Accessūs ad auctores*: Twelfth-Century Introductions to Ovid', *Allegorica*, 5.1 (1980), 6–48 (pp. 12–17). For the 'Vulgate' commentator's, see Coulson, 'Unedited Lives of Ovid', pp. 78–82.

Metamorphoses were written in an attempt to mollify the Emperor Augustus, who was incensed by the *Ars amatoria* wherein the poet had taught young Roman men how to be adulterers and young Roman women how to be unchaste. Arnulf proceeds to emphasize Ovid's moral *intentio* in describing transformation: the poet was not concerned with teaching about external, physical changes which result in good or bad corporeal forms, but rather with making us understand the nature of internal, spiritual change, so that we may be led from error towards knowledge of the true Creator. The work's *utilitas* or ethical usefulness is the instruction of divine matters which is achieved through its account of the transformation of temporal things.[8]

Elsewhere the apologetic, compensatory mission of the *Remedia amoris* is elaborated. According to the *accessus* to this work which has been edited by R. B. C. Huygens (Munich, Clm 19475 being taken as the base text), Ovid had written a manual of love, the *Ars amatoria,* 'in which he taught young men where to find mistresses', and how to be nice to them when they had found them, 'and he had given girls the same instructions. But some young men indulged their passion to excess' and were not in the least backward in having 'affairs with virgins, and even married women and female relatives, while the young women submitted themselves to married men just as much as to unmarried men. The result was that Ovid became very unpopular with his friends and with others. Afterwards he regretted what he had done, and, being anxious to be reconciled with those he had offended, he saw that the best way of achieving this was to discover the antidote for the love he had proffered to them'. So Ovid set about writing the *Remedia amoris,* in which he advises young men and women alike who have been 'trapped in the snares of love as to how they may arm themselves against unlawful love'.[9]

---

[8] The technical terms here cited are part of the lexical set associated with what Richard Hunt described as the 'type C' prologue, which usually discussed a text's title or name (*titulus*), intention (*intentio auctoris*), end or objective (*finis*), ethical utility (*utilitas*), material or subject (*materia*), organization (*ordo*), and method of stylistic and/or didactic procedure (*modus agendi*), together with the branch of learning (*pars philosophiae*) to which it pertained. For this and other types of academic prologue see Minnis, *Authorship*, pp. 15–33.

[9] *Accessus ad auctores*, ed. Huygens, p. 34; trans. in Minnis and Scott, *Medieval Literary Theory*, p. 25.

The poet's ultimate moral agenda was affirmed in *accessūs* to the *Heroides*.[10] William of Orléans is utterly typical in describing its *materia* as 'unlawful and foolish love', and its *intentio* as commendation and condemnation: commendation of certain girls who, like Penelope, practise legal love, but condemnation of illicit lovers like Phedra and foolish lovers like Phyllida and Oenone.[11] Similarly, in the second of the *Heroides* prefaces edited by Huygens, the work's intention is stated to be commendation of lawful marriage and love. It pertains to ethics (*ethice supponitur*), because Ovid is 'teaching good morality and eradicating evil behaviour. The ultimate end (*finalis causa*) of the work is this, that, having seen the advantage (*utilitas*) gained from lawful love, and the misfortunes which arise from foolish and unlawful love, we may shun both of these and may adhere to chaste love.'[12]

Moralizing scholarship of this type constitutes a rather vain attempt to police the meaning of Ovid's erotic poetry, by controlling it through moral structures and strictures. But of course the texts resist such imposition.[13] Ovid's amatory verse

---

[10] For glosses on the *Heroides* see the relevant material in Hexter, *Ovid and Medieval Schooling*. See further the copious materials transcribed by M. C. E. Edwards, 'A Study of Six Characters in Chaucer's *Legend of Good Women* with reference to Medieval Scholia on Ovid's *Heroides*' (B.Litt. diss., University of Oxford, 1970), esp. pp. 29–37.

[11] Cf. the text of this *accessus* from Vatican, MS Vat. Lat. 2792 as transcribed by Ghisalberti, 'Mediaeval Biographies of Ovid', p. 44.

[12] *Accessūs ad auctores*, ed. Huygens, p. 30; trans. Minnis and Scott, *Medieval Literary Theory*, p. 21. On Ovid as a champion of married love see H. A. Kelly, *Love and Marriage in the Age of Chaucer* (Ithaca, NY, 1975), pp. 75–8, 97–9.

[13] As Warren Ginsberg says, 'the strain to give Ovid scruples is evident'; he suggests that the 'explanations' which medieval commentators 'give to establish the utility of his poems are clear, if indirect, admissions of how unfit a dispenser of moral precepts Ovid is': '*Ovidius ethicus*? Ovid and the Medieval Commentary Tradition', in J. J. Paxson and C. A. Gravlee (eds.), *Desiring Discourse: The Literature of Love, Ovid through Chaucer* (Selinsgrove, 1998), p. 62. On the other hand, it should be recognized that medieval scholarship on the *auctores*—Ovid included—helped to make available to practising poets an array of possibilities which the standard commentaries could do little to contain. Cf. Nicolette Zeeman's insightful remark, albeit made in a rather different context, that the 'schools may have evolved for their own purposes of epistemological control propositions and theories about poetry which made it possible for writers outside the school to evade those very purposes of control'. She brings out superbly well the paradox that traditional teaching about poetry, despite its efforts at regulation, in some measure afforded a licence to poets: 'teaching may have had textual consequences which the most ingenious glossator could not have rendered safe': 'A License to Poets', pp. 156, 174.

was composed for a sophisticated audience of young Roman aristocrats who would find in the *Ars amatoria* 'a delicious incongruity and tension between form and content'.[14] A provocative presentation of love as 'a worthy and strenuous occupation, like farming or hunting', this poem nevertheless affords human desire a certain respect (though its pervasive irony prohibits the unequivocal emergence of such a serious sentiment): there was a strong Roman tradition of 'frankness in sexual matters'.[15] Along the way, it pokes fun at the political and moral values of Augustan Rome. A heady mixture indeed.[16] Which became even more volatile, so to speak, in the hands of its medieval readers. Ovid's words could be appropriated in a wide variety of ways by his glossators and imitators. This elasticity may be illustrated in the first instance by a review of relatively straightforward attempts to relocate the poet within different cultural perspectives, which, in addition to their inherent interest, will pave the way for the more complicated contestations of discourses which this chapter will proceed to investigate.

Textual transformations: Jacques d'Amiens, the Confort d'amour, *Guiart*

The following three French 'arts of love' do not exploit the *accessus* tradition as such, but certainly represent major ways in which Ovid was metamorphosed in the Middle Ages—as the poet of courtly compliment and as an authority in the sphere of ethics—while making very clear just how problematic such transformations could be. It was virtually impossible to rewrite Ovid's subtle and shifting texts in the often anodyne terms of

---

[14] A. S. Hollis, 'The *Ars amatoria* and *Remedia amoris*', in J. W. Binns (ed.), *Ovid* (London, 1973), p. 93.

[15] Ibid. 89, 84–5. Hollis comments: 'It was not really intended as a practical guide to ensnaring the opposite sex, any more than Virgil really intended his *Georgics* to be a practical handbook of farming' (p. 85).

[16] See further Peter L. Allen, *The Art of Love: Amatory Fiction from Ovid to the* 'Romance of the Rose' (Philadelphia, 1992), who describes how Ovid, the *praeceptor* and *vates*, chips 'away at his own credibility'. 'Each reversal' reveals 'that the world of the *Ars* is unstable and deceptive', and the reader has to seek 'a balance between the truth and falsehood, the illusion and disillusionment of the text' (p. 16).

fashionable flattery and refined self-display, and as a 'clerk' he
fell far short of the moral standards of Christian clericism,
despite the regular attempts (to which we have referred above)
to confine his works within the subject-area of ethics.

The first of our chosen translations is the work of a poet who
identifies himself as 'Jakes d'Amiens'.[17] He produced a French
version of the *Ars amatoria* in 2384 verses; a translation of the
Remedia amoris in 625 verses (usually known as the *Confort
d'amour*) was attributed to Jacques by Gustav Körting, but in
the face of scholarly opposition he later withdrew this claim.[18]
Jacques takes great liberties with the *Ars amatoria*, employing
the device of the amatory dialogue which had been used so elaborately by Andreas Capellanus. Here Ovid's text has been
pressed into the service of *fine amor*, and the poet-*persona* is
fully implicated in its performance: love for the 'debonnaire'
one who holds his heart in her prison was (he declares) what
prompted his poetry, and he hopes that it will further his suit.
May Love grant that it is agreeable to the 'tres douce dame' who
often makes his face pale (i.e. with love-suffering); indeed, without her love he cannot do anything that might ever please. In the
Epilogue to his *Art d'amors*, as a 'fine lover' Jacques addresses
everything in this book to his beloved, begging mercy with his
hands clasped in prayer, that she should take mercy and pity on
him, lest he should die.[19]

---

[17] I have used the edition by Gustav Körting, '*L'Art d'amors*' *und* '*Li Remedes
d'amors*' (Leipzig, 1868; repr. Geneva, 1976). There is also an edition by D. Talsma,
L'Art d'amours van Jakes d'Amiens (Leiden, 1925), repr. in A. M. Finoli, *Artes
amandi, da Maître Elie ad Andrea Capellano* (Milan, 1969), pp. 31–121. On
Jacques see further G. Paris, 'Chrétien Legouais et autres traducteurs et imitateurs
d'Ovide au moyen âge', *Histoire littéraire de la France*, 29 (1885), pp. 468–72, and
G. Kühlhorn, *Das Verhältnis der* '*Art d'amours*' *von Jacques d'Amiens zu Ovids* '*Ars
amatoria*' (Lepizig, 1908).

[18] The controversy is discussed well by Reginald L. Hyatte, 'The *Remedia amoris*
of Ovid in Old French Didactic Poetry' (Ph.D. diss., University of Pennsylvania,
1971), pp. 8–10. Hyatte's study concentrates on four texts: the *Confort d'amour*,
the final section of Guiart's poem, the adaptation of the *Remedia amoris* in the
Eschez amoureux, and a fifteenth-century translation of the *Remedia* (which he
edits).

[19] The atmosphere of courtly compliment created by this work is very similar to
that found in the anonymous *Clef d'amors* (dated 1280 by Gaston Paris), a poem of
some 3,200 octosyllabic lines which follows the *Roman de la Rose* in employing the
figure of the God of Love, who appears to the poet and orders him to write on the
art of loving. The poet hides his own name and that of his beloved in his text, which

Jacques's *Art d'amors* includes advice to women, though it should be noted that this draws on only a small part of Book 3 of the *Ars amatoria* itself; for the most part he adapts material from Book 2 to that purpose.[20] Even more remarkably, the anonymous poet of our second translation, the *Confort d'amour*, manages to direct his remedies against love to his lady—an action which, one may well think, is at variance with his own interests as her suitor.[21] The matter of this work, he asserts, relates to honesty and courtesy, and does not contain anything which is badly spoken or villainous. To blame those who should be praised is a waste of intelligence, and such behaviour wins neither praise nor glory; rather, those who act in this way make themselves hated by those who should love them. This is what happens when some-one writes ill of women, being unable to write either praise or good of them. The *Confort* poet does not say that women are without blemish, for there is no mortal who does not sin—even the heavens themselves are flawed. This attitude persists through-out his text, the result being that many of Ovid's misogynistic statements are softened. The *Confort* poet will seek to define love of a kind which is both wise and courtly, in opposition to that mad love which existed, for example, between Tristan and Isolde. In his view, true love between men and women is governed by charity, and will be rewarded in heaven.[22] Returning to the poet's statement of his purpose: the *Confort* poet explains that he sought matter from which he could make a poem that would profit and please, this being the objective at which all writers aim. Whether the poetry is good or bad the matter itself is subtle and noble enough and pleasing, he claims. It is not made of fable, the stuff of romance—'ne de Renart ne d'Ysengrin / ne de Biernart ne de Belin' (45–6)—rather it is drawn from pity and rhymed and made by love.

Fine amor, then, is what motivates this author's writing, and

---

represents a highly individual adaptation rather than a translation of the *Ars amatoria*. This work has been edited by A. Doutrepont, '*La Clef d'amors*': *Texte critique avec introduction, appendice et glossaire* (Halle, 1890); repr. in Finoli, *Artes amandi*, pp. 123–228.

[20] As is noted by Bruno Roy in the introduction to his edition of a work which we will be discussing later: *L'Art d'amours: Traduction et commentaire de l'Ars amatoria d'Ovide* (Leiden, 1974), p. 15.

[21] '*L'Art d'amors*' und '*Li Remedes d'amors*', ed. Körting, pp. 69–71.

[22] Cf. Hyatte, '*Remedia amoris* in Old French Didactic Poetry', p. 21.

gives him joy and happiness in his work. If his 'tres douce, cortoise et sage' lady, for whose love he has undertaken this enterprise, were pleased by it, he would take no notice of what anyone else thinks. Indeed, it should be agreeable to her, if she hears and knows it by heart—and not just to her, for all those who suffer the penance of love could obtain comfort and relief if they knew well this teaching. The *Confort* poet proceeds to emphasize how his text may help his lady's love-suffering. Seeing the very sweet one looking pale and lost because of the wounds of love's dart, and not knowing what to do about it, he set about providing a cure, so that she might be diverted and at least better able to bear her suffering even if she cannot put an end to it. So, he started to write out of pity for her. Henceforth, in the text which follows, the reader will be able to hear how 'one can have joy of love'— altogether a novel way to introduce remedies against love![23]

Our third Ovid translation is rather different from the ones discussed above, since it takes the Roman poet in a very different direction, in consolidating his position (as claimed in the *accessūs Ovidiani*) as a moral writer whose texts ultimately 'pertained to ethics'. Its translator, who refers to himself simply as 'Guiart, qui l'art d'amours vost en romanz traiter' (5), says he will first teach how one may find and conquer the beloved one, secondly, how one should behave during the affair, and thirdly, how one rids oneself of a lover who is no longer pleasing![24] This could be regarded as taking one step further the strategy outlined near the beginning of the *Ars amatoria*—

> Principio quod amare velis, reperire labore,
> Qui nova nunc primum miles in arma venis.
> Proximus huic labor est placitam exorare puellam:
> Tertius, ut longo tempore duret amor.
>
> (i.35–8)

[23] There is a certain awkwardness here, of course. On whose account has his lady been suffering? His? Someone else's? One possible rationalization is that his nominal mistress is so far above this humble clerkly poet that all he can expect from her at best is polite attention and perhaps patronage, her love-life being conducted within the highest ranks of society. Perhaps this is the wrong way to approach a poet who may have had no mistress but his muse; what we are dealing with here is conventional courtly language and rhetorical posturing. However, such discourses have their own logic and hence the question may be asked.

[24] Here I use the edition by Louis Karl, 'L'Art d'Amour de Guiart', *Zeitschrift für romanische philologie*, 44 (1924), 66–79, 181–7.

[First, strive to find an object for your love, you who now for the first time come to fight in warfare new. The next task is, to win the girl that takes your fancy; the third, to make love long endure.]

—in anticipating the objective of the *Remedia amoris*. However, Guiart comes up with a way of making 'love long endure' that was not recommended at this point by Ovid—namely, marriage.[25] If the target of one's Ovidian seduction strategies is worthy of respect, if she is loyal and good, then, in Guiart's view, that is the best course of action.

Guiart declares that a reproach which might be directed at him, that he is treating of the good and the evil at the same time, is not well founded. He proceeds just like the labourer who pulls out thistles and nettles in order to protect the seed, for earth which is poorly prepared yields little. Aristotle 'en son livre' says that a clerk may deceive his mistress, yet elsewhere in the same book he condemns such falsity. In the first instance, then, the writer wishes to demonstrate worldly vice; subsequently he will reveal the truth that consists in the service of God.

> Or vos voil je premier mostrer la fauseté,
> La vanité du monde et la desloiauté;
> Puis determinerai apres la verité,
> Coment on doit servir le roi de majesté.
>
> (25–8)

In sum, the work has basically a bipartite structure. Ovid functions within the first part, material from the *Ars amatoria* giving way to material from the *Remedia amoris* (now, Guiart declares, he will teach the lover how to leave his lady!), a transition which paves the way for the second, homiletic part of the poem. One should not lose God and His Mother just for a little pleasure which does not last long, as the Bible teaches. The world is old and full of falsity, lacking in either faith or loyalty. Whoever wishes to possess everlasting life must reject the works of the devil and worldly pleasures. And so forth. Guiart, taking over sixteen strophes from the poem *Des cinq vegiles*, advocates

---

[25] It should be recalled that Ovid was not deemed to be a particularly misogamistic writer, largely on account of the commentary tradition on his *Heroides*; see p. 38 above.

confession, repentance, and penance, and recommends the
virtues of humility, charity, patience, and respect for the church.
He proceeds to treat briefly of the seven sacraments and the Ten
Commandments, then offers a kind of love which is very different from the one described earlier: all men should be loved and
given good counsel, with hatred and war being despised.

> Porte pes et amor a toute gent en terre,
> Done loial couseil, s'on le te vient requerre,
> Envers touz les pechiez aies haine et guerre . . .
>
> (217–19)

The poem ends with a prayer to the Virgin as *mediatrix*. Apart
from the brief statement in the prologue in defence of his treatment 'ensemble bien et mal' (14), no attempt is made in ideological terms to reconcile this explicit Christian doctrine with
the teaching of the *Ars amatoria* as retailed earlier in the poem;
Guiart seems to assume that the text's structure will support the
burden of its meaning. And that structure very much reflects the
schematization of Ovid's works which is found in the *accessūs
Ovidiani*.

Scholia secularized: L'Art d'amours

Now we may move to consider a far more sophisticated 'Art of
Love' which makes substantial use of academic commentary
tradition, the *L'Art d'amours*, a translation into French of the
Ars amatoria along with gloss materials.[26] The first two books
of this work have been assigned to the period between 1214/15
and the end of the first third of the century, while the third book
seems to be an addition produced during the age of Philippe le
Bel (more precisely, some time between 1268 and the end of the
century). The specific set or sets of Latin glosses which the
translators followed have not yet been identified—which is
hardly surprising, given the present state of our knowledge, and
one of the many pieces of scholarly business which cannot be

---

[26] This work has been edited by Bruno Roy (cf. n. 20 above) and translated by
Lawrence B. Blonquist, *L'Art d'amours (The Art of Love)*, vol. 32 (New York,
1987). This translation has been drawn upon in the following discussion, though I
have made occasional alterations.

finished until such time as we have comprehensive editions of the medieval scholia on Ovid's poems.[27] What is perfectly clear, however, is that both the anonymous writers sought to go beyond the staple fare of the schools. In *L'Art d'amours* an impressive array of Latin and French texts are brought together. As well as citations of a substantial number of Ovid's other poems, along with the Bible, Horace, and the *De consolatione philosophiae* of Boethius, contemporary French songs and proverbs are liberally cited. Moreover, in the third book the *Roman de la Rose* is mentioned, while the first two books draw on French romances which were written towards the end of the twelfth century and the beginning of the thirteenth, namely Chrétien de Troyes's *Philomena, Athis et Prophilias, Li Fet des Romains,* and *Blancandin.*[28]

The following discussion will focus on the earlier translator. It may be inferred that he was a cleric who enjoyed considerable professional contacts with members of the aristocracy, whose interests and lifestyles were markedly different from those of a priestly caste which valued celibacy; certainly he himself was not in the business of implementing Ovid's 'commandments'. This comes across very clearly in his statement that 'Quant ilz sont riches et a gogues, si vuellent amer par amours et vuellent bouhourder et chevauchier et estre prisiez et alosés pour l'avoir et pour la richesse dont ils sont gros et enflez' ['When young men are at leisure, they want to practise the art of love. They want to amuse themselves, to ride horses, and to be prized and praised for having love and riches with which they are fat and puffed up'].[29] Here an element of clerical censoriousness has crept in. But in general such opinions are kept in check, as when Ovid's recommendation that 'the contest of noble steeds'[30] should not escape the lover, because there are many opportunities for courtship at that kind of event, prompts the citation of material from the romance of Blanchandin, who won the love

---

[27] A team of scholars comprising R. J. Tarrant, Frank T. Coulson, Ralph J. Hexter, and Ann Moss is currently engaged in the preparation of an annotated catalogue of the medieval and Renaissance commentaries on Ovid for the *Catalogus translationum et commentariorum.*

[28] Cf. *L'Art d'amours,* ed. Roy, pp. 49–53, 56.

[29] Ibid. 64; trans. Blonquist, p. 2.

[30] *Ars amatoria,* i.135–36; a passage much mangled in translation, though of course the French writer may have been misled by a gloss.

of his *amie* through a tournament.[31] Women, the French translator declares, take note of which of the *bachelliers* is the most
impressively armed and holds himself best on his horse, and
they are eager to see their menfolk bear certain tokens of their
love, though some knights dare not wear them openly for fear
of blame. Moreover, the translator offers an example of what
women sing in their dance-songs (*karoles*), and goes on to claim
that they are eager to take part in such things, this being a type
of amusement ('maniere de deduit') which is pursued solely for
the opportunities it affords them for display of their jovial qualities and their hearts' delights.[32] Indeed, he adds, the more they
are censured for such activities, the more they indulge in them.
But no thoroughgoing moral condemnation follows.

The hypothesis that the anonymous translator is, so to speak,
endeavouring to pull his punches finds further support in his
struggle with the meaning of Ovid's infamous *fallite fallentes*,
'deceive the deceivers' (i. 645), often read as a statement that since
all women are untrustworthy, men should have no scruples about
deceiving them. But in this case the anonymous Frenchman seems
to want to mute his original, at least initially;[33] his rendering
singles out as targets for deception only those women who want
to deceive 'you' (the addressee being constructed as male,
inevitably): 'Decevés ceulz que vous cuidiés qui vous vouldroient
decevoir: c'est droiture.'[34] The concomitant is that 'we must be
loyal to all those whom we expect to be loyal to us'. But then he
seems to defect to the other side: Ovid is credited with the belief
that since no woman is loyal to men we need not bear them any
loyalty. However, he continues, we must not deceive anyone else
('nul autre') if they do not deceive us before we deceive them.
Presumably he has in mind here certain males who do not seem
to deserve having pre-emptive 'traïson' being directed against
them? But his meaning is far from clear. Ecclesiastes 7:28 is then
brought in, 'Who will find a friend (*amie*) in a woman?', which is
interpreted 'as if he said openly: there is none'.

[31] *L'Art d'amours*, ed. Roy, pp. 84–5; trans. Blonquist, p. 16.
[32] *L'Art d'amours*, ed. Roy, p. 86; trans. Blonquist, p. 17.
[33] This can be read, of course, as a response to Ovid's recommendation to make
women fall into the snare which they themselves have laid (*Ars amatoria*, i.646),
which implies reactive rather than gratuitous or universal deception.
[34] *L'Art d'amours*, ed. Roy, pp. 144–5; trans. Blonquist, pp. 61–2.

That would seem to settle the issue. Yet later, when amplifying Ovid's advice about not reproaching a woman with her faults, the translator goes beyond the motivation of sexual self-interest in advocating chivalrous gallantry of a more general sort. 'Sur toutes riens gardés vous de dire villenie aux femme' ['Above all else be careful not to say churlish things to women'], and not only to the woman you love but to others, because if your beloved hears you speaking ill of another she will suppose that you really think the same of her.[35] The translator then refers to something which he has said elsewhere ('comme nous avons dit ailleurs'): the honour of the man who bears no honour to women must be dead.

> Qui aux dames honneur ne porte,
> La sienne honneur doit estre morte.
> (3384–5)

This seems to be a quotation from a poem (as yet unidentified, and perhaps lost) in which our anonymous writer spoke in the discourse of 'courtly love', a language which was often far more flattering to women than that found in the text of the Roman *praeceptor amoris*—as is indicated by (for example) the difficulties which Jacques d'Amiens had in trying to make Ovid into a poet of *fine amor*. Moreover, earlier in *L'Art d'amours* a song had been cited which youths sing when they want to show their ladies that they are prepared to serve them in word and deed—

> A ma dame servir
> Ay mis mon cuer et moy.
> (562–3)

—though a hint of cynicism is apparent in the remark that the lover must appear to be willing to serve in every way possible; that 'semblant' might imply 'faus semblant' (one may recall the figure of that name in the *Roman de la Rose*), the hypocritical demeanour of the man who will do and say anything in pursuit of his own pleasure.

It may therefore be concluded that the cleric responsible for the original *L'Art d'amours* is on the one hand making his Latin text more accessible to relatively uneducated readers and, on the

---

[35] *L'Art d'amours*, ed. Roy, p. 216; trans. Blonquist, p. 114.

other, adapting it to tastes which often were different from those of the schoolteachers who had compiled the Latin commentary on which, one may presume, he drew so substantially. However, the mark of the schools is very visible at the beginning of the text. The first twenty lines of our anonymous writer's preface follow the pattern of the *accessūs ad auctorem*.[36] It begins by identifying 'Trois choses furent pour lesquelles Ovide fu esmeüs a faire ce livre', the three reasons or causes which moved Ovid to write. This reflects *accessus* terms like *causae suscepti operis* and *causae scribendi*; by the middle of the thirteenth century the variant *causae moventes ad scribendum* was in use,[37] due to the impact of the 'Aristotelian Prologue' which followed the structural principle of the four causes (efficient, material, formal, and final).[38] In this case the *trois choses* consist of Ovid's wish to display his knowledge, to reveal the fickleness of his youth, and to teach the art of love, how to win over women and young girls.

The last of these reasons, the French translator continues, is 'neccessaire, convenable et profitable, car aucuns jouvenceaulx estoient qui tant amoient aucunes damoiselles et si ne les sçavoient prier ne requerre ne fere chose par quoz ilz les peüssent avoir' ['necessary, proper and profitable, for there are some young men who love young women very much, but they do not know how to court them, or how to find them, or how to do the things that would win them']. So they may despair, and either kill themselves or go mad. It was 'pour oster yceste desesperance des cuers aus jouvenceaulx' ['in order to remove

---

[36] *L'Art d'amours*, ed. Roy, pp. 63–4; trans. Blonquist, pp. 1–2. The first 12 lines or so (in Roy's edition) of this introduction are generally similar to the *accessus* to the *Ars amatoria* which may be the work of Fulco of Orléans, but the French version represents a considerable adaptation and amplification of the Latin text as published by Hexter, *Ovid and Medieval Schooling*, p. 219.

[37] On such terminology see Minnis, *Authorship*, pp. 31, 41, 80, 244n., 249n. For the *causae scribendi* in Ovid commentary specifically see e.g. Ghisalberti, 'Mediaeval Biographies of Ovid', pp. 52, 59; Hexter, *Ovid and Medieval Schooling*, p. 219; Minnis and Scott, *Medieval Literary Theory*, p. 26. For the term *causa intentionis* in Ovid commentary see further Ghisalberti, 'Mediaeval Biographies of Ovid', pp. 56, 58; Hexter, *Ovid and Medieval Schooling*, p. 224; Minnis and Scott, *Medieval Literary Theory*, pp. 25, 26.

[38] For a basic description of this prologue form see Minnis, *Authorship*, pp. 28–9. On the four causes in Ovid commentary see e.g. Ghisalberti, 'Mediaeval Biographies of Ovid', pp. 45, 50–2; Minnis and Scott, *Medieval Literary Theory*, pp. 361, 364.

this despair from the hearts of the young'] that Ovid wrote this book. Generally this is reminiscent of William of Orléans' remark that Ovid was moved to write the *Ars* when he saw young men suffering because they were doing the wrong things through ignorance of love.[39] Or the statement in an anonymous twelfth-century *accessus* to the *Ars amatoria* (as edited by Huygens, and described by Ralph Hexter as the 'canonical' introduction to that text)[40] that Ovid's *intentio* 'is to instruct young men in the art of love, and how they should behave towards girls when having a love-affair. . . . The way he proceeds in this work is to show how a girl may be picked up (*possit inveniri*), how when picked up she may be won over, and, once won over, how her love may be retained'.[41] Indeed, the French writer goes on to remark that once an attractive woman is found, her lover must know how to keep her, and so Ovid includes advice on this matter in his teaching. Such remarks derive, of course, from Ovid's own statement near the beginning of the *Ars amatoria* concerning the three tasks facing the lover: first, strive to find a love-object, second, win her, and third, 'make love long endure' (i. 35–8; cf. pp. 42–3 above).

The text's *tiltre* (cf. the Latin *titulus*)[42] is given as 'Cy commence l'Art d'amours', this being a version of the form commonly found in the *accessūs Ovidiani*.[43] And its *matiere* and *entent* (cf. *materia* and *intentio*) are described together as: 'Sa matiere si est hommes et femmes amoureux et ententis aus commandemens d'amours, dont il entent a introduire' ['His subject-matter is amorous men and women who are occupied with the commandments of love, which he intends to introduce'], though the earlier account of the *causae scribendi* had already offered a full explanation of the poet's intentions. Finally, the 'fin cause', 'c'est a dire l'accomplissement de ceste euvre', which is understood when one has read the book through in its

[39] London, British Library, Add. MS 49368, fo. 81ʳ.

[40] Hexter, *Ovid and Medieval Schooling*, pp. 46–7.

[41] *Accessūs ad auctores*, ed. Huygens p. 33; trans. Minnis and Scott, *Medieval Literary Theory*, p. 24.

[42] On this *accessus* term see Minnis, *Authorship*, pp. 19–20.

[43] See e.g. the *accessus* printed by Hexter, *Ovid and Medieval Schooling*, p. 219: 'Titulus talis est: O[uidii] Nasonis de amatoria arte liber primus incipit'. Cf. the specifications of the poem's *titulus* in the *accessūs* printed by Ghisalberti, 'Mediaeval Biographies of Ovid', pp. 45, 47.

entirety, is stated to be that we should keep the commandments
which Ovid provides. *Fin cause* translates the Latin *causa finalis*,
a term which could be used within the earlier *accessus* as largely
synonymous with the terms *intentio* and *utilitas* or indeed as an
extension of either or both of them.[44] (*Causa finalis* appeared
frequently as one of the 'type C' prologue headings, as R. W.
Hunt called it,[45] before becoming one of the four 'introductory
causes' that constituted the 'Aristotelian Prologue'.)

This *accessus* to his *auctor* having been completed, the
anonymous writer then remarks upon his own activity as translator. Rather coyly, he claims that had he wanted to he could
have given a more careful exposé and extracted more meaning
out of the text. But science which is open to everyone is
supposed to be worth nothing. By contrast, when words are
obscure one is more eager to pause over them in order to understand what is being said. The clear implication is that there is
much left to think about in *L'Art d'amours*. This is not, of
course, to be seen as some sort of invitation to delve deeply into
our text to discover some profound meaning hidden underneath
its literal sense. Rather, the translator is seeking to praise and
recommend his work by giving it a faint aura of mystery, in
claiming that it is replete with intriguing secrets; this was a
device often used by the writers of the day, even in cases in
which the meaning of what they had said was perfectly obvious.

The remainder of the French prologue and its greater part,
lines 28–109 in Roy's edition, follow another form which was
extensively used in the schools, this being what may be termed
the *accessus ad artem*, by which I mean a general discussion of
the art or science to which the text appertained rather than the
actual text under study. The distinction was well expressed by
Thierry of Chartres at the beginning of his *De Inventione*
commentary, in terms of what is necessary to know concerning
the art (*circa artem*) and concerning the textbook (*circa
librum*).[46] Concerning the art of rhetoric, he explains, ten things

---

[44] For examples of the use of the term *finalis causa* in *accessūs Ovidiani* see ibid.
45, 47, 50, 51; Hexter, *Ovid and Medieval Schooling*, pp. 16, 103, 111–12, 147,
158, 161, 220, 226; Minnis and Scott, *Medieval Literary Theory*, pp. 23, 24, 28,
361, 364.   [45] Cf. Hunt, 'Introductions to the *Artes*'.
[46] See N. M. Häring, 'Thierry of Chartres and Dominicus Gundissalinus', *MS* 26
(1964), 281; cf. 286.

must be considered: its genus, what the art is in itself, along
with its material, office, end, parts, species, instrument, master
or practitioner, and the reason why it is called rhetoric. Thierry
also used the *extrinsecus/intrinsecus* distinction to designate
respectively what must be known in advance before practising
an art and what must be known in practising the art itself. This
technical vocabulary is followed, for example, in Alan of Lille's
commentary on the *Rhetorica ad Herennium*, and it influenced
William of Conches' commentary on Priscian.[47] But within the
study of grammar the headings *extrinsecus* and *intrinsecus* took
over the functions performed by the headings *circa artem* and
circa librum in Thierry's paradigm: an 'extrinsic' discussion
comprised a discussion of the place in the scheme of human
knowledge occupied by grammar, together with a summary of
the defining characteristics of this art, while the heading *intrinsecus* introduced a systematic discussion of the text itself, often
in accordance with the vocabulary characteristic of the 'type C'
prologue, and which has in part been rendered into French in
L'Art d'amours.

In short, the anonymous translator has reversed the *extrinse-
cus/intrinsecus* order: the latter comes first, then the former,
with his own little piece of self-recommendation in between.
While he does not actually use the term *extrinsecus* (or *intrinsecus* either, of course) his concerns are those which were traditionally introduced by that heading, particularly the
specification of the place in the scheme of human knowledge
which is occupied by the art of love. A fundamental distinction
is made between the mechanical arts and the arts which
combine art and knowledge ('science'), the latter category being
divided into the liberal arts and the non-liberal arts ('ars non
liberaux'). There are only seven liberal arts practised at the
present time among Christians, he explains, these being
branches of study which may be pursued without the prohibition of the law or of the clergy. By contrast, there are certain
non-liberal arts which are prohibited either by earthly justice
and secular princes (including poisoning and killing by treason)
or by earthly justice and by the church (such as sorcery and

---

[47] See M.-T. d'Alverny, *Alain de Lille: Textes inédits* (Paris, 1965), pp. 52–5; also
Minnis and Scott, *Medieval Literary Theory*, pp. 122–4, 130–4.

divination). Moreover, the clergy in particular are barred 'by the church', meaning by canon law, from taking part in such arts as gaming, wrestling matches, and tournaments, along with games of dice, chess, and tables (elsewhere these are identified as aristocratic pursuits) and of course necromancy, 'qui est art d'enchantement'. Finally there are certain non-liberal arts which are not prohibited: these include astronomy (providing prediction ('sors') and necromancy are not involved) and the art of love. Here then, at last, is where the *ars amandi* fits into the scheme of things, the place it occupies within the *ordo scientiarum*. It is not forbidden for two reasons: first, it encourages love in certain people who, had they never read about the art, would have lacked the desire or the will to pursue it, and secondly, it ensures that the lover, who without the art would not know how to woo and win his lady, will avoid death. This is reminiscent of the treatments of the *finis* of the relevant art which were characteristic of the extrinsic prologues of rhetoricians and grammarians.

Moreover, the manner in which the anonymous translator actually began his excursus *circa artem* (i.e. ll. 28–41) seems to have been influenced by schoolteachers' discussions of the *artifex* or practitioner of the art under discussion. We are assured that love is rightly called an art, in accordance with the usual etymology and explanation of what an art is, since one who wishes to attain knowledge of love has 'moult de choses convient faire et dire et penser' ['to do, say, and think many things']. And because we are dealing with a true art, it can be known in several ways: *par nature, par coustume, par aprison*, and *par orgueil et folie*. Women and young men of the leisured class ('les femmes et les joennes hommes oiseux') know it by nature. (A few lines later the category *par nature* is amplified to include a specification of age; 'par nature et par jouvence'.) Love is known by custom to poor people and ribalds, a statement which presumably means that for such people it is merely a matter of habit, a crude mechanical exercise. Clerks know it by teaching inasmuch as they read the histories, books, and commandments (presumably he has Ovid's love-commandments in mind) of the ancients. Peasants ('villains') know it by folly and pride, which might mean that people of lower rank engage in foolish, untutored amatory practices on the one hand and on the other fall into the sin of pride by attempting to pursue a form of love which is far above their station.

Here, then, are the different ways in which love may be said to be practised, and the different kinds of practitioner. But clearly, it is the natural occupation of a small section of society: young men and women of the aristocratic élite who have time on their hands. And in this supposed fact we have found one of the major bases of the secularizing impulse of *L'Art d'amours*. For our French writer seems to be drawing on a discourse which counterbalances (or perhaps undermines) the moralizing discourse which he has inherited from the Latin commentary tradition on Ovid's love poetry. He speaks a language and conveys attitudes which often occur in, for example, commentaries on the chapter on 'heroic love' which is included in the *Viaticum* of Constantine the African (who died *c.*1087 at the abbey of Montecassino), a major textbook in university faculties of medicine.[48] Such material—which is quite absent from Jacques d'Amiens's courtly reworkings of Ovid—works in support of *fine amor*, lending at least some of its clichés genuine scientific substance. Of course, its approach and idioms are not identical with those of 'courtly love'; for example, in place of emotive affirmation of the pleasure and ennobling power of love is found detached analysis of a predictable and almost inevitable condition which afflicts aristocrats and can cause them much distress. Rather, the two discourses—of the court and the medical school, as it were—have forged an alliance, an alliance which works against the commonplace theological/ philosophical idioms which treat human desire as potentially (and often actually) sinful.

According to *L'Art d'amours*, love is known naturally by aristocrats, who moreover have the leisure (or is it idleness?) to indulge their pleasures; they enjoy being praised on account of their loves and their riches. But the illness can prove fatal. Male sexual frustration may lead to despair, which may lead to suicide. Some men hang themselves, explains the French translator, while

---

[48] In contrast with the beginning of *L'Art d'amours*, this medical discourse is not present in the remarks about the kinds of death love can cause which are found in the *accessūs* published by Ghisalberti, 'Mediaeval Biographies of Ovid', pp. 45, 47 (*re* the *Remedia amoris*) and Hexter, *Ovid and Medieval Schooling*, p. 219 (*re* the *Ars amatoria*).

others die by the sword, fire, or water. Still others lose their sense and memory on account of love.[49] Similarly, in the first *Viaticum* commentary to survive, the work of Gerard of Berry (late twelfth century), 'wealth and leisure—that is, pleasure in daily life—are the prerogatives of the nobility, and it is they who suffer the disease of love', to cite Mary Wack's cogent summary.[50] The Arabic medical texts that were the sources of such Western teaching do not mention a particular social class as more or less susceptible to the lovers' malady, but the medieval medical profession labelled 'love as an occupational hazard of the nobility. It became another mark of precedence, like wealth and leisure themselves'.[51] Thus, 'heroic' love—there was considerable confusion between the terms *eros* and *heros*—was specified to be the love that belonged to a lord or nobleman,[52] as in Gerard of Berry's statement that 'Heroes are said to be noble men who, on account of riches and the softness of their lives, are more likely to suffer this disease'.[53] Indeed, Constantine himself had said elsewhere (in his *De coitu*) that 'a leisured heart (*cor ociosum*) and daily joy increase libido'.[54] In his *Viaticum* he explains that 'if erotic lovers are not helped so that their thought is lifted and their spirits lightened, they inevitably fall into a melancholic disease'.[55] If untreated or unchecked, this could prove terminal. Cures recommended by Constantine included actual consummation of one's love (or,

[49] *L'Art d'amours*, ed. Roy, p. 63; trans. Blonquist, p. 1.

[50] Mary Frances Wack, *Lovesickness in the Middle Ages: The 'Viaticum' and Its Commentaries* (Philadelphia, 1990), p. 39.

[51] Ibid. 61. Love was linked with melancholy, also generated by the noble lifestyle; large amounts of leisure and pleasure allowed digestive products to collect which could in due course turn into black bile, and cause melancholy. Cf. the commentary on the *Eschez amoureux* (*c*.1398–1405) by the physician Evrart de Conty (the main subject of our final chapter), which speaks of the melancholy that is caused 'by loving excessively *par amours*, which malady is called in medicine *amor hereos*': *Eschez amour. moral.*, ed. Guichard-Tesson and Roy, p. 191. Later, Evrart quotes Avicenna as saying that the sickness which comes of loving *par amours* too foolishly 'is a kind of melancholy sometimes engendered by thinking too intensely about one's loves, and especially when the lover cannot attain or accomplish what he desires. It is not at all said without a reasonable cause that "love is a sickness of thought" ' (p. 544). On love as a mental illness cf. pp. 9–10 above.

[52] Wack, *Lovesickness*, pp. 46, 60. For the history of the term *amor heroicus* see further Danielle Jacquart and Claude Thomasset, 'L'amour "héroïque" à travers le traité d'Arnaud de Villeneuve', in *La Folie et le corps*, ed. Jean Céard (Paris, 1985), pp. 143–58.   [53] Wack, *Lovesickness*, pp. 202–3; cf. p. 60.

[54] Cited ibid. 61.   [55] Ibid. 188–9.

failing that, therapeutic sex with another woman—an idea which Christian *medici* found difficult to support!), recreational activities with friends, and the enjoyment of music, poetry, and beautiful gardens. Gerard of Berry does manage to include in his list of treatments 'consorting with and embracing girls, sleeping with them repeatedly, and switching various ones' (i.e. changing partners regularly).[56] But this apparent invitation to promiscuity is tempered by the thought that the lover's ardour may be lessened by instruction in the unlovely aspects of sex and the female body, which I presume is how this statement should be interpreted: 'the counsel of old women is very useful, who may relate many disparagements and the stinking dispositions of the desired thing'. At this point Gerard nears the territory occupied by Ovid's *Remedia amoris*.[57] The translator responsible for *L'Art d'amours* limits himself to the statement that his author Ovid wrote this treatise in order to 'remove despair from the hearts of the young'; here then is a courtship manual which may help its readers to achieve their amatory ends and preserve their health.

The concept of youth is vitally important in the French translator's account of love. It was the hearts of the young that Ovid sought to ease; there are some young men who love young women very much but do not know how to court them; when young men are at leisure they want to practise the art of love. But there is even more to it than this, for Ovid himself was a young man when he wrote the *Ars amatoria*.[58] The second of the three causes which lie behind this work is identified as Ovid's wish 'to reveal the fickleness of his youth'.[59] Later, after

---

[56] Ibid. 202–3.

[57] In the *accessus* to the *Remedia amoris* which has been edited by Huygens, Ovid is described as prescribing 'just like a doctor. For a good doctor gives medicine to the sick to heal them, and to the healthy so that they may escape illness' (trans. Minnis and Scott, *Medieval Literary Theory*, p. 25). Conversely, Ovid was quoted as an authority in certain medical commentaries. See e.g. the citation of his comments on the effects of wine by Egidius and Peter of Spain in their *Viaticum* commentaries in Wack, *Lovesickness*, pp. 208–9, 248–9.

[58] For Ovid as a poet who wrote love poetry in his youth and/or who addressed a youthful audience see the relevant remarks in the *accessūs* printed by Edwards, 'Chaucer's *Legend of Good Women*', pp. 32, 34, 35; Ghisalberti, 'Mediaeval Biographies of Ovid', pp. 44, 45, 47, 51, 57, 59; Hexter, *Ovid and Medieval Schooling*, p. 219; Minnis and Scott, *Medieval Literary Theory*, pp. 24, 25, 27, 362.

[59] *L'Art d'amours*, ed. Roy, p. 63; trans. Blonquist, p. 1.

his discussion *circa artem,* the translator develops this idea, in
stating that the poet, 'tant comme il fut adolescent en sa joen-
nesse, fist ce livre en la premiere fleur de son temps et de sa vie'
['when he was an adolescent and when he was a young man,
wrote this book in the first flower of his age and of his life'].[60]

Thus the *Ars amatoria* is put firmly in its place, as the expression of a young man, with all that implied in medieval culture.
When this translation was produced the notion that youth was
the age in which men were particularly susceptible to love, given
that this was the age in which their bodily heat was at its greatest, was an utter commonplace, along with the concomitant that
in one's maturity wiser counsels would, or at least should,
prevail. There was some dispute over when precisely *adolescentia* began and ended within a person's life-cycle (depending on
which scheme of the ages of man was being followed), but
general agreement that this was the *aetas amoris.* Sexuality, as
John Burrow puts it, 'was held to be a function' of that same
natural body heat 'whose gradual cooling, as the fuelling moisture ran out, caused the processes of ageing. Hence it was easy
to see why the fires of love should die down in the later ages of
life', when the colder humours dominated.[61]

Our French writer opts for the scheme of the seven ages of

---

[60] *L'Art d'amours,* ed. Roy, p. 69; trans. Blonquist, p. 4.

[61] J. A. Burrow, *The Ages of Man: A Study in Medieval Writing and Thought*
(Oxford, 1986), p. 157. 'Adolescence is of a hot and moist complexion,' declares
the ninth-century Arabic scholar who was known in the West as 'Johannitius' (cited
by Burrow, p. 22). Moreover, as Wack explains, a hot complexion was believed to
be the most important underlying cause of the lovers' malady (*Lovesickness,* pp.
98–100). 'We see that it befalls the young most,' asserts Peter of Spain in the B
version of his *Viaticum* commentary (Wack, *Lovesickness,* p. 243). See further the
A version of this commentary (ibid. 221–5), in which the time at which young men
most desire intercourse is investigated. (Unfortunately, Wack's summary of this
argument, on p. 86, is misleading.) Evrart de Conty has much to say about the characteristic virtues and vices of the young (and the old) in the extensive excursus on
the ages of man which forms part of his commentary on the *Eschez amoureux,* ed.
Guichard-Tesson and Roy, pp. 473–95. Aristotle is quoted as saying that young
people willingly follow their passions, i.e. the affections and pleasures of their
hearts. They ordinarily desire nothing but games, joy, delight, and worldly idleness.
(It is hardly surprising, then, that in the Judgment of Paris the young man should
have given the golden apple to Venus.) Because they have great natural warmth, they
willingly follow their passions and accomplish their desires, especially those of
sensuality. Young men do not possess great sense or reason, because of their lack of
experience, and change their minds easily, because the humours in their young
bodies are in themselves very changeable.

man, in providing an account of the sequence of the human life-cycle.[62] This scheme, which is Ptolemaic in origin, does not seem to have attained the level of popularity enjoyed in the Middle Ages by the 'four ages' model, which was reinforced by theories relating to the four humours and the four seasons. However, an elaborate version of the seven ages (related to the corresponding planets) is included in Jean Froissart's *Le Joli Buisson de Jonece* (1373), and we know that King Charles V of France possessed a tapestry representing 'Sept ars et estats des ages des gens'.[63] The translator of *L'Art d'amours* may have been prompted to use the seven ages scheme by his own earlier account of the seven liberal arts, but no such connection is made explicit in the text. And his interest is in the physiological and psychological changes which are characteristic of the various ages rather than their planetary associations. Thus he explains that the first age is infancy, when one is unable to talk; the second, boyhood, an age of innocence, wherein one can speak well; the third, adolescence, 'when one has his first beard'; the fourth, manhood, the time of full strength; the fifth, maturity, when a man has acquired all the virtues and enjoys 'all the beauty and natural sense that nature can give him'; the sixth, old age, when one is aged and white-haired; the seventh, decrepitude, when one 'drivels' and 'returns to the actions and speech of children'. The first age encompasses one year and a half; the second, seven years; the third, eighteen; the fourth, twenty-five; the fifth, fifty; the sixth, sixty to eighty years; the seventh, one hundred years, this being the time in which 'age chills man and woman, and they lose reason, strength, and memory'.

From our point of view, however, what is most important is that this account of the seven ages follows on from the translator's statement that Ovid wrote the *Ars amatoria* 'comme il fu adolescent en sa joenesse'. 'En la premiere fleur de son temps et de sa vie' he may have been, but this age had its limitations also, as a time of immaturity and passion. Hence the translator's remark near the beginning of his work that one of the reasons why Ovid wrote was to reveal the fickleness ('legiereté') of his

[62] *L'Art d'amours*, ed. Roy, p. 69; trans. Blonquist, p. 5.
[63] As is pointed out by Burrow, *Ages of Man*, pp. 40–1.

youth. While the translator's account of the seven ages does not
specifically link love with *adolescentia*, the implicit connection
is too obvious to miss. It may be inferred that this was the age
in which Ovid himself had acquired his amatory experience, for
the translator proceeds to gloss Ovid's claim that he is 'maistre'
of 'l'art d'amer' with the statement that no one can know sickness as well as the person who has experienced it: 'Nulx ne puet
si bien savoir la maladie comme cellui qui l'essaiee.'[64] Because
Ovid had tried love, he can 'speak better than anyone else about
what one must do to conquer it' ('A la conquerre' probably has
the sense here of 'to master it', though there is of course the
possibility of mild irony, a nod towards the tenets of the
Remedia amoris). In short, Ovid experienced and wrote about
lovesickness, what medieval writers could call *amor heros* or
hereos, in his adolescence, and it is up to the reader to contem-
plate the significance of that fact. He may have the authority of
experience, and love may be a quite natural activity for the
young. Hence his French translator declares that Ovid wished
'to prove that it is not a sin for a man and a woman to go to bed
with each other, for it is a natural thing, and nature bestows it,
nor is it an artificial thing'.[65] But the age of love is also a time
of *legiereté*, removed from the perfect age of man's life when he
is in possession of all the virtues and all the sense that nature
can give him.

Here is a source of contestation, a facet of instability of
meaning, of a kind which is recognizable in many medieval
poems about love, including the pseudo-Ovidian *De Vetula*, the
Roman de la Rose itself, and also those subsequent *dits
amoureux* which further cultivated several major areas of the
rose garden. In *De Vetula* an old woman substitutes herself for
the beautiful maiden with whom the poet-*persona* had an assig-
nation.[66] Some twenty years later 'Ovid' has another chance of
happiness with his beloved: the lady's husband having died, she

[64] *L'Art d'amours*, ed. Roy, p. 70; trans. Blonquist, p. 5.
[65] *L'Art d'amours*, ed. Roy, pp. 204–5; trans. Blonquist, p. 106.
[66] There are two recent editions, by Paul Klopsch, *Pseudo-Ovidius 'De Vetula':
Untersuchungen und Text* (Leiden, 1967), and Dorothy M. Robathan, *The Pseudo-
Ovidian 'De Vetula': Text, Introduction and Notes* (Amsterdam, 1968). See further
Robathan's article, 'Introduction to the Pseudo-Ovidian *De Vetula*', *Transactions
and Proceedings of the American Philological Association*, 88 (1957), 197–207.

is free to marry him. However, by this time she too has become old, a *vetula* reminiscent of the woman who originally had thwarted the *persona*'s passion. Disillusioned, he takes a crash course in mathematics, music, and philosophy, and seeks the consolations of religion. Finally 'Ovid' predicts the Virgin Birth of Christ (a passage which was frequently quoted as authoritative), and becomes a Christian. In this poem, then, the ephemeral nature of youth and its follies is made abundantly clear: physical beauty will not last, and when it goes, desire fades.[67]

In the *Jugement dou Roy de Behaingne* which Guillaume de Machaut composed shortly before 1342, the (female) personification Youth is described as being incapable of holding to any pledge or promise unless it is in accordance with her own desires. Here the fictional king of Bohemia laughs at her utterly predictable behaviour (she 'spoke only as she ought', Machaut declares) and accepts the grim advice of Raison, who teaches the hard lesson that human love is a corporeal thing which dies with the body (1848–99, cf. 1672–715).[68] Similarly, in Machaut's *Remede de Fortune* (*c*.1340) a man who has matured through the love of a good woman looks back to the time when 'Jonnesce me gouvernoit / Et en oyseuse me tenoit, / Mes oeuvres estoient volages; / Varians estoit mes courages' ['Youth governed me and kept me in idleness, my works were fleeting, my heart was changeable'] (47–50).[69] Even more damningly, in Froissart's *Le Joli Buisson de Jonece* an older I-*persona* (some 35 years of age, well into his maturity on any medieval theory of the ages of man) dreams his way back to past youth and love. But the personification Youth is confronted and interrogated: why, the I-*persona* asks, can his one-time mistress now be so young and fresh, as she was in the past? Youth replies by offering two *exempla*. One features lovers who are blinded by love to their own ageing; the other concerns a dead mistress who

---

[67] On the sexual politics of *De Vetula* see esp. Ralph Hexter, 'Ovid's Body', in James I. Porter (ed.), *Constructions of the Classical Body* (Ann Arbor, Mich., 1999), pp. 327–54.

[68] *'Le Jugement du Roy de Behaigne' and 'Remede de Fortune'*, ed. and trans. James I. Wimsatt and William W. Kibler (Athens, Ga., 1988), pp. 152–5, 144–7. For a discussion of Machaut's own reappraisal of this view see Minnis, *Chaucer's Shorter Poems*, pp. 158–9.

[69] *'Behaigne' and 'Fortune'*, ed. Wimsatt and Kibler, p. 170.

stays young only in her lover's dreams. This is hardly reassur-
ing. Froissart could be read as putting forward the proposition
that love is very much at home in the minds of those who are
ignorant of, or who wilfully ignore, reality. His *persona* awak-
ens to thoughts of approaching death and divine judgement; the
Joli Buisson ends with a prayer to the Virgin. It can be seen as
a more subtle reworking of the themes of *De Vetula*.

These highly sceptical realizations of Youth are particularly
remarkable since they feature in a genre which generally celebrates and recommends a refined version of the emotion with
which that age of man's life was irrevocably associated.[70] They
betray the clerical training of Machaut and Froissart inasmuch
as they evince theological distrust of the body and its pleasures,
not to mention the Boethian relegation of human desire as an
inferior good which must be left behind as the soul ascends
towards the *summum bonum*. But other discourses in their texts
often offer a more positive version, of *fine amor* as at once a
transformative experience and a learning process which en-
nobles the lover and makes him—for it is the male psyche which
is usually on display—superlatively sensitive and highly ambitious in every area of activity which befits his aristocratic station
in life. Turning to the issue of medical discourse, it must be said
that there is little if any of that in the *dits* mentioned above, but
the case is rather different in Machaut's *Jugement du Roy de
Navarre* (1349). This features the sad tale of a woman who, on
hearing that her beloved has been killed in a tournament,
becomes gravely ill (ll. 1863–2012).[71] A physician diagnoses her
ailment:

> Ses cuers est fermez en la tour
> D'amour, sous la clef de Tristesse,
> Ou elle sueffre grant destresse,
> Si que morir la couvenra
> Briefment; ja n'en eschapera.
>
> (1991–6)

---

[70] At the very least their existence gives the lie to what used to be an orthodoxy
of modern criticism, namely that the *dits amoureux* are merely pretty and precious.
On recent attempts to rehabilitate the *dits* see Minnis, *Chaucer's Shorter Poems*, pp.
100–1, 111.

[71] *The Judgment of the King of Navarre,* ed. and trans. R. Burton Palmer (New
York, 1988), pp. 84–91.

[Her heart is locked within the tower
of Love, by the key of Sadness,
And in this place she suffers great distress,
And thus she shall die
Soon; she'll never escape.]

And die she does. Here there is no moral condemnation, no theological or Boethian protest against an excessive love of the mortal in general and of corporeal things in particular. Moreover, this *exemplum* is vitally related to the central concern of the *Navarre*, namely the celebration of the poet-*persona*'s escape from the plague which is described in horrific detail at the beginning of the poem. Having taken care to avoid plunging into a deep melancholy while the plague raged,[72] once it has passed he dispels any lingering vestiges of such harmful thinking by going hunting—and subsequently engaging in a highly pleasurable debate with a lady called Bonneürté, who in large measure (whatever else 'she' may embody) personifies Good Fortune, Happiness, as her name suggests. Here Machaut is, in a sense, celebrating his own good fortune in being alive and well.[73]

The contestation between this medically oriented discourse and the theological/moral one which features prominently elsewhere in the *dits* affords a telling parallel to the situation in *L'Art d'amours*. And this contestation contributes significantly to making *L'Art d'amours* open to different readings. For in it Ovid's youthful poetry—poetry by a youth and for the young—is placed physiologically, and perhaps also morally. I say 'morally' because a reader could take the medical evidence as supportive of the action of the Emperor Augustus in exiling a man whose dangerous poetry was inciting passionate youth to promiscuity.[74] On the other hand, that same body of evidence could function in favour of a more positive and/or morally neutral reading of the behaviour to which the natural inclinations of a particular class led its members. The aristocrats who

---

[72] Which could have made him ill, perhaps even caused him to fall victim to the plague—to apply the usual medical assumptions. Cf. Minnis, *Chaucer's Shorter Poems*, pp. 149–55, for brief discussion and bibliography.

[73] Cf. pp. 213–14 below.

[74] On Ovid's exile as interpreted in medieval literature and literary theory see above, pp. 11, 13, and below, pp. 202 n.101, 239–40.

obviously formed a significant part of the target audience of
L'Art d'amours[75] may see themselves as the objects, perhaps
even the victims, of pressures which they have not wished on
themselves. (That is not to say that their moral responsibility is
in any way diminished—their priests and other spiritual advis-
ers would set them right on that score. Giving in to natural
tendencies could certainly be sinful. A disposition to do something did not destroy one's freedom of the will, since a person
had the choice of accepting or rejecting its promptings.) Being
noble meant being prone to a particular form of emotion which
could be enervating and even lethal, and a writer who offered a
cure for this disease—that being a definite part of the *Art
d'amours* author's self-promotion—should be given all due
credit.

In *L'Art d'amours*, then, the scholia have certainly been secularized. Even more remarkable is the fact that the grammar
masters' terms of reference have been supplemented by
discourses which take Ovid's art of love far beyond the restric-
tive hermeneutics of the schools into a world wherein clerical
values are confronted with the counter-claims of a body of
doctrine which treats desire as the object of medical diagnosis
rather than of moral condemnation (and in which fashionable
and self-fashioning courtship rituals enjoy a secure position).
Ovid's text and gloss has not simply been transliterated from the
Latin; rather, its vernacularization has entailed access to
doctrines from another Latin tradition of learning—doctrines
which enable the text to be placed in a rather different light, and
offer a legitimation of its appeal to people of secular estate.

*Sex and the sermon-prologue: Juan Ruiz and Richard de
Fournival*

In our next examples of medieval Ovidianism, vernacular trans-
lators/adapters have moved even further away from the text of
Ovid to exploit more fully the opportunities afforded by the

---

[75] Cf. the opinion of John W. Baldwin, who believes there is 'no doubt that the
intended audience was lay aristocracy'; *The Language of Sex: Five Voices from
Northern France around 1200* (Chicago, 1994), p. 23.

academic prolegomena which was such a major part of the medieval presentation of his poetry.

At the outset we must define yet another kind of prologue, as termed the 'sermon-type' by Beryl Smalley.[76] In prologues to twelfth-century biblical commentaries there was a formal development whereby a technique which for generations had been used in sermons was applied in textual exposition.[77] At the very beginning an *auctoritas* (i.e. an extract from an *auctor*) would be quoted, and divided up and discussed in the course of the prologue, at some stage (though not necessarily at the outset) being applied to the text. (It should be emphasized that the sermon prologue could follow either 'extrinsic' or 'intrinsic' principles (cf. pp. 50–2 above) or any combination thereof). Originally the *auctoritas* was a biblical one, which is hardly surprising, given the origins of this technique in the sermon and the fact that the prologues were introducing Bible commentaries. But in the thirteenth century secular *auctoritates* could be cited and used in the same way, Aristotle being a great source of pithy sayings.[78] By the end of the thirteenth century any kind of *auctoritas*, whether secular or sacred, could appear at the beginning of a commentary on any type of *auctor*, whether theological, philosophical, poetical or whatever.

Sermon-prologues made an appearance in Latin exegesis of Ovid. For example, Pierre Bersuire's *Ovidius moralizatus* begins with a quotation from 2 Timothy (4: 4): 'they will turn away from listening to the truth and will turn to fables'. St Paul's dictum is ingeniously interpreted—if not twisted—to mean that one may find truth in the fables of the poets, the moral exposition of Ovid on a grand scale thereby being rationalized.[79] The commentary on the *Metamorphoses* which Dante's friend and correspondent Giovanni del Virgilio wrote c.1322–3 begins its 'Aristotelian Prologue' with a biblical quotation, in this case Ecclesiasticus 47: 16: 'You were filled as a river with wisdom and your soul covered the earth, and you multiplied riddles in parables and your name is spread abroad even unto the islands.'

---

[76] Minnis, *Authorship*, p. 64.
[77] Beryl Smalley, 'Peter Comestor on the Gospels and his Sources', *RTAM* 46 (1979), 109–10.
[78] Minnis and Scott, *Medieval Literary Theory*, pp. 319–20.
[79] Ibid. 366–7.

'Although [here] the words are applied to something quite different from the matter at present under discussion,' he declares, 'yet they can be marvellously well adapted to our purpose, just as if they had here spoken in praise of Ovid.'[80] Giovanni manages to extract from them the four Aristotelian causes. The efficient cause, for example, is found in the first portion of this quotation, in the words 'you were filled'.[81] This 'may be spoken of Ovid, who was "filled with the river of wisdom", something which is quite obvious from all the works he wrote'. 'This could be made clearer, if it were the appropriate moment, by comparing him to a river,' Giovanni continues. 'But I pass over that.'[82] Instead he proceeds to identify the *causa efficiens* as being twofold—Ovid and God! This notion had first, as one would expect, been applied in commentary on the Bible, being used in discussion of the relationship between divine inspiration, and hence ultimate authorship, of the Bible, and the literary roles of the honoured human writers.[83] Giovanni's use of it indicates the degree of respect with which he believes Ovid should be treated. He proceeds to offer a life of the poet and review of all his works.

The 'Ovidian sermon-prologue' (if that somewhat oxymoronic label is acceptable) also appeared in vernacular literature, the most comprehensive—and certainly the most complicated—version known to me being the Spanish prose introduction in the Salamanca manuscript (dated 1343) of the *Libro de buen amor*. This is the work of either Juan Ruiz himself (as seems highly likely) or of some redactor who wished to exploit the conventions of Ovid commentary in the service of his text.[84] Such exploitation is at once utterly precedented and highly

---

[80] Minnis and Scott, *Medieval Literary Theory*, pp. 360–1.

[81] Such dividing up of the initial text (a version of what was called *divisio textus*) in order to provide the framework of the prologue means that Giovanni's introduction corresponds more closely to the 'sermon-type prologue' as defined above than does Bersuire's effort.

[82] Minnis and Scott, *Medieval Literary Theory*, p. 361.

[83] On the idea of the *duplex causa efficiens* in Bible commentary see Minnis, *Authorship*, pp. 79–80, 102, 118, 164–5, 173–5. Sometimes an even more complex causal system was described, involving a threefold or even fourfold *causa efficiens*; see pp. 80–1, 170, 175.

[84] The definitive study of the *accessus* in medieval Castile, together with Ruiz's prose prologue in relation to the *accessūs Ovidiani*, is John Dagenais, 'A Further Source for the Literary Ideas in Juan Ruiz's Prologue', *Journal of Hispanic Studies*, 11 (1986), 23–52. See further the discussion, largely of the first part of the prologue,

appropriate, given the substantial debt which the *Libro de buen amor* owes to Ovid, and indeed to that Ovidian comedy, the *Pamphilus*.[85] The 'Salamanca introduction' has, hardly surprisingly, provided a major challenge for modern criticism. It has been analysed with reference to the medieval dispute 'between the voluntarists and the intellectualists' (Ullman); the influence of 'medieval Castilian authors in the didactic tradition' (Kinkade); the *artes praedicandi* and sermon rhetoric (Ullman, Nepaulsingh, Chapman); the genre of 'erotic pseudo-autobiography' which conveys the message that 'Courtly Love is really greedy sensuality in hypocritical disguise' (Gybbon-Monypenny); and medieval theological, psychological, and indeed legal ideas (Jenaro-Maclennan).[86] Furthermore, the

---

in Dagenais's book, *The Ethics of Reading in Manuscript Culture. Glossing the 'Libro de buen amor'* (Princeton, NJ, 1994), pp. 86–97. Dagenais's position, as stated in his 1986 article, is that 'Jean Ruiz was acutely aware of the categories for thinking and talking about literature which the *accessus* contained' (p. 37), a view with which I heartily concur. Previously, Francisco Rico had argued that the text's autobiographical frame was influenced by the 'Medieval Ovid', and cited parallels between Ruiz's prologue and an *accessus* to the pseudo-Ovidian *De sompno*: 'Sobre el origen de la autobiografía en el *Libro de buen amor*', *Anuario de Estudios Medievales*, 4 (1967), 301–25. The possible relevance of *accessus* tradition to the *Celestina* of Fernando de Rojas (*c.*1465–1541) was postulated by Colbert Nepaulsingh in an article which discusses the prologues to both the *Celestina* and Ruiz's *Libro*: 'The Rhetorical Structure of the Prologues to the *Libro de buen amor* and the *Celestina*', *BHS* 51 (1974), 330–2. Nepaulsingh draws on E. A. Quain's 1945 article on the *accessūs ad auctores*, but neither relates the tradition to Ruiz nor considers the *accessūs Ovidiani*.

[85] The importance of Ovid for Juan Ruiz is vividly conveyed by G. B. Gybbon-Monypenny, 'Autobiography in the *Libro de buen amor* in the Light of Some Literary Comparisons', *BHS* 34 (1957), 66–8; see further Dagenais, 'Literary Ideas', pp. 44–8. Further discussion of the *Libro* as 'pseudo-autobiography' is provided by Laurence de Looze, *Pseudo-Autobiography in the Fourteenth Century* (Gainesville, Fla., 1997), pp. 43–65. On the influence of the *Pamphilus* on the Doña Endrina episode see esp. D. Seidenspinner-Núñez, *The Allegory of Good Love: Parodic Perspectivism in the 'Libro de buen amor'* (Berkeley, Calif., 1981), wherein the correspondences are usefully laid out in the form of parallel texts (pp. 95–149).

[86] In addition to the references already given, see: Pierre L. Ullman, 'Juan Ruiz's Prologue', *MLN* 82 (1967), 149–70; R. P. Kinkade, '*Intellectum tibi dabo* . . . : The Function of Free Will in the *Libro de Buen Amor*', *BHS* 47 (1970), 296–315; Janet A. Chapman, 'Juan Ruiz's "Learned Sermon"', in G. B. Gybbon-Monypenny (ed.), *'Libro de buen amor' Studies* (London, 1970), pp. 29–51; Gybbon-Monypenny, 'Autobiography in the *LBA*', pp. 77, 78; Luis Jenaro-MacLennan, 'Los presupuestos intelectuales del prologo al *Libro de buen amor*', *Anuario de estudios medievales*, 9 (1974–9 [=1980]), 151–86. Castilian prologue-literature is certainly very rich; see Margo Y. C. De Ley, 'The Prologue in Castilian Literature between 1200 and 1400' (Ph.D. diss., University of Illinois, Urbana-Champaign, 1976).

prologue has variously been seen as an exemplification in minia-
ture of the text's studied imprecision, contradiction, and ambiguity, this being taken as artistic achievement rather than 'slavish
imitation of didactic juxtaposition';[87] as establishing the credentials of a didactic text which 'in order to preach divine love,
assiduously asserts case-histories of worldly love';[88] as following
an 'Augustinian model' which Ruiz nevertheless transforms in
several ways;[89] and as 'an amalgam of many features of medieval
exordia'.[90] Its debt to the medieval sermon has often been
noted—hence it has been termed a *sermon parodique*[91] or
'burlesque sermon'[92] and discussed in respect of the traditions of
the so-called 'learned sermon'[93] and 'meditative sermon'.[94] But
the relationship between the first part of the prologue, which
seems to offer unimpeachable doctrine on memory, understanding and will, and the second part, which (at least at one point)
seems to promise a seducer's handbook, remains problematic in
these studies. Is one part supposed to dominate and control the
other, or are they locked in mutual contradiction?

My own suggestion is that the 'Salamanca introduction' may
be read, at least in part, as a sermon-type prologue which offers
both 'extrinsic' and 'intrinsic' material. Psalm 31: 10 is cited and
interpreted in terms of what 'some schooled in philosophy' have
identified as particularly pertaining to the human soul, namely
understanding, will, and memory.[95] The central theme is that by

[87] Anthony N. Zahareas, *The Art of Juan Ruiz* (Madrid, 1965), pp. 21–4. 'He
sacrifices clarity of intentions and theme, but he achieves variety and ironic appeal.
Technically, he introduces a well-known comment (*intellectum*) in order to achieve
initial clarity (avoid sin) but then dissolves this comment in a mist of plural meanings (either good or sinful).'

[88] Maria Rosa Lida de Malkiel, *Two Spanish Masterpieces: The 'Book of Good
Love' and the 'Celestina'* (Urbana, Ill., 1961), p. 29.

[89] Marina Scordilis Brownlee, *The Status of the Reading Subject in the 'Libro de
buen amor'* (Chapel Hill, NC, 1985), pp. 23–35.

[90] Dagenais, 'Literary Ideas', p. 37.

[91] Felix Lecoy, *Recherches sur le 'Libro de buen amor' de Juan Ruiz* (Paris, 1938),
p. 361. This view is supported by A. D. Deyermond, who believes that 'the parodic
note appears only at the end, but it retrospectively tinges the remainder, for it
changes the reader's attitude to what has gone before': 'Some Aspects of Parody in
the *Libro de buen amor*', in Gybbon-Monypenny (ed.), *LBA Studies*, pp. 56–7.

[92] Otis H. Green, *Spain and the Western Tradition* (Madison, Wis., 1968), i.46–7.

[93] Chapman, 'Ruiz's "Learned Sermon" '.

[94] James F. Burke, 'The *Libro de buen amor* and the Medieval Meditative Sermon
Tradition', *La Coronica*, 9 (1980–1), 122–7.

[95] *The Book of True Love: A Bilingual Edition,* ed. and trans. Saralyn R. Daly
and Anthony N. Zahareas (University Park, Penn., 1978), pp. 23–7.

true understanding man knows the good and consequently knows the bad. The biblical text is divided and discussed in the traditional manner. Finally, an 'intrinsic' treatment of the *Libro* itself is provided. Ruiz (assuming that this is by his own hand) declares that his intention is a good one; he has written 'in mindfulness of the good'; a man or woman with true understanding will choose and act upon it—which presumably means that such a person will understand what is good and what is evil as described in the book and behave accordingly.[96] However, this does not mean, Ruiz continues, that the book is dangerous for those of little understanding. In fact they will be educated by it, for

ca leyendo e coidando el mal que fazen o tienen en la voluntad de fazer, e los porfiosos de sus malas maestrías, e descombrimiento publicado de sus muchas engawoman with true understanding will choose and act upon it—which presumably means that such arán su fama . . . E desecharàn e aborresçeràn las maneras e maestrías malas de loco amor, que faze perder las almas e caer en saña de Dios . . .

[through reading and by realizing the evil that is done or is intended to be done by those who persist in their evil arts, and in discovering that their most clever, deceitful practices, which they use to sin and to deceive women, are made public, they will arouse their memory and not despise their reputation . . . And they will cast off and abhor the ways and evil arts of heedless love, which makes them lose their souls and fall under the wrath of God . . .]

These passages contain more explicitly Christian elaborations of notions which occur regularly in the *accessūs Ovidiani*, particularly the introductions to the *Heroides* and the *Remedia amoris*. The introductions to the *Remedia amoris* explain that, in order to make amends for the offensive *Ars amatoria*, on account of which he had been exiled, Ovid 'set out to write this book [i.e. the *Remedia*] in which he advises' those who are ensnared by love as to 'how they may arm themselves against unlawful love' (cf. p. 37 above). The poet's *intentio*, therefore, was to give 'certain precepts' by which 'unlawful love' may be removed.[97] Similarly, introductions to the *Heroides* argue that in this text Ovid has supplied positive examples of good behaviour and negative examples of evil behaviour, thereby illustrating what

---

[96] Ibid. 26–7.   [97] Minnis and Scott, *Medieval Literary Theory*, p. 25.

should be done and what should be shunned. The work's *intentio* is said to be the commendation of 'lawful marriage and love', and it pertains to ethics because here Ovid teaches good morality and seeks to eradicate evil behaviour. The final cause is that, 'having seen the advantage (*utilitas*) gained from lawful love' and the misfortunes which are occasioned by foolish and unlawful types of love, we are disposed to shun the latter and adhere to the former (cf. p. 38).

In similar vein, Ruiz declares that

mi intençión non fue de fo fazer por dar manera de pecar, ni por mal dezir, mas fue por reduçir a toda persona a memoria buena de bien obrar, e dar ensienpro de buenas contunbres e castigos de salvaçion. E porque sean todos aperçebidos e se puedan major guardar de tantas maestrias, como algunos usan por el loco amor.

[my intention was not to write this in order to give models for sinning or for speaking evil. But it was to guide every person back to the true memory of doing good, and to give an example of good behaviour and admonitions for salvation, and so that all might be warned and thus be better able to guard against such mastery as some use in the service of worldly love.]

St Gregory, he continues, says that arrows which are seen beforehand wound a man less, and we can protect ourselves better from what we have seen beforehand—here Ruiz is enlisting saintly support for a notion which had for generations been a cliché of Ovid criticism. Indeed, notions gleaned from his reading of the glossed Ovid could well have given Ruiz the idea of beginning his prologue with a discussion of how knowledge of both the good and the evil are necessary for true understanding.[98]

And this brings us to consider the main crux of the Ruiz introduction, the point at which, at the very centre of the 'intrinsic' prologue, there is what appears to be, on the face of it, an astounding volte-face—so sudden, indeed, is the transition that some have taken it as evidence that Ruiz was in some way parodying the techniques of the sermon. For, having warned against love, Ruiz proceeds to recommend his book as being a guide to it:

---

[98] The broad similarity between this argument and Guiart's underdeveloped defence of combining both the good and the bad in a single work is obvious.

Enpero, porque es umanal cosa el pecar, si algunos, lo que non los consejo, quisieren usar del loc amor, aqui fallarán algunas maneras para ello.

[However, inasmuch as it is human to sin, if anyone should wish (which I do not advise) to have a taste of this worldly love, here they will find some models for doing so.]

Therefore, this book can be said to give understanding (here Ruiz echoes his opening *auctoritas*) in two ways: those who would understand the good and do good works in the love of God will take it in one way, while those who desire 'foolish worldly love' will understand it in another. This ambivalence is not without precedent, however—for it reflects tensions within the medieval understanding of Ovid, that ambivalent *auctor* who could write as a moral philosopher in the *Metamorphoses* and the *Heroides* (so that Giovanni del Virgilio could suggest that God Himself was in a specific sense the ultimate efficient cause of the former) and yet be responsible for such a morally offensive work as the *Ars amatoria*. Ovid's purpose in his art of love, declares a typical commentator whom we have had cause to cite earlier, 'is to instruct young men in the art of love, and how they should behave towards girls when having a love-affair'; he proceeds by showing 'how a girl may be picked up, how when picked up she may be won over, and, once won over, how her love may be retained'.[99] Later, of course, Ovid retracted and wrote a remedy for such love. In other words, the art of love and its remedy are interrelated; the one presupposes the other. The ambivalence we are discussing could even enter into the analysis of a work which was relatively easy to justify, the *Heroides*. The intention of this work could be the identification of unchaste or foolish forms of love, declares one scrupulous and comprehensive commentator, 'or else to show how some women may be courted by letter, or how the results of living chastely may benefit us'.[100] Thus, some readers will find in the work models for love-letters, others will take it as an awful warning, and it may put some people off human love entirely! The transitions in the Ruiz prologue would have seemed far less surprising to those readers who knew the

---

[99] Minnis and Scott, *Medieval Literary Theory*, p. 24.   [100] Ibid. 23.

'Medieval Ovid' who was his source—i.e. Ovid as interpreted in the Middle Ages, entailing systematic moralization together with an ultimate harmonizing of discords by appeal to the poet's eventual repentance, as recorded in the *Remedia*, and indeed (for those who were prepared to take the pseudo-Ovidian *De Vetula* on trust)[101] to his conversion to Christianity.

Having said all that, it may be wondered if there is something intentionally amusing about the way in which this Spanish *accessus* puts the *remedium* before the *ars* (or, more accurately, the *ars* in the middle of the *remedium*), thereby disrupting rather than duplicating the standard *vita Ovidii*. This putative wit may confirm us in the belief that the Spanish prose introduction to the *Libro* was the work of Ruiz himself, though of course that is not proof positive. Had Ruiz kept to the traditional pattern, his obvious and direct appropriation of Ovidian criticism would have placed his *Libro* in a direct line of succession, as it were, from the Roman *praeceptor amoris*. But Ruiz was not content to be conventional in that way. And the *Libro* itself certainly does not follow a neat narrative sequence from *ars* through *remedium* to triumphal assertion of the values of the higher love, in the manner of Guiart; it is altogether too eclectic for such a structure to be read into it (except by the most determined and reductive of modern readers).

Moreover, one should note the structural impossibility of moving straight from a biblical quotation (as required by the sermon-prologue) into a recommendation of an *ars amatoria*—an initial emphasis on the remedial aspects would be far more appropriate, and hence Ruiz's procedure has an obvious logic. This does not, of course, diminish the effect of sharp transition as he moves to address those who wish to have a 'taste' of worldly love. But Ruiz ends the prologue by emphasizing the moral utility of his book, assuring us of his good *intençión* (in the passage quoted above) and recuperating the edifying sentiments of the first part of the prologue by claiming that he wished 'to guide every person back to the true memory of doing good'. *Ethice supponitur . . .* and ethics have the last word in

---

[101] On this work see pp. 58–9 above and pp. 71, 184–5 below.

this vernacular *accessus*, though certainly not (at least, not straightforwardly) in the variegated text which follows—there it is difficult if not impossible to find any 'last word', since the text resolutely resists closure.[102] And that resistance is, so to speak, in the best traditions of Medieval Ovidianism.

Our second example of an encounter between textual sexuality and the sermon-prologue is the work of one of the most significant and challenging Ovidian poets of the thirteenth century, Richard de Fournival. Particularly intriguing in view of our previous discussion of the importance of medical discourse in *L'Art d'amours* is the fact that Richard was a licensed surgeon (as well as being the son of a medical man, namely Roger de Fournival, who was personal physician to King Philip Augustus).[103] It need not be doubted that this background affected the way in which he approached his Ovid, although medical idioms are not writ large in the works here discussed. Richard may have been responsible for the Pseudo-Ovidian *De Vetula*, which was often taken as an original work of Ovid's.[104] Several amatory works in French have been attributed to him; the *Commens d'amours* and *Poissance d'amours* are probably

[102] As Dagenais says, subsequently Juan Ruiz draws from 'a wide variety of sources—goliardic, popular, lyric, perhaps Arabic and Hebrew, as well—without letting these elements (and their own generic intentions) become the dominant color of the work. They remain, almost by fiat, subservent to the higher didactic purpose.' However, he continues, Ruiz is 'acutely aware of the contradictions inherent in this system throughout this text, not just in the prologue. He seems to be pushing them to their limits, exploring, testing them': 'Literary Ideas', p. 48.

[103] It may be added that two other major figures in the history of medieval commentary tradition were physicians: Evrart de Conty, the author of the first substantial commentary on a text written originally in French, namely the *Eschez amoureux*, and the fourteenth-century scholar Dino del Garbo, who produced a commentary on Guido Cavalcanti's *Canzone d'amore*. On the former, see Ch. 6 below; on the latter, see the brief discussion and references in Minnis and Scott, *Medieval Literary Theory*, pp. 378–9.

[104] As e.g. in the glosses on *De Vetula* which are printed in the editions of this work by Klopsch (pp. 279–90) and Robathan (pp. 40–6); cf. Ghisalberti, 'Mediaeval Biographies of Ovid', pp. 50–1. It seems to have been accepted as a genuine Ovidian work by Roger Bacon, Thomas Bradwardine, Robert Holcot, Walter Burley, and Pietro Alighieri (cf. *De Vetula*, ed. Robathan, pp. 1–2, 13–14): the text's affirmation of the victory of Christianity over paganism was hard to resist. Robathan notes *De Vetula*'s interest in issues studied at the University of Paris at that time, and concludes that 'in many respects Fournival seems a likely candidate for the distinction of having written this pseudo-Ovidian poem' (pp. 4–10). Paul Klopsch also regards the authorship of Fournival as highly plausible; see his edition, pp. 84–99.

not from Richard's pen, but his authorship of the *Consaus d'amours* has been upheld.[105] There seems no doubt, however, that Richard was responsible for a love treatise of a rather different kind, this being the *Bestiaires d'amours,* wherein the pain of unrequited desire, which resonates through so much of Ovid's amatory poetry, finds expression with reference to beasts both real and imaginary.[106]

Li Bestiaires d'amours begins with the first sentence of Aristotle's *Metaphysics:* 'all men naturally desire to know'. That passage opens the prologues to many scholastic commentaries and treatises produced during the thirteenth century and beyond, and Dante was to use it at the beginning of his *Convivio,* a quite extraordinary instance of 'autoexegesis' in which the poet places the full weight of academic commentary-technique on three of his own *canzoni* (cf. Chapter 6 below). In the case of *Li Bestiaires d'amours* Aristotle's statement is at the head of an elegant 'extrinsic' prologue which discusses that faculty of mind which is called Memory, with its two doors, of Sight and Hearing.[107] Science gives way to sexuality when Richard declares that his beloved cannot depart from his memory, his love for her being incurable. And may he live forever in her memory! Throughout the work which follows he constructs himself as the typical 'fine lover' who 'mors de tel mort com a Amor apartient, c'est desperance sans atente de merci' ['dies the sort of death that is appropriate to Love, namely despair without expectation of mercy'],[108] but as usual his 'bele tredouce amie' can resuscitate him.[109] 'C'est la sovrainne medechine de moi aidier que de vostre cuer avoir,' he exclaims; the sovereign remedy to help me is to have your heart.[110] But this is sex in the head, for the beast lore and bestial analogies which follow effectively subvert and even ridicule the conventional antics of lovers,

[105] By G. B. Speroni, 'Il "Consaus d'amours" di Richard de Fournival', *Medioevo romanzo,* 1.2 (1974), 217–78.
[106] I have used the edition by Cesare Segre, *Li Bestiaires d'amours di Maistre Richart de Fornival e Li Response du bestiaire* (Milan and Naples, 1957). The earlier edition by C. Hippeau was reprinted in 1978 at Geneva.
[107] *Li Bestiaires,* ed. Segre, pp. 3–8.
[108] Ibid. 44; trans. Jeanette Beer, *Master Richard's Bestiary of Love and Response* (Berkeley, Calif., 1986), p. 15.
[109] *Li Bestiaires,* ed. Segre, pp. 54–5; trans. Beer, p. 19.
[110] *Li Bestiaires,* ed. Segre, p. 57; trans. Beer, p. 20.

presumably for the amusement of an audience which was wise and sophisticated enough to know better. As a whole the text makes abundantly clear that love is eminently curable, particularly since the animal imagery through which woman's nature is described is often highly derogatory.

An 'underlying acrimony' has been detected in this text by Jeanette Beer, who cites as an example the passage in which Richard's prayers to his lady are equated with dog's vomit that has flown out through his teeth.[111] But the writer's use of the beast-fable tradition may be said to have given him the licence to indulge in such far-fetched analogies. In this area a taste barrier divides our time from that of Richard's, a point which may be supported by consultation of, for example, the 'hunt of love' tradition in French literature, wherein imagery may be found of a kind which is far more grotesque than anything which Richard managed to invent.[112] Richard was probably far more interested in the construction of clever conceits, for the entertainment of his sophisticated audience, than in the conscious elaboration of misogynistic clichés. As Beer brings out very well, his underlying style is highly refined and often 'understated'; Richard exploits the literary traditions of *courtoisie*, and 'is not devoid of courtly preciousness either'.[113] All those elements, together with a certain graciousness, are very much evident in the style of, for example, the *Consaus d'amours* (here I assume that this was indeed written by Richard), which is altogether a more gentle affair. A 'tres douce suer' has asked him for advice about loving 'par amours',[114] and he obliges by giving her far more than what she had requested, seeking definitions of both spiritual and temporal love with the aid of quotations from not only Ovid but also

[111] Beer, *Master Richard's Bestiary*, p. xx.

[112] For example, in *L'amoureuse prise*, which Jean Acart de Hesdin wrote in 1332, the lover is imaged as the quarry in terms such as these: 'just as it was proper to feed the dogs after a hunt, so Love gave them the intestines and other matter woven about the entrails to devour. And he gave them my blood to drink . . . each of the hounds was led forth for the strewed feast that I was.' Quoted by Marcelle Thiébaux, *The Stag of Love: The Chase in Medieval Literature* (Ithaca, NY, 1974), p. 140. Jean Acart is cited in Evrart de Conty's commentary on the *Eschez amoureux*; see p. 292 below.

[113] Beer, *Master Richard's Bestiary*, p. xxi.

[114] Speroni, 'Il "Consaus d'amours" ', p. 242.

Cicero, Horace, Virgil, the Bible, and the modern masters John of Garland and Peter of Blois. Of particular interest in view of our previous discussion of the significance of youth in *L'Art d'amours* and several *dits amoureux* is the statement by Richard's *persona* that young lovers are the less reproachable on account of the tenderness of their years. 'Even our Lord, according to the Scriptures, pays less heed to the transgressions of youth than to all others'—a highly biased reading of the *auctoritas* here cited, Psalm 24: 7, 'The sins of my youth and my ignorances do not remember'! This deliberately outrageous remark contributes to the humour of the text which, one may imagine, was intended to entertain Richard's audience of clerics and aristocrats—the constitution of that audience mirroring his own dual status as church dignitary and surgeon.

Quite extraordinarily, that audience seems to have included a woman who wrote a spirited response to *Li Bestiaires d'amours*. At least, in a few manuscripts of the *Bestiaires* is found a short treatise by a writer who, having described herself(?) as 'a woman in conformity with Our Lord's good pleasure',[115] proceeds to offer a systematic critique of Richard's text. His initial citation of Aristotle prompts the argument that 'Hom qui sens et discretion a en soi ne doit metre s'entente ne son tans a cose nule dire ne faire par coi nus ne nule soit empiriés' ['A man who has intelligence and discretion must not employ his time or his attention to say or do anything by which any man or any woman may be damaged'].[116] The 'damage' described in the ensuing text is largely that caused to women by smooth-talking, mendacious men who say they are dying from unrequited love, in order to seduce the credulous objects of their lusts. The clear implication is that Richard (or rather his amatory *persona*) may be one of them, though at the end of the *Response* she politely grants that in fact he may have been trying to warn her against such men.

Adopting the *persona* of the woman to whom Richard had addressed the *Bestiaires*, the writer takes over his beast analogies and turns them against him. Of particular interest, in view of Richard's own status, is the writer's attack on certain 'dyables

---

[115] *Li Bestiaires*, ed. Segre, p. 106; trans. Beer, p. 42.
[116] *Li Bestiaires*, ed. Segre, p. 105; trans. Beer, p. 41.

oisiaus de proie' ['diabolical birds of prey'], meaning 'Clerc qui si s'afaifent en courtoisie et en leur beles paroles, qu'il n'est dame ne demoisele qui devant aus puist durer qu'il ne veullent prendre' ['clerics who are so decked out with courtesy and fine words that there is no woman or maiden who can withstand them, whom they do not wish to take'].[117] The attraction of these clerics is considerable: they have 'toute courtoisie, si que j'ai entendu' ['every courtesy, as I have heard']; moreover, they are the handsomest of men. But they are 'li plus soutil en malisse, et sousprendent les non sachans. Pour che les apele je oisiaus de proie, et bon feroit estre garnie contre aus' ['the most devious in malice. They take the ignorant by surprise. Wherefore I call them birds of prey, and it would be good to have protection against them']. The argument takes a highly practical turn when the writer notes that, in any case, clerics are not the best men for women to associate with, the clear implication being that marrying them is not a prudent course of action.[118] Far better to marry a knight, who will enable a woman to enjoy a superior lifestyle.

In *Li response du bestiaire*, then, the love object becomes the independent and highly vocal subject, declaring that she has no intention of clothing the suitor with her love, and warning against male deviousness of the type which was taught by Ovid and medievalized within the *fine amor* tradition. I myself see little evidence for the view that this putative woman writer was intimating a more philosophical defence of womankind in general, though certainly there are hints of that, as when at the beginning of the text it is pointed out that Eve was made of a better substance than was Adam, although she was not created equal.[119] In short, our mysterious 'feme . . . selonc che qu'il

---

[117] *Li Bestiaires*, ed. Segre, p. 133; trans. Beer, p. 56.
[118] *Li Bestiaires*, ed. Segre, pp. 134–5; trans. Beer, pp. 56–7.
[119] *Li Bestiaires*, ed. Segre, pp. 107–9; trans. Beer, pp. 42–3. Here the anonymous writer even puts forward the heterodox view that the original partner of Adam was created equal. However, Adam killed her, because she was nothing to him and so he could not love her. Thus God made a second wife for him, out of one of Adam's ribs, whereupon he loved her far too much—as is evidenced by the Fall. This could be a distant echo of the story of Lilith; on its development in medieval midrash see K. E. Kvam, L. S. Schearing, and V. H. Ziegler (eds.), *Eve and Adam: Jewish, Christian and Muslim Readings on Genesis and Gender* (Bloomington, 1999), pp. 162–3, 204, 207. *Li response* also puts forward the view that Eve was born of nobler stuff than Adam, since she was created from Adam's bone whereas he was created from

plaist a nostre Seigneur' was no Christine de Pizan. Christine's attack on Jean de Meun's section of the *Roman de la Rose*, which to some extent involves an attack on Medieval Ovidianism in general, is an altogether more substantial and thoughtful affair. This is due, in part at least, to Christine's obvious familiarity (and facility) with the clerical discourses of sexuality which she is confronting, thanks to her own training in Latin (which would inevitably have involved some understanding of academic literary theory) as well as her reading in medieval French translations of, or adaptations of material from, crucial Latin texts, including Ovid.[120] The writer of *Li response* seems to be innocent of the literary traditions which gave birth to *Li Bestiaires d'amours*.[121] And that could be taken as evidence in favour of the proposition that it was genuinely written by a woman rather than by a cleric *in persona mulieris*. At any rate, *Li response* betrays little if any vestige of the educated male voice.

In the *querelle de la Rose* an educated female voice speaks out powerfully, and speaks as a woman. Jean de Meun's archsupporter Pierre Col is forced into a defence of the *Rose* which emphasizes its value for women. The text is actually offering aid and advice to the defenders of the Lady's castle, he claimed.[122] Because they then knew how their fortress could fall, in the future they would block the gap or place better guards there and thus lessen the chances of the assailants. Jean made this information widely available by writing in 'the common language of

---

earth. Blamires, who identifies this as one of the traditional 'privileges of women', remarks that the writer 'disappointingly' goes on to defer to the male on the grounds that a created being must be obedient to that from which it derives (*Case for Women*, pp. 98–9). However, the passage may also be read as an elaborate profession of humility (offered only after the telling point has been made), designed to emphasize the woman's propriety and lack of presumption—and thus drive home the arguments she is making.

[120] To put it another way, she displays a substantial mastery of authoritative clerical (and therefore male) language. Cf. below, pp. 255–6.

[121] It is quite possible, however, that the remark that 'Richard' may have wished to warn 'her' against duplicitous suitors is an echo of the commonplace claim of the Ovid scholia (cf. the following paragraphs) that description of male seduction strategies may be intended to put women on their guard. The understated, sometimes enigmatic texture of crucial parts of *Li Response* makes appraisal of its author's intellectual accomplishments very difficult. Cf. n. 119 above.

[122] *Le Débat*, ed. Hicks, pp. 104–5; trans. Baird and Kane, p. 108.

men and women, young and old, that is, in French ('en franssois'). By contrast, the *Ars amatoria* exclusively sought to teach men how to assault the castle—being in Latin this work was not available to women. Therefore Ovid, according to Col, served only the assailants, whereas Jean de Meun has taken the side of the defenders in preparing them for the stratagems which they will face.

This is an utter anachronism, of course. The high-caste women of Ovid's day were certainly not barred from reading his poems by a failure to understand Latin; Col has been misled by the general cultural situation of women in his own day. Moreover, Col's argument seems to depend on a reading of the *Ars amatoria* which quite ignores the third book, wherein Ovid sets out to give women the same sort of instruction as he had provided for men in the first two books. Intriguingly, in the *accessus* to the *Ars amatoria* printed by Huygens Ovid's aim for the first two books is expressed, as if the entire work were addressed to men only, and its final cause is analysed only in terms of Ovid's male addresses.[123] Could Col have been influenced by an account such as this, wherein the contents of the *Ars amatoria* are imperfectly represented? By contrast the *accessus* in Copenhagen, Kongelige Bibliotek Gl. Kgl. S. 2015 4 o (late twelfth century?), which may be the work of the scholar Fulco who was criticized so roundly by Arnulf of Orléans,[124] declares with far greater accuracy that Ovid sought to teach both young men and young women in the art of love ('intendit iuuenes et puellas in amorem instruere'), a view reiterated in his account of the work's *materia* ('materia eius sunt iuuenes et puelle, quos uult docere et instruere in arte amandi').[125] Similarly, in the *accessus* to the *Remedia amoris* which we have had cause to cite earlier, it is noted that Ovid had not only taught young men how to acquire and keep mistresses but also given girls the corresponding instruction.[126] Clearly, Col does not reflect this tradition of glossing. Moreover, the person responsible for the third book of *L'Art d'amours*, in explaining

---

[123] *Accessūs ad auctores,* ed. Huygens, p. 33; cf. Hexter, *Ovid and Medieval Schooling,* pp. 46–7.
[124] See Shooner, 'Les *Bursarii Ovidianorum*', pp. 408–9 (esp. n. 12), 410–11 (n. 17), 423 (n. 47); cf. Hexter, *Ovid and Medieval Schooling,* p. 43 (n. 85).
[125] Ed. Hexter, ibid. 219.   [126] *Accessūs ad auctores*, ed. Huygens, p. 34.

why Ovid wanted to give women the same teaching as men, asserts that 'it would be an ugly thing for men to conquer those who do not know how and would not be able to defend themselves'.[127] Here the anonymous French translator claims for the final part of the Ars amatoria a function and purpose which Pierre Col claims is not to be attributed to that work but rather to the Roman de la Rose.

That having been said, it must be admitted that Col's realization of the Ars amatoria is broadly in line with what is commonly found in French translations of that Ovidian text. The original L'Art d'amours ended with the second book, the translation of Book 3 being a later addition, as explained above. Even Jacques d'Amiens, who was so concerned to address his Ovid translations to a 'douce dame', preferred to draw on the second book of the Ars amatoria rather than the third. Moreover, there is the testimony of an Ars translation which we have not as yet mentioned, the work of a certain 'Maistre Elie' who seems to have been a contemporary of the writer of the original L'Art d'amour. Elie was interested only in the first two books of Ovid's poem (though he goes no farther than line 336 of Book 2).[128] His poem of 1,305 octosyllabic lines adapts and amplifies parts of the original (while omitting a large number of passages), modernizing it considerably with reference to Parisian locations, manners, and styles of dress. The third book of the Ars is utterly ignored.

The reasons for this reluctance to engage with Book 3 can only be guessed at. Bruno Roy makes the eminently plausible suggestion that here we are dealing with 'un phénomène d'ordre sociologique, celui de la répugnance qu'éprouvaient les auteurs

---

[127] L'Art d'amours, ed. Roy, p. 228; trans. Blonquist, p. 123. Similarly, at the end of the translation of Book 3 it is asserted that from this text both men and women may learn how to guard and protect themselves. However, there follows a rather different (from the one quoted above) view of the usefulness to women ('est il pour les femmes prouffitablez') of the text: by this they can conquer men 'et mectre dedens leurs loys' ['and put them under their laws']. Moreover, first comes the statement that it is 'Prouffitables pour les hommes, car par icel ilz puent savoir les cautelles et decepcions des femmes, et ainssi ilz se puent mieux garder' ['beneficial for men, for by this they can know the ruses and deceptions of women, and thus they can be more careful']: ed. Roy, p. 281; trans. Blonquist, p. 184.
[128] Maître Elies Überarbeitung der ältesten französische Bearbeitung der Ars amatoria des Ovids, ed. H. Kühne and E. Stengel (Marburg, 1886); repr. in Finoli, Artes amandi, pp. 1–30.

didactiques à s'adresser directement aux femmes', which is certainly true of the earlier thirteenth century,[129] though by the end of that same century change was well on the way. Roy's statement, however, raises the issue of what exactly a 'didactic' work was in the period under discussion; the poet of the *Ars amatoria* always sat uneasily among 'les auteurs didactiques', and as we have seen this work could easily be adapted to serve the ends of *fine amor*, a tradition wherein direct address to a woman or women was utterly commonplace. In this regard one need only think of how Jacques d'Amiens managed to recommend the *Remedia amoris* to a female love-sufferer, albeit with considerable ingenuity. Then again, women were regularly addressed as readers—and sometimes as patrons—of French romances, which often contained highly didactic passages.[130] The *romans antiques* are an obvious case in point (and, incidentally, are highly indebted to the Ovidian tradition of female complaint. But that is another story).[131] In general, however, Roy's suggestion that the medieval *ars amandi* tradition had a mainly male audience may be accepted,[132] though it is going too far to say that '*Toute* la littérature des arts d'aimer . . . s'adresse aux hommes'.

Another reason for the relative neglect of the third book of the *Ars amatoria* could have been that writers were reluctant to treat of, or unable to use in their own literary works, its blatant sexuality; particularly its unblushing accounts of different types of intercourse, which are far more explicit than anything found

---

[129] Introduction to his *L'Art d'amours* edition, p. 16. For one exception, see the major corpus of English treatises produced for women in the period 1190–1230, in part edited by Bella Millett and Jocelyn Wogan-Browne, *Medieval English Prose for Women* (Oxford, 1990).

[130] On this controversial subject see especially Roberta L. Krueger, *Women Readers and the Ideology of Gender in Old French Verse Romance* (Cambridge, 1993). [131] See esp. Nolan, *Chaucer and the 'Roman Antique'*.

[132] Just as in the medieval tradition of 'heroic love' the patients were, for the most part, assumed to be male. However, female victims of lovesickness were not unknown, and more attention is paid to them in the later tradition of *Viaticum* commentaries, starting with Peter of Spain. See Wack, *Lovesickness*, pp. 7, 9, 110–15, 121–5, 174–6; also the cogent comments by Joan Cadden, *Meanings of Sex Difference in the Middle Ages: Medicine, Science, and Culture* (Cambridge, 1993), pp. 138–41. See further the elaborately detailed account of a woman who dies of the disease despite the ministrations of many physicians and the correct diagnosis by one of them, which is included in Guillaume de Machaut's *Jugement dou Roy de Navarre* (cf. pp. 60–1 above).

in the first two books. The disapproval of the author of Book 3 of *L'Art d'amours* becomes evident occasionally. Introducing Ovid's 'lessons' on how a woman must perform the 'labeur de Veneris' ['work of Venus'] he remarks that 'Pluseurs y sont si soubtilles qu'il ne leur fault point de doctrine' ['There are many so clever that no teaching is necessary for them'].[133] A brief review of the sexual practices of experienced women is broken off with the comment, 'il sut pluseurs autres faussetez, yquelles scevent mieux de moy' ['there are many other perversions, which they know better than I'].[134] Ovid's text seems to be confirming some of his worst suspicions about women. He is not above seeing the funny side of the business, however, as when he glosses Ovid's recommendation of alternative sexual positions (the woman on top or the man on top) with a citation of Galatians 6: 2, 'Bear ye one another's burdens, and so you shall fulfil the law of Christ'.[135] But that, of course, is a very donnish, male joke. Despite the hope expressed at the very end of his translation, that no one can bear him any ill will because his work is of benefit to both men and women, it seems aimed at an audience which is largely, though probably not exclusively, male. Which is hardly surprising.

John Baldwin has described the author of *L'Art d'amours* as having 'positioned himself at the border of the clerical and aristocratic worlds';[136] the same could be said (though with some specific variations) of most if not all of the medieval Ovidians described in this chapter. It is also true—elaborately and elusively true—of the highly controversial authors of the most popular of all the medieval *artes amandi*, the *Roman de la Rose*, the construction and consumption of which will be the subject of the following four chapters. By writing in the vernacular Guillaume de Lorris and Jean de Meun made their amatory fiction available to an audience which ranged far beyond the clerical, to people who had life-choices, aspirations, and tastes which differed markedly from those of clerics, particularly on matters relating to celibacy and sexuality. And that audience included at least some women who refused to kowtow to the

---

[133] *L'Art d'amours*, ed. Roy, p. 277; trans. Blonquist, p. 179.
[134] *L'Art d'amours*, ed. Roy, p. 277; trans. Blonquist, p. 180.
[135] *L'Art d'amours*, ed. Roy, p. 278; trans. Blonquist, p. 180.
[136] *Language of Sex*, p. 23.

clerics. The female *persona* of *Li response du bestiaire* deni-
grates them as possible partners in marriage—wealthy knights
are far better! Christine de Pizan exploited clerkly constructions
of woman for her own ends, setting in opposition to male
textual authority the authority of female experience. Such
responses were facilitated by the activities of certain well-
educated male writers who had stripped the *auctores* (sources of
eroticism and misogyny both) of their protective Latin clothing,
thereby exposing them to wider availability and even to attack.
Some of the implications of such sexual/textual nakedness may
now be addressed.

CHAPTER 2

Lifting the Veil: Sexual/Textual Nakedness in the Roman de la Rose

'An open and naked exposition of herself (*apertam nudamque expositionem sui*) is distasteful to Nature', declares Macrobius, in explaining why certain philosophers make use of 'fabulous narratives'. Just as Nature 'has withheld an understanding of herself from the vulgar senses of men by enveloping herself in variegated garments (*tegmine*)', he continues, she 'has also desired to have her secrets handled by more prudent individuals through fabulous narratives'. Thus, 'her sacred rites are veiled in mysterious representations so that she may not have to show herself naked even to initiates. Only eminent men of superior intelligence gain a revelation of her truths . . .'.[1]

In the Twelfth-Century Renaissance various eminent men of superior intelligence, including Bernard of Chartres, William of Conches, and Bernard Silvester, set about widening the Macrobian category of fables which merited the approval of philosophers,[2] through a process of 'integumental' interpretation whereby the veils or garments of allegory were judged to

[1] Macrobius, *In somnium Scipionis*, I.ii.17–18; trans. W. H. Stahl, *Commentary on the Dream of Scipio by Macrobius* (New York, 1952; repr. 1990), pp. 86–7. When expounding this passage in his commentary on Macrobius, William of Conches explains 'naked' as 'that is, without an *integumentum*' and claims that 'only the wise should know the secrets of the gods, [arrived at] through the interpretation of *integumenta*. As for churls and foolish men, let them not know but only believe.' Cited by Peter Dronke, *Fabula: Explorations into the Uses of Myth in Medieval Platonism* (Leiden, 1974), p. 48. As Baswell says, 'Macrobius here never distinguishes . . . between the mysteries of the fabulous text and the covered body of nature. The two elements remain densely interplicated, a near-unification of world and text . . .' (*Figuring the 'Aeneid'*, p. 98).

[2] On this widening process see Minnis and Scott, *Medieval Literary Theory*, p. 119. Here the editors illustrate how William of Conches was prepared to find scientific truths in fables which Macrobius would probably have dismissed as base and unworthy (cf. *In somn. Scip.* I.ii.11) with William's integumental reading of the castration of Saturn. See further Dronke's excellent discussion, *Fabula*, pp. 25–30.

clothe profound truths relating to physics or ethics.[3] In the
Aeneid commentary sometimes attributed to Bernard it is
claimed that Virgil was both a poet and a philosopher, the latter
because of his integumental discourse,[4] and a few generations
after these scholars flourished, Arnulf of Orléans extrapolated
from Ovid's *Metamorphoses* a series of *allegoriae* which were to
enjoy considerable popularity.[5] Moreover, in his *Anticlaudianus*

[3] The term *integumentum* basically meant a garment or covering: for medieval
definitions see above, pp. 15–16. The most important discussions include Edouard
Jeauneau's 1957 study, 'L'Usage de la notion d'*integumentum* à travers les gloses de
Guillaume de Conches', repr. in his *Lectio philosophorum: Recherches sur l'école de
Chartres* (Amsterdam, 1973), pp. 127–92; Brian Stock, *Myth and Science in the
Twelfth Century* (Princeton, NJ, 1972), pp. 49–62; Winthrop Wetherbee, *Platonism
and Poetry in the Twelfth Century* (Princeton, NJ, 1972), pp. 36–48, 54–6; and
Dronke, *Fabula*, pp. 4, 5, 23–5, 32, 36, 37, 48–52, 119–22, etc. For the related term
involucrum (again meaning a 'covering' or 'wrapping') see esp. M.-D. Chenu,
'*Involucrum*: Le mythe selon les théologiens médiévaux', *AHDLMA* 22 (1955),
75–9; and Dronke, *Fabula*, pp. 56–7, 120.
[4] Minnis and Scott, *Medieval Literary Theory*, p. 150. The argument that this
commentary is not the work of Bernard but rather of English origin is included in
the study by C. Baswell, 'The Medieval Allegorization of the *Aeneid*: MS
Cambridge, Peterhouse 158', *Traditio*, 41 (1985), 181–237. Peter Dronke has
defended the attribution to Bernard in his article 'Bernardo Silvestre' in
Enciclopedia Virgiliana, ed. F. della Corte (Rome, 1984–91), i.497–500. E. R. Smits
suggested that the commentary might be the work of Bernard of Chartres (d.
c.1130), who taught at the cathedral school there from before 1117: 'New Evidence
for the Authorship of the First Six Books of Virgil's *Aeneid* commonly attributed to
Bernardus Silvestris?', in M. Gosman and J. Van Os, *Sed Nove: Mélanges de civilisation médiévale dédiés à Willem Noomen* (Groningen, 1984), pp. 239–46. In an
article published in the same year, which includes an edition of a *Timaeus* commentary here ascribed to Bernard of Chartres, this possibility is ruled out: see P. Dutton,
'The Uncovering of the *Glosae super Platonem* of Bernard of Chartres', *MS* 46
(1984), 210–11, 220 n. Jeauneau cautiously says that if the author is not Bernard
Silvester it is someone who resembles him closely, someone who has read the same
texts and interpreted them in the same spirit. See his recent article on his discovery
of another (fragmentary) copy of the 'Bernard Silvester' *Aeneid* commentary,
'Berkeley, University of California, Bancroft Library MS 2', *MS* 50 (1988), 452.
(This manuscript should in fact be referred to as MS 95; see Hexter, 'Ovid's Body',
pp. 350–1, n. 62.) Julian W. Jones 'doubts that the master of Tours was responsible
for it': 'The So-Called Silvestris Commentary on the *Aeneid* and Two Other
Interpretations', *Speculum*, 64 (1989), 835 n. Exemplarily even-handed comments
on opposing positions are included in Baswell, *Figuring the Aeneid*, pp. 108–10,
112, 355–6 nn.
[5] On Arnulf as Ovid commentator see Ghisalberti, 'Arnolfo d'Orléans' and
Coulson, 'Sources of the *Accessus* of Arnoul d'Orléans to the *Metamorphoses*'.
Arnulf's *allegoriae* were drawn on by the compiler of the major thirteenth-century
'Vulgate' commentary on the *Metamorphoses*, on which see *Vulgate Commentary*,
ed. Coulson, and Coulson's article, 'The "Vulgate" Commentary on Ovid's
Metamorphoses'.

and *De planctu naturae* Alan of Lille put integumental theory
into literary practice. Here, as Alan said of the *Anticlaudianus*,
'the sweetness of the literal sense' is meant to soothe the ears of
boys, while 'the moral instruction' will 'inspire the mind on the
road to perfection'. Most important and elevated of all,
however, is 'the sharper subtlety of the allegory', which is
designed to 'whet the advanced intellect'.[6]

The use, or relative lack of it, which is made of such
garments of style in a later text which is highly indebted to *De
planctu naturae*, namely Jean de Meun's portion of the *Roman
de la Rose*, is at the centre of this chapter. The stylistic differences between the two works could hardly be greater. Alan's
ornate and richly articifial *modus loquendi*, with its dazzling
rhetoric, convoluted allegory and heavy dependence on classical myth and grammatical metaphors, distances the reader
from empirical reality and *temporalia*. And the reader presupposed by *De planctu naturae* is a privileged individual indeed;
the knowledge required for comprehension of this text in its
entirety, for appreciation of its donnish innuendoes as much as
its profoundly learned allusions, ensures that it will remain
caviar to the general.[7] In this case Dame Nature need not
worry about being exposed to the uninitiated; her secrets
remain safe within a clerical coterie. Jean de Meun, however,
sought to tell tales out of school (to some extent at least). His
'mirror for lovers' was very much a product of the age which
fostered the *Speculum maius* of Vincent of Beauvais, a formidable compilation which boasts (for example) 171 chapters on
herbs, 134 chapters on seeds and grains, 161 chapters on birds,
and 46 chapters on fishes, all written in a straightforward Latin
prose which eschews ambivalence and artifice. While in *De
planctu naturae* the book of Nature was 'an infinite book of
secrecy',[8] in the *Speculum naturale* Nature's secrets are being

---

[6] Alan of Lille, *Anticlaudianus*, trans. J. J. Sheridan (Toronto, 1973), p. 40.

[7] On those donnish innuendoes see esp. Jan Ziolkowski, *Alan of Lille's
Grammar of Sex: The Meaning of Grammar to a Twelfth-Century Intellectual*
(Cambridge, Mass., 1985). See further the important development of key ideas by
Eugene Vance, *Marvelous Signals: Poetics and Sign Theory in the Middle Ages*
(Lincoln, Neb., 1986), pp. 230–55, and Robert Myles, *Chaucerian Realism*
(Cambridge, 1994), pp. 118–32.

[8] To borrow a phrase from F. J. E. Raby, '*Nuda Natura* and Twelfth–Century
Cosmology', *Speculum*, 43 (1968), 77.

inventoried one by one, divided and conquered by scholastic *divisio* and *distinctio*. And Jean's *Speculum amantis* (cf. *Rose*, 10621) shares some of the formal techniques of the thirteenth-century *compilatio*. *Nuda natura*—for thus may Jean's construct be regarded—describes directly and clearly her own creation, planetary motions and powers, destiny and free will (following Boethius), the influence of the heavens, the properties of mirrors and glasses, dreams and frenzies, and true gentility, concluding with a commendation of all creation, man excepted, for its ordered obedience.

In short, an ornate, richly artificial high style has made 'plain and open', to adopt a phrase from a typical description of the kind of translation which Jean de Meun is sometimes said to have practised in *Li Livres de confort*, his French rendering of *De consolatione philosophiae*.[9] Jean was a plain-style poet whose main (though by no means only) modes of procedure are narration and exemplification rather than enigmatic fable and allegory ('personification allegory' or prosopopoeia being, of course, a different thing altogether, and fundamental to the poem).[10] The language of the *Rose* is frequently outspoken, explicit, literal.

That statement is a controversial one for me to make, however, given that John Fleming has objected to an earlier remark of mine to the effect that Jean de Meun's text frequently evinces an attitude which is 'unflinchingly literal'.[11] Jean's theory of love, I went on to say, is expressed in perfectly literal terms. Here I was seeking to align myself with H. R. Jauss, who had suggested that in the *Rose* Jean de Meun no longer took seriously the allegorical mode which he inherited from Alan of

---

[9] On the style of *Li Livres de confort* see A. J. Minnis and T. W. Machan, 'The *Boece* as Late-Medieval Translation', in A. J. Minnis (ed.), *Chaucer's 'Boece' and the Medieval Tradition of Boethius* (Cambridge, 1993), pp. 172–3.

[10] Good working definitions of allegory (not prosopopoeia) and exemplification are offered in John Burrow's cogent remarks: 'These two modes often overlap in practice, but in theory there is a fundamental distinction between them. Exemplification treats facts or events (real or imagined) as examples which demonstrate some general truth; whereas allegory treats facts or events as metaphors which represent some truth or some other event. Allegory requires the reader to translate; exemplification requires him to generalize': *Medieval Writers and Their Work: Middle English Literature and Its Background 1100–1500* (Oxford, 1982), p. 87.

[11] A. J. Minnis, *Chaucer and Pagan Antiquity* (Cambridge, 1982), p. 16.

Lille,[12] and with Winthrop Wetherbee, who had elaborated that point in the following statement, with which I still warmly concur:

Certainly the effect of his [i.e. Jean's] allusive dialogue with Alain and the *De Planctu* is to prohibit any naïve attempt to educe a higher *significatio* from the facts of human behaviour by resource to the sort of poetic typology which unifies the former poem, realigning its imagery and cosmology with the archetypal pattern which man's depravity had obscured. Raison cites Plato and seeks recourse to *integumanz* in defence of her plain speaking on sexual matters, but the unflinching literalism of La Vielle and Genius dominates, and reveals how thoroughly Jean has 'de-allegorized' his materials.[13]

Fleming retorts by reiterating the fundamental principle which informs his 1969 and 1984 monographs on the *Rose*: that Jean de Meun expects his audience (an extraordinarily consistent and consensual interpretative community, according to Fleming) to decode the classical fables within his text with the aid of the moral allegories transmitted by the Latin mythographic tradition.[14] It is emphasized that the lover's winning of the Rose is described not literally but obliquely through (*inter alia*) the imagery of a pilgrim worshipping at the shrine of his beloved saint and (with the aid of his stiff and stout staff) entering into her pudendal sanctuary—an allegory which, in Fleming's view, presents Amant's cupidinous behaviour as contemptible idolatry.

But of course, neither Jauss, Wetherbee, nor I would or could deny that Jean sometimes drew on mythographic materials and displayed an awareness of the allegorical or 'integumental' method of interpreting them, and I can safely say that none of us would dream of confusing a pilgrim's staff with a penis. The end of the *Rose* features allegorical expression which is far removed from the harshly 'literal' way in which the sex act is

---

[12] H. R. Jauss, 'La Transformation de la forme allégorique entre 1180 et 1240: d'Alain de Lille à Guillaume de Lorris', in *L'Humanisme médiéval dans les littératures romanes* (Paris, 1964), pp. 107–46.

[13] Winthrop Wetherbee, 'The Literal and the Allegorical: Jean de Meun and the "De Planctu Naturae" ', *MS* 33 (1971), 286.

[14] John V. Fleming, 'Jean de Meun and the Ancient Poets', in Brownlee and Huot (eds.), *Rethinking the Rose*, pp. 81–100. Cf. Fleming's two monographs, *Allegory and Iconography* and *Reason and the Lover*.

often described in the *fabliaux*. It remains, however, perfectly possible to speak of the 'literal' and 'literalizing' manœuvres in the *Rose*, as a major feature of Jean de Meun's part of the poem—whilst, it may be added, recognizing that the category of the 'literal' is neither uncomplicated nor uncontested.[15] We would expect no less from a poet who was exercised by the artificial nature of the linguistic sign—a point to which we will return in Chapter 3. Indeed, it may be argued that, in the *Rose*, literal and allegorical trajectories serve and enable each other. Medieval commentators on the *auctores* tended to promote an 'either/or' approach to the respective discourses of 'veiled' and 'unclothed' language (Ovid's *Metamorphoses* versus Juvenal's *Satires*); Jean de Meun brings them together, in a vital opposition which reveals how much they depend on each other for their distinctive operations. What is at stake, then, is not which of two major impulses, the integumental or the satiric, wins out in the *Rose*, but rather the status and significance which Jean affords them at different stages within his total project. That is the issue which will now be addressed, in considering the positioning and contestation of literary-theoretical discourses within the *Rose*.

Competing theoretical discourses: allegorical covering versus satiric stripping

At one point in the *Rose* Jean de Meun quite unmistakably uses the language of integumental hermeneutics. His character

---

[15] At several points in the present book we will have cause to remark upon the slippery, shifting status of the *sensus litteralis* within late medieval textual culture. A positivistic approach which postulates a hard-and-fast category is doomed to failure, given that, e.g. the literal sense came to dominate territory which once had been occupied by allegorical senses, and certain types of 'transferred' or 'improper' signification—e.g. scriptural parables—could be judged as falling within the parameters of the literal sense. Cf. A. J. Minnis, 'Fifteenth Century Versions of Literalism: Girolamo Savonarola and Alfonso de Madrigal', in *Neue Richtungen in der hoch- und spätmittelalterlichen Bibelexegese* (Munich, 1996), pp. 163–80. By the same token, the scholastic definition of *integumentum* was not capacious enough to comprise all the relevant vagaries of linguistic and literary practice. A broader sense of allegory may be postulated, whereby the 'irreducibly figurative nature of language' is foregrounded. See Nicolette Zeeman, 'A License to Poets', pp. 154–5, and also Howard Bloch's investigation of the implications of the fact that the very 'idea of metaphor connotes alienation, denaturalization, or usurpation of linguistic property': *Etymologies and Genealogies: A Literary Anthropology of the French Middle Ages* (Chicago, 1983), pp. 118, 160.

Raison declares that in the *integumanz aus poetes* one will see 'une grant partie / des secrez de philosophie' ['a large part of the secrets of philosophy'] (7137–40). Trained clerics have access to those secrets. In our schools, she declares, many things are said *par paraboles* which are very beautiful to hear; however, one should not take them *a la letre* (7121–7). The fables of the poets in particular offer 'deliz mout profitables / souz cui leur pensees covrirent, / quant le voir des fables vestirent' ['very profitable delights beneath which they cover their thoughts when they clothe the truth in fables'] (7145–8).

Here Raison is going back a long way in the text, to her version of the fable of how Saturn was castrated by his son Jupiter, the result of which was the birth of Venus (5505–12). In this typical case, she assures us, 'La verité dedenz reposte / seroit clere, s'el iert esposte' ['The truth hidden within would be clear if it were explained'] (7135–6). But the promised exposition is not being provided here (I mean, in Raison's disquisition on *integumanz*). Instead Raison makes the point that certain words should be taken 'a la letre . . . sanz glose' ['according to the letter . . . without gloss'] (7151–4). Here she has in mind 'two words', *coillon* and *viz/vit* (6936, 7087), which she had used to designate the male genitalia; in turn these words refer back to her previous naming of Saturn's *coilles* or 'balls' (5507). According to her forceful argument Raison is perfectly justified in naming such noble things (noble because made by God) in plain text, without need of gloss. Glossing is again rejected just before Raison launches into her praise of the integuments of the poets, as cited above. You want me to gloss ('me requierz de gloser', 7052), she tells Amant scornfully, but why shouldn't I name such parts of the human anatomy directly or 'properly' (*proprement*), i.e. in language which is precise and appropriate, special to the things thereby designated (7095, cf. 7049)?[16] Are

---

[16] An interpretative problem is created here by semantic slippage between two senses of *gloser*, the technical sense 'to expound' (which one would expect in a discussion of the interpretation of integuments) and the sense 'to gloss over, to equivocate', the development of which was probably prompted by reaction against exposition which was deemed to be over-elaborate (or even deliberately misleading); cf. Christine de Pizan's remark about 'the glosses of Orléans which destroyed the text' and my related discussion, on pp. 138–40 below. The looser sense seems to be operating at l. 7052—to make matters even more complicated, and perhaps yet another instance of Jean's incessant linguistic playfulness! The technical sense is

they not the works of my Father? In sum, here—at the very (and only) point in the entire text at which integumental allegoresis is described, and immediately before the passage which modern panallegorizers regularly cite in justification of their totalizing readings—is a defence of 'proper' language and plain speaking which seems to be quite at variance with a language of secrecy and concealment that bespeaks the coterie knowledge of the privileged few who have studied long in the schools. This claim holds good irrespective of what view one takes of the possibly shifting meaning of the terms *glose, gloser*, and *gloseré* in the passages discussed above.[17] Surely passages such as these may appropriately be described as 'unflinchingly literal':

> cui [i.e. Saturnus] Jupiter coupa les coilles,
> ses filz, con se fussent andoilles,
> (mout ot ci dur filz et amer)
> puis les gita dedanz la mer . . .
>
> (5507–10)

[Saturn, whose balls Jupiter, his hard and bitter son, cut off as though they were sausages and threw into the sea . . .]

> mist Dex en coillons et en viz
> force de generacion
> par merveilleuse entencion . . .
>
> (6936–8)

[God in his wonderful purpose put the generative power into the pricks and cocks . . .]

> Coilles est biaus nons et si l'ains,
> si sunt par foi coillon et vit . . .
>
> (7086–7)

unequivocally present at ll. 7162 and 7166. We would *expect* it to be present also at l. 7154, since this statement follows immediately on from Raison's account of the *integumanz aus poetes* (7123–50), and since the technical sense of *proprement* (on which see below) operates in l. 7154. But it is perfectly possible to read ll. 7151–4 as meaning, 'But afterwards I gave you two words which you well understood and which must be taken literally and "properly", without equivocation' (which in this case may be particularized as, 'without substitution of euphemisms for obscene words'). Granted this possibility, however, I would wish to make the case that some vestige of the technical meaning remains at l. 7154. A few lines later (to heap irony upon irony) Amant will be using *gloser* and *gloseré* in their technical senses. However, his speech at ll. 7169–74 clearly echoes ll. 7151–4 (with 7174 cf. 7154), and the looser sense makes its presence felt once more.

[17] Cf. the previous note.

['Balls' is a good name and I like it, and so, in faith, are 'prick' and 'cock' . . .][18]

My purpose in labouring this point is not to be dismissive of integumental allegoresis, but rather to suggest that it is not the only hermeneutic process in operation. Indeed, there are several distinct but related theoretical discourses functioning within the *Rose* which justify language that is direct, plain, and open. One turns on the technical distinction between 'proper' and 'improper' speech, another on the relationship between words and deeds; yet another celebrates a style which presents truth as standing naked, stripped of the veils which conceal the harsh facts of human folly and depravity. The first two of these discourses will be discussed in Chapter 3 below; the last—which defines the objectives of the medieval literary theory of satire— is the subject of the present chapter.

The Roman satirists, Horace, Juvenal and Persius, were believed to have cut through falsehood and subterfuge to reveal facts about society that were unobscured by poetic invention or ornamentation.[19] Hence, a representative twelfth-century

[18] Here I alter Frances Horgan's translation, by using 'balls', 'prick', and 'cock' in preference to her terms 'testicles', 'testes', and 'penis', to bring out the deliberately obscene force of Jean's language. Cf. Ch. 3, below. David Hult has suggested to me (private communication) that Raison is distinguishing between her use of *coilles* in telling of Saturn's castration (5507) and her subsequent discussion of *coillon* and *vit* (6936 and 7087) as sexual organs: the first use is meant to be understood philosophically, and thus as an *integumentum* to be glossed, while the second is directly significative speech. That is to say, Raison speaks integumentally at one point of the poem and plainly in another, and, moreover, with a term used incidentally on the earlier occasion (where her interest is rather in fortune, justice, and the Golden Age) becoming the centre of attention in the later, due to Amant's prompting. I take all these points completely, but would suggest that Raison still has a case to answer for her initial use of *coilles*—a highly provocative act, and one designed (within Jean de Meun's comic economy) to provoke a response, however much later it may come. Raison may want to see her first use of the term as part of an integumental discourse, but such a usage is of course unprecedented in the Latin mythographers' treatments of the fable of Saturn, and in the *Rose* it retains its 'literal' force as an example of 'dirty talk' and has considerable shock value. One may contrast the use of the term *genitaires* in the *Ovide moralisé* and Christine de Pizan's *Epitre Othea*, and of the term *membres* in Evrart de Conty's commentary on the *Eschez amoureux*, in their explanations of the same *integumentum*.
[19] On the medieval literary theory of satire see esp. Minnis and Scott, *Medieval Literary Theory*, pp. 116–18; Paul. S. Miller, 'The Mediaeval Literary Theory of Satire and its Relevance to the Works of Gower, Langland and Chaucer' (Ph.D. diss., Queen's University of Belfast, 1982), also his article 'John Gower, Satiric Poet', in A. J. Minnis (ed.), *Gower's 'Confessio Amantis': Responses and*

commentator on Juvenal can declare that 'satire is naked . . . because it censures the vices of the Romans nakedly, and openly, and clearly, and without circumlocution and periphrasis, and without an *integumentum*'.[20] And Conrad of Hirsau, in comparing satyrs with satiric poets, explains that while the former are not embarrassed to expose themselves publicly without care for clothing (*nichil tractantes de tegumentis*), the latter are not restrained from their objective of making 'the depraved suffer under the naked outspokenness of their words'.[21] That is to say, it is unnecessary (indeed impossible) to interpret Roman satire allegorically because it conveys its moral message 'at the first, literal level of meaning', as Paul Miller puts it.[22] Obscure and obscuring *integumenta* were not deemed to be part and parcel of the style characteristic of satirists; here were no veils for the commentators to remove. Hence, in the *Ars versificatoria* which he composed in the middle of the twelfth century, Matthew of Vendôme could depict satire as a female figure who is garrulous, shameless—and naked: 'she presumes to keep so little of her sense of shame because she does not blush at all at her own nakedness'.[23] Here all the positive symbolic aspects of the decorous concealment of Nature, the desire to keep her nakedness hidden from the vulgar senses of men (as in the quotation from Macrobius which opened this chapter), have been reversed within a positive personification of outspoken, bold (even brash) moral discourse which exposes itself to all beholders.

Little wonder, then, that the satirists' literalism often expressed itself in language which was plain, blunt, and got straight to the point, even to the extent of being quite rude on occasion. Hence their discourse could be described as *fetidus, turpis*—and *obscenus*.[24] A striking example of what 'obscenity'

Reassessments (Cambridge, 1983), pp. 79–105; U. Kindermann, *Satyra: Die Theorie der Satire in Mittellateinischen: Vorstudie zu einer Gattungsgeschichte* (Nuremberg, 1978).

[20] Cited from Oxford, Bodleian Library, MS Auct. F.6.9 by Miller, 'Literary Theory of Satire', p. 27; cf. Minnis and Scott, *Medieval Literary Theory*, p. 116.
[21] Ibid. p. 61.   [22] Miller, 'Literary Theory of Satire', p. 27.
[23] *Ars versificatoria*, ii.6, in *Mathei Vindocinensis opera*, ed. F. Munari (Rome, 1977–88), iii.135; trans. Roger P. Parr (Milwaukee, Wis., 1981), p. 63.
[24] See the quotations assembled by Miller, 'Literary Theory of Satire', p. 382, n. 70.

could mean in this context has been provided by Suzanne
Reynolds, who cites a description of satire as being naked
'because it does not speak through circumlocutions (*circumlo-
qutiones*) like Virgil and Ovid, who, when discussing the hole
... [say] "whoever through the lips of chaste Diana ..." '. [25]
This seems to refer to the 'lips of Diana' as mentioned in Ovid's
Ibis, 479, which the scholia often gloss as 'the vulva'. Given,
then, that Ovid is here seen as referring to human genitalia in a
roundabout manner, the commentator's point seems to be that
the satirist's distinctive task is, *au contraire*, to speak of such
things directly. From which one might deduce that he is licensed
to use words like *coilles*, *coillon*, and *vit*. The outspokenness of
Jean's Raison, her wish to call a spade a bloody shovel (or, to be
more exact, to call testicles 'balls'), may be seen as following in
this satiric tradition, perhaps even being a conscious development of it. Jean de Montreuil sought to defend his dear master
by declaring that, thanks to the *satirici officium*, Jean de Meun
is 'permitted many things which are prohibited to other writers'.[26] Perhaps de Meun's use of 'obscene' language should be
taken as one, albeit the most extreme, case for which such
special permission needs to be claimed.[27]

The full flavour of the *accessūs ad satiricos* may be conveyed
by one comprehensive example, this being the introduction to
Juvenal glosses which have been attributed to William of
Conches by their modern editor, though this has proved controversial.[28] The vices of the Romans are identified as Juvenal's
subject-matter (*materia*), and his mode of treatment (*modus
agendi*) as reprehension (*reprehensio*), while the text's usefulness (*utilitas*) consists in the fact that it draws the reader or
hearer (*auditor*) from the clutches of those vices. Our anonymous glossator proceeds to define satire in general as 'reprehension composed in metre' and then offers a possible
explanation of the name: 'According to some, "satire" is so
called from the satyrs, who were woodland gods, because the

[25] Reynolds, *Medieval Reading*, p. 145.
[26] *Le Débat*, ed. Hicks, p. 42; trans. Baird and Kane, p. 154.
[27] The problem of obscenity in the *Rose* will be discussed in Ch. 3 below.
[28] *Guillaume de Conches: Glosae in Iuvenalem*, ed. Bradford Wilson (Paris,
1980). For important criticisms of this edition see the review by H. J. Westra in
Mittellateinisches Jahrbuch, 18 (1983), 368–9.

two are perfectly matched in all their characteristics', which include being naked and having 'an unbridled tongue'.

> . . . illi nudi et hec nuda, sunt enim quidam qui reprehensiones suas velant, ut Lucanus de pinguedine Neronis ait: *Sentiet axis honus* et tunc *obliquo sidere Romam*. Satira vera nude et aperte reprehendit. Dicaces sunt satiri. Satira nihil tacet et nulli parcit . . .

[They are naked and it is naked. For there are some writers who cover up (*velant*) their reprehension, as when Lucan, speaking of Nero's obesity, says: 'the axle will feel the weight' and then '[Nero will gaze on] Rome with oblique ray'. True satire consists of naked and open reprehension. Satyrs have an unbridled tongue; satire passes over no person in silence, and spares no one . . .][29]

Other *accessūs* explain that the satirist was motivated by righteous anger (*indignatio*) or some similarly commendable reaction which led to an abrupt outburst (*ex abrupto*) against the ills of society.[30] While sparing no one from his censure, he was careful to avoid spreading slander about particular individuals, and was fully prepared to admit his own failings.[31] Irony, here denoting a form of wit in which one says the opposite of what is meant, is often identified as a feature of satire, and mockery and laughter are said to function to confute the vices: 'Deridendo etiam omnia redarguit vitia.'[32] Indeed, irony may be

---

[29] *Glosae in Iuvenalem*, ed. Wilson, pp. 89–91; trans. Minnis and Scott, *Medieval Literary Theory*, pp. 136–7. The point being made here is that Lucan is criticizing Nero in an indirect and circumlocutory manner, in contrast with the open and direct ethical discourse of satire.

[30] For example, the Persius commentary attributed to Remigius of Auxerre speaks of the indignation, shock, and urge to reprehend which motivated Persius' outburst at the beginning of his first satire: 'Reprehendo cum indignatione et admiratione inchoavit et ipse ex abrupto, i. ex aspero docens . . .'. Cited by Dorothy M. Robathan and F. Edward Cranz (with P. O. Kristeller and B. Bischoff), 'A. Persius Flaccus', in F. Edward Cranz and P. O. Kristeller (eds.), *Catalogus translationum et commentariorum*, iii (Washington, DC, 1976), pp. 238. For similar statements see pp. 216, 219, 221. Cf. Miller, 'Literary Theory of Satire', pp. 101–3, 112.

[31] 'The satirists are in the habit of censuring even themselves', declares the *Scholia Pseudoacronis* on Horace; cited by Miller, 'John Gower, Satiric Poet', p. 93, who provides other examples of this view (see further p. 95).

[32] Robert John Barnett, Jr., 'An Anonymous Medieval Commentary on Juvenal' (Ph.D. diss., University of North Carolina at Chapel Hill, 1964), p. 2. Barnett dates this commentary to either the end of the twelfth century or early in the thirteenth; his edition is based on two manuscripts in the Bern Burgerbibliothek, MSS 666 and A61.

identified as satire's characteristic form of mockery: 'derisoria est, quod ironice loquitur'.[33] Moreover, the genre features a 'low' and 'light' (*levis*) rather than an elevated style: 'satira est levis quia constat vulgaribus verbis et cotidianis'.[34] Similarly, in an *accessus* to an exposition of Juvenal which represents the second of the vulgate commentary traditions, a distinction is made between satire which, as it were, lives in the country and hence uses common words (*vulgaribus utitur verbis*) and tragedy, which always uses elevated words (*regalibus utitur verbis*).[35] Those last remarks, incidentally, point to the great potential of satiric writing *in vulgari*. One could be more vulgar in the vernacular, so to speak, a fact which was fully appreciated by Walter of Châtillon (*c*.1135–after 1189), who composed several highly effective macaronic satires.[36]

Satiric discourse such as this—what Miller has called the 'vocabulary of censure'[37]—is vitally important for an understanding of both Jean de Meun's *apologia* and the style and strategy of his entire part of the *Rose*. In order to acquire the relevant discourse Jean did not have to know the Roman satirists directly (though he certainly had read some Juvenal, on which more later), for the schoolroom scholia on those authors had helped to create a medieval satirical tradition which flourished in the twelfth century, comprising texts by Walter of Châtillon and Walter Map and the *De contemptu mundi* of Bernard of Cluny (who died *c*.1140); an obvious later example is afforded by John of Garland's *Morale scolarium* (1241), which was also known as the *Opus satiricum* or *Liber satiricum*. Bernard of Cluny's debt to the *accessūs ad satiricos* is particularly marked.[38] He explains that while the first book of

---

[33] Quoted from a thirteenth-century Persius gloss (in Bern, Burgerbibliothek, MS 539b) by Miller, 'Literary Theory of Satire', p. 382, n. 71.

[34] Barnett, 'Anonymous Medieval Commentary on Juvenal', p. 1.

[35] Cited from Bern, Burgerbibliothek MS 539b (thirteenth century) by Miller, 'John Gower, Satiric Poet', p. 97. On the two vulgate traditions of Juvenal commentary see E. M. Sanford, 'Juvenalis, Decimus Junius', in F. E. Cranz and P. O. Kristeller (eds.), *Catalogus translationum et commentariorum*, i (Washington, DC, 1960), 182–92.

[36] Cf. Miller, 'John Gower, Satiric Poet', p. 86: 'Many poets found that the "low" style and abrasive tone of satire were more readily achieved in the vernacular languages than in the Latin of the Middle Ages from which vituperative colloquialisms had been refined.'   [37] Miller, 'Literary Theory of Satire', p. 94.

[38] As noted by Miller, 'Gower, Satiric Poet', p. 83.

De contemptu mundi is the contempt of the world, in Books 2 and 3 his subject (*materia*) is censure (*reprehensio*) of vices and his intention (*intentio*) is 'to recall from vices'.[39] Near the beginning of Book 2 he declares, 'here I follow satire (*hic satiram sequor*)'. Satire has a 'wide way' open to it, and modesty must forbear: 'Much that follows is indecent (*inhonesta*)', which is justified by his concern 'to prevent wicked deeds and to encourage virtuous deeds (*honesta*)'.[40] Bernard soon shows us what he means by this, launching an attack on an age which is fettered by lust, deceit, and vanity, some of his most extravagant strictures being directed at women: 'Woman is a guilty thing, a wickedly carnal thing, or rather all flesh, quick to betray and born to deceive, taught to deceive, the lowest ditch, the worst serpent, beautiful rottenness, a slippery path, a wickedly common thing, plunder and plunderer, a horrid night-owl, a common doorway, sweet poison. She knows nothing honestly; she is fickle and impious, a vessel full of clay . . .'.[41] And so forth, for there is much more—this anti-feminist diatribe being far more extravagant and extreme than anything found in the *Rose*.

Bernard's editor attempts to defend him in some measure by suggesting that this passage 'should be viewed less as an example of genuine misogyny . . . than a conformity to the tradition of satire'.[42] Whether that argument be accepted or not—one can imagine Christine de Pizan having little truck with it—Bernard of Cluny may certainly be identified as an author who, having been influenced by academic literary theory relating to satire, set about writing in the distinctive style which medieval *magistri* had theorized from the practice of the Roman satirists, and also sought to accommodate this discourse within a larger value system and a more elaborate textual structure, wherein

---

[39] *Scorn for the World: Bernard of Cluny's 'De contemptu mundi'*, ed. Ronald E. Pepin, Medieval Texts and Studies, 8 (East Lansing, Mich., 1991), pp. 8–9. Bernard was a Cluniac monk during the abbacy (1122–56) of Peter the Venerable. Pepin suggests that 'two sentiments are abundantly revealed: rage and regret'. 'Bernard's verses evidence his Christian zeal for reform and his Juvenalian indignation over vices themselves' (p. xii). [40] Ibid. 82–3.

[41] Ibid. 102–3.

[42] Ibid. p. xvii. Admittedly, this excursus was influenced by Walter Map's *Epistola Valerii ad Rufinum* and Juvenal's sixth satire. On Jean de Meun's use of these same sources in the jealous husband's harangue see below, pp. 99–100.

pagan laceration of vice is assimilated to Christian contempt of the world. I believe that the same process of assimilation and adaptation of satiric theory and tradition may be found in the *Rose*. We are not dealing here with an all-determining influence, to be sure—too many other literary theories and practices jostle for position and privilege within the protean *Rose*. But its major contribution should be given more credit than it has received thus far in the poem's modern reception.

Wherever Jean de Meun got the relevant theoretical ideas from (academic theory, textual practice, or both), they are manifest in his *apologia*, an excursus ostensibly prompted by Jean de Meun's desire to offer some sort of defence for the negative things said about women thus far in the poem, in particular (one may presume) within the speeches of Ami and La Vielle. 'Satire is the naked censure of vices, sparing no-one', declares a twelfth-century gloss on Juvenal.[43] The 'William of Conches' Juvenal commentary explains that 'satire passes over no person in silence, and spares no one'.[44] And Walter of Châtillon's macaronic satire which begins 'A la feste sui venue' describes the poet-satirist as being 'like a sword sparing no guilty man'.[45] Similarly, Jean's self-construction professes himself to be no respector of status or of persons (15221–6). Rather, he seeks to wound hypocrites wherever they may be, whether they live in the world or in the cloister. It does not matter how they are clothed ('que robe qu'il se queuvre'), i.e. what office or role in society they perform—perhaps Jean was thinking here of satire's concern with the naked truth. *Nichil tractantes de tegumentis . . .*

However, it was not his *entencion,* Jean declares, to speak against any living man who follows holy religion or performs good works. He does not wish to harm anyone other than those who deserve his censure (15243–4). Instead of having any specific target he shoots his arrows in a general fashion ('generaument'; 15227–30), using a volley—rather, one may presume, than aiming single shots at specific targets (cf. 15245). Moreover, it is possible that the lines in which he declares that he does not wish to attack any 'fame qui seit en vie . . .' (15174–8) should be

[43] MS Auct. F.6.9, fo.1ʳ, cited by Miller, 'John Gower, Satiric Poet', p. 84.

[44] Minnis and Scott, *Medieval Literary Theory*, p. 137.

[45] Karl Strecker (ed.), *Moralisch–Satirische Gedichte Walters von Chatillon* (Heidelberg, 1929), p. 123 (no. 13); cf. Miller, 'John Gower, Satiric Poet', p. 84.

interpreted in a similar way, as meaning that the poet never said anything, or intended to say anything, against any living woman in particular. Even Bernard of Cluny had claimed that he was not seeking to target any wicked woman in particular: 'Her I regard as good, but her acts I condemn, and therefore I censure them.'[46] All this is reminiscent of the satirists' professed desire to avoid slandering individuals, their targets being people in general and indeed the vices in general. 'Vices are the subject-matter of the satirists, not the vices of a certain definite person considered individually (*non singulariter alicuius determinatae personae*), but rather those of the populace considered collectively (*populi communiter*).'[47] And the opening lines of the *Morale scolarium*[48] profess John of Garland's intention not to lacerate anyone in particular but rather to employ a style which will 'play' in general, this presumably intimating the 'light' ('satira est levis . . .') quality of satiric writing and its use of mockery:

> Scribo novam satiram, set sic ne seminet iram,
> Iram deliram, letali vulnere diram,
> Nullus dente mali lacerabitur in speciali,
> Immo metro tali ludet stilus in generali.
>
> (1–4)

[I am writing a new satire, but in order not to spread anger which is maddening, terrible, deadly and wounding, no one in particular will be slandered by the sharp words of a wicked man, but rather in such a style my pen will amuse itself in general terms.]

Jean de Meun's phrasing and choice of expression are very much within this universe of discourse. Similar ideas, it may be added, are part and parcel of standard late medieval theory of preaching.[49] In the eyes of some of their Christian readers, the

[46] *De contemptu mundi*, ed. Pepin, pp. 102–3. Generally speaking, Pepin argues, Bernard's verses 'show him in the grip of the Christian satirist's dilemma, to love the sinner while hating the sin' (p. xii).

[47] From a twelfth-century Juvenal commentary found in Cologne, Dombibliothek MS 199; cited by Sanford, 'Juvenalis, Decimus Junius', p. 198. Cf. Miller, 'John Gower, Satiric Poet', p. 85.

[48] Ed. and trans. Louis Paetow, Memoirs of the University of California, 4. 2 (Berkeley, Calif., 1927), pp. 65–273.

[49] For a brief discussion, and references, see A. J. Minnis, 'Chaucer's Pardoner and the "Office of Preacher" ', in P. Boitani and A. Torti (eds.), *Intellectuals and Writers in Fourteenth-Century Europe* (Tübingen, 1986), pp. 107–8.

Roman satirists seemed to anticipate the didactic techniques and appropriate lifestyles of the preachers of their own day. Indeed, the satirists sometimes were regarded as the preachers of antiquity.[50]

Finally, far from adopting a 'holier than thou' attitude, the first-person speaker of Jean's *apologia* frankly admits that he himself is a sinner ('quex que pechierres que je soie', 15228). Similarly, the Carolingian *Scholia Pseudoacronis* on Horace had declared that self-censure was commonly practised by the satirists,[51] a sentiment often echoed in later commentaries. For example, 'William of Conches' follows the 'Vulgate Scholia' by interpreting the opening lines of Juvenal's first satire as the poet's accusation of himself for having stayed silent for so long, this being done so that he could reprehend others the more freely: 'ut liberius consortes suos reprehendat, seipsum in principio de nimia taciturnitate reprehendit'.[52] In another version of this same gloss, the rhetorical question is asked, 'How can a man who does not spare himself spare either you or me?'[53] By refusing to spare himself, therefore, Jean de Meun is justifying his refusal to spare others.

Given the evidence here reviewed, it is little wonder that that great defender of Jean de Meun in the *querelle de la Rose*, Jean de Montreuil, should describe him as a 'very severe satirist' (*satiricum perseverum*).[54] This is, of course, meant as a great compliment, as is made utterly clear by the fact that it is accompanied by the affirmation that truth will conquer, while false things do not last. It may be concluded, therefore, that

[50] As Miller says, they 'illustrated and censured the moral shortcomings of their pagan society in words that would endear them to many a Christian apologist. Like the preachers of the Christian Middle Ages, the Roman satirists recognised the spiritual deficiencies of their world and, through admonition, attempted to rectify its moral shortcomings': 'Literary Theory of Satire', pp. 26–7. See further Bernard Bischoff's account of a Juvenal commentary (*Catalogus* i, 196 ff.) in which Christian equivalents are found for the rites and tenets of pagan religion: 'Living with the Satirists', in R. R. Bolgar (ed.), *Classical Influences on European Culture, A.D. 500–1500* (Cambridge, 1971), pp. 89–90.   [51] See p. 93 above.

[52] From the text represented in Paris, Bibliothèque Nationale, MS Lat. 2904; *Glosae in Iuvenalem*, ed. Wilson, p. 92.

[53] Found in Baltimore, Walters Art Gallery, MS 20; *Glosae in Iuvenalem*, ed. Wilson, p. 92.

[54] *Le Débat*, ed. Hicks, p. 38; trans. Baird and Kane, p. 44. For de Montreuil's remark about the 'office of satirist' see above, p. 92.

knowledge of medieval notions about the naked text of satire played a significant role in Jean de Meun's self-fashioning as a poet.

Ovid among the satirists

Jean's indebtedness to satiric theory, as understood in his day, was not limited to the *apologia*, but may be said to have touched his text at many significant points. Raison is not the only figure in the *Rose* who speaks with a directness which is blunt to the point of rudeness. Moreover, Jean demonstrates direct knowledge of passages from the Roman satirists themselves, his love of Juvenal being particularly obvious. For example, at 8251 ff., when Ami is complaining about how women are not satisfied until they have got everything they possibly can out of their lovers, he follows the general statement of 'Juvenaus', 'Never will you find a woman who spares the man who loves her; for though she be herself aflame, she delights to torment and plunder him' (*Satura* vi. 208–10).[55] This is conflated with Juvenal's specific attack on Hibernia, who is not satisfied with one man any more than she would be satisfied with one eye (*Satura* vi. 53–4), here misunderstood (or should one say reworked?) to mean, she would rather 'un des euz perdre / que soi a un seul home aherdre' ['lose one of her eyes than be attached to one man'] (8259–60). Jean then moves on to praise the Golden Age (8325 ff.) in which women had other customs: loves were loyal and pure then, without greed or rapine (8329–30). This echoes the opening lines of Juvenal's sixth satire, in which the poet looks back to the 'days of Saturn' in which 'Chastity still lingered on the earth' (1–2).

Given that this is the Roman poet's most thoroughgoing piece of antifeminist writing, it is quite understandable that Jean should move on to have Ami present the figure of the Jealous Husband as commending Theophrastus' 'Golden Book' on marriage (8531 ff.), known only through Jerome's citations in that other classic of misogyny, the *Adversus Jovinianum*. And in

[55] Here I have used the edition and translation by G. G. Ramsay, *Juvenal and Persius*, rev. edn. (Cambridge, Mass., 1940).

turn this is followed by Walter Map's *Dissuasio Valerii ad Ruffinum philosophum ne uxorem ducat* (8575 ff.).[56] Jean de Meun may well have read Map's epistle as a satire. For it begins *ex abrupto*, in the best satirical manner: 'I am forbidden to speak, and I cannot keep silence.'[57] That phrasing recalls Juvenal's first satire, commonly interpreted by the glossators as the Roman poet's profession of his compulsion to write (in view of the vices of his contemporaries, which cried out for censure) despite the pressures on him to keep silent.[58] 'I hate the crane and the screech-owl's voice,' Map continues; 'I hate the owl and the other birds that dismally shriek their prophecies of the woes of winter and mud.'[59] That is to say, he has no wish to act like

---

[56] Jean actually draws on 'Valerius' before his ostentatious naming of him at ll. 8659, 8689 and 8697. Ll. 8575–8 and 8621–2 follow the *Dissuasio*, expanding it with the story of Lucrece as told by Livy (cf. Lecoy's note, on p. 273). Juvenal himself is named again at 8705: here Jean is following *Satura* vi. 28–32; he seems also to have used Juvenal at 8674–86 (cf. *Sat.* vi. 165, 47–9) and maybe at 8665 (cf. *Sat.* vii 202).

[57] Walter Map, *De Nugis curialium: Courtiers' Trifles*, ed. and trans. M. R. James, rev. C. N. L. Brooke and R. A. B. Mynors (Oxford, 1983), pp. 288–9.

[58] See e.g. the two versions of the relevant 'William of Conches' gloss as published by Wilson, *Glosae in Iuvenalem*, p. 92. As already noted, the Paris manuscript reads, 'Sed ut liberius consortes suos reprehendat, seipsum in principio de nimia taciturnitate reprehendit'. Thus in the usual satiric manner Juvenal begins with an exclamation which is prompted by indignation: 'ita more satirico ex indignatione clamando incipit'. Cf. the typical glosses on Persius' opening exclamation, as cited in n. 30 above, and also Bernard of Cluny: 'When I note such baseness, so many impieties which are the evils of the earth, although my tongue is unskilled, I cannot keep silence' (*De contemptu mundi*, ed. Pepin, pp. 82–3). In his general prologue, Bernard makes a similar point in explicitly Christian terms, explaining that he has 'expressed in speech what, concealed in my mind, I had long concealed within myself. . . . And the Lord said to me: Open your mouth and I shall fill it. Therefore, I opened my mouth, which the Lord filled with the spirit of wisdom and understanding' (pp. 6–9).

[59] Aesculapius was changed into a screech-owl for reporting that Proserpine had violated Pluto's law by eating three apple seeds: an exemplum of being forbidden to speak yet being unable to keep silent. Perhaps Map had this *fabula* in mind. It appears in Ovid, *Metamorphoses,* v. 539–52, where the screech-owl is described as a bird 'which heralds impending disaster, a harbinger of woe for mortals' (trans. Mary M. Innes (Harmondsworth, 1955), p. 130). On the owl as a prophet of doom see further Alan of Lille, *De planctu naturae*, ii, pr. 1 (trans. Sheridan, pp. 89–90), and the early Middle English poem (perhaps of the twelfth century) *The Owl and the Nightingale*, ll. 329 ff., 925, 1261–8; ed. E. G. Stanley (Manchester, rev. edn. 1970), pp. 59–60, 76, 85. The crane was commonly regarded as a bird with a strong, complaining cry; the leader of a flock of cranes would force the others to fly away, 'crienge as hit were blamynge' with her voice: see the *De proprietatibus rerum* of Bartholomaeus Anglicus (begun between 1225 and 1231 at Oxford), bk. xii, ch.

those proverbial prophets of doom. Yet speak out he must—
and, of course, he does.

This combination of materials, therefore, has its own logic.
What may seem less comprehensible is why Ami should wish to
follow those particular authorities in the first place. Given that
his ostensible mission in the poem is to help the lover into his
desired rose-bed, why should so many of Ami's remarks be of a
type which could well put the lover off women altogether? The
basic answer is that in the *Rose* the agendas of satire and of
seduction seem remarkably intertwined on occasion. We may
focus our attention on the problem by noting that, shortly
before the specific citations of Juvenal's sixth satire as discussed
above, Ami had offered over 500 lines of advice, culled from
Ovid's *Ars amatoria*, on the best methods of courtship (*Rose*,
7277 ff.). These involve making strong promises, swearing
vehement oaths, weeping profusely (with some tips on how to
fake it, if need be), and winning over the lady's guardians with
gifts, flattery, or any other means necessary. In short, this is a
training in the art of deception, as Amant himself points out
(though subsequently, of course, he will do what his friend
suggested). It leads naturally enough into a derogatory account
of the ways of women.

Here we are in the world of *Ovidius minor*, a very different
writer from the revered *auctor* of that 'pagan Bible', the
Metamorphoses, a work which was highly susceptible to
Christian appropriation and moralization. The highly volatile
nature of Ovid's amatory poetry, with which, in their scholia,
successive generations of medieval *magistri* had fought a losing
battle, has been described in our previous chapter. The implications of those facts of medieval literary scholarship for interpretation of the *Rose* are many and various. What is most obvious,
I hope, is that a structure which is built on so unstable a structure as the *Ovidius minor* is itself likely to be extremely unstable, offering materials which are capable of being taken in
many different ways. Given that Jean de Meun greatly amplified
all of the contesting Ovidian elements, it may be suggested

15 (Frankfurt, 1601; repr. Frankfurt a.M., 1964), pp. 534–5. Cf. *On the Properties
of Things: John Trevisa's Translation of Bartholomaeus Anglicus, De Proprietatibus
rerum*, ed. M. C. Seymour et al. (Oxford, 1975), p. 626 (which is quoted here).

(certainly, it is what I believe) that he magnified that instability rather than bringing it under control.

Two specific points may be ventured here. First, given the ambivalent nature of the *Ars* itself (a courtship manual which nevertheless reveals the follies of youth), along with the fact that in medieval scholarship the *Ars* and the *Remedia amoris* went together like the proverbial horse and carriage, Ovid being regarded as the expert on both the pursuit and the eradication of love, material from his shorter poems could be taken as emitting either positive or negative signals about human desire—or indeed, confused signals, which could be decoded either way. Given this pliancy of *Ovidius minor*, it is hardly surprising to find him, in Ami's monologue, rubbing shoulders with Juvenal, Jerome, and Walter Map. They are definitely in agreement about the deficiencies of womankind—and the question of whether those deficiencies are to be condemned or exploited is less important than that large measure of agreement. Theorists sometimes distinguished between Ovid and the satirists on the grounds that the intention of the former was solely to delight and of the latter to teach;[60] practising poets, however, often recognized that they had spoken with one voice.[61] Hence the conflation of Ovid and Juvenal, as noted above, with perhaps some help from the *Dissuasio Valerii*, particularly if Jean de Meun had recognized its formal affinities with the genre of satire. Ovid has become, it could be said, an honorary satirist.

Further evidence of the occasional consonance (from Jean's point of view) of these poets' style and substance may be illustrated by Jean's citation of *Satura* i. 38–9 at *Rose* 21409–12: 'Juvenaus meïsmes affiche / que, qui se met en vielle riche, / s'il

---

[60] For discussion see below, Ch. 5.

[61] This was, albeit in a negative sense, the view of Jean Gerson, who lumped together Juvenal and Ovid, along with other sources of the *Rose*, in a thoroughgoing condemnation: 'L'Art d'amour, laquelle escript Ovide, n'est pas seulement toute enclose ou dit livre, mais sont translatés, assemblés et tirés come a violance et sans propos autres livres plusseurs, tant d'Ovide come les autres, qui ne sont point moins deshonnestes et perilleux (ainssy que sont les dis de Heloys et de Pierre Abelart et de Juvenal . . .)' ['this romance contains not only Ovid's *Art of Loving* but also other books which are there translated, brought together, and drawn in by force and to no purpose. Meun used both Ovid and the works of others, which are not any the less dishonourable or dangerous, like the writings of Heloise and Abelard, and of Juvenal . . .']: *Le Débat*, ed. Hicks, pp. 76–7; trans. Baird and Kane, p. 83.

veust a grant estat venir' ['Juvenal declares that if a man wants to gain a great fortune he can take no shorter road than to take up with a rich old woman']. This, as the context of this declaration in Juvenal's text makes clear, is one of the many things which today's guilty age presents to his gaze in the open street (cf. ll. 63–4), arousing his indignation and obliging him to write 'angry rhymes'.[62] But Jean de Meun connects it to Ovid's recommendation of women of 'a later age' (*Ars amatoria*, ii. 667–8).[63] Ovid was making the point that older women make better lovers; Jean de Meun, however, follows Juvenal's lead in emphasizing the financial rather than the sexual rewards. Then he declares that older women are harder to trap because they have passed the time of their youth, when they were very susceptible to flattery and liable to be taken in and tricked; the implicit conclusion is that it is better for a man to try his luck with young women, who are less wary of the traps—women, it may be inferred, like the virgin Rose herself. Here it is difficult if not impossible to decide if Ovid has once again been made (or allowed) to speak like a satirist or if, thanks to Jean's (or is it Amant's?) casuistry, Juvenal has been enlisted in the ranks of the *praeceptores amoris*.

Whichever discourse (the erotic or the satiric) one judges to be dominant in such passages, it seems abundantly clear that it is not integumental, the meaning being very much on the surface, made manifest in an aggressively direct and frank manner; there seems no wish to bury significance deep under the surface where it can be reached only by the expert probing of *cognoscenti*. And that is my second specific point regarding Jean de Meun's exploitation of materials from the *Ovidius minor*, and of the various resonances which they struck in the minds of medieval scholiasts.

I would suggest further that, to some extent, in Jean's poem the mythographic language of the *Ovidius maior*, with all its potential for allegoresis, has been assimilated to the *modus loquendi* characteristic of the *Ovidius minor*. This argument may be advanced through an investigation of his exploitations of several *fabulae poetarum* which owed much of their medieval reputation to their inclusion in the *Metamorphoses*.

---

[62] Here I draw on the translation by William Gifford, *Juvenal, Satires, with the Satires of Persius* (London, 1992), pp. 6, 11.

[63] *'Art of Love' and Other Poems*, trans. Mozley, pp. 110–11.

Ovid unveiled

The fable of Venus and Adonis (as recorded in *Metamorphoses* x) is referred to by way of introduction to Venus, when Jean's narrative reaches the point at which that deity's aid is sought by the Castle's attackers. In his *Metamorphoses* commentary Arnulf of Orléans, following and elaborating upon Fulgentius, had declared that the death of Adonis signifies the extinction of love's pleasure, whether it be in the work of Venus or in any other activity; his transformation into a flower is taken as an affirmation of the superiority of charitable love over the love of Venus.[64] In the *Rose*, however, the 'moral' which is drawn (as part and parcel of Jean's erotic *comedia*) is that lovers should believe their sweethearts; moreover, he pokes fun at the protagonists by depicting Venus as a scold and Adonis as a childish character who turns a deaf ear to her constant nagging (cf. 15645 ff.).

A similar process is at work in Jean's appropriation of the fable of Hercules and Cacus, as alluded to in *Metamorphoses* ix and treated more fully in *Aeneid* viii and *De consolatione philosophiae* iv, met. vii. Fulgentius had explained that 'Cacus' is from the Greek word *cacon*, which means 'evil'.[65] He 'covets the property of Hercules, because all evil is opposed to virtue', and hides Hercules' cattle 'in his cave because evil is never frank or open-faced; but virtue slays the evil ones and redeems its own possessions'. Thieves like Cacus create smoke in an attempt to conceal their wrongdoing; thus evil 'puts out either what is contrary to the truth, that is, light, or what is offensive to those who see it, as smoke is to the eyes, or what is dark and dismal raillery. And so evil in its manifold forms is two-faced, not straightforward . . .'. In the thirteenth-century revision of William of Conches' Boethius commentary,[66] the episode of

---

[64] Ghisalberti, 'Arnolfo d'Orléans', p. 223. Cf. Fulgentius' account of the fable of Myrrha and Adonis, *Mitologiarum libri tres*, iii.8; trans. Whitbread, *Fulgentius the Mythographer*, p. 92.   [65] *Mit.* ii. 3; trans. Whitbread, pp. 68–9.

[66] Jean de Meun seems to have known a version of this thirteenth-century commentary, and used it both in the *Rose* and in his translation of *De consolatione philosophiae*: see A. J. Minnis, 'Aspects of the Medieval French and English Traditions of the *De consolatione philosophiae*', in M. T. Gibson (ed.), *Boethius. His Life, Thought and Influence* (Oxford, 1981), pp. 315–34. For proof that this

Hercules and Cacus is interpreted in terms of how evil seeks to lead right reason astray and wishes to hide under malice, but Hercules, i.e. the wise man, extracts, kills, and despoils Cacus (literally 'strips him', *denudatur*), thus bringing hidden malice out into the open.[67] Similarly, William of Aragon talks of how the *sapiens* diligently shuns evil in all things, avoiding it himself and also teaching its avoidance to others;[68] once again, the actual extraction and killing of Cacus is interpreted as all that is sordid and invidious being brought into the open.[69] All this is a far cry from lines 15526–62 of the *Rose*, where Seürtez ('Security'), in criticizing Poor ('Fear'), recalls how Poor fled with Cacus when he saw Hercules come running towards him with his club. And from lines 21589–602, when Amant's difficult penetration of his virgin rose is likened to the force which Hercules has to use to break into the cave of Cacus. The first passage offers exemplary narrative, which needs to be read *litteraliter*; the second, a very literal joke. In both these cases, as in the Ovidian narrative of Venus and Adonis, Jean's text seems to have divested *fabulae* of the integuments in which moralizing clerics had clothed them.

When the *Rose* does indeed appear to be drawing on traditions of moralizing mythography, the effect is often quite different from that found in the earlier texts. Jean de Meun, and indeed Guillaume de Lorris before him, were not content to passively reflect those traditions, but rather made vital contributions to them. Excellent examples are afforded by the uses to which the *fabulae* of Narcissus and Pygmalion (cf. *Metamorphoses* iii and x respectively) are put in the poem.

commentary is not the work of William of Conches himself, see A. J. Minnis and Lodi Nauta, '*More Platonico loquitur*: What Nicholas Trevet Really Did to William of Conches', in Minnis (ed.), *Chaucer's 'Boece' and the Medieval Tradition of Boethius* (Cambridge, 1993), pp. 1–33. See further Lodi Nauta's appendix, on pp. 189–91.

[67] London, British Library, MS Royal 15.B.III, fo. 122ʳ. A similar account is given in William's own commentary, with *denudatur* appearing in the majority of manuscripts; see the edn. by Lodi Nauta, *Guillelmi de Conchis, Glosae super Boetium*, CCCM 158 (Turnhout, 1999), p. 285.

[68] For Jean de Meun's knowledge of at least the prologue to the Boethius commentary of William of Aragon (who flourished in the second half of the thirteenth century) see Minnis, 'Medieval French and English Traditions', pp. 314, 315–34.

[69] Paris, Bibliothèque Nationale, MS Lat. 11856, fo. 111ʳ.

There is a remarkable degree of consensus among its modern readers regarding the status of the fountain of Narcissus as 'an emblem of destructive self-love',[70] though it must be said that this interpretation is at variance with, for example, Arnulf of Orléans' integumental analysis of that Ovidian fable. For Arnulf Narcissus can be understood as arrogance, while Echo means a man's good fame. She speaks well of arrogance, who, however, rejects her and prefers himself. For this he is turned into a flower, i.e. a useless thing, because he quickly passes away in the manner of a flower.[71] In short, Guillaume de Lorris pays more attention to the fable's *sensus litteralis* than Arnulf does, the theme of self-love being utterly apparent if the Ovidian text is read as exemplary narrative.

Even more remarkably, Jean de Meun sets up Pygmalion as the antithesis of Narcissus, this being part and parcel of a systematic recapitulation and redirection of Guillaume's major terms of reference which begins around line 20339. Initially at least, Pygmalion is no less a fool than Narcissus, despite his foolish protestation that his situation is different, since Narcissus could not possess what he saw in the fountain whereas he, Pygmalion, can take, embrace, and kiss his beloved ivory statue (20843–58). But this is, of course, no genuine possession, as Pygmalion himself admits a few lines later: 'je truis m'amie autresinc roide / conme est uns pex, et si tres froide / que, quant por lui besier i touche, / toute me refredist la bouche' ['I find my love as rigid as a post and so very cold that my mouth is chilled when I touch her to kiss her'] (20871–6). It would have been the easiest thing in the world for Jean to have depicted Pygmalion as a simple emblem of perverted desire—a figure just like Narcissus. After all, Arnulf of Orléans had stated that 'In truth, Pygmalion the wonderful artificer made an ivory statue which he began to misuse as though it were a living woman (*cepit abuti ad modum vere mulieris*)'.[72] However, Jean

---

[70] As Thomas D. Hill puts it; 'Narcissus, Pygmalion, and the Castration of Saturn: Two Mythographical Themes in the *Roman de la Rose*', *Studies in Philology*, 71 (1974), 407. Cf. Wetherbee, 'Literal and Allegorical', pp. 268–9, 285–6.   [71] Ghisalberti, 'Arnolfo d'Orléans', p. 209.
[72] Ibid. 223. This type of interpretation may have influenced Evrart de Conty's version of the Pygmalion story in his *Eschez amoureux* commentary. Evrart describes how Pygmalion made the beautiful image a companion of his table and of his own bed, and played with her as if she were alive ('jouoit a elle come se elle fut

does not present Pygmalion as doing disgusting things with a sex toy. He follows not the gloss of Arnulf but the text of Ovid, wherein Venus answers Pygmalion's prayers and turns the statue into a living woman, who bears him a child, Paphos, from which the island of Paphos takes its name.[73] In short, the farcical courtship of an inanimate object (which may well be taken as emblematic of the ridiculous adulation which some lovers profess in order to win their ladies) nevertheless results in the continuation of a man's divine self through progeny, to borrow a phrase from Raison (4373–80), and as such is a cut above the sterile self-love exemplified by Narcissus, which had no issue.[74] Moreover, as regarded in these terms, Jean's version of the Pygmalion legend rightly precedes the consummation of Amant's love for his Rose, an encounter which results in her impregnation (that being how I interpret ll. 21699–700) and certainly involves 'natural' heterosexual practice of the type recommended by Alan de Lille.[75] However, Jean problematizes rather than follows the prescriptive sexuality of *De planctu naturae* by intermingling the discourse of aggressive Ovidian

vivre'): *Eschez amour. moral.*, ed. Guichard-Tesson and Roy, p. 419. (Ovid had limited himself to remarking that Pygmalion kissed his statue and embraced it; placing his creation on a couch he made it his bedfellow.) However, Evrart goes on to offer more positive interpretations: she may represent (1) a young girl who, upon reaching physical maturity, is able to reciprocate Pygmalion's desires, (2) the process by which a man chooses one woman from among many others and she eventually responds (following his successful courtship), and (3) more literally ('plus pres de la lectre'), how man loves (non-sexually) the image of himself that he sees in his own daughter (pp. 419–21).

[73] This point is emphasized by Hill, who argues that the tradition whereby Pygmalion 'is an emblem of sterile and perverted concupiscence, is simply not relevant to the *Roman de la Rose*': 'Narcissus, Pygmalion', pp. 409–10.

[74] The episode remains ambivalent, of course, with different readings being possible—as is intimated by its variegated textual history. In the *Rose* of the KMN manuscripts, Pygmalion is presented as one 'driven mad by the erotic feminine presence he has created', according to Huot (*Rose and Its Readers*, p. 177). In his substantial rewriting (on which see pp. 259–60 below) Gui de Mori deletes the episode altogether, but 'his previous work on the poem had established the groundwork for a morally acceptable erotic relationship', and Amant is allowed his pleasurable impregnation of the Rose (ibid. 105). The episode is maintained in B-group manuscripts, although with some of its controversial elements pruned, and indeed enjoys more prominence, due to other revisions and deletions (ibid. 137, 143–4).

[75] On Alan's doctrine of sexuality see the discussion by Sheridan in the introduction to his translation of *De planctu naturae*, pp. 40–1, 59–62, and esp. Cadden, *Meanings of Sex Difference*, pp. 209, 221–5, together with Mark D. Jordan, *The Invention of Sodomy in Christian Theology* (Chicago, 1997), pp. 67–91.

eroticism, replete with its cross-currents of misogyny and cynicism.[76]

It could be argued, then, that in large measure Jean has lifted the veils from Ovidian *fabulae*, the possibilities for integumental allegoresis being spurned in favour of *exemplum*, and indeed of euhemerism, by which I mean a strategy of humanization.[77] However, integuments are indeed to be found in the *Rose*. And they come not from Raison (despite her mention of the theory of the interpretative method) or indeed from the narrator/Amant despite the suggestion that he may gloss the poet's sentences, fables and metaphors in time (7160–68). Others may defer, but the figure who delivers is—Genius.

Integumanz *at last: the garments of Genius*

Of course, Genius's credentials as exegete have been viewed with intense suspicion. 'Genius, like Amis, La Vielle, and above all the Lover himself' is regarded as 'unregeneratedly carnal and literal' by John Fleming, who reads the 'comedy and ironic inadequacy' of his 'pontifical pronouncements' as part of a strategy which seeks to direct the text's readers towards moral condemnation of the priest of Venus.[78] And yet: the 'sermon' of Genius contains the most substantial use of allegoresis in Jean's text, comprising not only *integumanz aus poetes* but theological symbolism as well. For it is Genius who, *inter alia*, describes the life of the blessed in Paradise, and affirms the superiority of the Good Shepherd's Park over the Garden of Mirth (as described at the beginning of the poem, by Guillaume), a critique which is of course central to the panallegorists' reading of the poem. Surely they should give Genius the credit for that, at least? Not that they do, of course.

True, on occasion Jean seems to want to remind us of who is actually speaking here. For instance, Genius recommends the *Rose* as a book which will ensure that its readers need not fear

[76] For discussion of Amant's richly problematic consummation at the end of the *Rose*, see Ch. 4 below.

[77] For a cogent introduction to medieval euhemeristic techniques, see John D. Cooke, 'Euhemerism: A Medieval Interpretation of Classical Paganism', *Speculum*, 2 (1927), 396–410.   [78] Fleming, *Allegory and Iconography*, p. 210.

the judgement of Rhadamanthus, Aeacus, and Minos, going on
to claim that the leading of a good life involves loyalty in love,
with each lover pleasing the other (19855–60). Later, he
declares that those who teach Nature's doctrine will not be kept
out of Paradise (19901 ff.): the winning of heaven is indubitably
a more complicated business than that. And Genius indulges his
castration complex (20007–52), even making the absurd
threat—a joke that has fallen flat for many modern readers—
that mass castration should be inflicted on those who fail to
follow Nature's laws. But the proposition that therefore everything he says should be regarded as suspect is simply too much
to swallow. Indeed, even Fleming admits that some of his
comments have some value: 'while Genius himself is totally
amoral he knows (rather than understands) that the path of
mythography leads very quickly to Christian morality, so he
also knows that the likely consequence of following the dispen-
sation of Jupiter is eternal damnation in a hell which is the nega-
tion of the Good Shepherd's Paradise'.[79] Not bad for a
'buffoon' who knows nothing of grace, and whose appropriation of symbolic language is 'unregeneratedly carnal and
literal'![80]

The following brief review of Genius's sermon will, I hope,
serve to demonstrate that this construct is better regarded as a
site occupied by several, sometimes competing, discourses
rather than as a figure who must always speak 'in character'; or,
to put it a little differently, that in Jean's *Rose* discourses are not
strictly constrained by the requirements of *persona* definition.[81]
Nature sends Genius out to preach that those who strive against
her will face excommunication while those who repent, and
vigorously strive to multiply the human race, will receive a total
pardon for all their sins against her. But what begins as an
exhortation to Love's barons to practise natural sex (as opposed
to the perversions which Alan of Lille had attacked), and
thereby save their family lines from oblivion, moves into a
forceful account of the three fatal sisters who bear, spin, and cut
the thread of life, along with Cerberus, the hound of hell who
longs to feed off men's flesh. This evocation of the terrors of the

---

[79] Ibid. 222.   [80] Ibid. 210; cf. p. 208.
[81] On medieval *persona* theory see below, Ch. 5.

other world, wherein the denizens of the classical Hades are
given qualities characteristic of those tormenting devils who
inhabit the Christian Hell, goes far beyond what is necessary for
the encouragement of Cupid's army.

It is as if the discourse relating to the underworld is following its own logic. Talk of the unavoidable pagan inferno
prompts an affirmation of the infinitely preferable Christian
alternative, when the hope is expressed that God, who is
Nature's master, may save the narrator when Atropos buries
him. 'Cil est saluz de cors et d'ame'; he is the salvation of body
and soul (19867–9). Soon the text is elaborating the attractions
of the Christian (Heavenly) Paradise, a land of beautiful fields
wherein the offspring of a virgin ewe leads His white sheep
along a scarcely trodden, narrow path which is covered with
flowers and herbs. There they can eat their fill, and no harm will
befall them, thanks to the attentions of the Good Shepherd
(19877 ff.). After this excursus, the text returns to secular
symbolism, in recuperating the myth of the Golden Age which
came to an end with the castration of Saturn—a *narratio fabulosa* which, of course, was first introduced by Raison (20053
ff.). The final verses of Genius's description of the Fall from that
pagan Eden link with the previous narrative block, in distinguishing between two kinds of sheep, the black ones with
meagre fleeces who never will be released by the infernal gods
(described as having taken the broad path, which has led to the
miserable dwelling they now occupy),[82] and the white, smooth,
and sleek ones who enjoy life in the Shepherd's Park (20179 ff.).
Genius then proceeds to offer a thoroughgoing critique of the
Garden of Mirth (20305 ff.), with special emphasis being placed
on the 'perilous fountain, so bitter and poisonous' which killed
Narcissus (20379–82). By the time he has finished no one could
possibly doubt that the Park's Fountain of Life is superior in
every way. Then the narrative reasserts itself; Genius remembers
who 'he' is. The text speaks once more of Nature's promise of
Pardon and threat of excommunication, and Love's barons
prepare for the final assault on the Castle of Jealousy (20653
ff.).

---

[82] In contrast with the narrow path taken by the above-mentioned white sheep.
Of course the image of the two roads derives from Matt. 7: 13–14.

The subsequent narrative is a far cry from, say, the symbolism of the carbuncle placed in the Fountain of Life, which is perfectly round (betokening eternity) and of three facets, an obvious image of the Trinity (20495–503). What Genius (of all people, so to speak) has given us is no less than a powerful vision—a *visio imaginaria*, to use the technical term—of the final judgement, with heaven and hell being presented in all their stark opposi-tions.[83] Moreover, it is perfectly possible to find in his words an affirmation of the superiority of heavenly love over all earthly love (though it is also possible to argue, in the light of what comes next in the poem, that sterile, unproductive earthly love is being specifically criticized by Jean). Whatever view one takes on that issue, it seems remarkable that Genius, whose domain is earthly love and generation, should have pronounced on matters which are far beyond his ken.[84] Here is no figure who simply and exclusively lends 'spurious authority' to the 'devious plot' being hatched by those 'forces of carnal license who have installed him as a puppet bishop'.[85] For at least some of the things Genius says are redolent of real authority, possess genuine spiritual value. At any rate, many of Jean's early readers seem to have been quite unworried by the fact that his amalgam of paradisal imagery from scriptural and secular sources is attrib-uted to Genius. For, as Fleming himself notes, certain illumina-tors were very interested in highlighting this eschatology.[86] It may be added that several fourteenth-century scribes 'could gloss the discourse of Genius as an allegory of Christian Heaven and salvation',[87] while Pierre Col, within the *querelle de la Rose*,

[83] But imaginary vision was not the highest type of vision; that was the intellec-tual vision, which precluded imagery, though it could be argued that *visio imagi-naria* included a certain amount of *visio intellectualis*. See A. J. Minnis, 'Langland's Ymaginatif and Late-Medieval Theories of Imagination', *Comparative Criticism*, 3 (1981), 92–4.

[84] As Huot remarks, 'it is one of the ironies of Jean's poem—a point noted, if unappreciatively, by Gerson—that Nature and Genius speak at far greater length and far more explicitly about theological matters than Reason does' (*Rose and Its Readers*, p. 97).

[85] Fleming, *Allegory and Iconography*, p. 211.

[86] Ibid. 222 (and fig. 7). See further Huot, *Rose and Its Readers*, pp. 30–1. Her subsequent discussion brings out very well how the discourse of Genius 'had always been susceptible of divergent readings'; cf. n. 74 above.

[87] Ibid. 175. On rubrication in early *Rose* manuscripts which highlight the theo-logical aspects of his sermon and present him as a moral authority, see ibid. 29–31. Huot further comments that, whilst evidence certainly exists 'in the textual history

could read Genius's criticism of the Garden of Delight as a direct statement of the views of the author, proof positive that Master Jean de Meun was not himself a foolish lover:

Conment pouroit il mieux monstrer qu'il n'estoit pas fol amoureux et qu'il amoit Raison que en blasment le vergier Deduit et les choses qui y sont, et en louant Raison et mettant ung aultre parc (ung autre parc ou vergier), ouquel il figure si notablement la Trinitey et l'Incarnacion par l'escharboucle et par l'olive qui prant son acroissement de la rousee de la fontainne, etc.?

[How could he show better that he was not a foolish lover and that he loved Raison than by blaming the Garden of Delight and the things that are in it; and by praising Raison and by putting another part in the Garden, in which he depicts so nobly the Trinity and the Incarnation by the carbuncle and by the olive tree which takes its growth from the dew of the fountain, etc.?][88]

Indeed, Col ends this particular document by echoing that very same disquisition:

. . . laquelle nous ottroit a tous toison si blanche que nous puissiens, avec le dit de Meung, brouter de herbes qui sont ou parc a l'aignelet saillant.

[And may the Trinity grant us all a fleece so white that we may, with the said de Meun, crop the grass which grows in the park of the little gambolling lamb.][89]

of the *Rose* for discomfort with the sermon of Genius, evidence also exists for a "straight" reading of the sermon as an unveiling of the poem's moral and spiritual significance' (p. 174). In one group of manuscripts the text is altered to bring Raison and Genius closer together; thus 'Genius argues for natural, procreative sexuality in accordance with Reason' (p. 177). Furthermore, in Gui de Mori's version of the *Rose* Genius's sermon is revised in such a way that 'his exhortation to procreate can be understood in the context of marriage' (p. 104). On the other hand, it must freely be admitted that elsewhere the 'theological content of Genius's discourse is almost entirely omitted' and he 'appears as the voice of active and fruitful sexuality' (p. 186).

[88] *Le Débat*, ed. Hicks, pp. 94–5; trans. Baird and Kane, p. 98. Huot concludes that 'when he defended the discourse of Genius' Col was 'speaking for a significant portion of medieval *Rose* readership' (*Rose and Its Readers*, p. 75). She also notes Col's argument that 'Nature and Genius urge not foolish love, but rather "les euvres de Nature" [the works of Nature]', these being 'legitimate for the purposes of procreation and of avoiding homosexuality': if Genius 'urges engagement in heterosexual relations' for these two purposes, Col sees 'nothing wrong with it' (pp. 174–5).

[89] *Le Débat*, ed. Hicks, p. 112; trans. Baird and Kane, p. 115.

And surely it was the sermon of Genius which moved Laurent de Premierfait to compare the *Rose* with Dante's *Comedy* as texts which treated of heaven and hell.[90]

In short, to this *persona* is entrusted the allegorical centre-piece or climax of the entire text, an excursus which in its spirituality far transcends everything which has come before, or indeed which will come after. Here are integuments at last—and Jean has not been content with second-hand clothes, but instead has produced something unique in making a pattern which incorporates both secular and sacred imagery of the most sobering kind. After this, Amant's sexual climax may well appear as something of an anticlimax, his elaborate innuendo trivial and bathetic. Here is not so much lifting the veil as looking up skirts. In structural terms, Jean de Meun was taking an extraordinary risk. Maybe the *Rose* never recovers from it.[91]

The specific interpretative problems—and they are legion—raised by the ending of the poem will be addressed in a later chapter. At this point we may consider some of the wider-reaching implications of satire's concern with the unveiled truth. Suzanne Reynolds has suggested that this genre, 'by virtue of its naked moral intention, allows for the development of a mode of exposition that investigates the surface of a text; it attends to the text's materiality for its own sake, not for a hidden moral which the text merely adumbrates'. She then looks forward to thirteenth-century literary theory, wherein (most obviously within

[90] On this comparison see esp. Badel, *Rose au XIVe siècle*, pp. 486–9.

[91] That certainly was the view of Christine de Pizan. She declares that 'ce mesle il paradis avec les ordures dont il parle' ['he brings paradise into the filthy things that he describes'] in order to give greater credibility (*plus foy*) to his book, and (in contrast to the view of Laurent de Premierfait as quoted above) compares the *Rose* unfavourably with the *Divine Comedy*: 'Mais se mieulx vuelz oïr descripre paradis et enfer, et par plus sublitz termes plus haultement parlé de theologie, plus prouffitablement, plus poetiquement et de plus grant efficasse, lis le livre que on appelle le Dant . . . et ou tu pourras plus prouffiter . . .' ['If you wish to hear paradise and hell described more subtly and, theologically, portrayed more advantageously, poetically, and efficaciously, read the book of Dante . . . I say that you will find there sounder principles . . .'] (*Le Débat*, ed. Hicks, pp. 134–5, 141–2; trans. Baird and Kane, pp. 132, 138). More broadly, Gerson states that Jean de Meun added a 'tres orde fin' ['most shameful conclusion'] but also a 'moien desraisonnable contre Raison' ['irrational middle in opposition to Raison'] to what Guillaume de Lorris had begun; like Christine, he believed that the poet had not ultimately condemned vice with the requisite clarity and thoroughness (*Le Débat*, ed. Hicks, pp. 85–6; trans. Baird and Kane, p. 89).

the new 'Aristotelian' academic prologue)[92] notions of causality
and agency 'served to promote the discussion of human as
opposed to divine authorship, to allow theorists to focus on
human literary activity', and suggests that 'in the twelfth
century, the conjunction of naked satire and an intentionalist
hermeneutics represents a similar development', whereby the
usefulness and value of texts is not located in what they veil.[93]
Indeed, one may argue that these phenomena are part and
parcel of a general development within the history of reading, a
trend to which many other factors contributed, including the
decline in prestige of the 'spiritual sense' of Holy Scripture
within scholarly exegesis, and the increasing popularity of
exemplification (which wore its ethics on its sleeve, so to speak)
as a mode to be found in biblical and other authoritative texts—
hence the identification of the *modus exemplorum suppositivus*—and, indeed, which a moralist could adopt in his own
writing.[94] Other literalistic types of writing, such as history and
its sub-category tragedy, also played a part.

But the total picture is far more complicated than this.
Biblical allegories were recognized as having the power to move
if not to prove, and believed to be useful in preaching and other
means of popularizing Christian doctrine of the kind deemed
suitable for mass, including lay, consumption (the *Bible moralisé* being a major case in point).[95] Then again, at the same time

---

[92] On this prologue-paradigm see Minnis, *Authorship*, pp. 28–9; Minnis and
Scott, *Medieval Literary Theory*, pp. 2–4, 197, 198–200, 314, 321.

[93] Reynolds, *Medieval Reading*, p. 77. See further Malcolm Parkes's account of
how the increasing emphasis on *sensus litteralis* affected the actual punctuation of
biblical texts: *Pause and Effect: An Introduction to the History of Punctuation in
the West* (Berkeley, Calif., 1993), pp. 72–6.

[94] On the *modus exemplorum suppositivus*, see Minnis, *Authorship*, pp. 123–4,
125, 182 n., 261 n.

[95] The situation should not be seen as a simple conflict between the literal and
spiritual senses; we are dealing not with devaluation but rather with revaluation.
Sensūs scripturae became subjected to the requirements (whether real or supposed)
of different audiences, and the demands of the different professionals who had to
cater for those audiences. The issue of the proliferation of hermeneutic discourses
and the relative status of the various *sensūs* was resolved not intellectually but practically, in suiting the text and technique to the auditor. Furthermore, the parameters
of the various senses themselves shifted. It became fashionable to include within the
sensus litteralis various figurative expressions (including parables and prefigura-
tions) which previously had been regarded as aspects of the spiritual sense. Cf. pp.
135–6 below.

that biblical exegesis was displaying an increased interest in the individual historical situations and intentions of *auctores humani*, classical scholarship disclosed 'a growing exegetical independence from the historical situation of the author, a tendency to register but then ignore authorial intention'.[96] This may be seen in Giovanni del Virgilio's commentary on Ovid's *Metamorphoses*, as described in Chapter 1, the anonymous *Ovide moralisé* (written between 1316 and 1328),[97] and the *Ovidius moralizatus* which forms book 15 of Pierre Bersuire's *Reductorium morale* (book 16, it may be added, offers a moralized Bible). Bersuire's enthusiastic moralizations of fables from the *Metamorphoses* are pursued with utter disregard for the Roman poet's own ambitions or the belief-system of his age, as when 'the satyrs, the gods of the fields' are moralized as 'prelates', particularly 'bishops with their horns and mitres, who should, out of feelings of deep affection, run to and fro around that Diana, that is, around the Blessed Virgin, serving her with devotion, and frequenting her altar with devotion, love, and the desire to serve her', repeating the words of the Song of Songs 1: 3: 'Draw me after you. We will rush to the fragrance of your perfume'.[98]

These 'two parallel but interestingly contrary developments in readership', as Christopher Baswell has called them,[99] must be given their due; each deserves an extensive chapter, so to speak, in the history of late medieval reading. And the very fact of their unresolvable contestation merits full consideration, with any temptation to totalize the one at the expense of the other being resisted. Furthermore, there is a way in which they may

---

[96] To borrow a phrase from Christopher Baswell's cogent comparison and contrast between the findings published in my own monograph *Authorship*, which concentrates on biblical exegesis, and those offered by the studies of Paule Demats and Judson Allen, which are largely concerned with late medieval classical scholarship (Baswell, *Figuring the Aeneid*, p. 165).

[97] On this poem's interpretative techniques see esp. Paule Demats, *Fabula: Trois études de mythographie antique et médiévale* (Geneva, 1973), pp. 61–105.

[98] Minnis and Scott, *Medieval Literary Theory*, pp. 371–2. On Bersuire's hermeneutic techniques see esp. the study by Ralph Hexter, 'The *Allegari* of Pierre Bersuire: Interpretation and the *Reductorium Morale*', *Allegorica*, 10 (1989), 51–84. As Hexter says of the *Ovidius moralizatus*, 'Whether as multiple interpretations of the same fable or of successive fables, the range of possibilities for the same figure or set of figures is dizzying' (p. 58). Bersuire 'seems to have been untroubled by the possibility of infinitely postponable closure, permanent incompleteness' (p. 69).

[99] Baswell, *Figuring the Aeneid*, p. 165.

be seen as ultimately connected: the impetus of claiming and affirming textual prestige is clearly a force in both situations. One of the results was what I have described elsewhere as a 'coming together' of pagan and scriptural *auctores*, at least in terms of their shared *modi agendi*: scriptural *auctores* were being read with close attention paid to their poetic and rhetorical methods, pagan *poetae* were being read integumentally and allegorically—and thus the twain could meet.[100] Not everyone approved of such fraternization, of course. Writing in 1491, the Italian Dominican Girolamo Savonarola attacked certain 'poets' who in their effort 'to prove that the art of poetry is of equal worth to Holy Scripture' use the argument that poetry has allegorical senses, just like the Bible. In fact, says Savonarola, 'no branch of learning except the Holy Scriptures properly and truly has a spiritual sense'. Unfortunately, 'some of our contemporaries try to allegorise the histories of the Romans and other pagans, thinking that they contain allegories in the same way as the Holy Scriptures do'; this should not be done, for those writings 'were by no means ordained with this meaning in mind'.[101] Thus Savonarola applies the principle of historical *intentio auctoris* as a means of suppressing inappropriate interpretation of pagan texts and preserving the superiority of sacred Scripture. But scholars like Albertino Mussato, Petrarch, and Boccaccio took pleasure in discovering 'thousands' of poetical expressions in the Bible and held that theology itself 'is simply the poetry of God'.[102] In his *Genealogia deorum gentilium*, Boccaccio read the fable of Persius' killing of the Gorgon in line with the traditional four senses of scriptural exegesis.[103] Dante,

---

[100] Cf. Minnis, *Authorship*, p. 142.

[101] See Minnis, 'Savonarola and de Madrigal', pp. 166–7. Compare the criticisms of Giovannino of Mantua (*fl. c.*1315), discussed by C. C. Greenfield, *Humanist and Scholastic Poetics, 1250–1500* (London, 1981), pp. 80–5, 87–9; cf. Minnis and Scott, *Medieval Literary Theory*, p. 390.

[102] See Minnis, *Authorship*, pp. 216–17; Minnis and Scott, *Medieval Literary Theory*, pp. 387– 91. See further the views of Pierre Bersuire, as expressed in the prologue to his *Ovidius moralizatus*, trans. in Minnis and Scott, *Medieval Literary Theory*, pp. 366–7; cf. Minnis, *Authorship*, pp. 142–3.

[103] However, this is the exception rather than the rule in this treatise. Cf. Charles G. Osgood, *Boccaccio on Poetry, being the Preface and the Fourteenth and Fifteenth Books of Boccaccio's 'Genealogia deorum gentilium'* (Princeton, NJ, 1956), p. xviii. It is impossible to identify who Savonarola's targets may have been—and, of course, he may have engaged in rhetorical exaggeration to strengthen his point.

arguably the greatest 'self-commentator' of the Middle Ages, distinguished between the 'allegory of the poets' and the 'allegory of the theologians' in a way which brought out their similarities, and found in the integumental reading characteristic of the 'allegory of the poets' a means of claiming textual authority for his own *canzoni*.[104] If, on one strategy of valorization, it was important to proclaim the absence or the lifting of veils, on another it was vital to keep them in place.

A full discussion of these matters is, unfortunately, beyond the scope of the present book. Suffice it to return to the quotation with which this chapter began, wherein Macrobius declares that an open and naked exposition of herself is distasteful to Nature. This passage seems to have been the inspiration for the twelfth-century Latin poem *Nature talamos intrans reseransque poeta*.[105] Here a poet who had entered the house of Nature, and dared to reveal her secrets, is castigated. This figure finds himself in a dark wood, threatened by wild beasts. But in a small clearing an old house stands, all by itself, and the poet can discern a naked maiden within. On asking for shelter, he is refused. Hiding her nakedness with her hair and hands, the woman accuses him of having broken faith with her: 'Stand afar off, and do no more wrong to my modesty. Only with difficulty did I bring myself to allow you to enter into my mysteries. You ought to have kept perpetual faith. Why, then, have you not been afraid to make me common, and, by spreading abroad what you knew about me, prostituted me, as though I were worthy of the name of a harlot? For this reason I will not suffer

---

[104] See Minnis and Scott, *Medieval Literary Theory*, pp. 382–3, 396–7. Dante thinks of the 'allegory of the poets' in terms of 'that which hides beneath the mantle (*manto*)' of such fables as Ovid's story of Orpheus; in such cases 'a truth' is 'hidden beneath a beautiful falsehood' (p. 396; cf. p. 383).

[105] Edited and discussed by Raby, 'Nuda Natura'. As he points out, the poem was almost certainly influenced by Macrobius's anecdote concerning the philosopher Numenius, who 'had revealed to him in a dream the outrage he had committed against the gods by proclaiming his interpretation (*interpretando vulgaverit*) of the Eleusinian mysteries. The Eleusinian goddesses themselves, dressed in the garments of courtesans, appeared to him standing before an open brothel, and when in his astonishment he asked the reason for this shocking conduct, they angrily replied that he had driven them from their sanctuary of modesty and had prostituted them to every passer-by' (*In somn. Scip.*, I.ii.19; trans. Stahl, p. 87). See further William of Conches' commentary on this Macrobius passage, quoted and discussed by Dronke, *Fabula*, pp. 53–5.

you any longer to look closely upon me, but I will cast you out and leave you to death and the beasts.' Here, as F. J. E. Raby puts it, 'that what Nature commands to be hidden is to be expounded only to the few who are fit to receive it, lest it should become of no account when heard by the vulgar'.[106]

Who was that poet? We may never know (assuming for the moment that a particular individual was being criticized here), but for our purposes he may be identified as someone rather like Jean de Meun. For Jean could be said to have made known the secrets of Nature to the vulgar, and in the vulgar tongue at that. (Over half a century later, Boccaccio was to celebrate the time when 'the Muses began to walk naked in the sight of men', i.e. the appearance of poetry in the vernacular.)[107] In the *Rose* we see Nature leaving her old house, and taking faltering steps in search of a new audience, an interpretative community wider and more diverse than that presupposed by Alan of Lille. Like W. B. Yeats long after him, Jean was content—in parts of his poem at least—to leave to others the 'embroideries / Out of old mythologies', believing that 'there's more enterprise / In walking naked'.[108]

---

[106] Raby, 'Nuda Natura', p. 77.   [107] See p. 274 below.
[108] 'A Coat', in *The Collected Poems of W. B. Yeats* (London, 1965), p. 142.

CHAPTER 3

Parler proprement: *Words, Deeds, and Proper Speech in the* Rose

In one of the most heavily quoted passages in the entire corpus of medieval literature, the first-person narrator of the *Canterbury Tales* asks his audience to forgive him if he should 'pleynly speke' (I(A) 727). Anyone who wishes to 'reherse' the words of other men must keep as close as possible to the *ipsissima verba*, or else the report will be imprecise, even false. Accurate reporting involves speaking their words 'proprely' (729)—i.e. repeating the actual expressions which are the property of the individual people—even though certain statements may be 'large' and 'rude' (725–38). Here 'large' means 'unrestrained', 'free'. 'Rude' has the general sense of 'uncultivated', though the context makes it clear that the more specific sense of 'vulgar', 'uncivil', and perhaps even 'obscene', is also operating. The Chaucer *persona* proceeds to cite two top authorities in defence of his position. Jesus Christ himself spoke 'ful brode' in Holy Writ, and no one dares to regard *that* as 'vileynye' ('rudeness', 'vulgarity', 'churlishness'). Plato is on his side also:

> Eek Plato seith, whoso kan hym rede,
> The wordes moote be cosyn to the dede.
> (I(A), 741–2)[1]

This discourse of words and deeds, of 'proper' speech and 'bad language' (as the modern idiom would have it), is heavily indebted to one source in particular—Jean de Meun's part of the *Roman de la Rose*. Of course, Chaucer's debt to the *Rose* has been widely acknowledged in modern scholarship. But it is, I think, fair to say that many details of that influence—and

---

[1] All Chaucer quotations are from *The Riverside Chaucer*, ed. Larry D. Benson et al. (Oxford, 1988).

perhaps even its profundity—have been somewhat occluded in recent criticism.[2]

The French poem draws on a variety of genres; it is marked by competing styles and strenuous attempts to yoke together heterogeneous source texts. In this cornucopia—some would call it confusion—Chaucer found several distinct but related theoretical discourses that justify language which is direct, plain, and open. That may sound surprising to those who believe that the *Rose* is determinately indebted to the traditions and techniques of integumental interpretation and/or allegory. However, as argued in the previous chapter, no consistent allegorical programme may be found in the *Rose*. Rather than clothing his entire text in the *integumenta* which medieval mythographers (and commentators on Latin *auctores*, particularly Virgil, Ovid, and Boethius) had found in pagan fable, Jean de Meun makes his own, often highly original if not eccentric, use of the actual narrative strands of classical tales. Here are no second-hand clothes; the poem is no second-hand rose. Furthermore, often he prefers *exemplum* to allegory, straightforward narration to the encoding of meaning, and engages in that naked outspokenness which medieval theorists deemed to be characteristic of the medieval literary theory of satire. Above, we have dealt with Jean's engagement with blunt and sometimes bawdy satiric language. Here our subject is his pronouncements on speech which is plain, 'proper', and directly significative of its referents. But the issue of obscenity arises here also, inasmuch as Raison claims the right to use a risqué word—*coilles,* roughly equivalent to 'balls' in modern vulgar English—on the grounds that this is the plain, 'proper', and direct way of referring to the male sexual organs. In order to elucidate the issues at stake here, we must turn to late medieval theory of signification, as found in commentaries on texts both sacred and secular and also in the logical treatises of such figures as Peter Abelard, Peter of Spain, William of Sherwood, and Lambert of Auxerre. It is indubitable that Jean de Meun was conversant with current

    [2] Two exceptions, which include discussion of issues treated in the present chapter, are the essays of Marc M. Pelen, 'The Manciple's "Cosyn" to the "Dede" ', *Chaucer Review*, 25 (1991), 343–54, and 'Murder and Immortality in Fragment VI(C) of the *Canterbury Tales*: Chaucer's Transformation of Theme and Image from the *Roman de la Rose*', *Chaucer Review*, 29 (1994), 1–25.

doctrine concerning the *voces significativae*, the 'signifying sounds' which constitute human speech. What he did with that doctrine, however, was far from common, as I now hope to show.

The notion that theory based on, and taught with reference to, the Latin language could be applied directly to French would not have troubled Jean in the slightest, given the widespread belief in a 'universal grammar'. '*Grammatica* is the same for all men and for all languages', confidently asserts the Parisian *artista* Jean le Danois in his *Summa grammatica* (1280).[3] In the *accessus* to a commentary on *Priscianus maior* attributed to Robert Kilwardby,[4] it is explained that the art of grammar may be regarded as divided into species in accordance with the various languages in which it is displayed.[5] Hence one may speak of Latin grammar, Greek grammar, Hebrew grammar, and Chaldean grammar—and the number could increase if the distinctive names and figures 'in Gallica lingua' or in any other language were inventoried.[6] But the clear understanding is that, although different words are used in different languages, the art of grammar is single and unified. As William of Conches puts it, 'arts are general and the same for everyone, although Greek explains them differently with different *voces*'.[7] Hence, in terms

---

[3] *Summa grammatica,* ed. Alfred Otto (Copenhagen, 1955), p. 54

[4] This attribution is highly dubious. See Osmund Lewry, 'The Problem of Authorship', in Jan Pinborg, O. Lewry, K. M. Fredborg, et al., 'The Commentary on *Priscianus maior* ascribed to Robert Kilwardby', *Cahiers de l'Institut du moyen-âge gret et latin*, 15 (1975), pp. 12–17+. The treatise may have been written in the 1250s. Kilwardby (d. 1279), an Englishman, taught arts at Paris; on his return to England he joined the Dominican order, and subsequently (in 1273) was consecrated Archbishop of Canterbury.

[5] Alfonso Manierù explains that 'the universality of grammar, which is common to all languages', was sometimes seen as being 'like a genus shared by all species'. See 'The Philosophy of Language', in *History of Linguistics*, ii: *Classical and Medieval Linguistics*, ed. Giulio Lepschy (London, 1994), pp. 280–1.

[6] 'Commentary on *Priscianus maior* ascribed to Kilwardby', selected texts, ed. Pinborg et al. (cf. reference in n. 4 above), pp. 47–8. See further Serge Lusignan, *Parler vulgairement: Les intellectuels et la langue française au XIIIe et XIVe siècles* (Paris, 1987), p. 23. Here 'Kilwardby' is elaborating a passage in the *accessus* to Peter Helias' highly influential *Summa super Priscianum*, as Lusignan points out (pp. 21, 23; cf. p. 190). Vincent of Beauvais drew heavily on this work, including its *accessus*, in compiling the second book of his *Speculum doctrinale*.

[7] K. M. Fredborg, 'Universal Grammar according to some Twelfth-Century Grammarians', in *Studies in Medieval Linguistic Thought Dedicated to G. L. Bursill-Hall*, ed. K. Koerner, H.-J. Niederehe, and R. H. Robins (Amsterdam, 1980), p. 71.

of semantics, or what was supposed to be 'the general meanings of words',[8] what worked for Latin supposedly went for French. And of course Latin set the standards by which medieval grammarians and logicians, 'living in constant bilingualism', measured other languages.[9] To *parler vulgairement*, to speak in French, was to employ a language system governed by principles and precepts that were analysed with reference to Latin and in Latin.[10] That certainly is the assumption made by Dame Raison, Jean's spokesperson on semantics. Here in the *Rose* Latin theory and vernacular practice are forcefully brought together[11] in a way which I personally find hilarious, *pace* the reading of the passages in question as constituting a serious justification of accurate, robust expression and 'telling it how it is'. Jean de Meun pushed to the limits what it is to *parler vulgairement*.

Vulgar talk and vernacular revaluation

In the apology for poetry which Jean provides at lines 15129–272 of the *Rose* the hope is expressed that 'seigneur amoreus' ('amorous lords') will support him against certain slanderers who may protest that his text contains speeches which are too bawdy (*baudes*) or foolish (*foles*). He seems to have in mind his earlier use of the term *coilles* in the course of Dame Raison's account of the castration of Saturn by his son Jupiter (see 5507–8; cf. 6898–900 and 7076–88). At line 7087 *coillon* and *vit* are added, which may be rendered as 'prick' and 'cock'.[12] Defending such words against the charge that they are

---

[8] See N. Kretzmann, A. Kenny, and J. Pinborg (eds.), *The Cambridge History of Later Medieval Philosophy* (Cambridge, 1982), p. 169.

[9] Cf. Manierù, 'The Philosophy of Language', p. 280.

[10] See esp. the discussion by Lusignan, *Parler vulgairement*; Bursill-Hall, *Speculative Grammars*, p. 38; P. Swiggers, 'Les premières grammaires des vernaculaires gallo-romans face à la tradition latine: stratégies d'adaptation et de transformation', in *L'Héritage des grammairiens latins de l'antiquité aux lumières* (Paris, 1988), pp. 259–69.

[11] Here I echo Gerson's remark that in the *Rose* various sources are 'assemblés et tirés come a violance', but apply the idea in a more positive way. *Traité contre le Roman de la Rose*, in *Le Débat*, ed. Hicks p. 76; trans. Baird and Kane, p. 83. Cf. Introduction.

[12] Cf. p. 88 above. I am working on the assumption that such language would indeed have been regarded as 'talking dirty' in Jean de Meun's day. This seems to be the consensus in current criticism of the *Rose*, but in the past some doubts were

ugly and villainous (*lez et vilain*), Raison adduces the principle
that *maniere* should be appropriate to *matire*. Sallust is credited
with this view, the essential point being that words that are
neighbours with things must be cousins to their deeds:

> 'Car quiconques la chose escrit,
> se du voir ne nous velt ambler,
> li diz doit le fet resambler;
> car les voiz aus choses voisines
> doivent estre a leur fez cousines.'
>
> (15161–2)

[Whoever does the writing, if he is not to deprive us of the truth, his
words must echo the deed, for when words rub shoulders with things,
they should be cousins of the deeds.]

This follows a passage in the *Bellum Catilinae*, iii, wherein it is
declared that not only those who have actually done things ('qui
fecere') but those who have written down the actions of others
('qui facta aliorum scripsere') are sometimes to be praised.
Although the recorder ('scriptorem') and the doer ('actorem'; in
some manuscripts 'auctorem') are not of equal repute, yet
Sallust insists that the writing of history ('res gestas scribere') is
'one of the most difficult of tasks', because for a start 'the style

expressed. For instance, John Fleming suggested that *coilles* is the 'proper name' for
testicles, this being justified by 'the etymological history of Latin *culleus* in the
Romance languages': *Reason and the Lover*, p. 106. To which Douglas Kelly
responded: 'if he means by "etymological history" the history of usage and semantic range, he should cite his sources; the phonological and morphological development alone of the word into the Romance languages will tell us nothing about its
usage proper or improper' (*Internal Difference*, p. 47). Kelly goes on to cite
instances of the 'obscene juxtaposition' of *coilles* and *andoilles* (meaning 'sausage
chitterlings'; cf. *Rose*, 5507–8) in *fabliaux* and in what he describes as a 'blatantly
obscene' passage in François Villon's *Testament* (pp. 49, 169–70 nn.). He also
points out that an (apparently) more polite French word was available to Jean,
namely *genitaires*, which is used in the accounts of the castration of Saturn found in
the *Ovide moralisé* and Christine de Pizan's *Epitre Othea*. Furthermore, the term
'membres' is used in Evrart de Conty's commentary on the *Eschez amoureux*
(*Eschez amour. moral.*, ed. Guichard-Tesson and Roy, p. 66). I myself feel that, as
used by Raison, the words in question *had* to appear shocking, or else the fuss made
of them in the *Rose* would have seemed inexplicable. Cf. David Hult, who suggests
that Jean de Meun is 'acutely aware both of the incendiary nature of his writing, and
of the linguistic means by which it is carried out': 'Words and Deeds: Jean de Meun's
Romance of the Rose and the Hermeneutics of Censorship', *New Literary History*,
28 (1997), 352. Furthermore, it is surely significant that, in various revisions and
rewritings of the *Rose*, the term *coilles* has vanished: see below, p. 259.

and diction must be equal to the deeds recorded' ('facta dictis exaequanda sunt').[13]

However, as has often been pointed out, Jean may also have had in mind Boethius, *De consolatione philosophiae*, iii pr. xii, 111–12.[14] There Dame Philosophy, in explaining to the Boethius *persona* how her arguments have been consonant with the stage that their inquiry has reached, remarks that there is no reason to be surprised by this, since he has learned under Plato's authority that words should be akin (*cognatos*) to the things being spoken about: 'il couvient que les paroles soient cousinez aus chosez dont il parlent', to quote the corresponding passage in Jean's own *Consolatio* translation, *Li Livres de confort*.[15] The Boethian allusion is to Plato's *Timaeus*, 29B. Here, in discussing the secondary reality of the physical world, Timaeus strives to account for the similarities between this world and its eternal exemplar by declaring that 'the words in which likeness and pattern are described will be of the same order as that which they describe',[16] although a 'description of a likeness of the changeless' as offered in myth, 'being a description of a mere likeness', will be 'merely likely': it is impossible for us to 'render a consistent and accurate' verbal account of such matters. (In the Calcidius Latin version of the *Timaeus* the crucial passage is, 'Causae quae, cur unaquaeque res sit, ostendunt, earundem rerum consaguineae sunt . . .'.)[17] Clearly, Boethius' application of Plato's statement has taken it some distance from this particular context, and allowed it wider applicability. What was originally a statement of the difficulties inherent in talking about eternal verities has become a catch-all *sententia* on the desirability of suiting style to subject. Which is how Jean de Meun may have thought of it. But to adapt it for a defence of bawdy or foolish words on the grounds that the subject may require such expression is to take an extraordinary liberty with his authoritative source.

---

[13] *Sallust*, ed. J. C. Rolfe (Cambridge, Mass., 1971), pp. 6–7.

[14] *Boethius: The Theological Tractates and 'The Consolation of Philosophy'*, ed. H. F. Stewart, E. K. Rand, and S. J. Tester (Cambridge, Mass., 1973), pp. 306–7.

[15] *Li Livres de confort*, iii pr. xii, 102–3, in 'Boethius' *De Consolatione* by Jean de Meun', ed. Dedeck-Héry, p. 232.

[16] *Plato: Timaeus*, trans. H. D. P. Lee (Harmondsworth, 1965), p. 41.

[17] Both the terms *cognatos* (Boethius) and *consaguineae* (Calcidius) have the sense of a blood relationship or 'cousinage', so the difference here is one of choice of word rather than of sense.

There is, however, yet another parallel to Jean's reference to the relationship of words and deeds, which must be given full weight in any discussion of this topic, particularly since it confronts the issue of what Jean de Meun really did to Alan of Lille.[18] I am referring to a passage in *De planctu naturae* (viii, pr. iv) which records Nature's initial response to the I-*persona*'s request for an explanation of why mankind alone has rebelled against her laws. She declares her intention of treating of the subject in an oblique and indirect fashion, in a more excellent style, away from 'the plain of plain words' ('plana uerborum planicie'), and refusing 'prophanis uerborum nouitatibus prophanare prophana', i.e. to 'profane the profane' or heap vulgarity upon vulgarity by using lowly neologisms, novel expressions far removed from the best ancient practice.[19] Rather she will 'gild things immodest with the golden trappings of modest words' and 'clothe them with the varied colours of graceful diction': 'uerum pudenda aureis pudicorum uerborum faleris inaurare uariisque uenustorum dictorum coloribus inuestire' (839). As a result, the 'dross of the above-mentioned vices will be beautified with golden phrases and the stench of vice will be balsam-scented with the perfume of honey-sweet words'; thanks to this, that 'great dung-hill stench' will not cause the audience to vomit 'from sickening indignation'. Here Nature seems to be coming close to the discourse characteristic of satire, with its emphasis on the *indignatio* which motivated, say, Persius or Juvenal to write so scathingly about the vices of mankind. Then the argument takes a different tack. Despite what she has just said, Nature continues, since the language in which we speak should show a kinship with the matters which are being spoken about ('quia rebus de quibus loquimur cognotas oportet esse sermones'), 'there should be at times an uncouthness of style to conform to the ugliness of the subject-matter' ('rerum informitati locutionis debet deformitas conformari'). But the wish to avoid giving offence takes priority: 'to prevent a poor quality of diction from offending the ears of readers or anything foul finding a place on a maiden's lips (*in*

[18] We will return to this question in Ch. 4 below.
[19] I have used the edn. of *De planctu naturae* by N. M. Häring, *Studi medievali*, 3rd ser., 19.2 (1978), 797–879, and the translation by Sheridan.

ore uirginali)' she will place 'a mantle (*pallium*) of fair-sounding words' upon 'the above-mentioned monsters of vice'.

Alan is obviously following Boethius in phrasing, while the context in which he has placed the *sententia* may well reflect the *Timaeus* passage as quoted above. But the significance of Alan's statement is markedly different. Whereas Boethius was noting the consonance of the language of myth with its eternal referent whilst at the same time emphasizing just how approximate such description is, Alan is, at it were, looking in the other direction, at *temporalia* rather than transcendent realities. For him at this point, myth-making, and ornate language in general, is a means of decently covering up what is base. That is Alan's dominant stylistic strategy; however, he has occasionally—this being the exception rather than the rule—used uncouth style as suitable for uncouth subject-matter. To put it another way, for the most part his words are not cousins to the deeds in question, but rather their distant relatives, who remain superior and aloof. For Jean de Meun, who was far more concerned with *temporalia* than Alan, the opposite is true, most of Jean's words being full cousins to the deeds which they signify. Here, then, is a substantial rethinking of Alan of Lille's policy on 'vulgar language'. Rather than placing 'a mantle of fair-sounding words' upon the vices, Jean often performs the office of the satirist in stripping them naked so that their monstrosity may be apparent to all, as has been argued in our previous chapter. Uncouth style is *frequently* used as suitable for uncouth subject matter, Jean being quite content to linger on the *plana uerborum planicie*. And the *Rose* often intimates a preference for 'proper' rather than oblique and indirect language— that being the main subject of the present chapter.

The distance between the writers is amusingly marked by the use to which Jean put Dame Nature's expression of concern about 'anything foul finding a place on a maiden's lips' (as quoted above). In the *Rose* it is Amant who worries about foul speech finding a place in the mouth of a courteous girl, which is how he addresses Dame Raison in these crucial lines:

> 'Si ne vos tiegn pas a cortaise
> quant ci m'avez coilles nomees,
> qui ne sunt pas bien renomees
> en bouche a cortaise puchele.'
>   (6898–901)

[Moreover, I do not consider you courteous when just now you named the balls; they are not well thought of in the mouth of a courteous girl.][20]

However, far from being put out by this suggestion that she has been 'talking dirty', Raison forcefully defends her chosen words as being noble and beautiful. It is Raison who is speaking here, and no ordinary woman. Therefore Amant's concern that her language should conform to the standards of polite society, and be in keeping with the courteous behaviour deemed to be appropriate to gentlewomen, seems hilariously misplaced. Thus Jean enjoys a moment of play with Alan's text; confrontation of the feminine gender of a personification is always good for a clerical laugh.[21] But there is a serious point here for literary hermeneutics—or, at least, concerning the attitude to literary hermeneutics which is being adopted at this point in Jean's text. Alan's Nature had decorously adorned immodest things with golden trappings and clothed them with colourful diction; by contrast, Jean's Raison wishes to speak plainly and 'without gloss' ('par plein texte sanz metre gloses', 6928). It is actually the Lover, Amant, who wants to gloss at this point, and to Raison this smacks of equivocation and hypocrisy. Therefore she refuses to have anything to do with such obscurantism.

This emphasis is reinforced by lines 7067–75. Raison quotes

[20] Here I follow the translation by David Hult, 'Language and Dismemberment', p. 116, which brings out the possible innuendo in Amant's speech—the words or the things are not well thought of . . . Here, then, in the very act of accusing Raison of obscenities, Amant may well be committing one himself. However, I have replaced Hult's term 'testicles' with 'balls', to recreate the vulgar shock-effect which Jean de Meun seems to want (cf. n. 12 above). The fact that Amant invokes a young woman (*puchele*) is significant, given that, as Jan M. Ziolkowski puts it, 'over the past two millennia one particular class of people has conventionally embodied modest speech in western Europe', i.e. 'young women and especially young virgins. One common measure of the propriety or impropriety of a given word or topic has been to see if it brings a blush to the cheeks of an innocent girl.' In contrast, if 'any collection of individuals was implicated strongly in obscene language and was perceived to be habitual offenders, that group was old women'—old women, it may be added, like Ovid's Dipsas, the heroine of the pseudo-Ovidian *De Vetula*, Jean's La Vielle, and Chaucer's Wife of Bath. See Ziolkowski, 'The Obscenities of Old Women. Vetularity and Vernacularity', in Ziolkowski (ed.), *Obscenity*, p. 73. Consequently, in the *Rose* one would expect dirty talk from La Vielle but not from Lady Raison.
[21] Cf. Sarah Kay, 'Women's Body of Knowledge: Epistemology and Misogyny in the *Romance of the Rose*', in Sarah Kay and Miri Rubin (eds.), *Framing Medieval Bodies* (Manchester, 1994), pp. 211–35.

Plato as saying in his *Timaeus* that speech was given to us for teaching and for learning—

> Et ce que ci t'ai recité
> peuz trover en auctorité,
> car Platon lisoit en s'escole
> que donee nous fu parole
> por enseignier et por aprendre.
> Ceste sentence ci rimee[22]
> troveras escrite en *Thimee*
> de Platon, qui ne fu pas nices.

[And you may find authority for what I have told you, for Plato taught in his school that speech was given to us to make our wishes understood, to teach, and to learn. You will find this idea, here expressed in verse, in the *Timaeus* of Plato, who was not stupid.]

—as indeed he did, but this is a wonderful example of a *sententia* taking on a new import when it is quoted out of context. For, of course, the *Timaeus* valorizes mythic language as a means of expressing something about things which are in fact inexpressibly transcendent. Yet here is Jean de Meun citing this text as authorizing the view that speech should say exactly and plainly what we mean. Secret language, comprehensible only to the cognoscenti, has given way to the public language of teaching and learning.

Geoffrey Chaucer was to take this process of broadening, demystification, and empiricization even further, accommodating the *sententia* regarding the kinship of *voiz* and *fez* to the words and deeds of a far wider (fictional) group of speakers and listeners, which included male and female *personae* who spoke *ful brode*. In the first instance, it should be noted that lines 15161–2 of the *Rose* have been reworked, and the result attributed not to Sallust but to Plato:

> Plato seith, whoso kan hym rede,
> The wordes moote be cosyn to the dede.
>   (I(A), 741–2)

---

[22] The use of 'rimee' here, apart from the obvious advantage of affording Jean a word which rhymes with 'Thimee', may reflect the fact that Plato was believed to have used a *modus loquendi* (viz. *integumentum*) that was characteristic of the poets. Cf. below, pp. 135–6.

This probably reflects the influence of *De consolatione philosophiae*, iii pr. xii, 111–12.[23] In Nicholas Trevet's Boethius commentary, on which Chaucer had drawn sporadically in the course of his translation of the *Consolatio*, it is asserted that here Plato is excusing himself for offering not rational demonstrations but assertions which are consonant with the thing or subject ('assertiones magis esse rei de qua loquimur consentaneas'), Boethius' term 'cognatos' being glossed as 'proprios et consentaneos'.[24] Applying the same principle a few lines earlier (iii pr. xii, 100–2), Boethius had invoked divine aid in order that he might speak about the most important matters of all both appropriately and decently. Perhaps it was Trevet's emphasis on the relationship between the status of the material and the style in which it should be treated which inspired Chaucer to cite the Boethian version of the relevant *sententia* in the General Prologue to *The Canterbury Tales* (I(A) 741–2; cf. p. 128 above), and also in the Manciple's Tale:

> The wise Plato seith, as ye may rede,
> The word moot nede accorde with the dede.
> If men shal telle proprely a thyng,
> The word moot cosyn be to the werkyng.
> (IX(H) 207–10)

---

[23] Cf. P. B. Taylor, 'Chaucer's *Cosyn to the Dede*', *Speculum,* 57 (1982), 324. However, I am sceptical of his claim that 'The insertion of the epigram at the very end of his apology in the General Prologue does much more than evoke authority for "rudeliche" speech. That apology as a whole moves from pleading the necessity of a vernacular and base speech to a suggestion—in citing both Christ and Plato—that words both clothe morality and reflect in their particular references a world of universals.' I myself believe that Chaucer's purpose is far removed from such Boethian epistemology; rather, a highly innovative English poet is indeed trying to 'evoke authority' for vernacular speech (no matter how 'rude' it can sometimes be). The sayings of Christ and Plato are being appropriated to that end (see further the concluding paragraphs of the present chapter). At the very least, Taylor's statement that Chaucer's 'view of language is that of a Christian Platonist' overstates and oversimplifies the case. A more nuanced discussion is provided by Myles, *Chaucerian Realism*, pp. 20, 22–7.

[24] Here I have used the typescript edn. of Trevet's commentary on Boethius by E. T. Silk, kindly provided to me by Prof. Silk, who was still working on it at the time of his death. Trevet's commentary is believed to have been written *c.*1300. See Lodi Nauta, 'The Scholastic Context of the Boethius Commentary by Nicholas Trevet', in J. F. M. Hoenen and Lodi Nauta (eds.), *Boethius in the Late Middle Ages: Latin and Vernacular Traditions of the 'Consolatio philosophiae'* (Leiden, 1997), pp. 41–67.

Indeed, Trevet's glosses 'consentaneas'/'consentaneos',
'proprios' and 'rei de qua loquimur' could lie behind Chaucer's
phrasing 'cosyn' and 'proprely a thyng',²⁵ although the case for
the influence of Jean de Meun's 'cousinez' (*Livres de confort*, iii
pr. xii, 102–3) may also be made.²⁶ But Chaucer was certainly
indebted to the *Rose* for the general context in which such high-
sounding assertions can be placed, the purpose to which they
may be put. As already noted, Jean's poem had managed to shift
the agenda from discussion of eternal verities to talk of *coilles*.
Chaucer was apparently very happy to go farther down the
route here indicated, towards a vernacular revaluation of vulgar
talk. In *The Canterbury Tales* he presents a defence of 'villainous' speech as used by the lower social orders who are his tales'
tellers and, to some extent, their subjects—this takes us very far
from Lady Raison, but the English poet (ostensibly) wants her
principles to apply. In the Miller's Prologue the narrator
declares that

> this Millere
> He wolde his wordes for no man forbere,
> But tolde his cherles tale in his manere.
> (I(A) 3167–9)

—and proceeds to apologize to 'every gentil wight' for the
language which will ensue, for which he takes no personal
responsibility. He must serve as a faithful reporter of the words
of others (I(A) 3173–5).²⁷ Chaucer's own *vileynye* (cf. I(A) 726)
is not at issue here but rather that of his 'villainous' *personae*.²⁸

> The Millere is a cherl; ye knowe wel this.
> So was the Reve eek and othere mo,
> And harlotrie they tolden bothe two.
> Avyseth yow, and put me out of blame;
> And eek men shal nat maken ernest of game.
> (I(A) 3182–6)

---

²⁵ Cf. Minnis and Nauta, '*More Platonico loquitur*', pp. 28–9.
²⁶ In Chaucer's translation of Boethius, which was influenced by both Jean's
Livres de confort and Trevet's commentary, the crucial phrase is rendered, 'thow
hast lernyd by the sentence of Plato that nedes the wordis moot be cosynes to the
thinges of whiche thei speken' (*Boece*, iii pr. xii, 205–7; *Riverside Chaucer*, p. 439).
²⁷ On the precedent for Chaucer's 'defence of the reporter' in Jean de Meun's
apologia see Minnis, *Authorship*, pp. 198–9.
²⁸ On medieval theory of *personae* see below, Ch. 5.

The language of 'harlotrie' is appropriate for churls, due to the nature of what is being described. In defence of that proposition Chaucer could well have cited Sallust's plea (as he had encountered it in the *Rose*) for recognition of the historian's artistry in suiting style and language to the events being recorded. In Jean's text there is perhaps an element of the ridiculous in an eminent historian's defence of his professional skill being appropriated within an *apologia* for bawdy or foolish deeds and their related words. In Chaucer the discourse seems to be used, and developed, rather more seriously. The English poet seems prepared to respect the words and deeds of the lowly as well as those of the great, and to treat them (or so it is implied) with something like the care and attention which traditionally had been afforded to the ancient Latin writers of great authority. Chaucer's churlish tale-tellers are therefore, in a sense, 'vernacular authors' of the most 'vulgar' kind—and 'authors' not only in the legal sense of being responsible for certain words and deeds[29] but also inasmuch as they have been put in the position usually reserved (within the rhetoric of deference to source materials) for the traditional *auctores*. Thus Chaucer problematizes the different senses of the term *auctor* and the concomitant types of 'authorship'.

Improper speech and the politics of interpretation

The notion of 'proper' speech, as inherited by Chaucer from Jean de Meun, requires fuller definition in view of its complexity. When Chaucer justifies his practice of speaking 'proprely' the Canterbury pilgrims' words (I(A) 729) and of telling 'proprely a thyng' by ensuring that the word is 'cosyn' to the 'werkyng' (IX (H) 207–10), he is personalizing language theory which tended to be applied to speech acts as opposed to speakers. For him 'propre' speech is speech belonging to certain individuals, rather than a quality which belongs to the speech, and speaking plainly is something which people do rather than something relating to

---

[29] In Roman antiquity the term *auctor* had a juridic connotation; e.g. the *auctor* was the person who transferred to another a right for which he could vouch. See M.-D. Chenu, 'Auctor, actor, autor', *Bulletin du Cange*, 4 (1927), 81–6; also his *Introduction à l'étude de Saint Thomas d'Aquin*, 2nd edn. (Montreal, 1954), p. 109.

the spoken word itself. In order to appreciate that manoeuvre—
which is not uncommon, and has a precedent in *De consolatione
philosophiae*, iii pr. xii[30]—we will have to delve more deeply into
medieval semantic theory, to seek illumination of the relationship between 'pleyn' speech and 'propre' words.

For both Jean de Meun and Chaucer, 'proper' speech meant
language of a kind which is direct and to the point as opposed to
being oblique or circumlocutory, clearly and plainly significative
rather than elaborately (or indeed obscurely) metaphorical. In
the scholarship of their day, the adjective 'proper' was often used
to describe the discourse of cool and rational science, no-
nonsense logical language as opposed to the fables of the poets
on the one hand and the loose, untechnical speech of the
common herd on the other. Matters were considerably complicated, of course, by the fact that the Bible and many works by
the Church Fathers made heavy use of figurative and 'improper'
speech.[31] Besides, pagan texts also could be figurative or allegorical, and to comparably good effect—behind the stylistic
garments or 'integuments' of Plato and the poets lay profound
truths of natural philosophy or human morality.[32] Yet late
medieval schoolmen prided themselves on the scientific, rigorously logical nature of their deductions from texts, whether those
texts were secular or sacred. St Thomas Aquinas, John of Paris,
Nicholas of Lyre, and William of Ockham (to name but a few)
approvingly cited Augustine's comment that only from the literal
sense of Scripture can a sound argument be drawn, and not from
those things said through allegory.[33] This point may be illustrated with reference to Jean de Meun's contemporary John of
Paris (1250/4–1306), who wrote a treatise *De potestate regia et*

[30] Cf. Myles, *Chaucerian Realism*, p. 24, who points out that the Boethian
emphasis 'is on the will of the speaker, not on the words themselves'.

[31] Peter Abelard quotes a definition wherein 'improper locution' is understood as
involving the use of a word 'in another sense from the one it normally or properly
has'. In medieval grammatical and rhetorical doctrine it was common to describe a
trope as a *modus orationis* which features a 'transference' of meaning from a proper
to a non-proper signification. See W. J. Courtenay, 'Force of Words and Figures of
Speech: The Crisis over *Virtus Sermonis* in the Fourteenth Century', *Franciscan
Studies*, 44 (1984), 113.   [32] Cf. above, pp. 15–16, 82–3.

[33] These citations are discussed by A. J. Minnis, 'Material Swords and Literal
Lights: The Status of Allegory in William of Ockham's *Breviloquium* on Papal
Power' (forthcoming). The Augustine passage may be found in *Epistula* xciii. 8 (*PL*
33, 334).

papali in support of King Philippe le Bel, to whom Jean would dedicate his Boethius translation. Philippe had been in dispute with the papacy since 1296 over the right of princes to tax the clergy within their realms and subsequently concerning the issue of clerical immunity from the jurisdiction of secular courts. The 'two swords' of Luke 22: 38 had been allegorized as the two major powers, of church and state, in a manner contrary to the king's interests. John attacked with the authority of St Augustine, who 'in his *Letter to Vincent*' had said that 'allegory is insufficient to prove any proposition unless some clear authority can be produced from another source to substantiate it'.[34] There is nothing in his opponents' argument, he concluded, 'except a certain allegorical reading (*adaptatio allegorica*)'—from which 'no convincing argument can be drawn'.

Such was the context in which the distinction between 'proper' and figurative or 'improper' speech functioned. Its commonplace nature may be demonstrated by the citation of three statements which are some distance apart in time. The first is from Henry of Ghent, a leading light in the arts faculty of the University of Paris and subsquently (from *c.*1275 until 1292) in its faculty of theology. In his *Summa quaestionum ordinariarum* Henry explains that certain passages of Scripture require not 'proper' but figurative interpretation ('non proprie sed figurative exponendus est'). At Judges 9: 8 we read of how the trees of the forest elected a king. 'That text has no true historical sense of its own,' declares Henry, 'but the words are put there figuratively for the sake of the mystical sense.' The true signification of the passage should be discovered by this approach, just as in the case of straightforward accounts we should take the truth as that which is expressed in normal language (*propriis verbis*) and revealed by the obvious signification of the words (*secundum significationem vocum*).[35]

---

34 *De potestate*, xviii; ed. Jean Leclercq in *Jean de Paris et l'ecclésiologie du XIIIe siècle* (Paris, 1942), p. 232; trans. J. A. Watt, *On Royal and Papal Power* (Toronto, 1971), p. 196. Watt believes that John of Paris (or Quindort) probably emerged 'from merely pupil status in the Parisian theological world in the later 1270s'; 'by 1300 he was established as one of the most prominent of the teachers and preachers of the leading theological school of Christendom' (pp. 9, 10).

35 See Minnis and Scott, *Medieval Literary Theory*, p. 264; for the Latin text see Henry of Ghent, *Summa in tres partes praecipuas digesta* (Ferrara, 1646), pp.

Our second statement is found in the *Summa de arte praedicandi* of Thomas of Chobham (*c.*1158/68–*c.*1233/6).[36] Words are used in their 'proper' signification when, for example, Hannibal's wars with Rome are described. In metaphor, however, there is *impropria significatio*, as when *principium*, which is used 'properly' to refer to the beginning of the world, as in 'In principio creavit Deus celum et terram' (Gen. 1: 1), is 'transferred' (*transumitur*) so it refers to the Son of God, with *celum* signifying the angels and *terra*, the other creatures. *Impropria significatio* has various names, Thomas continues, such as *tropus, tropologia, metonomia* (or *transumptio*), and *metaphora* (or *transformatio*), because each of the words or sayings in question 'is said to be converted or transferred or transformed from '"proper" signification to "improper" metaphor'. Grammar and dialectic deal with words in their 'proper' significations, inasmuch as they are instituted for signifying, while rhetoric deals with metaphors, teaching how by various 'colours' words are shifted from 'proper' to 'improper' significations.[37]

Our third witness is a passage from a text of the early fourteenth century, the *De sacramento altaris* of William of Ockham (*c.*1285–*c.*1347). The statements of authorities cannot always be taken 'according to the propriety of speech' (*secundum proprietatem sermonis*), says Ockham, for many figurative expressions were employed by philosophers, saints and scriptural writers.

268–9. This analytical language represents a modernization of earlier terminology as used, e.g. by St Augustine in *De doctrina christiana* and elsewhere. As Courtenay notes ('Force of Words', pp. 112–13), Augustine described literal meaning through such phrases as *ad litteram, locutio propria, in verbis propriis*, and *ad proprietatem verborum*. Figurative meaning is described as *tropos, modus locutionum, locutio translata, locutio figurata*, or *in verbis translatis*. Furthermore, in his *De schematibus et tropis*, the Venerable Bede explains that 'tropic expression' (*tropica locutio*) involves a transfer of meaning from 'proper signification' (*propria significatio*) to a 'non-proper similitude' or comparison (*non propria similitudo*); see PL 90, 175B.

[36] 'De modo significandi in theologia', in *Thomae de Chobham, Summa de arte praedicandi*, ed. F. Morenzoni, CCCM 82 (Turnhout, 1988), pp. 4–11. Cf. Gillian Evans, *The Language and Logic of the Bible: The Earlier Middle Ages* (Cambridge, 1984), pp. 57–8. On Thomas's life, see the Introduction to his *Summa confessorum*, ed. F. Broomfield, Analecta mediaevalia Namurcensia (Louvain, 1968), pp. xxviii–xxxviii. He seems to have read arts and theology at Paris before joining the episcopal *curia* of the bishop of London; some time between Oct. 1206 and *c.*1208 he was appointed sub-dean of Salisbury.

[37] *Summa de arte praedicandi*, ed. Morenzoni, pp. 6–7.

Moreover, they are also to be found in everyday speech. Ockham proceeds to explain what the grammarians have to say on the subject. According to them, 'transferences' (*translationes*) from 'proper' to 'improper' speech are made for three reasons: for the sake of metre, as in poetry; for the sake of ornament, as in rhetoric; and for the sake of necessity, either brevity or utility, as in philosophy. In all of these ways 'transferences' occur in Holy Scripture.[38]

Similar formulations are often found in theologians' attempts to define the boundaries and stylistic range of the literal/historical sense of Scripture. Thus Henry of Ghent can remark that 'the historical truth is sometimes expressed by a "proper" style (*sermone proprio*) and sometimes by a "transferred" and figurative style (*sermone translato et figurativo*)'.[39] Thomas Aquinas, whose second Parisian regency (1269–72) coincided with the period in which Jean de Meun seems to have been working on the *Rose*, says that within the *sensus litteralis* words can signify something properly (*aliquid proprie*) on the one hand, and something figuratively (*aliquid figurate*) on the other. Aquinas concludes that 'the parabolical sense' may therefore be regarded as 'contained in the literal sense'.[40] Furthermore, in his commentary on Job he affirms that 'the literal sense is that which is first intended by the words, either speaking properly (*proprie dicta*) or figuratively (*figurate*)'.[41] Similar vocabulary is found in discussions of Platonic *integumenta*. Commenting on the *Consolatio philosophiae* of Boethius, Nicholas Trevet describes how Plato, in transmitting his philosophy according to the manner of ancient theologians, conveyed his meaning under coverings and 'improper' words (*sub integumentis et verbiis impropriis*). It is the custom of the poets, he adds, to use fables

[38] *De sacramento altaris*, ed. and trans. T. B. Birch, Lutheran Literary Board (Burlington, Ia., 1930), pp. 40–5. Cf. Minnis, *Authorship*, p. 74. The sense of *translatio* as found here goes back at least to the rhetorical textbooks of the late Roman world; for discussion of its use across several medieval centuries see Evans, *Language and Logic of the Bible*, pp. 110–14.

[39] *Summa*, art. 16, qu. 3 (p. 265). Cf. Minnis and Scott, *Medieval Literary Theory*, p. 262.

[40] *Summa Theologiae*, 1a qu.1, art.10, ad 3um; here quoted in the Blackfriars edn. (London, 1964–81), i. 40–1; cf. Minnis and Scott, *Medieval Literary Theory*, pp. 242–3.

[41] *Expositio in librum B. Iob*, cap. i, lect. 2; in *Aquinatis opera* (Parma, 1852–72), xiv. 4.

and integuments and 'improper' locutions, and therefore Boethius' *modus loquendi* is consonant with that of the poets.[42]

In the light of these remarks, Jean de Meun's Raison may be identified as a speaker with considerable respect for the literal sense (as expressed in the greater part of her disquisition). For she claims divine sanction for her habit of speaking 'properly' of things when she pleases, without imposing any glosses: here the term *gloses* has the pejorative connotation of inappropriate concealment, implying a failure to face the facts.

> Par son gré sui je coutumiere
> de parler proprement des choses
> quant il me plest, sanz metre gloses.
>   (7048–50)[43]

[It is by his [i.e. my Father's, God's] will that I am accustomed to call things by their names when it pleases me, without glossing them.]

This echoes line 6928 ('par plein texte sanz metre gloses'), as already quoted. One can hardly ignore the implication that glossing is connected to, and necessary for understanding of, metaphorical and 'improper' language of the kind found in the integuments of the poets, as referred to by Raison herself at lines 7137–48[44]—here a negative implication, despite the positive estimation afforded *integumanz* in that later passage as offering a great number 'des secrez de philosophie / ou mout te vodras deliter, / et si porras mout profiter' ['of the secrets of philosophy, in which you will gladly take delight and from which you will also be able to gain great benefit'] (7139–42). But let us return to lines 7048 ff. When Amant opposes her, Raison continues, he

[42] *In Cons. phil.* iii, met. 11, ed. Silk (unpublished). Cf. the discussion by Minnis and Nauta, '*More Platonico loquitur*', p. 12. Here Trevet is expanding on the statement in William of Conches' Boethius commentary—a primary source of his own—which criticizes those who fail to realize that here the author is speaking in a Platonic manner 'by integument' ('nescientes modum Platonis loquendi de philosophia per integumentum'). *Glosa super Boetium*, ed. Nauta, p. 190.

[43] With the sense of 'quant il me plest' here cf. what may be the more technical meaning of 'a mon plesir' at l. 7062, as discussed on p. 141 below.

[44] Cf. Daniel Poirion, 'De la signification selon Jean de Meun', in L. Brind'Amour and E. Vance (eds.), *Archéologie du signe* (Toronto, 1983), p. 175. Poirion goes on to discover in Jean de Meun 'une méfiance pour la glose' (p. 176), and a desire for 'un système de signes dont la *lettre*, le signifié immediat, serre au plus près la réalité des choses, la richesse et le mouvement de la vie' (p. 179).

is asking her to gloss, i.e. to give up this right to speak *proprement* (7049, cf. 6920), to express the plain truth in language which is straightforward and direct, which of course she is not prepared to do. Here, then, is further evidence of the Protean nature of the *Rose*, its perpetual play with competing discourses.

Jean de Meun's notion of speaking plainly and properly lies behind Chaucer's somewhat different application of the terms in *Canterbury Tales*, I(A) 727–9 and IX(H) 207–10, as quoted above. Furthermore, in the Middle English tradition of the *Rose* the 'nakid text' is opposed to the 'glose':

> And if men would ther-geyn appose
> The nakid text, and lete the glose,
> It myghte soon assoiled be . . .
>
> (6555–7)

Here we quote from the C fragment of the *Romaunt of the Rose*, which is probably not the work of Chaucer; however, similar idioms occur in work which is indisputably his. In the G Prologue of the *Legend of Good Women*, Chaucer's intention is stated to be the declaration of 'The naked text in English' of many stories as told by 'autours' (85–8), which I take to mean that his narratives will use language that is plain, literal, and relatively unembellished, being devoid of elaborate rhetoric and the fabulous garments of style which had adorned the *integumenta poetarum*. (Approximately fifty years after Chaucer's death, John Lydgate was using the phrase 'plain English'.)[45] In the Summoner's Tale an unscrupulous interpreter of Scripture, who professes that 'Glosynge is a glorious thyng' (III(D) 1793), is held up for ridicule. In this tale obscurantist and opportunistic exegesis is shown as being motivated by greed and hypocrisy. It has been suggested that such a privileging of literalism was, at least in part, motivated by the controversial views on Bible interpretation which prompted the translation of the entire Bible into English. But one did not have to be a Lollard to be convinced of the crucial importance of the *sensus litteralis*. Several generations before John Wyclif's time it was already quite fashionable to emphasize its significance, with theologians even claiming to have discovered a 'double literal sense' in key

---

45 See Minnis, *Chaucer: Shorter Poems*, pp. 331–6.

passages.[46] Moreover, suspicion of clever glossing of a kind which supposedly twisted the meaning of the text had been around for a long time; scholars were very aware of the many directions in which the waxen nose of authority could be bent.[47] And it continued to persist, as when Christine de Pizan cited the 'common proverb' about 'the glosses of Orléans which destroyed the text'—a reference to the hermeneutic practices of the school of Orléans, that great centre of classical studies in the twelfth and thirteenth centuries. Presumably Christine had particularly in mind the integumental interpretation of pagan fables of the type found in Arnulf of Orléans's *Metamorphoses* commentary.[48]

But the limits of such unease about over-interpretation should be recognized. Critiques of the allegorical method were often made by the very same people who elsewhere practised it. Here we may recall the fact that Nicholas of Lyre, arguably the greatest literal interpreter of Scripture in the later Middle Ages, produced a *Postilla moralis,* largely for the use of preachers.[49]

[46] See Minnis and Scott, *Medieval Literary Theory,* pp. 205-6; cf. Minnis, 'Savonarola and de Madrigal', pp. 172–4. Wyclif himself propounded a quite radical version of the distinction between 'proper' and 'improper' speech, arguing in effect that since God is the *auctor* of sacred Scripture, *all* its language is effectively 'literal' and 'proper' in respect of the unique divine style: see A. J. Minnis, ' "Authorial Intention" and "Literal Sense" in the Exegetical Theories of Richard FitzRalph and John Wyclif', *Proceedings of the Royal Irish Academy,* 75, section C, no. 1 (Dublin, 1975), pp. 14, 25–7, and Rita Copeland, 'Rhetoric and the Politics of the Literal Sense in Medieval Literary Theory: Aquinas, Wyclif, and the Lollards', in Piero Boitani and Anna Torti (eds.), *Interpretation: Medieval and Modern* (Cambridge, 1993), pp. 1–23 (esp. p. 18).

[47] Cf. Alan of Lille's remark that an authority 'has a wax nose, which means that it can be bent into taking on different meanings': *De fide catholica,* i. 30 (*PL* 210, 333); cf. Chenu, *Thomas d'Aquin,* pp. 122–3.

[48] On which see above, pp. 83, 106–7, and with Christine's remark cf. Alexander of Villa Dei's attack on Orléans in general and Arnulf in particular: *The 'Ecclesiale' of Alexander of Villa Dei,* ed. L. R. Lind (Lawrence, Kan., 1958), pp. 2–3, 10–11.

[49] Cf. Minnis, 'Savonarola and de Madrigal', pp. 173–4, 178–9. De Madrigal had grand plans to produce fuller versions of both Lyre's literal and moral commentaries. For a valuable comparison of the ways in which, within his *Reductorium morale,* Pierre Bersuire moralized in turn the *Metamorphoses* and the Bible to provide material for preachers, see Hexter, 'The *Allegari* of Pierre Bersuire', esp. pp. 62–4. See further Judson Allen's discussion of the way in which certain English 'classicizing friars' promoted what he calls 'a spiritual sense of fiction': *Friar as Critic,* pp. 53–116. The foundational study of this 'group' is, of course, Beryl Smalley's *English Friars and Antiquity in the Early Fourteenth Century* (Oxford, 1960).

Returning to John of Paris's *De potestate regia et papali*, it may be noted that, having enlisted the support of Augustine on the insufficiency of allegory in proof of propositions, he moves quickly into a critique of the specific mystical sense which his opponents have offered, believing that he can offer better ones.[50] Or at least ones that serve the cause of Philippe le Bel. Furthermore, Christine de Pizan herself engaged in sophisticated mythographic glossing and self-glossing in the *L'Epistre d'Othéa* and *Livre de la mutacion de Fortune* respectively. In the former, Ovidian fables are interpreted in no fewer than three ways, with reference to their literal/historical, moral, and allegorical/spiritual senses. In the latter, Ovid's *Metamorphoses* provides models for her own metamorphosis into a man (as transformed by Fortune), following her husband's death and subsequent assumption of masculine roles. Then again, in her *Cité des Dames* Christine (on Earl Jeffrey Richards's reading) 'applied the Augustinian scheme of an earthly and a heavenly city in which the literal, historical experiences of women allegorically represent all humanity and anagogically represent the City of God'.[51] And, as already said, within the *Rose* itself the *integumanz aus poetes* are spoken of approvingly, even though Jean's Raison expresses grave suspicions about the value of *gloses*. The existence of 'improper', metaphorical or 'fabulous' speech was certainly not being called in question. It was its epistemological status, rhetorical uses, and appropriate audiences that were under discussion, all aspects of what may be termed the politics of interpretation.

The issues at stake here may be clarified with reference to Rita Copeland's important work on the relationship between medieval rhetoric and hermeneutics. She has shown how the commentary tradition appropriated the tools of late antique rhetoric and assumed much of its force. Rhetorical strategies of composition were transformed into strategies of reading, and an

[50] However, William of Ockham, whose *Breviloquium de principatu tyrannico super divina et humana* is influenced by John's treatise, at this point proceeds to present a general devaluation of allegory in the sphere of expert discussion. This is one of a series of tracts produced by Ockham during his exile in Munich, between 1332 and his death in 1347(?). See Minnis, 'Material Swords and Literal Lights'.

[51] 'Christine de Pizan and Sacred History', in M. Zimmermann and D. De Rentiis, *The City of Scholars: New Approaches to Christine de Pizan* (Berlin, 1994), p. 21.

abundance of *modi agendi*—considered in relation to their
didactic effectiveness—was sought in authoritative texts. Just as
the orator invented a speech that was governed by the 'circumstances' of time, place, and audience, the exegete reworked his
text to suit the specific descriptive and evaluative objectives of
hermeneutics.[52] But in the situation under review here, this
trajectory seems to be reversed. Exegesis moves outward rather
than inward, turns away from the text to address its target audience. And the way in which the waxen nose of textual authority is bent is a political decision, made with regard to the needs,
as judged by the interpreter, of his intended recipients.

'Improper' speech was thereby licensed on a large scale. Here,
then, is the (limiting) perspective within which those powerful-
sounding claims for the virtues of plain truth and unglossed text
should be understood. This caveat having been entered,
however, there is no doubt that certain late medieval trends in
linguistic and literary theory did nurture the emergence of a
discourse wherein notions of plainness, directness, and 'propriety' of speech were brought together and valorized. The history
of those trends is far beyond the scope of this chapter; suffice it
to say that Jean's *Rose* and Chaucer's *Canterbury Tales* have
their part in the story.

Reasonable shame and the human institution of speech

The ideological justification of Jean de Meun's theory of
'proper' speech rests on the belief that language is a sign-system
of human construction. Raison makes that point by declaring
that God has left it to man to assign names to things:

> ainceis m'opposes
> que, tout ait Dex fetes les choses,
> au meins ne fist il pas le non,
> ci te respoing: espoir que non,
> au meins celui qu'eles ont ores
> (si les pot il bien nomer lores
> quant il prumierement cria
> tout le monde et quan qu'il i a),

---

[52] See Copeland, *Rhetoric, Hermeneutics*, pp. 7, 64–5, 70–1, etc.

mes il vost que nous leur trovasse
a mon plesir et les nomasse
proprement et conmunement
por craistre nostre entendement . . .
(7053–64)

[. . . you do in fact object that although God made things, at least he
did not make their names—this is my reply: perhaps he did not, or at
least not the names they now have (although he could certainly name
them when he first created the whole world and everything in it), but
he wanted me to find proper and common names for them as it pleased
me [i.e. Raison], in order to increase our understanding . . .]

Sermo significativus was deemed to be 'the beginning of learning' (as Gillian Evans puts it),[53] very much devised *por craistre
nostre entendement*. To employ the then contemporary jargon,
impositio, the act of imposing a name on an object, of assigning
to a word the task of signifying,[54] was an artificial activity
rather than something 'natural' which could not be otherwise.
Many of the logical treatises of Jean's time routinely divided
significant sounds into those which signify naturally (*natu-
raliter*) and those which have their meaning determined by
convention, the common consent and usage of speakers (*ad
placitum*; cf. Jean's *a mon plesir*).[55] Examples of natural sounds
include the groaning of the sick and the barking of dogs. An
example of 'signifying sound' would be the Latin term *homo*
('man'); in other languages different words are employed to

[53] Evans, *Language and Logic of the Bible*, p. 79.
[54] The 'signification' of a term may be defined as 'the conventional (*ad placitum*)
representation of a thing by a vocal expression (*vox*)', to follow Peter of Spain,
'Tractatus', *called afterwards 'Summulae Logicales'*, ed. L. M. de Rijk (Assen,
1972), p. 79; trans. Francis P. Dinneen, *Language in Dispute: An English
Translation of Peter of Spain's 'Tractatus'* (Amsterdam, 1990), p. 69. Cf. Kretzmann
et al., *Cambridge History of Later Medieval Philosophy*, p. 169.
[55] See e.g. Peter of Spain, 'Tractatus', ed. de Rijk, pp. 1–2; trans. Dinneen, p. 2;
also William of Sherwood, *Introduction to Logic*, trans. Norman Kretzmann
(Minneapolis, 1966), p. 23. Peter, who studied arts at Paris and subsequently
became Pope John XXI, was born around 1205 and died in 1277; William was a
Master at Oxford in 1252. See further the cogent discussion by Ross G. Arthur,
Medieval Sign Theory and 'Sir Gawain and the Green Knight' (Toronto, 1987), pp.
22–5. This interesting book unfortunately leaps from semiotic subtlety and linguistic variation to a reductive moralism of a kind for which there is no precedent in the
medieval language theorists Arthur cites, as I argue in my review in *Studies in the
Age of Chaucer*, 12 (1990), 244–8.

designate a man, which proves that here we are dealing with
signification of a kind which is determined by the will of the
institutor or 'imposer' (*ad voluntatem instituentis* or *secundum
voluntatem imponentis*), fixed through human custom or institution (*ex humana institutione*).[56] It is in this sense that Peter
Abelard (writing in his *Dialectica*) claims that only *voces* which
signify *ad placitum* are the object of logic, for only they are
devised by men as elements of human speech, and have imposed
upon them the designation of things. A natural sign such as the
barking of a dog, by which we understand that it is angry, is far
removed from any kind of logic. Jean's Raison demonstrates the
ad placitum principle graphically, by explaining that if she had
used the term 'relic' rather than 'balls' to designate the male
genitalia, and the term 'balls' to designate relics, we would now
be calling balls 'relics' and relics 'balls' (7076–85). (At the end
of the *Rose*, Jean de Meun will return to this theme, in using
'pilgrim's staff' to mean 'penis', and so forth, the vocabulary of
pilgrimage being substituted for the language which 'properly'
and conventionally denotes sexual intercourse.)

Once Raison has fixed the *impositiones* of language, however,
they are here to stay. Of course she had to 'nomer / proprement
les euvres mon pere' ['name "properly" the works of my father']
(7095): without such specification of meaning, people would not
be able to talk about things (7097–100). *Ad placitum* signification did not, the logicians emphasize, imply a semantic free-for-
all, with meanings being in a state of constant flux.[57] For in the

---

[56] See L. M. De Rijk, *Logica modernorum: A Contribution to the History of
Early Terminist Logic* (Assen, 1962–7), ii.1, 191. Similarly, in his *Logica nostrorum
petitioni* Abelard emphasizes the human activity involved in *impositio* (*Logica
modernorum*, pp. 191–2).

[57] Many of the issues raised here have been discussed cogently by Howard
Bloch, who relates 'nominalistic' linguistic theories, said to be 'disruptive of any
naturalized attachment of word to physical property', to troubadour lyrics and
certain Old French romances. In my view he posits too sharp a contrast between
these and an 'early medieval grammar' of 'proper' signification. See *Etymologies
and Genealogies,* esp. pp. 34–63, 115–19, 159–60; cf. the brief critique of Bloch's
dichotomy in Zeeman, 'A License to Poets', p. 161. Furthermore, Bloch is probably too sensationalist in positing an 'anguished ambiguity provoked by a deep
split' between what medieval writers knew scientifically about verbal signs, i.e.
that they were conventional, and what they wanted to believe about them, i.e. that
a quasi-Cratylistic connection existed between words and things (p. 44). Cratylus
was the Platonic character who put forward the view that there was a ' "natural",
inherent, direct relationship between a word and a thing, regardless of the will or

process of *impositio* the human will is guided by right reason, which ensures a measure of permanence for her decisions. In the logical treatise which he probably published around 1260 at Paris, Lambert of Auxerre makes the point very nicely by distinguishing between two ways in which 'freedom of choice' (*voluntas*) may be understood.[58] A man may choose to sit or not sit; if this type of willing functioned in language use then a word could mean one thing on one occasion and another on another. But language does not work like that, Lambert declares confidently. We may also speak of will 'in so far as it is considered by right reason or derived through reason', and thus understood will is not a changeable principle. Here, then, is the way in which 'will is the principle of imposing utterances (*voces*) for the purpose of signification'.[59]

There was some discussion concerning whose reason-guided will should do the imposing. In the 'Kilwardby' commentary on *Priscianus maior* the various possibilities are considered. Should it be done by a philosopher? And not just by any philosopher, but rather one who has authority over all other wise men, a veritable 'prime philosopher'? Should it be done by the grammarian or logician, or left to the specialist (*artifex specialis*) to institute *voces ad significandum* in his particular

intention of the person who speaks that word', to quote Robert Myles's summary, *Chaucerian Realism*, p. 6; see also his discussion of Bloch, pp. 10–11. I myself hold that medieval writers had no problem at all in accepting that 'the bond between signifier and signified ... was merely conventional', believing, with Eugene Vance, that 'people of the Middle Ages were basically anti-Cratylistic in their conception of verbal signs'. Vance goes on to emphasize that 'medieval thinkers' had fully grasped 'not only the relationship between free will and signification but also the *contractual* basis of signification (*secundum id pactum et placitum, quo inter se homines ista signa firmarunt* [Augustine, *Confessions*, I.xiii.35])': *Mervelous Signals*, p. 258.

[58] *Logica (Summa Lamberti)*, ed. Franco Alessio, Pubblicazioni della Facoltà di Lettere e Filosofia dell'Università di Milano (Florence, 1971), pp. 7–8. On Lambert see further L. M. De Rijk, *Through Language to Reality: Studies in Medieval Semantics and Metaphysics*, ed. E. P. Bos (Northampton, 1989), item ix: 'The Development of *Suppositio naturalis* in Mediaeval Logic', pp. 89–102. De Rijk suggests that Lambert's treatise may have been written at the court of Troyes or Pamplona between 1253 and 1257 and published in Paris between 1257 and 1276, most likely about 1260.

[59] 'Sic voluntas non est principium transmutabile, et hoc modo voluntas est principium imponendi voces ad significandum. . . . Nam ut in plurimus voces imponuntur ad significandas res secundum rerum proprietates et etiam secundum rationem . . .' (*Summa Lamberti*, pp. 7–8).

science?[60] 'Kilwardby' has it both ways by concluding that, while in every science a 'proper' and specifically instituted vocabulary is used (each and every *artifex specialis* cannot be allowed to institute his individual vocabulary), as far as vocabulary 'common to all' is concerned,[61] that should be left to the *philosophus primus*. But Jean de Meun does not go onto that level of detail. What is abundantly clear, I hope, is that it was quite appropriate for an account of the conventional nature of human language to be assigned to Raison, and this in itself makes the point that mankind is not condemned to live in a world of slippery signifiers. If Raison is talking, she must be talking reason. What she is saying about language implies that it is under rational control.

Moreover, the logicians generally supposed that in at least some cases there was a connection between a word and the nature and qualities of the thing which it designated. According to a representative passage in the *Logica ingredientibus* attributed to Peter Abelard, in the first instance the *inventor nominum* 'considered the nature of the thing on which he imposed the name by which it was to be indicated'.[62] All of this helps to explain why Jean's Raison is so convinced of the value of her *impositiones,* assigned *ad placitum* but rationally (of course!) and with an awareness of the *naturae rerum* (that principle of control being implied rather than stated).

Hence she is justified (according to the ideology prevailing here) in criticizing women for not using such words as she has chosen. First she speculates that the problem is one of lack of usage. Custom is a powerful thing—as already noted, it is custom, *institutio*, which establishes the common usage of

[60] 'Commentary on *Priscianus maior* ascribed to Kilwardby', ed. Pinborg et al., pp. 76–9. The *quaestio* 'Cuius sit voces instituere ad significandum' is included in 2.1.11. Cf. the conclusion of 2.1.12: 'necesse fuit unum sapientem magistrum et doctorem omnium aliorum voces ad significandum instituere' (p. 79).

[61] 'Communi ad omnes'; cf. Raison's term *communement* (7063; quoted on p. 141 above).

[62] De Rijk, *Logica modernorum*, ii.1, 192. On the notion of the *primus inventor* or *impositor* of language see Hunt, *History of Grammar*, ed. Bursill-Hall, p. 19 n., and E. Vineis, 'Linguistics and Grammar', in *History of Linguistics*, ii, ed. Lepschy, pp. 176–7, 235 n. Vineis places emphasis on the belief that 'every word must be judged not so much for the way it is used in a certain construction, but on the basis of the nature and purpose for which it was created, as an "appropriate" designation imposed by the *primus inventor* on a specific reality' (p. 176).

speech—and if women used the 'proper' names (*propres nons*) for the male sexual organs more frequently, they would cease to be ashamed of naming them thus *proprement* (7101–6). Secondly, Raison considers the possibility that female hypocrisy is at work in this case: women do not want to use the words (and so they adopt all kinds of extraordinary euphemisms for male members) even though they are perfectly willing to do the deeds, finding that 'pricks' are not so painful after all (7107–16). If women refuse to engage in proper naming (*proprement nomer*) that is their business, concludes Raison; she will 'not make an issue' of it: 'je ne leur en feré ja force' (7117–19). However, she herself will not hold back when she wishes to *parler proprement* (7120–22). All this is quite impeccable semantic theory, and no doubt Abelard, Peter of Spain and the others would have approved. But they might well have been surprised, and probably amused, to discover that their doctrine was being used in defence of talking dirty.

Having made her case for 'proper' speech, for words understood in their primary and immediate significations, Raison launches into praise of the *integumanz aus poetes*, wherein words (according to the scholastic ideas which we have summarized above) are used in a manner which is 'improper', indirect, and figurative. Consistency of theoretical discourse is compromised even further when Amant refuses Raison's invitation (7139–50) to engage in integumental interpretation: 'ne bé je pas a gloser ores' ['I do not now hope to gloss them' (i.e. the poets)] (7162). Here glossing is seen as something desirable, something which Amant should be doing, whereas a few lines previously it smacked of evasion, petty squeamishness, hypocrisy. Indeed, at the beginning of this particular excursus Amant had expressed surprise at Raison's failure to gloss the word *coilles* with some courteous utterance (6902–6), which she roundly refused to do.[63] Yet now, in lines 7137–50 and 7162–74, the situation is reversed, as we hear Raison asking Amant to gloss and him refusing.

[63] At this point the sense of *gloser* as 'to gloss over' (here, specifically 'to provide euphemisms') is present—and yet the fact that a *mot* is being glossed with other words (euphemisms to be sure) recalls the technical, expository sense of the term. At ll. 7162 and 7166 Amant uses *gloser* and *gloseré* in that technical sense—yet at l. 7174 (which echoes l. 7154) the sense of 'providing euphemisms' resurfaces. Cf. pp. 88–9 above.

However, he does at least promise that he shall gloss them all in time ('bien les gloseré tout a tens', 7166), that he will return to provide the necessary exegesis. What, if anything in particular, Amant is referring ahead to here is highly debatable. But it could be argued that at the very end of the *Rose*, when he talks of his pilgrim's staff and sack, and how he scattered a little seed upon the rosebud, he is doing just that: engaging in 'glossing' of a kind which obscures the text, using 'improper' rather than 'proper' speech. True, he could be regarded as inventing his own integuments, clothing the facts with garments of his own making rather than investigating the old *integumanz aus poetes*, but at least he seems to be managing language in a manner which is consonant with Raison's recommendation. Of course, that argument will not survive a moment's analysis. For Amant's linguistic activity is of a kind which Raison would find reprehensible: is his 'improper' speech not on a par with the euphemistic language which, in the passage we have just discussed, she criticized women for using? If that connection were emphasized, soon we might be talking of Amant's 'womanly' and concupiscible linguistic corruption as a sign and symptom of his spiritual depravity. However, any temptation to take a leaf out of the books of D. W. Robertson and John V. Fleming may be tempered by recollection of Raison's relatively tolerant view of women's linguistic 'impropriety'. She refuses 'to make an issue' of this matter. Why, then, should we make a major issue of Amant's similar speech acts?

It could be concluded that gender-specific euphemism is afforded relatively minor status in Raison's rather rambling disquisition. But Christine de Pizan, as one of Jean de Meun's posthumous opponents in the *querelle de la Rose*, was prepared to make a major issue of it. Her intervention has proved almost as controversial as Jean's dubious language itself. According to Sheila Delany, Christine's 'main complaint against the *Roman* is that its author talks dirty', this being seen as an instance of stifling self-righteousness and prudery.[64] It seems to me that

---

[64] 'Mothers to Think Back Through': Who Are They? The Ambiguous Example of Christine de Pizan', repr. in Delany, *Medieval Literary Politics: Shapes of Ideology* (Manchester, 1990), p. 98; cf. p. 91. 'French popular literature must have been agony for Christine', given its use of bawdy language, claims Delany; 'it was not, by and large, a prudish age' (pp. 98–9). Similarly, Robertson claims that 'the art and

such a claim at once trivializes Christine's concern and misrepresents the significance of what she has to say on the poem's supposed obscenity by detaching it from the larger argument of which it forms one part, albeit an important one. As Christine Reno has said, 'Christine's main objection to the *Rose* was not that it contained some dirty language, but rather that it promulgated misogyny', and this was far from preciosity or priggishness, since there is a clear recognition in her contribution to the

exegesis of the Middle Ages show no qualms about the members of generation' (*Preface to Chaucer*, p. 361). But a 'change of taste' occurred in the fifteenth century, according to Robertson and Fleming, who believe that the reactions of Gerson and Christine open a period in which 'humanists would find themselves frequently put on the defensive by the attacks of the righteous' (ibid. 364; cf. Fleming, *Allegory and Iconography*, p. 47). One may recall the claim of 1960s cultural historians that 'the relative freedom of sexual expression in Elizabethan England' was followed by 'the rise of Puritanism', which in its turn was followed by 'successive waves of stigmatisation and legal repression'; 'sexual expression' was supposedly 'driven underground where, divorced from reality, it went bad, finally to re-appear in the form of the pornography of perversions'. Here I follow the brief historical sketch by Ian Hunter, David Saunders, and Dugald Williamson, *On Pornography: Literature, Sexuality and Obscenity Law* (Basingstoke, 1993), p. 3. They go on to argue that, 'far from being a sign of cultural backwardness, the concept of obscenity has today resumed its place as a central category in the analysis of pornography. Today, in some circles, pornography is less likely to be regarded as an expression of the truth of sex than as a harm or discrimination perpetrated by a systematic campaign to cast women as sexual, according to the *diktat* of male interest, imagination and desire' (pp. 3–4). Such thinking is encapsulated in the MacKinnon/Dworkin ordinance (1983), which claimed that pornography is 'a form of discrimination on the basis of sex'; thereby women are reduced to their private parts, presented as whores by nature, and dehumanized as sexual objects who e.g. experience sexual pleasure in rape. This may be seen, at least in part, as a reaction against what Foucault has termed the hysterization of women's bodies, i.e. the process whereby the feminine body is analysed as being thoroughly saturated with sexuality. (Though passed by the Minneapolis City Council, the MacKinnon/Dworkin ordinance was subsequently ruled 'unconstitutional' by the Supreme Court.) See Sharon Grace, *Testing Obscenity: An International Comparison of Laws and Controls Relating to Obscene Material*, Home Office Research Study 157 (London, 1996), p. 12, and Joseph Bristow, *Sexuality* (London, 1997), pp. 150–7. A substantial amount of medieval literature, including vast parts of the *Rose*, would certainly fail the MacKinnon/Dworkin test, and hence one might be led to feel some sympathy for Christine's attack on obscenity, however partial and conservative it is judged to be, and despite the awkwardness of her subject-position between the desire to claim expert knowledge of the despised object (the *Rose*) and the wish to profess ignorance of its details and its power to affect her (cf. David Hult's telling argument, 'Words and Deeds', pp. 361–4). Such an act of historical imagination may, of course, be difficult for anyone who supports Nadine Strossen's line that 'censoring sexual speech is really a detour, or, worse, a dead end' on the route to 'equality and safety for women': see her *Defending Pornography: Free Speech, Sex, and the Fight for Women's Rights* (London, 1995), p. 279.

querelle that 'derisive attitudes with regard to women lead inevitably to abusive behaviour directed against them'.[65] Furthermore, Christine looked behind the words themselves to consider their speaker's underlying intent, and, above all else, moved beyond the referentiality of language to focus on how it operates in society, on what might be called the sociolinguistics of smut (or what is alleged to be such).

'Le nom ne fait la deshonnesteté de la chose, mais la chose fait le nom deshonneste,' Christine assures Jean de Montreuil; the name does not make the thing dishonourable, but the thing, the name. Hence there is no point in trying to avoid the indecent name by substituting the word 'relics' for it (as Jean does in describing Amant's sexual consummation).[66] It would seem,

---

[65] 'Christine de Pizan: "At Best a Contradictory Figure?" ', in Margaret Brabant (ed.), *Politics, Gender, and Genre: The Political Thought of Christine de Pizan* (Boulder, 1992), p. 184. Here Reno alludes to Christine's anecdote of how a violently jealous husband would follow his reading of the *Rose* with an assault on his wife (see below, p. 200). *Pace* Hult, who suspects that 'Christine did not take the anecdote seriously, or at least not as a crucial component of her argument' ('Words and Deeds', p. 355), I believe that she took it very seriously indeed, and that it was a vital part of her argument in the text in question, which is the longest letter of the *querelle* and her most sustained and carefully argued critique of the *Rose*. Hult is absolutely right, however, to take previous criticism to task for its reduction of Christine to a one-issue debater in the *querelle*, that issue being 'the attack on women' found in the writings in question (p. 356). In fact, like Gerson's, her strictures 'were predominantly based on Christian moral grounds'—a view with which I would concur, though I believe that Christine should be given the credit for a vision of society which is more comprehensive than has sometimes been allowed. As in her *Livre de corps de policie*, certain flaws in her thinking in the *querelle* may be seen as stemming 'from the attempt to conjoin a life of practical politics with the desire for the Good, for the love of wisdom': cf. Kate Langdon Forhan's introduction to her edition and translation of *The Book of the Body Politic* (Cambridge, 1994), p. xxiv.

[66] *Le Débat*, ed. Hicks, p. 14; trans. Baird and Kane, pp. 48–9. Here Christine may be offering a view similar to that expressed in the *Speculum universale* of the Parisian theologian Raoul Ardent (d. *c.*1200): a word is 'shameful or honest' only 'according to the shamefulness or the honesty of the thing signified'. Cited by C. Casagrande and S. Vecchio, *Les Péchés de la langue: Discipline et éthique de la parole dans la culture médiévale*, trans. P. Baillet (Paris, 1991), p. 282. Cf. Howard Bloch, 'Modest Maids and Modified Nouns: Obscenity in the *Fabliaux*', in Ziolkowski (ed.), *Obscenity*, pp. 304–5. The 'sins of the tongue' have been discussed in relation to Middle English Literature by Edwin D. Craun, *Lies, Slander and Obscenity in Medieval English Literature: Pastoral Rhetoric and the Deviant Speaker* (Cambridge, 1997). See further Ruth Mazo Karras, '*Leccherous Songys*: Medieval Sexuality in Word and Deed', in Ziolkowski (ed.), *Obscenity*, pp. 233–45. Drawing on materials from the same tradition, she argues that pastoral writers were concerned 'about the effect on the souls of the men and women who engaged in or

then, that any name for certain body parts, no matter how euphemistic or polite, would offend against decency. Yet Christine shows herself to be fully aware of the principle that sometimes an ugly thing is appropriately designated by an ugly word (a principle affirmed in satiric theory and conceded by Alan of Lille's Nature), and she also believed that certain words which designate ugly things are less ugly than others. Thus, speaking of the word *meretrix* as applied by Christ to the women sinners at Matthew 21: 31–2 and Luke 15: 30, Christine says that this name 'n'est mie deshonneste a nommer selon la vilté de la chose' ['is not particularly dishonourable to utter considering the vileness of the thing named']. Furthermore, 'plus vilment pourroit estre dit mesmes en latin' [' it could have been more basely said even in Latin'], which I take to mean that a harsher Latin word for the *chose* could have been found. (I suspect the further implication, that even harsher words could have been found in the vernacular.) In sum, it is important not to reduce Christine's views on linguistic frankness and obscenity to the crude notion that she condemned all words which she regarded as *vile*.

Her most important statement on the subject comes in the form of a response to Pierre Col's justification of the naming of private parts in the *Rose*.[67] She emphasizes that, because of the corruption of the human will which accompanied the Fall of our first parents from Paradise, it would be impossible to speak honourably of a dishonourable thing.[68] It is the thing (*fait*) which makes the name (*non*) dishonourable. If, under present (rather than prelapsarian) conditions, the thing—whether the *secrés membres* or some other *chose deshonneste*—is dishonourable, then there is no way in which any name applied to it

listened to obscene or titillating speech'. Hence their interest differed from Catharine MacKinnon's (cf. n. 64 above), whose focus is on the effects of pornography within the human community—but they share the view that in this area 'the words and the imagination did not only lead to but constituted crime' (pp. 234–5). Karras characterizes MacKinnon as 'the most forceful advocate of the view that writing or depicting sexual violence is the equivalent of doing it: words are the same as deeds' (p. 233).

[67] For the argument that here, as elsewhere in the *querelle*, Pierre Col actually exacerbated Jean de Meun's misogynistic remarks, see Brown-Grant, *Moral Defence*, pp. 25–8.

[68] *Le Débat*, ed. Hicks, p. 117; trans. Baird and Kane, pp. 117–18.

would not become dishonourable. But this general linguistic corruption, Christine avers, is to be distinguished from personal purpose and motivation—a vital point, ignored by too many recent scholars who have effectively isolated her concern for smutty talk from the specific contexts in which it was expressed. If she fell ill and, in trying to describe her condition, referred to the 'secret members or whatever else' by a certain name (i.e. a name other than the 'proper name', *propre non*), then that name would not become dishonourable, because her purpose was not dishonourable. On the other hand, if on such an occasion she were to designate those things by their proper names, then anything which was dishonourable about those words would continue to exist but would not be her fault. They could not escape the taint of dishonour, since 'la premiere entencion de la chose a ja fait le non deshonneste' ['the primary associations of the thing have already made the name dishonourable'], but Christine herself would not be to blame. (In other words, the impact of those words would be determined by custom and the common usage of speech, which no individual speaker can over-throw.) By the same token, Christine says, Jean de Meun is to blame for what he wrote; the same appeal to personal purpose must be made. He was writing to excite lust. Or, to be as gener-ous to him as one possibly can, whatever his intention may have been, in actual fact his writing is of such a kind that it 'sonne mal a ceulx qui ne se delittent en telle charnalitey' ['sounds evil to people who do not delight in such carnality'].[69]

This same emphasis on personal responsibility for one's speech acts is at the centre of Christine's subsequent critique of the argument that Jean is justified in his use of 'proper' names since 'la sainte Escripture et la Bible' use them, where appropri-ate, and this is without sin. Her response is that, if that is indeed the case, then the *maniere de parler* and the purpose (*propos*) of

---

[69] *Le Débat*, ed. Hicks, p. 121; trans. Baird and Kane, p. 120. Here Christine crucially moves from locating obscenity within the *speaker*'s intent to the idea that the *hearer*'s reaction is crucial for the definition of obscenity, whatever the speaker's purpose may or may not have been. Christine's point is, of course, that people who are not amused by 'dirty talk' will find Jean's words offensive. It may be added that such words may have a bad effect on those who are less correct in their behaviour. As Kelly puts it, 'joking about *coilles, andoilles*, or any other sexual member before a passionate young man like Amant is situationally and rhetorically improper' (*Internal Difference*, p. 47); cf. Gerson's version of this argument in his *Traité* (*Le Débat*, ed. Hicks, pp. 84–5; trans. Baird and Kane, pp. 88–9).

such holy writings are entirely different from those of the *Rose*: their matter is far removed from carnal enticement. And if one appeals to the argument from custom and usage (as described in the Latin semantic treatises in terms of the *humana institutio* of language and *ad placitum* signification), then it should be noted that nobody has said 'que en tout le monde femmes ne hommes mesmement en parlent plainnement et en publique' ['that women and men anywhere speak thus plainly and publicly'] about their genitalia. Here Christine appeals to the principle of 'reasonable shame' (*honte raisonnable*) which, as she had explained a little earlier in this letter, has existed in the postlapsarian world from the time when Adam and Eve hid their secret members.[70] Similarly, Jean Gerson's *Traité contre le Roman de la Rose* emphasizes the vast difference between the State of Innocence and ours, 'combien que ce n'est mie pareil pour l'estat d'innocence et pour le nostre'. In the present state

... veoir ou oïr aucunes choses charnelles neument et selonc leur premier estat esmouveroit les pecheurs regardans a tres villains desirs, et pour l'esta d'innocence n'eust pas ainssy esté: tout cecy apert, car avant pechié Eve et Adan estoient nus sans honte, puis pecharent, et tantost se mussierent et couvrirent a grant vergoingne.

[... seeing or hearing carnal acts moves those sinners who see and hear to the most shameful desires, but within the state of Innocence it would not have been so. This is clearly apparent, since before sin Adam and Eve were naked and unashamed; after they sinned, they immediately hid and covered themselves with great shame].[71]

---

[70] *Le Débat*, ed. Hicks, p. 117; trans. Baird and Kane, p. 118.

[71] *Le Débat*, ed. Hicks, p. 84; trans. Baird and Kane, p. 88. St Augustine, in *De civitate Dei* xiv. 23, had famously declared that, before the Fall, matters relating to sex and generation could have been talked about openly, 'unhampered by any fear of obscenity'. Discussion 'would then range freely over all that might come to mind in relation to bodily organs'; 'nor would there be any words which might be called obscene: rather, whatever was said on this subject would be as honourable as what we say when speaking of the other parts of the body'. However, Augustine is very clear about the decorums which must appertain after the Fall. To summarize his point of view with the use of some of his own expressions, nowadays 'modesty' has a perfect right to suspect anyone 'wishing to discuss this subject', and be ready to compel one to 'ask pardon, with an apology to chaste ears'. Hence Augustine feels obliged to assure the 'modest and religious reader' of his good intentions. For a start, he shall not be 'mentioning and condemning damnable obscenities'. In respect of what he actually *will* be explaining, i.e. 'the processes of human generation', he promises to try 'to avoid the use of obscene words': *The City of God against the Pagans*, ed. and trans. R. W. Dyson (Cambridge, 1998), p. 625. Therefore it is

The principle of *honte raisonnable*, Christine affirms, must be respected. On its basis she directly challenges Pierre Col. If he is so keen to endorse the view of Jean's Raison that 'they should be called plainly (*plainnement*) by name', why does not Col himself 'name them plainly' in his own writing?

Il me samble que tu n'es pas bon escolier, car tu n'en suis pas bien la doctrine de ton maistre. Qui te muet a ce? Se tu dis que ce n'est la coustume, si as doubté d'en estre repris. . . . Veulz tu vivre a oppinion de gent? Suy la bonne doctrine: si monstre aux autres qu'ilz doivent fere; . . . et se on t'en blasme au premiers, tu seras aprés loué . . . Ha! Par Dieu! autremant va! Tu ne le pues nyer.

[It seems to me that you are not a good pupil, for you do not follow well at all the doctrine of your master [i.e. Jean de Meun], who teaches you to name them. If you say that this is not the custom, are you then afraid of being criticized . . .? Do you wish to live by the opinion of other people? Rather, follow good doctrine, in order to show them what they ought to do . . . And if someone blames you at first, you will be praised for it later . . . Ha! My God! You do not do so. You cannot deny that shame keeps you from it.][72]

This substantially addresses Raison's argument at *Rose*, 7101–10, to the effect that if women do not use certain 'proper names' for God's works in France then it is simply because they are not used to this practice:

potentially misleading to read Augustine's account as justifying 'openness to frank language', *pace* Jan M. Ziolkowski, 'Obscenity in the Latin Grammatical and Rhetorical Tradition', in Ziolkowski (ed.), *Obscenity*, p. 48. Gerson's awareness of the 'vast difference between the State of Innocence and ours' in respect of appropriate speech acts may be regarded as perfectly Augustinian.

[72] *Le Débat*, ed. Hicks, pp. 123–4; trans. Baird and Kane, p. 123 (with minor alterations). The effectiveness of this challenge was recognized and praised by Gerson: this lady, he declares, has shrewdly pointed out that 'your own writings, whether you like it or not, show that you have the same sense of shame: for your naturally good disposition would not permit you to utter obscenity (*obscenum loqui*) therein' (*Le Débat*, ed. Hicks, p. 168; trans. Baird and Kane, p. 148). In her turn, Christine seems to have been developing ideas canvassed by Gerson in his *Traité contre le Roman de la Rose*. The personification 'Theological Eloquence' asks, 'is it not madness to say that one should speak fully and openly without shame, no matter how dishonourable the words are in the judgment of all men?' She moves into heavy irony: 'Teach them [your daughters and sons] the way to every evil if they are not able to find it themselves. If they do not speak according to the teachings of that Reason, beat them!' (*Le Débat*, ed. Hicks, pp. 81–2; trans. Baird and Kane, pp. 87–8).

Se fames nes noment en France,
ce n'est fors desacoutumance,
car li propres nons leur pleüst,
qui acoutumé leur eüst;
et se proprement les nomassent,
ja certes de riens n'i pechassent.
Acoutumance est trop poissanz,
et se bien le sui connoissanz,
mainte chose desplest novele,
qui par acoustumance est bele.

[If women do not name them in France, it is only because they are not accustomed to do so, for they would have liked the proper name had it been made familiar to them, and in giving them their proper name they would certainly have committed no sin. Habit is very powerful, and if I am any judge, many things that offend when they are new become beautiful through habit.]

Basically, Raison is appealing to the principle of *institutio*: if the terms in question were used more they would become more common and so a custom would be established, hence any element of embarrassment would vanish. Clearly, this is a highly casuistic argument, as Christine realizes—and she calls Pierre Col's bluff. Given the emphasis placed on *acoutumance* and *coustume*, why does not Col contribute to the establishment of the custom that his master had advocated? This might be difficult at first, she taunts him, but if he persists in proper naming of private parts then no doubt he will eventually be praised for it! But of course, Col will not do so; he is as much bound by the existing *coustume* as is anyone else. So much, then, for Jean's Raison, who can easily be defeated by such a feeling of shame.

Et ou est la Raison maistre Jehan de Meung? Elle a pou de puissance quant honte la desconfit. Benoitte soit tele honte qui desconfit tele Raison! Et se je te haisse je diroie: 'Pleust a Dieu que tu l'eusses fait!', mais je t'ayme pour ton bon sens et le bien que on dist de toi (non obstant ne te cognoisse): si ne voulroie ta deshonnour. Car parler honneste avec les vertus moult advient en bouche de louable personne.

[And where is Master Jean de Meun's Raison? She has little power when shame defeats her. Blessed be such shame that defeats such Raison. If I hated you, I would say, would to God that you had gone against custom in this matter. But I love you for your good sense and the good that people say of you (although I scarcely know you): I do not wish you the dishonour. For honourable and virtuous speech is the mark of a praiseworthy person.][73]

The parameters of Christine's argument should be appreciated. For her the key issues concern *humana institutio* rather than *significatio* and *impositio*; her interest is in behavioural and linguistic propriety (to use that word in its modern English sense) rather than speaking *proprie* in the technical medieval sense of that concept. That is to say, in Christine's thought there is no blanket condemnation of, or general worry about, plain and precise speech. The point at issue rather concerns the appropriateness of a certain *usus loquendi* on a certain occasion, whether textual or social, with Christine putting great emphasis on the public performance of language, how words function in social exchange. Having shifted the argument onto the ground on which she feels strongest (or better, having chosen her ground from the alternatives offered by the *Rose*'s shifting narrative), she uses those common assumptions about decorous behaviour, which of course Col shares, against him. Shame keeps her opponent from linguistically practising what he and his master preach, and thereby the value of their *parler proprement* doctrine is seriously called in doubt.[74]

Alternatively, one could characterize Christine's objections as presenting a challenge to Jean de Meun's protestation that his controversial words 'were called for by my subject-matter (*matire*), whose inherent properties drew me to such language' (*Rose*, 15142–5). The first article from a Parisian arts faculty statute of December 1340 cites the proposition—apparently regarded as a truism—that speech (*sermo*) has no power (*virtus*) 'except by imposition (*impositio*) and by the common usage of authors and others, therefore the virtue of speech is such as authors commonly employ it and as the subject-matter demands, since expressions (*sermones*) are to be received according to the subject-matter'.[75] Now, Christine tacitly drives a wedge between what 'the subject-matter demands' and the 'common usage' of

---

[73] *Le Débat*, ed. Hicks, p. 124; trans. Baird and Kane, p. 123 (with minor alterations).

[74] Christine uses the phrase *parler proprement* at *Le Débat*, ed. Hicks, p. 123, l. 254.

[75] Quoted by R. Van der Lecq and H. A. G. Braakhuis in the introduction to their edition of Jean Buridan's *Questiones elencorum* (Nijmegen, 1994), p. xxii.

speech. Whatever the requirements of the former may be, if *usus communis*—which in her terms is influenced by reasonable shame and the honourable intentions of social convention—militates against them, they cannot hold sway.

One consequence of this must be the failure of the attempt to single out women as being inhibited by hypocritical prudery in their use of language. As Christine said in an earlier letter (to Jean de Montreuil), *nobody* who loves virtue and honour ('personne aucune amant vertus et honnesteté') will listen to the *Rose* without being totally 'confus de honte et abhominé d'ainsi oïr discerner et desjoindre et mectre soubz deshonnestes ficcions ce que raison et honte doit reffraindre, aux bien ordonnéz, seulement le penser' ['confounded by shame and abomination at hearing described, expressed, and distorted in dishonourable fictions what modesty and reason should restrain well-bred folk from even thinking about'].[76] Hence, the reactions of virtuous women in particular are quite justified:

Et dont que fait a louer lecture qui n'osera estre leue ne parlee en propre forme a la table des roynes, des princesses et des vaillans preudefemmes—a qui convendroit couvrir la face de honte rougie?

[Who could praise a work which can be neither read nor quoted at the table of queens, of princesses, and of worthy women, who would surely, on hearing it, be constrained to cover their blushing faces?][77]

Apparently, Amant was right after all to profess that no well-bred young woman should call *coilles* by that name (*Rose*, 6898–901; cf. p. 126 above). But Christine does not go so far as to ally herself with that dubious *persona*. Rather she affirms the importance of supporting 'la noble vertu de honte' ['the noble virtue of modesty'], which by its very nature restrains 'les goliardises et deshonnestetés en dis et fais' ['indecency and dishonourable conduct in words and deeds'].[78]

In his *Institutio oratoria*, Quintilian had criticized those 'who do not think it necessary to avoid obscenity on the ground that no word is indecent in itself'. He then professes his own objective

[76] *Le Débat*, ed. Hicks, p. 20; trans. Baird and Kane, p. 53.
[77] *Le Débat*, ed. Hicks, p. 20; trans. Baird and Kane, p. 54.
[78] *Le Débat*, ed. Hicks, p. 14; trans. Baird and Kane, pp. 48–9.

of 'following the good old rules of Roman modesty'.[79] It could be argued that Christine was seeking to follow those same 'good old rules'. But Quintilian's cultural milieu was, of course, very different from Christine's, and so such a comparison will not get us very far. A more robust argument would relate her protests to a major development within the history of 'courtliness': that 'new sense of obscene or vulgar language' which, according to Charles Muscatine,[80] had developed substantially by the early thirteenth century. In a passage in Guillaume de Lorris's part of the *Rose* which Christine de Pizan could hardly have objected to, the God of Love gives Amant a lesson in *cortoisie* which includes a warning against the use of dirty words or coarse expressions: 'Je ne tien pas a cortois home / qui orde chose et laide nome' ['I do not consider a man to be courteous if he names filthy, ugly things'] (2097–102). Muscatine compares this to a statement in Jean Renart's *Lai de l'ombre* wherein the author claims that his *cortoisie* is revealed by his telling of 'a pleasing tale that has in it nothing offensive or ugly', and with Henri d'Andeli's *Lai d'Aristote*, which at the outset promises to offer fine words free from any taint of vulgarity: 'a work that runs to vulgarity should never be heard at court'.[81] Against this argument, however, may be pitted the large number of late medieval romances and *fabliaux* containing obscene elements, which were produced or consumed within courtly circles. R. Howard Bloch has argued powerfully that 'Courtliness and obscenity are not . . . antithetical'; rather, on occasion obscenity 'seems to be inferred by narrative produced within a court setting, especially when that narrative uses euphemism for a

---

[79] *Institutio oratoria*, VIII.iii.38–9; ed. H. E. Butler (Cambridge, Mass., 1920–2), iii.232–2; cf. Ziolkowski, 'Obscenity in the Latin Grammatical and Rhetorical Tradition', p. 42, who goes on to discuss what 'indecency' may have meant to Quintilian.

[80] 'The Fabliaux, Courtly Culture, and the (Re)Invention of Vulgarity', in Ziolkowski (ed.), *Obscenity*, pp. 281, 284. On the 'body language' of the *fabliaux*, see further Simon Gaunt's chapter 'Genitals, Gender and Mobility: The *fabliaux*' in his *Gender and Genre in Medieval French Literature* (Cambridge, 1995), pp. 234–85.

[81] Muscatine, 'The (Re)Invention of Vulgarity', p. 285. The *Lai d'Aristote* challenges the stereotypes by treating a rude tale (the story of how Alexander's Indian mistress tricked the philosopher Aristotle into allowing her to ride him like a horse) in a studiously polite manner. A lively translation may be found in John DuVal, *Fabliaux Fair and Foul* (Binghamton, NY, 1992), pp. 85–98.

comic effect, which is also pleasurable'.[82] While this may well be true, I think there is much life in Muscatine's argument—courtly culture certainly did sustain an ideal (however much in contestation with other pressures it may have been) wherein high value was placed on 'clean courtly (*cortays*) conversation free from filth', as the Middle English *Gawain*-poet puts it (*Sir Gawain and the Green Knight*, 1013).This is, in my view, part of a larger picture, which also includes the transformation of Ovidian *amors* into *fine amors*, wherein the predatory stratagems of the *Ars amatoria* give way to an ideal of civilized behaviour which, indeed, is utterly accommodating of marriage.

We have already discussed aspects of this phenomenon in Chapter 1 above, and further evidence will be offered in our treatment of the text and gloss of the *Eschez amoureux* in Chapter 6. What is most crucial here, however, is the fact that strictures against dirty talk often go together with recommendations to honour the virtues of women. The passage from Guillaume's *Rose* which we partly quoted above moves from a warning against naming filthy, ugly things to the following exhortation: 'Serve to honour all women, toil and labour in their service, and if you hear any slanderer speaking ill of women, reproach him and tell him to be quiet' (2103–7). Guillaume de Machaut's *La Fonteinne amoureuse* features a God of Love who tells the poet to take 'special care' not 'to write anything immoral ('A faire chose ou il ait villennie'), / And don't ever vilify a lady; / But always praise and glorify them' (Prologue, 75–8).[83] The Machaut *persona* readily accedes to this request, declaring that he will uphold 'l'honneur des dames' (286) and exclude anything ugly ('laide') from his work; his purpose is 'to renounce / All things immoral (*villeinne*), putting them aside' (*Fonteinne amoureuse*, 23, 28–9).[84] It would seem, then, that Christine de Pizan found ready-made a discourse which linked clean courtly conversation with *commendatio mulierum*. Her contribution to it—or rather, her appropriation of it—is, of course, quite remarkable. But she was not alone.

---

[82] Bloch, 'Modest Maids and Modified Nouns', p. 307.
[83] *The Fountain of Love (La Fonteinne amoureuse) and Two Other Love Vision Poems*, ed. and trans. R. Burton Palmer (New York, 1993), pp. 6–7.
[84] Ibid. 90–1.

Hence, moves to identify her as a prudish exception to the general rule, or as the herald of some major shift in taste at the turn of the century, tend to produce a mere caricature.

From Latin to vernacular: broadening the discourse

Christine de Pizan called Pierre Col's bluff. Some of Jean de Meun's recent readers have failed to call *his* bluff, preferring to read his account of naming human genitalia as if it were an utterly serious and sober scientific disquisition.[85] In the *Rose* the term *coilles*—a word straight from the common herd if ever there was one—is offered as a 'proper' term. Its very power to shock, its forceful vulgarity, seems to lend it a sort of authenticity as a verbal sign closely related to the thing it signifies. But here, surely, is an element of sleight of hand, linguistic science having been pressed into the service of donnish humour. If Raison is right, then presumably one is free to imagine Adam going around the garden of Eden cheerfully using the primordial equivalents of terms like 'shit' and 'fuck' (if I may work further Jean's vein of humour). Doubtless someone may retort that such terms would have been innocent in Paradise—which rather misses the point that, particularly when imagined in such a context, they are a source of amusement to Adam's not-so-innocent descendants. To make the same point in a different way, a modern-day professor could be envisaged as straight-facedly propounding some elaborate theory of semantics—which in itself was utterly respectable academically—in which every example was a swear-word. That would occasion amusement among some of the students and certainly in the senior common room. Others would, no doubt, suffer 'reasonable shame' or embarrassment, or feel that the teacher was misusing his/her position. The more earnest souls might solemnly take notes, having missed the joke. If some of those remarks sound elitist and preciously donnish, I hope they may be permitted as an attempt to convey those very qualities as constitutive of Jean's humour (as I see it) in the passage under discussion.

[85] D. W. Robertson believes that 'Jean offers a very reasonable account of his use of words like *vit* and *coilles*' and assures us that 'the art and exegesis of the Middle Ages show no qualms about the members of generation, so that Christine's stricture represents a change in taste': *Preface to Chaucer*, pp. 206, 361.

Jean de Meun's excursus on words and things concerns 'faits d'ordre logique', declares Gustav Ineichen; 'le problème qu'il vise est celui de la connaissance et du statut possible des choses'.[86] I have no quarrel with that; I agree entirely with the proposition that Jean's semantics echo the technical logical and epistemological discussions of his age. However, the playful nature of so much of the *Rose* must never be forgotten, the extraordinary way in which the subversive clerical laughter of sexual comedy[87] interweaves with the morally righteous laughter of satire to produce effects in which earnest and game are virtually impossible to segregate. Therefore, in my judgment Daniel Poirion is perfectly justified in exclaiming, with reference to Raison's commentary on *coilles*, 'Voila une souriante leçon de philosophie du langage! Evidemment notre poète s'amuse en la développant'.[88]

Tantalizingly, and sometimes frustratingly, Jean de Meun vacillates freely between various idioms without investing exclusively in any single one. There is no master discourse relating to linguistic and literary theory which can be seized upon and made the hermeneutic key to Jean's entire text. The *Rose* moves from words which are plain and 'proper' to expression which is richly 'improper' and metaphorical, from use of the bluntest satiric language to affirmation of the value of the *integumanz aus poetes*, from historical and exemplary narration to mythographic innovation. (It is perfectly possible to appreciate this

---

[86] 'Le Discours linguistique du Jean de Meun', included in the Proceedings of the Göttingen 'Colloque sue le *Roman de la Rose'*, published in *Romanistiche Zeitschrift für Literaturgeschichte*, 2 (1978), 245–53. Here Ineichen critiques the article by Daniel Poirion, 'Les Mots et les choses selon Jean de Meun', *Information littéraire*, 26 (1974), 7–11, on the grounds that 'une interprétation littéraire' is given there of a discussion in the *Rose* which should rather be analysed with reference to the medieval sciences of logic and epistemology. But Ineichen merely affirms rather than proves the relevance (which I myself would utterly endorse) of the discussions of signification in medieval logical treatises. After a very cursory analysis he leaps to the conclusion that Jean's semantic thinking is conservative in respect of the 'initiatives linguistiques' of his time. In my view, Jean draws on logical categories and terminology which were in vogue both before and after his time, and so we should be careful about designating him as 'un clerc conservateur'. Poirion's lively response to Ineichen, which respects both the 'faits d'ordre logique' and 'interprétation littéraire', unfortunately limits itself to brief citation of the language theory of Peter Abelard, as described in J. Jolivet's monograph *Arts du langage et théologie chez Abelard* (Paris, 1969; 2nd edn., 1982): Poirion, 'De la signification selon Jean de Meun', pp. 174–5.   [87] This will be discussed in Ch. 4 below.
[88] 'De la signification selon Jean de Meun', p. 173.

range whilst believing that the main stylistic thrust of the poem is literalistic.) And yet—that range has definite limits. The *Rose* seems to be uncertain and curiously unconfident about its vernacularity. It may be written 'in Gallica lingua', but it is carrying on the business of Latin literature. Let us listen again to that hostile yet perceptive witness Jean Gerson:

Itaque memini me pridem gustasse iam ab adolescentia fontes illos omnes aut fere omnes a quibus actoris tui dicta velud rivuli quidam male traducti prodierunt; Boecium, Ovidium, Therencium, Juvenalem, Alanum, et de Sancto Amore, Abelardum cum sua Heloyde, Marcianum Capellam et si qui sunt alii.

[I first drank long ago in my youth all, or almost all, those fountains from which the writings of your author have poured forth badly translated, like little streams: such as Boethius, Ovid, Terence, Juvenal, Alanus [de Insulis], [Guillaume] de Saint-Amour, Abelard and Heloise, Martianus Capella, and many others.][89]

Gerson's point is that his dislike of the *Rose* was certainly not due to ignorance, since he has read all its sources. My point is that it took someone as highly educated as Gerson to recognize all those sources, and to be in a position to confront what Jean de Meun had done with them (even if he did not like what he saw). Now, while Geoffrey Chaucer drank from most if not all of those fountains from which the writings of his French predecessor had poured forth translated, he was also capable of taking his refreshment elsewhere, as *The Canterbury Tales* demonstrates so magnificently. A wider range of genres is accommodated, and the stylistic range is much more ambitious, as *fabliaux* rub shoulders with high-art romances and saints' lives, and the northernisms in the speech of the Reeve's students are inscribed with as much care as are the idioms of *curtesye* which feature in the tales of the Knight and Squire. The social mix of texts and tellers is as successful as it is unprecedented, and it is reasonable to assume that Chaucer envisioned a far wider audience for his work than had actually been achieved by the *Rose*,[90] though one should be wary of confusing Chaucer's characters with his actual or potential readers.

---

[89] *Le Débat*, ed. Hicks, p. 172; trans. Baird and Kane, p. 151.

[90] However, it should be recognized that the text does turn up in the most unlikely of places; cf. the two standard studies of the reception of the *Rose*, Badel, *Rose au XIVe siècle*, and Huot, *Rose and Its Readers*.

Christ spoke *ful brode* in holy Writ, declares Chaucer (I(A) 739), who daringly claims that alleged fact as a precedent for his reportage of the *brode* speech of his 'vileins'. The term *brode* in this context may owe something to the Latin word *grossus*, which indicates on the one hand (and yet again) the class origins of standards of taste and artistic value, and on the other an awareness on Chaucer's part of how a negative, derogatory term can be turned to personal advantage. Consider the introduction to Giles of Rome's highly popular *De regimine principum*, a work which was written around 1285 for the future king Philippe le Bel, and subsequently translated into several European vernaculars, including French and English. In the sphere of moral teaching the *modus procedendi* is figurative and broad (*grossus*), declares Giles, citing Aristotle as his authority for that proposition. That is to say, in such matters one should use types and figures rather than any more precise form of language. The populace as a whole forms the audience for this sort of treatise, Giles continues. And since they are simple and unsophisticated (*grossus*) and cannot understand subtleties, one must proceed 'in a figurative and broad way', using arguments 'which are superficial and appeal to the senses'.[91] Chaucer is, I believe, making a similar point about Christ's preaching and teaching. In order to appeal to a wide and 'gross' audience the Saviour of mankind had to adopt an appropriate style, which avoided subtleties and functioned in a manner which was 'gross', figurative and parabolic. (This assertion is in line with statements found in late medieval Bible commentaries and the *artes praedicandi*.)[92] And what was right for Christ cannot be

---

[91] Minnis and Scott, *Medieval Literary Theory*, pp. 248–50.

[92] Particularly significant was Gregory the Great, who said that Jesus employs such mundane comparisons in order that the spirit can ascend from the things that are known and familiar to those that are unknown. The influence of Aristotle also fed this tradition; Albert the Great appropriates him in arguing that, because of the 'rudeness' of the human intellect, Christ had to offer similitudes in order that his teaching could be understood. See Stephen L. Wailes, 'Why Did Jesus Use Parables? The Medieval Discussion', *Medievalia et humanistica*, 13 (1985), esp. 50–1. In brief, parables and *exempla* are linked as literal and mundane forms of speech which appeal to the populace at large—and, indeed, are specially efficacious in the teaching of simple souls whose intellectual capacity is limited. There is no contradiction in describing such figurative expression as 'literal', given the common thirteenth-century classification of parable as a type of *sensus litteralis*: see Minnis and Scott, *Medieval Literary Theory*, pp. 205, 222–3, 242–3, 262; also Minnis, 'Savonarola

wrong for Chaucer—though of course this claiming of precedent is highly casuistical, given that the *harlotrie* of certain Canterbury Tales is very far removed from the edifying figurative language of the son of God:[93] any category which can include both of these must be *brode* indeed! But it seems reasonable to assume that Chaucer believed his 'gross' *modus procedendi* would help his writing to reach a broad cross-section of the populace.

We have some firm evidence concerning the 'gross' reception of that medieval writer who most consciously had constructed himself as a 'vernacular author', namely Dante Alighieri. The fact that he had written his master work in Italian did not impress everyone. With the knowledge of hindsight the *Comedy* can be seen as a powerful forerunner of, and stimulus to, the great literary achievements of the European vernaculars in the Renaissance, but things seemed rather different to those Italian humanists who were embarrassed by Dante's tacit rejection of Latin. Why are you wasting such serious themes on the common masses? asks Giovanni del Virgilio in a Latin verse epistle addressed to Dante. Similarly, Petrarch was worried lest the *Comedy* had put serious subjects into the mouths of 'ignorant oafs in taverns and market places'—one can only wonder at what he would have made of a poem in which a tavern-keeper is chosen as the judge of the best story.[94] And Boccaccio, who gave public lectures on the *Comedy* in 1373 (in Florence), was attacked by a humanist friend who said that he was prostituting the Muses by sharing their secrets with the 'volgo'. But the

and de Madrigal', pp. 170–2. However, as Wailes points out, there was another way of approaching parables, this being in response to the statement at Mark 4: 11–12 that they were for the benefit of the chosen few, and intended to conceal rather than clarify knowledge. This tradition connects with the discourse of allegorical or integumental language which could be penetrated only by the *cognoscenti*—quite the opposite to what Chaucer means at General Prologue, I(A) 739. However, it may be close to how Jean de Meun regarded *paraboles* at l. 7124 of the *Rose*, this use of the term being at the beginning of his discussion of the *integumanz aus poetes*. Here Jean has in mind language which is not to be taken *a la letre* but rather explained so that the truth hidden within may be revealed and the 'secrets of philosophy' uncovered. In sum, it would seem that Chaucer and Jean de Meun are exploiting different traditions concerning parabolic speech.

[93] Cf. Taylor, 'Chaucer's *Cosyn to the Dede*', p. 320.

[94] Cf. David Wallace's discussion in Minnis and Scott, *Medieval Literary Theory*, pp. 440, 457–8.

'volgo' fought back. As N. R. Havely has noted, the term *grosso* recurs several times in the discourse of semi-learned Florentine appropriators of Dante, who set about popularizing some of his stories (and produced a popularized life story of the poet himself).[95] For instance, in his prologue to the *capitulo* on Dante in the *Centiloquio*, Antonio Pucci—bellringer, auditor and town crier—speaks of his limited intellect (*grosso ingegno*) and inability to cope with this high theme. Similarly, in the *Trecentonovelle* Pucci's friend, Franco Sacchetti, 'claims to be following in some respects the example of the *vulgare poeta fiorentino Dante*, whilst in the same breath describing himself as a *fiorentino* who is *discolo e grosso* ("ignorant and coarse")'.[96]

It would seem, then, that one should not underestimate the *volgo*. Chaucer appears not to have done so, if we can judge by the manner in which, in the General Prologue to *The Canterbury Tales* and in the Miller's Prologue, he treats the speech of his motley *dramatis personae* with that deference which for generations had been the due of the ancient *auctoritates*. 'There should be at times an uncouthness of style to conform to the ugliness of the subject-matter', Alan's Dame Nature had declared,[97] her distaste for that ugly subject-matter, and the exceptional nature of such commerce with that uncouth style, being crystal clear. In Chaucer the uncouth style and ugly subject-matter are at the centre of textual attention rather than on the margins, and value judgements like 'uncouth' and 'ugly' are implicitly called in question. The predecessor who, more than any other, pointed him in that direction was Jean de Meun. Chaucer owed much to his French master's deliberately provocative disquisition on words, deeds, and proper speech. Indeed, Jean may be regarded as a pivotal figure in the history of the use of *brode* speech in self-consciously serious literature *in vulgari*.

---

[95] N. R. Havely, 'Muses and Blacksmiths: Italian Trecento Poetics and the Reception of Dante in *The House of Fame*', in A. J. Minnis, C. C. Morse, and T. Turville-Petre (eds.), *Essays in Ricardian Literature in Honour of J. A. Burrow* (Oxford, 1997), pp. 77–8. [96] Ibid. 79.

[97] Cf. p. 125 above.

CHAPTER 4

Signe d'estre malles: *Genre, Gender, and the End of the* Rose

'To assign an Author to a text', declares Roland Barthes, 'is to impose a brake on it, to furnish it with a final signified, to close writing.' By contrast, what is produced by the modern-day 'Scriptor' should be seen as 'a multi-dimensional space in which are married and contested several writings, none of which is original: the text is a fabric of quotations, resulting from a thousand sources of culture'.[1] This distinction is simply unworkable as far as much medieval literature is concerned. Many readers of the *Roman de la Rose* (particularly Jean de Meun's section), Juan Ruiz's *Libro de Buen Amor,* or Geoffrey Chaucer's *Canterbury Tales* would wish to retort that there is nothing particularly modern about texts wherein many types of writing marry and contest, which bear the marks of thousands of sources of culture. And it is the failure of such medieval texts to achieve closure which inhibits any claim to *auctoritas* which they may have, and/or which their writers may have wished to make, however fleetingly or furtively (the latter because of the requirements of decorum).

The aim of this chapter is to identify and discuss some of the semantic cross-currents which problematize the ending or terminus of the *Roman de la Rose,* rendering closure impossible and consequently undermining the text's occasional aspirations towards historical, moral, or metaphysical truth. Previous chapters have argued that the poem draws upon two major authorizing discourses, of *integumentum* and satire, but

---

[1] 'The Death of the Author', in *The Rustle of Language,* trans. Richard Howard (Oxford, 1986), pp. 52–3. Aspects of the crucial relationship between *auctoritas* and closure are explored in A. J. Minnis, '*De vulgari auctoritate*: Chaucer, Gower and the Men of Great Authority', in R. F. Yeager (ed.), *Chaucer and Gower: Difference, Mutuality, Exchange* (Victoria, BC, 1991), pp. 36–74.

Jean refuses to pursue either of them with full commitment and consistency. Neither discourse is dominant; indeed, they compete with each other and with the various genres that appear and disappear within the text of the *Rose*, including the 'art of love', *planctus*, tragedy,[2] and comedy. The last of these is the main focus of the following discussion, which will concentrate on the ending of the poem, considering the laughter which surrounds Amant's sexual consummation. 'Th'ende is every tales strengthe,' affirmed Chaucer's Pandarus (*Troilus and Criseyde*, II.260), and according to Christine de Pizan a work stands or falls by its conclusion: 'a la conclusion tient tout'.[3] Jean Gerson was in no doubt that it had fallen. *Videatur finis!* he warns; the end of the *Rose* is filthy, and its claim that lechery follows nature is disgusting.[4] Christine found it abominable,[5] and argued that Jean de Meun had not left the reader with clear ethical instruction, by failing to 'fait sa conclusion en meurs de bien vivre' ['conclude in favour of the moral way of life'].[6] The causes of the text's terminal disruption of its moral impulses will now be addressed.

Phallocentric exegesis: the emasculation of Orpheus

Jean de Meun's strategy of bringing integumental meaning to the surface, reiterating it in a manner which is aggressively plain

---

[2] Obviously inspired by the theory and practice of Boethian tragedy, Jean de Meun chronicles the falls from prosperity to adversity of several great men, namely Seneca, Nero, Croesus, and Manfred, king of Naples and Sicily. The misfortunes of several great women, Phyllis, Oenone, and Medea, are also described (the influence of the *Heroides* being obvious), though as part of La Vielle's excursus they serve as *exempla* of how men trick women (the 'moral' being that women should trick men in turn), rather than being placed within the perspective of Fortune's operations. Jean's contribution to medieval tragedy is not included in H. A. Kelly's quite comprehensive study, *Ideas and Forms of Tragedy from Aristotle to the Middle Ages* (Cambridge, 1993).

[3] *Le Débat*, ed. Hicks, p. 134; trans. Baird and Kane, p. 132.

[4] *Le Débat*, ed. Hicks, pp. 180, 184; trans. Baird and Kane, pp. 159, 168. Gerson speaks of 'la laidure de la fin' and declares that what the *Rose* says through Genius is said by the author in his own person 'plus ordement en la fin'.

[5] *Le Débat*, ed. Hicks, p. 136; trans. Baird and Kane, p. 133. Christine attacks 'the horrible things in that most abominable conclusion' ('les orribletés qui sont en la fin tant abhominables').

[6] *Le Débat*, ed. Hicks, p. 135; trans. Baird and Kane, p. 132.

and direct,[7] is nowhere more obvious than in his treatment of the *fabula* of Orpheus and Eurydice. In Ovid's *Metamorphoses* (x.1–85, xi.1–66) a full account is given of how Orpheus, having failed to rescue his beloved Eurydice from the underworld, shrank from contact with any woman, preferring to centre his affections on young boys of tender age, a practice which he introduced into Thrace. Subsequently he was dismembered by the Ciconian women, who were infuriated by his rejection of them. Arnulf of Orléans interpreted those women as people who live in a 'womanly' (meaning morally weak) and vicious fashion; Orpheus' change of sexual preference becomes a commendable association with those who act in a 'manly' way (*viriliter*). Hence the Ciconians kill him by stoning, i.e. by behaving lecherously. 'For women', explains Arnulf, 'are more prone to lechery and to vices than men.' Having killed Orpheus (i.e. the wise man), the women (i.e. the lecherous) were transformed into diverse shapes; this fiction, declares Arnulf, indicates the many forms which lechery can take.[8] Nothing in this moralization seems to be of interest to Jean de Meun's Genius. What he concentrates on is the identification, in Ovid's narrative, of Orpheus as one who sinned against nature—which is how Alan of Lille had regarded him in *De planctu naturae*, wherein Nature protests that 'man alone turns with scorn from the modulated strains' of her own cithern 'and runs deranged to the notes of mad Orpheus's lyre' (viii, pr. 4).[9]

Another part of Arnulf's interpretation, which is reiterated by the later 'Vulgate Commentary' on the *Metamorphoses*, identifies Eurydice as that 'good judgment' to which the superlatively wise man adheres since he makes judgements concerning the most noble things.[10] Having been bitten by the serpent, i.e. taken in by the deceits of this life, good judgment descends *ad inferos*, i.e. inclines to vices; she is followed by her husband when he is diverted to the vices not only in thought but also in deed. Therefore this transformation (*mutacio*) is a moral one, the anonymous commentator concludes, here referring to a

---

[7] As argued in Ch. 2 above.
[8] Ghisalberti, 'Arnolfo d'Orléans', p. 222.
[9] *De planctu naturae*, ed. Häring, p. 834; trans. Sheridan, p. 133.
[10] *Vulgate Commentary*, ed. Coulson, p. 139.

distinction[11] which he had explained in his *accessus*, between natural, moral, magical, and spiritual *mutaciones*. But none of these matters to Genius. The only transformation he has in mind is the physical one of castration,[12] a mutilation which he regards as a fitting punishment for those men who in their sexual behaviour emulate Orpheus. Hence the dismemberment of Orpheus becomes a prefiguration of the fate deemed appropriate to those who are guilty of homosexual behaviour. Jean identifies the testicles as the defining signs of maleness ('signe d'estre malles'). Their possession and correct sexual use are requisites for masculinity, and anyone who does not use them correctly deserves to lose them.

> cil qui les .II. marteaus reçoivent
> et n'an forgent si con il doivent
> droitemant seur la droite anclume,
> cil que si leur pechiez anfume
> par leur orgueill qui les desraie
> qu'il despisent la droite raie
> du champ bel et planteüreus,
> et vont conme maleüreus
> arer en la terre deserte
> ou leur semance vet a perte,
> ne ja n'i tandront droite rue,
> ainz vont bestournant la charrue
> et conferment leur regles males
> par excepcions anormales,
> quant Orpheüs veulent ansivre . . .
> o tout l'esconmeniemant
> qui touz les mete a dampnemant,
> puis que la se veulent aherde,
> ainz qu'il muirent, puissent il perdre

[11] An elaboration of Arnulf's; see Ghisalberti, 'Arnolfo d'Orléans', p. 181. Texts of the Vulgate Commentator's *accessus* are printed by Coulson in *Vulgate Commentary*, pp. 24–9, and in Coulson, 'Unedited Lives of Ovid', pp. 177–82.

[12] In similar vein, for Jean Le Fèvre at the beginning of his French translation of *De Vetula* the crucial Ovidian *mutacioun* is the author's castration! The tale of Ovid's dismemberment—maybe the result of contamination of the *vita Ovidii* with the story of Abelard's misfortunes in love—also appears in Le Fèvre's *Livre de leesce*; cf. Helen Solterer, *The Master and Minerva: Disputing Women in French Medieval Culture* (Berkeley, Calif., 1995), pp. 143–4; cf. p. 246. And Christine de Pizan declares that Ovid, despite being allowed to return from exile, persisted in his faults, on account of which he was 'castrated and disfigured': see *The Book of the City of Ladies*, i. 9; trans. Brown-Grant, pp. 20–1.

et l'aumosniere et les stalles
don il ont signe d'estre malles! . . .
Les marteaus dedanz estachiez
puissent il avoir arrachiez!

(19610–42)

[. . . those who receive the two hammers and do not forge with them as they justly should on the straight anvil; those who are so blinded by their sins, by the pride that takes them off their road, so that they despise the straight furrow of the beautiful, fecund field and like unhappy creatures go off to plough in desert land where their seeding goes to waste; those who will never keep to the straight track, but instead go overturning the plough, who confirm their evil rules by abnormal exceptions when they want to follow Orpheus . . . may they, in addition to the excommunication that sends them all to damnation, suffer, before their death, the loss of their purse and testicles, the signs that they are male! . . . May they have the hammers that are attached within torn out!]

Similarly, a little later in the text, Genius's declaration that 'Granz pechiez est d'ome escoillier' ['It is a great sin to castrate a man'] (20020) leads into an account of the consequences of Jupiter's castration of Saturn, namely the introduction of an epicurean ethic that held that delight is the sovereign good.[13] Here once again Jean is choosing not to draw on the traditional mythographic moralization of a pagan *fabula*. We are very far from, for example, William of Conches' assertion that Saturn's testicles 'signify the fruits of the earth, through which, in the course of time, the seed from the bowels of the earth is diffused more and more . . . this is nothing but that the warmth of the upper element ripens the fruits and makes them ready for cutting off and gathering'.[14] And from

---

[13] This account recalls and extends the earlier—infamously vulgar—statement by Raison that Jupiter cut off Saturn's balls (*coilles*) 'con se fussent andoilles, . . . puis les gita dedanz la mer' ['as if they were sausages and threw them in the sea'] (*Rose*, 5507–10; cf. 7086–7), on which see Ch. 3 above. Following Daniel Poirion, David Hult notes that forms of the avowedly obscene word *coille* reappear in two accounts of clerical dismemberment in the *Rose*, the castrations of Abelard and Origen; thus 'an illicit or socially inappropriate linguistic usage' necessarily 'induces us to attend to, and associate, these three moments': 'Language and Dismemberment', p. 113. Cf. Le Fèvre's reference to the castration of Ovid: 'Car on reconte en verité / Qu'on lui coupa ambdeux les couilles . . .' (*Livre de leesce*, ll. 2710–11).

[14] See Dronke, *Fabula*, p. 26. Cf. Fulgentius, *Mitologiae*, i.2, ed. R. Helm, *Fulgentii opera* (Leipzig, 1898), p. 18. See further the useful anthology of 'Birth of Venus' texts (which include description and moralization of Saturn's emasculation) in Kay, 'Venus in the *Rose*', pp. 29–37.

the following interpretation—which manifests the influence of William's—from the 'Bernard Silvester' *Aeneid* commentary:

Mare corpus humanum intelligitur quia ebrietates et libidines que per aquas intelliguntur ab eo defluunt et in eo sunt commotiones vitiorum et per ipsum ciborum et potus meatus fit. Secundum hoc legimus Venerem ex virilibus Saturni natum fuisse in mari. Her virilia in mare deiciuntur quoniam ciborum et potus superfluitates in corpore aguntur. Hec autem in corpore per cibos acta libidinem movent. Ideo dictum est 'sine Cerere et Bacco friget Venus'.

[The sea is understood as the human body, because drunkenness and desire (which are the waters) flow from it, and the turbulence of vice is in it, and there are channels for food and drink through it. Because of this, we read that Venus was born from Saturn's genitals in the sea. For Saturn's genitals are the qualities of heat and moisture by which time creates things. Saturn's genitals are cast into the sea, since the excess of food and drink affects the body. The genitals, warmed by food in the body, produce lust, and it is therefore said that 'without Ceres and Bacchus, Venus freezes'.][15]

What we are offered instead is an interpretative strategy which could best be summed up as 'phallocentric demythologization'. Stylistic equivocation and polite euphemism are stripped away to lay bare the insistent demands of male desire and men's preoccupation with their sexual potency. What David Hult has termed 'Jean de Meun's unrelenting fascination with castration and, in broader terms, physical dismemberment'[16] functions within a complicated matrix of ideas which highlight male anxieties relating to emasculation and frustrated or fractured virility. The resultant writing comprises the coital comedy that is the main subject of this chapter.

It could, of course, be protested that such phallocentricity is precisely what one may expect from Genius, whose exegesis is highly suspect, given what he represents. My response would be that a blanket condemnation of Genius is quite impossible. For a start, the passage regarding Orpheus which I quoted above is

---

[15] *Commentary on the First Six Books of the Aeneid of Virgil*, ed. J. W. Jones and E. F. Jones (Lincoln, Neb., 1977), pp. 10–11; trans. Earl G. Schreiber and Thomas E. Maresca (Lincoln, Neb., 1979), p. 12 (to which I have made one alteration). The quotation may derive from Terence, *The Eunuch*, 732. Cf. the similar interpretation of this fabulous event in the 'Bernard Silvester' commentary on Martianus Capella, ed. Westra, pp. 56–7.   [16] 'Language and Dismemberment', p. 115.

part of a disquisition that draws heavily on the protestations of Dame Nature in *De planctu naturae*—a text with impeccable credentials, wherein male refusal of the imperative of procreation (through homosexual behaviour) is roundly condemned.[17] Jean has Genius protest that 'Les jaschieres, qui n'i refiche / le soc, redemourront an friche' ['if no one thrusts the ploughshare into the fallow fields, they will remain fallow'] (19543–4); those that don't plough straight with their ploughs and ploughshares should have their bones broken in pieces so that they never can be mended (19647–9). Genius proceeds to urge his 'barons' to 'Arez, por Dieu, . . . arez, / et voz lignages reparez' ['Plough, for God's sake, . . . plough and restore your lineages'] (19671–2). All of this is in the spirit of Alan's *planctus*. Moreover, such counsel pursues, albeit in a more exaggerated form, a principle which had been given the blessing of a figure universally respected by panallegorist critics, Dame Raison. She asserts that whoever lies with a woman should wish, as best he can, to perpetuate his divine essence and to maintain himself in his likeness so that the succession of generations should not fail, given that all men are subject to decay. Nature wills that children should rise up to continue the work of replenishment. For this reason she made the work pleasurable, ensuring that the workman will take pleasure in his task, and neither flee from it nor hate it (4385–8). Hence one can well imagine Raison agreeing with Genius's statement (as quoted above) that 'It is a great sin to castrate a man'. But, of course, there are morally dubious implications in having Genius say this. One could argue—though Jean never actually says it—that for Genius *any* generation is good, no matter what the circumstances (rape included). And it should be noted that castration was a well-known punishment for rape, inflicted upon the perpetrator by the victim's family, or enforced judicially.[18] Therefore, those most at risk of castration are those

---

[17] It must be admitted, however, that Alan's argument is often incoherent and logically problematic, due in some measure to the difficulties inherent in its presentation through Dame Nature. Hence Jordan can argue that there are crucial 'gaps in the covering that is supposed to be the main moral teaching of the text—the condemnation of same-sex copulation'. *Invention of Sodomy*, p. 68.

[18] See M. T. Clanchy, *Abelard: A Medieval Life* (Oxford, 1997), pp. 197–200, and Martin Irvine, 'Abelard and Remasculinization', in Jeffrey J. Cohen and Bonnie Wheeler (eds.), *Becoming Male in the Middle Ages* (New York, 1997), pp. 88–90.

who are, so to speak, spreading their seed around most vigorously and indiscriminately, thereby engaging in work of which Genius would heartily approve, at least in terms of its potential consequences. That irony is, I believe, alive and well in Jean's text. But this need not necessarily imply that Genius is urging barons to 'plough and restore' their 'lineage' through promiscuous behaviour; that phrase could well connote preservation of aristocratic lineage and transmission of privilege and property within the legal sanctions and protection of marriage.

This is not, to be sure, to make the (quite absurd) suggestion that Genius is an unproblematic voice for the expression of the whole truth and nothing but the truth. He does make certain ridiculous claims (the hyperbole is outrageous and presumably intended as hilarious), as for example when it is affirmed that the person who strives hard to love well, without any base thoughts, should enter paradise crowned with flowers (19505–8). But a little later we hear Genius chronicling the joys of the delectable fields where those who have succeeded in following the path of the lamb live eternally, drinking from the fair spring that is so sweet and bright and healthful that anyone who drinks its waters will never die (20618–25). To say that Genius has covered ideas 'with religious trappings in order to distort, to violate, them'[19] is to make a sweeping generalization which the facts and fissures of the text simply do not bear out.[20]

At any rate, it seems perfectly possible to allow some value to his fascination with male potency, and his anxieties regarding emasculation and other threats to the fulfilment of male desire, particularly since Nature and Raison seem in some measure to share his views on such matters. The consensus is that manliness requires the possession, and proper use, of testicles. The significance of this point may be elaborated further through reference to another major medieval 'castration narrative', namely the story of Abelard and Heloise, which was often alluded to in literature composed in French academic milieux during the late twelfth and thirteenth centuries.[21] Jean de Meun took a special

[19] Heather M. Arden, *The Romance of the Rose* (Boston, 1987), p. 66.
[20] Cf. the discussion in Ch. 2 above, pp. 108–13.
[21] For a full account see Peter Dronke, 'Abelard and Heloise in Medieval Testimonies', in his *Intellectuals and Poets in Medieval Europe* (Rome, 1992), pp. 247–94; see also Clanchy, *Abelard*, pp. 154–7. Abelard's own embarrassment

interest in it. In the *Rose* the Jealous Husband figure (as ventril-oquized by Ami) refers to the removal of Abelard's testicles, 'a Paris en son lit de nuiz' ['in his bed in Paris, at night'] (8766–8): this occurs in the context of an account of the lovers' relation-ship in which, remarkably, the correspondence between them is mentioned, this being the first testimony we have to the exis-tence of that body of material. Indeed, around 1380 Jean trans-lated the letters of Abelard and Heloise into French, a work which survives in a unique manuscript in the hand of Gontier Col, one of Jean's arch-defenders in the *querelle de la Rose*.[22]

The crucial point is that throughout the Middle Ages castration normally meant the removal of the testicles but not the penis, a fact which is often ignored in modern discussion of medieval castration narratives. Therefore eunuchs retained feeings of sexual desire—they could have penile erections, and indeed there was a view (here exemplified by the words of St John Chrysostom) that 'far from assuaging the lusts of the flesh', castration 'exacerbates them'. Here I am quoting a well-documented study by Yves Ferroul.[23] However, the matter was more confused, and is more confusing, than Ferroul seems to allow. As Michael Clanchy says, whatever the medical facts, and despite the views of some medieval authorities that 'castration in adulthood does not necessarily

about the speed with which the news of his 'extraordinary mark of disgrace would spread throughout the world' (*Historia calamitatum*, trans. J. T. Muckle, *The Story of Abelard's Adversities* (Toronto, 1964), p. 39) seems to have been well founded. Writing over ten years before Abelard had composed his own record of events, his opponent Roscelin of Compiègne gloatingly commented that 'your misery is already widely known' (*PL* 178, 369); cf. Irvine, 'Abelard and Remasculinization', p. 91.

[22] It has even been argued that Jean de Meun forged those letters: see H. Silvestre, 'Réflexions sur la thèse de F. J. Benton relative au dossier "Abélard-Héloïse" ', *Recherches de théologie ancienne et médiévale*, 44 (1977), 215–16. For recent defences of their authenticity see Dronke, 'Medieval Testimonies', pp. 247–57, 278; Barbara Newman, 'Authority, Authenticity, and the Repression of Heloise', in her *From Virile Woman to WomanChrist: Studies in Medieval Religion and Literature* (Philadelphia, 1995), pp. 46–75; and Constant J. Mews, *The Lost Love Letters of Heloise and Abelard* (Basingstoke, 1999), pp. 47–53. The last of these publications takes the debate into pastures new by proposing that the *Epistolae duorum amantium* found in Troyes MS 802 (fifteenth century) uniquely preserves a further collec-tion of 'lost' love letters of Abelard and Heloise.

[23] 'Abelard's Blissful Castration', in Cohen and Wheeler (eds.), *Becoming Male in the Middle Ages*, p. 136.

cause impotence', it 'is evident from their writings that Abelard and his contemporaries believed it did'.[24] Hence Abelard, who, as Ferroul says, seems to have retained his penis,[25] believed that he had 'been deprived of the part' of his body 'that was the centre of voluptuous desires, the prime cause of the lusts of the flesh';[26] in other words, apparently he held that his testicles were the 'centre' of his 'voluptuous desires'. Peter of Spain (who taught medicine at Sienna during the period 1246–50) seems to throw some light on the subject. In the B-version of his commentary on Constantine's *Viaticum* he declares that, while 'sexual desire' (*desiderum in coitu*) comes from the liver, the 'act of love is in the testicles' and the natural 'stimulation to intercourse' is located 'in one member, and this is in the testicles'.[27]

What does seem perfectly clear is that the removal of the testicles was widely believed to put an end to the male's ability to emit true seed (allegedly produced by the brain, whence it passed into the spinal marrow and finally to the sexual organs). Clearly, this ties in with Jean de Meun's precise relation of the possession, and 'natural' use, of *coilles* to procreation and the future survival of the human race. More generally, it would seem that medieval medical tradition fully supports the *Rose*'s assumption that possession of testicles is essential to maleness. For instance, Arnold of Villanova (who produced a substantial number of medical treatises at Montpellier in the 1290s) quoted 'the ancients' as believing that the testicles were the principal organs inasmuch as they supplied the *virtus* (virility, power) of the whole body'.[28] Little wonder, then, that castration was constructed as a major threat to male integrity and identity. Such fears are addressed and quelled, the crisis of masculinity resolved, at the end of the *Rose*. There, I wish to argue, Jean de Meun prepares a stage for Amant's star performance of normative masculinity.

[24] Clanchy, *Abelard*, p. 224. [25] 'Abelard's Blissful Castration', p. 136.
[26] PL 178, 206D. [27] See Wack, *Lovesickness*, pp. 234–7.
[28] *De coitu* (Basel, 1585), pp. 307–8; cf. Ferroul, 'Abelard's Blissful Castration', p. 141.

Rewriting nature: insular values and their revision[29]

The *Rose*'s partial participation in the playful and pleasure-affirming genre of *ars amatoria* makes it difficult if not impossible to read its ending as an amplification of the moral recommendation of natural sex which Alan of Lille had made in *De planctu naturae*, and hence the type of closure achieved by Alan's text is simply not possible for Jean's. For a start, Alan's discourse admits the pleasure principle (as already noted) but crucially appeals to the authority of God and his vice-regent on earth, Dame Nature; the functional pleasure thus allowed to those engaged in the natural work of procreation is very different from the type which is writ large in the *Ars amatoria*. But it is important to consider how far an 'Insular' reading of Jean de Meun can go. After all, one of Jean's defenders in the *querelle de la Rose*, Jean de Montreuil, declared that the 'end' (*finis libri*) of the *Rose* was 'the propagation of the species'—which is very much the *finis* of *De planctu naturae*.[30] Against this may be set the trenchant view of Jean Gerson, who, in attacking Jean de Meun's use of the figures Nature and Genius, declares that this poetic fiction is a corruption of what the great Alan of Lille had written.[31] The question must therefore be posed, what role—if any—does Alan's *finis libri* actually play at the end of the *Rose*?

Alan's Nature, as noted above, had stridently protested about homosexual activity, censuring the man 'who hammers on an anvil which issues no seeds . . . his ploughshare scores a barren strand'. She proceeds to wonder aloud why 'so many kisses lie fallow on maidens' lips while no one wishes to harvest a crop from them'.[32] *Au contraire*, Amant relishes the fact that his hammers, cunningly crafted by Nature, are in excellent working order within his scrip; changing Alan's sexual metaphor he says—twice—that his pilgrim's staff required no metal tip to

---

[29] The adjective 'insular' is here formed from the Latin form of Alan of Lille's name, 'Alanus de Insulis'.

[30] *Le Débat,* ed. Hicks, p. 44; trans. Baird and Kane, p. 154. On the use of the term *finis libri* in medieval commentary tradition, see Minnis, *Authorship*, pp. 20, 29, 31, 32, 41, 52, 92, 93, 120, 126–7, 129–30, 132, 147–8, 179, 217, 340 n. For the occurrence of the term elsewhere in the *querelle*, see Ch. 6 below.

[31] *Le Débat,* ed. Hicks, p. 80; trans. Baird and Kane, p. 86.

[32] *De planctu naturae*, i met. 1; trans. Sheridan, pp. 70–1.

strengthen it (21355, 21558). Nature is thanked for her gifts to him, which he puts to their natural use. Amant places his seed exactly where it should be (no sodomy or *coitus interruptus* here!),[33] and the Rose is duly impregnated.

Presumably Alan of Lille would have been pleased with that. However, one can imagine him being less pleased with Amant's subsequent speculation that, while he was the first to possess the Rose, he may not have been the last. Indeed, the woman may subsequently have charged for her favours—the implication being that she may have become some kind of prostitute (or, less shockingly, earned herself a husband with them). In passages such as this, 'Insular' values have undergone revision in the light of alternative discourses:

> Et se bien l'estre du pas sé,
> nus n'i avoit onques passé,
> car g'i passai touz li prumiers,
> n'oncor n'iere pas coustumiers
> li leus de recevoir paages.[34]
> Ne sai s'il fist puis d'avantages
> autant aus autres comme a moi;
> mes bien vos di que tant l'amoi
> que je ne le pou onques croire,
> nels se ce fust chose voire,
> car nus de legier chose amee
> ne mescroit, tant soit diffamee;
> ne si ne le croi pas oncores.
>
> (21625-37)

---

[33] On *coitus interruptus* as a widely practised form of contraception, and church condemnations thereof, see P. P. A. Biller, 'Birth Control in the West in the Thirteenth and Early Fourteenth Centuries', *Past and Present*, 94 (1982), 3–26; cf. Angus McLaren's brief treatment in *A History of Contraception, from Antiquity to the Present Day* (Oxford, 1990), pp. 119–20. I raise this matter here to emphasize the fact that in Jean's text there is no hint of either 'deviant' sexual practice or sinful withdrawal. Amant, so to speak, does it the 'natural' way, and according to the prevailing mores deserves some sort of credit for that. On the normativity of Jean de Meun's positions (both intellectual and sexual), see Michael Camille, 'Manuscript Illumination and the Art of Copulation', in K. Lochrie, P. McCracken, and J. A. Schultz (eds.), *Constructing Medieval Sexuality* (Minneapolis, 1997), pp. 82–4.

[34] On the ability of the penetrating male to feel the difference between a virgin and a sexually experienced woman, cf. the pseudo-Ovidian *De Vetula*, ii.669–72, and the discussion of this passage by Hexter, who brings out well 'the fictive Ovid's obsession about the feel of a virgin as opposed to a *mulier fracta*' ('Ovid's Body', p. 341).

[Indeed, if I knew the state of the passage, no one had ever passed there; I was absolutely the first. The place was still not common enough to collect tolls. I don't know if, since then, it has done as much for others as it did for me, but I tell you indeed that I loved it so much that I could hardly believe, even if it were true, that the same favours had been given to others. No one lightly disbelieves what he loves, so dishonoured would it be; but I still do not believe it.]

This passage has, unsurprisingly, been the subject of considerable comment. René Louis sees in it the destruction of the love-ideal proffered by Guillaume de Lorris: 'On atteint ici ... à l'insinuation la plus infâme par laquelle le continuateur achève de détruire et de piétiner avec mépris l'idéal si poétique et si délicat du premier auteur du *Roman*'; 'l'admirable allégorisme érotique que Guillaume avait conçu et mis en scène achève de tomber en ruines et de s'écrouler sous les coups répétés de l'ironie méprisante du continuateur'.[35] Per Nykrog envisions an older and experienced man talking here; not necessarily a person who has become corrupted, but one who is in a position to regard 'ses débuts dans sa jeunesse timide avec une certaine distance ironique quoique affectueuse'.[36] According to Jean's theory of love, he suggests, sexual relationships cannot last; the lovers must inevitably part and enter into liaisons with others, in a manner quite unlike that love-until-death exemplified by Tristan and Isolde. By contrast, Thomas D. Hill cites lines 21621–36 as proof of the 'fact' that 'the lover speaks of a continuing relationship with his love in the concluding episode of the poem'.[37] What prompts that (quite incredible) statement is Hill's utterly valid emphasis on the similarities between Pygmalion and Amant, both of whom beget a child: 'The lover, like Pygmalion, is irrational and yet at the same time he achieves

[35] René Louis, *Le Roman de la Rose. Essai d'interprétation de l'allégorisme érotique* (Paris, 1974), p. 140.
[36] Per Nykrog, *L'amour et la Rose. Le grand dessein de Jean de Meun* (Cambridge, Mass., 1986), p. 77.
[37] Hill, 'Narcissus, Pygmalion', p. 415, n. 17. Apparently Hill wishes to believe that this is no one-night stand. However, there is nothing said about the duration of the relationship, and no indication whatever that Amant enjoyed his Rose on subsequent occasions. All we have is his dubiously sentimental hope that he was the only man she ever knew sexually; the remark that he could never believe otherwise is probably meant as evidence of his foolish vanity, with the implication that she indeed went on to have other partners.

what Raison defines as the rational end of sexuality.'[38] This view, moreover, could be seen as a reading of the *Rose* in which the terms of reference of *De planctu naturae* are given top priority (though Hill does not put it like that). But working against this view, particularly as applied to Amant, is a priapic posturing and self-conceit which allows male sexual satisfaction rather more textual space than the natural imperative of procreation which had so concerned Alan of Lille.[39] Indeed, the account of the Rose's impregnation occupies a mere four lines—

> Si fis lors si meller les greines
> qu'el se desmellassent a peines,
> si que tout le loutonet tandre
> an fis ellargir et estandre.
>
> (21697–700)

[I thus mingled the seeds in such a way that it would have been hard to disentangle them, with the result that all the rose-bud swelled and expanded.]

—so cursory that some have refused to believe that it has actually taken place.[40] What dominates in Amant's description of

[38] Ibid. 417.

[39] Hence John Fleming can easily ridicule the 'procreation justification' for Amant's actions; see his *Allegory and Iconography*, pp. 243–4. A fresh look at the problem has recently been taken by Kevin Brownlee, 'Pygmalion, Mimesis, and the Multiple Endings of the *Roman de la Rose*', *Yale French Studies*, 95 (1999), 193–211. Pointing out the obvious fact that the courtly discourse which Jean inherited from Guillaume of 'a man in love with a flower' makes 'both narrative closure and sexual fulfillment equally impossible', Brownlee goes on to, in effect, posit the reciprocal and fulfilled desire of Pygmalion and Galatea as a surrogate consummation which engages in a dialectical relationship with the terminal 'projection of male desire' wherein 'the female role is limited to that of recipient' (pp. 195, 207–8). Might one, then, more appropriately locate the 'procreation justification' in the Pygmalion and Galatea narrative, arguing that *this* is the true exemplification of heteronormative 'Insular' values, rather than Amant's impossible coupling with a flower? Another part of Brownlee's discussion would militate against this, however. As he brings out well, the scene of Pygmalion 'holding his beloved naked in his arms functions in important ways against a key program operative from very early on in the conjoined *Rose* text, a program that had repeatedly presented [this type of] image as a dream, a lie, or both' (p. 199). Here as elsewhere in the *Rose*, total heterosexual 'success' remains elusive—a prickteasing illusion or masturbatory fantasy forever doomed to remain just that (my words, not Brownlee's, since I am even more convinced than he is of the dominance of self-centred male desire in Jean's text).

[40] Personally I am in no doubt that it has. Jean's reference to the mingling of seeds (21697–8) is conclusive, given that conception was believed to take place when the male sperm or seed came together with the female seed. See Cadden, *Meanings of*

his sexual union is, as Nykrog says, the account of a ' "perfor-mance" érotique mâle vue du côte masculin exclusivement'.[41] And that performance is marked by a strong element of sexual comedy, of a kind which is exclusively masculine. In particular, this humour is obsessed with male potency and the gratification or frustration of male desire. Therefore it is utterly congruous with that phallocentric hermeneutics which Jean de Meun brings to bear on classical mythology.

For this and other reasons the humour present in the poem's ending cannot be rationalized with reference to that moral irony which, according to the readings of D. W. Robertson and John Fleming, is the *Rose*'s main stylistic strategy.[42] Neither can it be reduced to that strident, superior mockery which medieval commentators regarded as one of the most powerful weapons in the satirist's armoury.[43] Little wonder, then, that Christine de Pizan could condemn the text for not having concluded clearly in favour of the moral life. Much of its wit remains uncon-trolled, subversive—though operative within certain definite limits, which are those of what may be identified as a medieval clerical sense of humour, the product of an exclusively male academic environment. Such was the humour which prompted a response to something in Ovid that could not readily be pressed into the service of ethical teaching: 'in Arte Amatoria dat precepta de amore, in hoc opere ludicra tractat et iocosa'.[44] It also features in the group of texts which we will be consider-ing next, the Latin *comediae* which flourished around 1150 in the Loire valley. They constituted a genre which had developed (however improbable it may seem) under the influence of the Roman comedians Terence and Plautus, though the Ovidian influence on verse form, style, and ideology is very strong. Here they are treated as affording analogues to the ending of the

Sex Difference, pp. 11–165 (esp. pp. 93–4). For the view that mere arousal is taking place here, see Marc M. Pelen, *Latin Poetic Irony in the 'Roman de la Rose'* (Liverpool, 1987), p. 155, n. 65, and Kelly, *Internal Difference*, p. 78.

[41] Nykrog, *L'amour et la Rose*, p. 74.

[42] Robertson, *Preface to Chaucer*, pp. 198–207, 442–3, 448 (the latter discus-sions largely concern Andreas Capellanus, but Robertson's view of Jean de Meun is similar); and see esp. Fleming, *Allegory and Iconography*, pp. 50–1.

[43] See above, pp. 93–4.

[44] From an *accessus* in Paris, Bibliothèque Nationale, MS Lat.7994 (thirteenth century), printed by Ghisalberti, 'Medieval Biographies of Ovid', p. 46.

Rose; direct influence of the genre is possible but unprovable. Particularly interesting is the fact that in the *comediae* the spectre of male impotence (or at least inadequacy) sometimes looms, together with the dark suspicion that learning emasculates a cleric.Taking a voluntary vow of celibacy was one thing; being unmanned by one's professional duties was something else. Clearly, this prospect remained a site of deep male anxiety. It is certainly shared by some of the Latin comedies, Richard de Fournival's *Bestiaires d'amours,* and the *Rose,* as I now hope to show.

Sis homo semper: *being male in the Latin* comediae

In the *comediae* academic in-joking interweaves with sexual humour of an aggressive (and sometimes violent) kind, to create a stylistic blend which is often highly reminiscent of what we find in the *Rose*.[45] A good example is afforded by the *Amphitrion* (also known as the *Geta,* after the work's main protagonist) of Vital of Blois, which dates from the last third of the twelfth century.[46] While Amphitrion is away following the 'studies of the Greeks', i.e. learning logic, in Athens (which here stands for Paris), his beautiful wife Alchema comes to the attention of Jupiter. As a master of disguise the licentious god easily takes on the form of Amphitrion and comes to Alchema as her husband. Jupiter brings with him Mercury; disguised as Amphitrion's servant Geta, he guards the door while his master is with Alchema. Then Amphitrion returns, accompanied by Geta, who soon makes it clear that he has picked up a little learning while in Athens: for instance, he can prove that a man is an ass. When Geta is confronted by the false Geta he becomes convinced that this impostor is the real Geta, and therefore he himself must be nothing—and launches into a series of specious

[45] On occasion what gives the academic wit of the *comediae* its particular spice is a palpable distaste for certain types of study (particularly logic and dialectic) which at that time were particularly associated with Paris. Generally these texts are very much on the side of the poets in the battle of the liberal arts, expressing something of the spirit of the schools of Blois, Orléans, and Vendôme in opposition to the values of the emerging universities.

[46] F. J. E. Raby, *A History of Secular Latin Poetry in the Middle Ages* (Oxford, 1934), ii. 55–8.

syllogisms in an attempt to cope with the situation. On meeting his master he assures him that they had both come home long ago. When he hears these apparent ravings Birria (Alchema's slave) concludes that Greece has made the two men mad, and vows never to have anything to do with logic: 'They were sane when they went to Greece, but they've come back as lunatics. Logic drives any fool mad. I hope you never learn that art, Birria. It's good not to know an art that uses some kind of gobbledegook to make men into asses or to wipe them out altogether. If someone wants to be a logician, let him; as for you, Birria, always be a man (*sis homo semper*).'[47] This is followed by the statement that Geta 'takes pleasure' in 'being a man'. Vital of Blois does not specify what kind of identity crisis is envisaged for Geta at this point—relief at being a person rather than nothing (as he feared when he met 'himself', in the false Geta) or pleasure in those virile activities which (thanks to the false Geta, who, so to speak, brought him to recognize his true masculine self) he now accepts as his natural behaviour. For their parts, Birria is content with the smell of the kitchen, and Amphitrion with Alchema. Contrary to the conventions of Roman comedy, the master is ridiculed every bit as much as the slave/servant: for all his philosophical learning, Amphitrion cannot comprehend what has happened to his wife, even when she stands before him with dishevelled clothes and talks of just having been to bed with him.

This sort of donnish wit and sexual humour was not, of course, confined to the Loire valley, and neither was the genre of the Latin *comedia*. The *Babio* seems to have been written by an Englishman around 1150. Its hero, a rustic named Babio, pursues his stepdaughter Viola, but loses her to his master, the soldier Croceus. Meanwhile Babio's slave/servant Fodius embarks on an affair with Babio's wife. Throughout Babio is portrayed as having extraordinary pretensions to learning, particularly in the areas of grammar and logic, this being a major source of humour in the text, as for example when he remarks, 'I have studied logic: I can prove that Socrates is

---

[47] Translated by Ian Thomson and Louis Perraud in their anthology, *Ten Latin Schooltexts of the Later Middle Ages: Translated Selections* (Lewiston, NY, 1990), p. 211.

Socrates and that a man is a man.'[48] Quite predictably, this
knowledge does him little good. In the end, having been outwit-
ted, beaten as a thief on two occasions, and even castrated (by
Fodius), Babio gives up women altogether and turns to religion,
announcing his intention of becoming a monk. F. J. E. Raby
remarks that 'the Christian note comes in strangely at the end,
for the tale is set in a pagan world'.[49] However, this could be
explained by a possible sub-text: the *Babio* may be recalling
Abelard's pursuit of Heloise, which resulted in his castration
and subsequent entry into the Benedictine order.[50] There could
also be an allusion to those same events in the *Amphitrion*,
though it has been questioned whether or not Abelard's castration is specifically being implicated.[51] What is indubitable is
that in that text 'being a man' is jocularly being set in opposition to being a logician. Logic erodes the difference between
men and asses, indeed turns them into asses. Moreover, learning
hinders a man's sexual performance, in various ways: while
Amphitrion is away studying his place in his wife's bed is taken
by the sexually rapacious Jupiter, and Geta's ridiculous attempts
at logical thinking are seen as being at variance with what, for

[48] *La 'Comédie' Latine en France au XIIe siècle*, ed. G. Cohen (Paris, 1931), ii.36
(ll. 135–6). The contrast between the social positions of figures in the *comediae* and
the elevated discourses they often use is discussed by Stephen L. Wailes, 'Role-
Playing in Medieval *Comediae* and Fabliaux', *Neuphilogische Mitteilungen*, 75
(1974), 640–9. He speaks of characters being 'humorously miscast through diction
and rhetoric' (p. 645). In my view this is a reflex of their coterie milieu rather than
some major literary principle which can be justified on universalizing aesthetic
grounds.   [49] Raby, *Secular Latin Poetry*, ii.130.
[50] *Three Latin Comedies*, ed. Keith Bate (Toronto, 1976), p. 8. There is, of
course, one major difference, in that Babio fails in his attempt at seduction: but he
shares Abelard's fate nevertheless. Peter Dronke has questioned the allusion in its
entirety: 'If Abelard, with Heloise's help, had castrated Fulbert, one just *might* be
tempted to see a certain parallel between this plot and the events recounted in the
Historia calamitatum.' Here he is critiquing the study by D. Fraioli, 'Against the
Authenticity of the *Historia calamitatum*', in *Fälschungen im Mittelalter* V, MGH,
Schriften, Bd. 32, v (Hanover, 1988), pp. 167–200. However, Dronke concedes that
'it is nonetheless possible that, in mid-twelfth-century England, *any* comic mention
of a man who becomes a monk because he's been castrated could have brought to
mind, at least for some of the audience, Abelard's *moniage* a generation earlier'. See
'Heloise, Abelard, and Some Recent Discussions', in Dronke's *Intellectuals and
Poets*, p. 333.
[51] See Keith Bate's review of F. Bertini (ed.), *Le commedie latine*, in *Latomus*, 35
(1976), 163–4, and the response by Thomson and Perraud, *Ten Latin Schooltexts*,
pp. 195–6.

him, is appropriate virile behaviour. The false Geta (who proudly describes his 'prick' as 'never satisfied' and 'too big to measure') gives the real Geta a quick lesson in being a real man: get what you can out of your master by deceit, and be highly active sexually. Find an ugly woman who won't mind your ugliness; besides, women don't care about your face if they like your sex![52] From such humour it could be inferred that Abelard's castration is being seen as one, and unquestionably the most extreme, among several instances of loss of manhood through learning. This suggestion finds some, though not conclusive, support in the possibility that certain passages in the *Amphitrion* may be referring to Abelard's *Sic et non*.[53]

Many of the women in the *comediae* are credulous recipients of male desire and/or rather casual in their lack of discrimination between partners, yet in their own way adept at concealing their transgressions. The parameters within which they move are very much those assigned to women in Ovid's love poetry. Hence we discover the peasant Babio wooing Viola with words which echo the *Metamorphoses* and, when he has lost her, consoling himself with notions taken from the *Remedia amoris*.[54] Nowhere is this more evident than in the highly popular *Pamphilus* (which may be yet another product of the Loire valley, though this theory has been challenged by Peter Dronke).[55] The text begins with Venus advising Pamphilus as to how he may court and win Galatea; her doctrine is heavily indebted to the *Ars amatoria*, and anticipates many of the things which Jean de Meun's Ami has to say to Amant.[56] Having received only mild encouragement from his beloved, Pamphilus buys the help of a go-between, an Old Woman, who is an obvious descendant of Ovid's Dipsas (*Amores* i) and an ancestor of

---

[52] Trans. ibid. 208–9.

[53] Bate, review of Bertini, p. 164; Thomson and Perraud, *Ten Latin Schooltexts*, pp. 194, 195–6.   [54] Cf. Wailes, 'Role-Playing', p. 641.

[55] For the opposing views see Bruno Roy, 'Arnulf of Orléans and the Latin "Comedy" ', *Speculum*, 49 (1974), 258–66, and Peter Dronke, 'A Note on *Pamphilus*', *Journal of the Warburg and Courtauld Institutes*, 42 (1979), 225–30. Dronke would locate the work in Germany, perhaps the Bavarian monastery of Tegernsee, and date it as early as *c.*1100.

[56] Specific verbal echoes of Ovid are listed in *La 'Comédie' Latine*, ed. Cohen, ii. 173–5, but this is certainly not exhaustive; besides, apart from the close literal parallels many ideas and precepts from Ovid's amatory works have been thoroughly assimilated into the text.

La Vielle in the *Rose*. Particularly important from our point of view is Venus's Ovidian statement that women actually enjoy rape. 'You may use force; women like you to use it', the *praeceptor amoris* had declared; 'they often wish to give unwillingly what they like to give' (*Ars amatoria*, i.673–4). In the case of the rapes of Phoebe and Hilaira, Ovid continues, 'each ravisher found favour with the ravished' (679–80).[57] Similarly, Venus claims that Galatea would rather lose her virginity by force than by saying, 'da me fac modo uelle tuum' ('take me if you wish'; 114).[58] And force is indeed used. There is no physical description of the episode; as is common in the *comediae* the action has to be inferred from the character's rhetorical set pieces (presumably a fossil of the genre's origin in theatrical performance art):

Pamphile, tolle manus! . . . te frustra nempe fatigas!
Nil ualet ille labor! . . . quod petis esse nequit! . . .
Pamphile tolle manus! . . . male nunc offendis amicam! . . .
Iamque redibit anus: Pamphile tolle manus! . . .
Heu michi! quam paruas habet omnis femina uires! . . .
Quam leuiter nostras uincis uttasque manus! . . .
Pamphile! nostra tuo cum pectore pectora ledis! . . .
Quid me sic tradas? . . . est scelus atque nephas! . . .
Desine! . . . clamabo! . . . quid agis! male detegor a te! . . .
Perfida, me miseram, quando redibit anus?
Surge! precor! . . . nostras audit uicinia lites! . . .
Que tibi me credit non bene fecit anus! . . .
Hujus uictor eris facti, licet ipsa relucter,
Sed tamen inter nos rumpitur omnis amor!

(681–96)

[Pamphilus! Take away your hands! You're trying in vain! . . . This effort's for nothing . . . What you wish can't be. Pamphilus, hands off! Now you're seriously offending your lover! The old woman'll soon be back! Hands off, Pamphilus! Alas, what little strength women have! How easily you overcome both my hands. Pamphilus! You're hurting my breasts with your chest! Why do you handle me like this? It's a sin and an outrage! Stop, I'll call out! What are you doing? It's nasty to undress me like this! Woe is me, when will that deceitful woman come back? Get up!

---

57 On Ovid's 'highly ambivalent' attitude toward women, see esp. Allen, *Amatory Fiction*, pp. 24–6, 32.
58 *La 'Comédie' latine*, ed. Cohen, ii.198. I have drawn on the partial translation of the *Pamphilus* included in *Medieval Comic Tales*, trans. Peter Rickard, Alan Deyermond, et al. (Cambridge, 1972), pp. 114–27.

Please! The neighbour'll hear our struggles! The old woman did a foul deed in entrusting me to you! I'll never be caught again with her, and she'll never again deceive me as she did now! You'll be the victor in this fight—although I struggled!—but all love between us is now broken off!]

The text then leaps to a point in time after the rape, with Pamphilus calmly remarking, 'Having finished the course, our racehorse takes a breather' (697–8; perhaps inspired by one of Ovid's sexual metaphors, *Ars amatoria*, ii.732). The text ends with the old woman recommending marriage to Pamphilus and Galatea—perhaps this is an attempt to ameliorate the rape, but what is perfectly clear is the assumption that Galatea (as is typical of a woman, the text implies) did not mean what she said when she asserted that 'all love between' them 'is now broken off'. The principle which here dominates is, 'They often wish to give unwillingly what they like to give'. Pamphilus, it would seem, is set fair to join the ranks of ravishers who 'found favour with the ravished'.[59]

The figure of the old woman who is expert in the art of love appears yet again in the Pseudo-Ovidian *De Vetula*, possibly the work of Richard de Fournival, which postdates the *Pamphilus* but might have been known to Jean de Meun (proof of influence is difficult if not impossible, given their common debt to Ovid). *De Vetula* is a prime example of academic Ovidianism; the joke was given even more spice (albeit unwittingly) when this text itself became the subject of scholastic commentary.[60] If it be

[59] I cannot therefore accept the argument of Alison Goddard Elliott that Galathea is genuinely unwilling to become involved with Pamphilus, and that marriage to him would be an utter misery; *Seven Medieval Latin Comedies* (New York, 1984), p. xxix. Far more to the point is the view of Thomson and Perraud, *Ten Latin Schooltexts*, pp. 159–60, that her 'coyness' is meant to be seen as 'only a spur to ardor. Galathea's angry protests during the climax of the seduction are not inconsistent with a hidden willingness to comply'. By the same token, I would dispute the reading of this rape scene in terms of social realism (as held e.g. by Elliott, p. xxix). Like Marjorie Curry Woods I believe it is largely a site of rhetorical and pedagogic convention; cf. her article 'Rape and the Pedagogical Rhetoric of Sexual Violence', in Rita Copeland (ed.), *Criticism and Dissent in the Middle Ages* (Cambridge, 1996), pp. 56–86. This radical study argues that 'scenes of erotic violence were an established pedagogical tool for teaching verbal skills' to young men in the Middle Ages, as in late antiquity; a continuous classroom 'tradition of using rape' and love poetry of a type which valued male sexual aggression had long been in place (p. 66). Thus, 'medieval schoolboys' worked out 'their anxieties about adulthood on the bodies of literary ladies (or rather girls)' (p. 73).

[60] See e.g. the glosses on *De Vetula* referenced on p. 71, n. 104.

granted that Richard was responsible for *De Vetula*, he stands as one of the major Ovidian writers of the thirteenth century. Among the attributions of several French love treatises to him, his authorship of the *Consaus d'amours* seems definite. We shall return to that work later; here our interest is in Richard's *Bestiaires d'amours* (which accompanies the *Rose* in four manuscripts), because of the way in which it brings together that clerkly and often scurrilous humour which we have been discussing and a quite remarkable piece of ironical self-construction which merits comparison with Jean de Meun's realization of Amant at the end of the *Rose*.

Imaging clerical potency: cocks and other creatures

In the *Bestiaires* traditional beast lore is ostensibly being compiled and interpreted for the benefit of lovers. However, what we are dealing with here is very far from *fine amor*, for the conventional antics of lovers are consistently undermined and even on occasion ridiculed to such an extent that the amatory fiction threatens to break down, and lay bare the traditional misogyny which it flimsily covers. Presumably this was composed for the amusement of an audience which was educated and wise enough to know better; the familiars of the chancellor of the chapter of Notre Dame in Amiens would perhaps have found in the *Bestiaires* a *remedium amoris* thinly disguised as an *ars amatoria*.

The beginning of the treatise itself is particularly revealing, in that it presents five animals as images of frustrated male desire, namely the cock, wild ass, wolf, cricket, and swan. Since the cock is the very first animal to appear in the bestiary, presumably it has special significance. It has been argued that the *gallus* (i.e. a cock, or alternatively a priest of Cybele, to follow Isidore of Seville's etymology) was traditionally associated with castration, and hence that is the implication here, the writer depicting 'himself' as impotent in the face of his lady's rejection.[61]

---

[61] Trans. Jeanette Beer, *Master Richard's Bestiary of Love and Response* (Berkeley, Calif., 1986), p. xvii. Cf. Isidore of Seville, *Etymologiae*, ed. W. M. Lindsay (Oxford, 1911), XII.vii.50. See further Rabanus Maurus, *De universo*, viii.6 (*PL* 111, 248A-B), and the twelfth-century bestiary trans. T. H. White, *The Book of Beasts, being a translation from a Latin Bestiary of the Twelfth Century* (London,

Furthermore, there is a second and quite explicit image of castration in the *Bestiaires*, involving the unfortunately well-endowed beaver, hunted because its virile member contains healing medicine. In order to escape death the creature mutilates itself: 'il set bien c'on ne le cace se pour celui membre non: si gete les dens et l'esrace et le laisse caoir enmi la voie; et quant on le treuve, se le laisse on aler . . .' ['it knows well it is being pursued only for that member, so it sets upon it with its teeth, tears it off and drops it in the middle of the path. When it is found, the beaver is allowed to escape . . .'].[62] Somewhat bizarrely, Richard uses this beast lore to figure female, rather than male, behaviour: if only the lady would give up her heart, on account of which the lover is pursuing her, then he would stop, for that is the medicine he needs, the *sovrainne medecine* ('sovereign remedy') which would rescue him from *mort d'amours* ('death by love').[63] But it seems eminently reasonable to take the graphic beaver narrative, along with the implications (as identified by Beer) of the image of the cock, as crucially revelatory of male sexual insecurity and frustration. I believe that Helen Solterer goes too far in identifying 'the image of torn male genitalia' (in the beaver narrative) as 'the high point of the *Bestiaire*'s commentary':[64] in my view the text has other priorities. However, it is certainly important, as a particularly dramatic way of focusing the significance of the lady's ongoing silent denial of her would-be lover—a process which may advisedly be described as his emasculation. For she (at least from his perspective) has unmanned the narrator by placing him in the inferior subject position, as traditionally occupied by the woman in relation to her male superior. And what better way to

1954): 'The cock (*gallus*) is called the cock because it gets castrated. It is the only member of the bird family whose testicles are removed. Indeed, the ancients used to call the Galli (the priests of Cybele) the "cut-offs" ' (p. 150).

[62] *Li Bestiaires*, ed. Segre, pp. 57–8; trans. Beer, p. 20.

[63] *Li Bestiaires*, ed. Segre, pp. 58–9; trans. Beer, p. 21. See further the discussion by Solterer, *The Master and Minerva*, who notes that two other animals 'used to illustrate woman's necessary self-sacrifice are identified as male', i.e. the pelican and the lion (p. 89). Physical mutilation also features in the story of the father pelican, which resuscitates his babies 'with the blood he draws from his side. In this way he brings them back to life'. Similarly, if the lady gave his lover her heart this would revive him (trans. Beer, p. 20).

[64] Solterer, *The Master and Minerva*, p. 89.

emphasize this role reversal than by figuring through distinctively male creatures certain ways in which he would like her to act, as in the *Bestiaires'* tales of the the lion, pelican, and beaver? Thus, features of the male body and male behaviour paradoxically become figures of desired female submission.

In other words, allusions to castration in the *Bestiaires* function to evoke frustrated potency rather than actual impotence or failure of virility. This suggestion finds some support in the ambivalent nature of the cock, the creature given pride of place by Richard, as described in medieval beast lore.[65] There was some confusion between the cock and the capon, and a strong convention certainly existed which emphasized the rooster's sexual prowess.[66] Petrus Alfonsi (1062–1110?) was unequivocal. In his *Disciplina clericalis* he describes how Balaam advised his son not to be less vigilant than the cock: if this creature could satisfy his ten wives, then surely the son could control his one and only spouse.[67] Although the section *De gallo* in the

[65] The following discussion of imagery relating to the cock is indebted to discussion with Luuk Houwen (of the Department of English at the Ruhr-Universität Bochum). I am particularly grateful to him for allowing me to consult his database on medieval beast lore, and for pointing out the partial parallels between the accounts which Richard de Fournival, Gregory the Great, and Hugh of Fouilly provide of the manner in which the rooster varies its song.

[66] The strong iconographical tradition (in classical antiquity and the early Christian centuries) of the cock as a fertility symbol is discussed by Lorrayne Y. Baird, 'Priapus Gallinaceus: The Role of the Cock in Fertility and Eroticism in Classical Antiquity and the Middle Ages', *Studies in Iconography*, 7 (1981/2), 81–111. In particular, the cock appeared as an animal which accompanied the great fertility- and creator-god, Priapus—and even at times served as the embodiment of the god himself. She notes that, in a 'curious reversal' of this tradition, certain written sources (Latin poems and patristic texts) feature the cock as eunuch. While on the one hand suggesting that 'the cock as Christian eunuch priest all but supplanted the cock who lent his form to Priapus', on the other Baird notes the survival of the priapic cock as 'a symbol of lust and perversion' (pp. 96–7). Jerome's mistranslation of Prov. 30: 31 ('A cock girded about the loins', *gallus succinctus lumbos*) certainly contributed to the 'cock as eunuch' tradition. But Baird suggests that the early Christian tendency to use the cock as a symbol of Christ was suppressed by later writers 'because the popular domestic fowl not only was flagrant in his everyday salacity, but he also came trailing erotic associations': see her later article, 'Christus Gallinaceus: A Chaucerian Enigma; or the Cock as Symbol of Christ in the Middle Ages', *Studies in Iconography*, 9 (1983), 19–30 (esp. pp. 24–5).

[67] *The Scholar's Guide: A Translation of the Twelfth-Century 'Disciplina Clericalis'* of Pedro Alfonso, by J. R. Jones and J. E. Keller (Toronto, 1969), p. 36; *The 'Disciplina clericalis' of Petrus Alfonsi*, ed. Eberhard Hermes with an English translation by P. R. Quarrie (London, 1977), p. 105. As Jones and Keller say (p. 16), this work had an

thirteenth-century *De proprietatibus rerum* of Bartholomaeus
Anglicus begins with the Isidorean notion that the bird had that
name because 'of geldinge', it proceeds to describe the creature
as a 'ful bolde and hardy' fowl that dearly loves his wives, and
fights for them against other roosters. He likes to have the hen
that is fattest and most tender perch beside him; in the morning
he engages in an elaborate courtship ritual to invite her 'to
tredinge'.[68] Geoffrey Chaucer's bold and hardy Chauntecleer is
similarly amorous:

> He fethered Pertelote twenty tyme,
> And trad hire eke as ofte, er it was pryme.
> (*Nun's Priest's Tale*, VII.3177–78)

In his version of the same Aesopic fable, Robert Henryson has
'Pertok' refer to the fact that 'In paramouris he wald do us
plesing' (i.e. 'in sexual love' the rooster 'would give pleasure to
us'; l.506), though a few lines later she reveals her libidinous
nature by claiming that his best efforts were unable to satisfy
them sexually (525–9). Another hen, Coppok, then speaks like
'ane curate', claiming that Chantecleir's abduction by the fox
was divine punishment for his 'lous' (i.e. wanton) and 'lecherous' nature (530–6).[69] Given this reputation, it is hardly surprising that the cock often featured in sexually risqué or downright
obscene contexts, as in the fifteenth-century Middle English
lyric which begins as follows:[70]

'astonishing vogue', and enjoyed a very substantial vernacular reception. See e.g. 'The
Fables of Alfonce' as included in *Caxton's Aesop*, ed. R. T. Lenaghan (Cambridge,
Mass., 1967); Balaam's advice to his son appears on p. 193. On the tradition of the
wisdom of Balaam (who is mentioned in Numbers 22–24) see John Tolan, *Petrus
Alfonsi and His Medieval Readers* (Gainesville, Fla., 1993), pp. 76–8.

[68] *De proprietatibus rerum*, pp. 535–7; cf. Trevisa, *On the Properties of Things*,
ed. Seymour, p. 627 (from which the above quotations are taken).

[69] *The Poems of Robert Henryson*, ed. Denton Fox (Oxford, 1981), pp. 23–4.

[70] *Medieval English Lyrics*, ed. R. T. Davies (London, 1963), p. 153. For discussion of this poem see esp. Louise O. Vasvári, 'Fowl Play in My Lady's Chamber', in
Ziolkowski (ed.), *Obscenity*, pp. 108–35, who shows that the phallic rooster also
features in riddles in many other languages. See further Lorrayne Y. Baird's listing
of puns on 'cock'/gallus = penis in French, Italian, German, Slovak, etc.: 'O.E.D.
Cock 20: The Limits of Lexicography of Slang', *Maledicta*, 5 (1981), 213–25; also
Alan Dundes, 'Gallus as Phallus: A Psychoanalytic Cross-Cultural Consideration of
the Cock-Fight as Fowl Play', in Dundes (ed.), *The Cockfight: A Casebook*
(Madison, Wis., 1994), pp. 251–3.

> I have a gentle cock
> Croweth me day:
> He doth me risen erly[71]
> My matins for to say.

And ends with quite blatant innuendo:

> His eyen arn of cristal,
> Loken all in aumber:[72]
> And every night he percheth him
> In mine lady's chaumber.

By the same token, it could be argued that the masculinity of Richard de Fournival's narrator is not in question; his problem is lack of opportunity or occasion, given his beloved's aloofness, rather than some physical impediment. In a tradition which goes back to Pliny's *Natural History* at least, when cocks are gelt they stop crowing.[73] Given the vocal virtuosity of Richard's rooster, there seems no reason to doubt his physical virility.

Pliny also depicts the cock as a heroic creature which holds royal sway in whatever household it lives; through its victories in cock-fights it brings honour to the region whence it came, and even the lion, noblest of wild animals, is frightened by its intimidating appearance.[74] Little wonder, then, that the cock's courage and potency constituted a rich source of imagery and metaphor—a point of considerable importance for *Li Bestiaires d'amours*. As has already been noted, Richard begins his text with an extrinsic prologue which describes how Memory's House guards the treasury of knowledge acquired by the mind

---

[71] 'He causes me to rise early'.   [72] 'All set in amber'.

[73] *Natural History*, x.25. Cf. Dundes, 'Gallus as Phallus': 'A capon—a rooster that has been castrated to improve the taste of the meat—seldom crows, never notices hens, and will hit nothing with spur or beak. But a game fowl is the ultimate blend of balls and skill, all of which is inextricably bound up with the man who bred it and fed it and handles it in the [cock-fighting] pit' (p. 253). Cf. the following note.

[74] Pliny, *Natural History*, x.24. On the erotic associations of the cockfight, see Baird, 'Priapus Gallinaceus', and also Dundes, 'Gallus as Phallus'. Dundes categorizes cock-fighting among games in which 'one male demonstrates his virility, his masculinity, *at the expense of a male opponent*', and proceeds to offer the following hypothesis: 'the cockfight is a thinly disguised symbolic homoerotic masturbatory phallic duel, with the winner emasculating the loser through castration or feminization' (pp. 250–1). He quotes a criminological study by F. F. Hawley (of cockfighters as a deviant recreational subculture) as claiming that 'The cock is, to all appearances, a walking unselfconscious set of eager genitals . . . the cock represents male sexuality raised (or lowered) to the most primitive extremity' (p. 254).

of man by virtue of his intelligence. The cock often features as a figure of intelligence, following Job 38: 36, 'Who hath put wisdom in the heart of man? Or who gave the cock under-standing?'[75] In his *Moralia in Iob* Gregory the Great declares that the cock utters 'its louder and longer-drawn strains in the deeper hours of the night', but when the morning approaches 'it utters altogether more gentle and feeble notes'.[76] He moralizes this in terms of how discreet preachers suit their style to their audience. When preaching to the wicked, they speak 'with loud and great voices'—'they cry out, as it were, in the darkness of the profound night'. However, when 'the light of truth is already present to the hearts of their hearers', they speak in gentler tones, as it were bringing forth 'the allurements of rewards', and moreover as the morning approaches they sing 'within dimin-ished tones', this being a figure for the preaching of 'all the subtlest mysteries'. An amplified version of this excursus is provided in Hugh of Fouilly's extensive *Aviarium* (dated between 1132 and 1152). The question 'by whom is he [the cock] granted intelligence?' is swiftly answered, Hugh declares, by 'the blessed Gregory'. 'The cock is granted intelligence from heaven', he explains, 'because the virtue of discernment is divinely provided to the teacher of truth, so that he should know to whom he might offer what, when or by what means. For one and the same exhortation does not suit all people, because an equal quality of character does not bind all people.'[77]

The cock's long and well-attested association with divinely given intelligence could well have inspired Richard to follow on from his extrinsic prologue into an account of the nature of this creature. In *Li Bestiaires d'amours*, however, the traditions (as described above) concerning the modulations of the rooster's song have been transformed into a contrast between 'more frequent song closer to daybreak' and 'more forceful song closer to midnight'. For Richard the former phenomenon signifies 'l'amour dont on n'a del tout essperance ne del tout desesperance'

---

[75] In fact, Jerome's *gallo* is a mistranslation of the Hebrew, as is noted by Baird, 'O.E.D. Cock 20', p. 218.

[76] *Moralium libri*, xxx.iii.14; *PL* 76, cols. 531–2.

[77] *Hugh of Fouilly's 'Aviarium'*, ed. and trans. W. B. Clark (Binghamton, 1992), pp. 180–3.

['the love where one has neither complete confidence nor complete despair']; the latter, 'l'amour del tout desesperee' ['totally despairing love']. When the lover had hope, it was like twilight; now he has none, and so he must sing louder.[78] The variations of song relate to differences in the speaker's feelings rather than to the different needs of different audiences. Here we are far from the heroic preacher, master of his craft, who sizes up his auditors and decides how best to address and affect them. According to the fiction of *Li Bestiaires d'amours* the male speaker has no control over his female addressee, and it is her (unknown but probably negative) reaction which holds sway rather than his linguistic action. In place of the power of the preacher's rhetoric we have the frustrated potency of unfulfilled male desire. The Lover is no capon-figure; he is in full possession of his vocal and physical faculties: the problem is rather that his beloved is rejecting his invitation 'to tredinge'.

Such contrasts between priestly Gregorian cock and amatory Ricardian rooster, between Aristotelian prologue ('All men naturally desire knowledge')[79] and Ovidian text (all men naturally desire sexual knowledge), bring us to consideration of what might be termed the vocational impediment—should a cleric be propositioning a woman in this way? And this becomes particularly problematic if we wish to read Richard's clerical status in, or into, his self-construction. This issue is touched on in the extrordinary *Response* to *Li Bestiaires d'amours*, which is written *in persona mulieris* and may indeed be the work of a woman. At one point the writer criticizes clerics who are so decked out 'en courtoisie et en leur beles paroles' ['with courtesy and fine words'] that there is no woman or maiden who can withstand them.[80] Although they are the handsomest of men they are 'li plus soutil en malisse' ['the most devious in malice'], since they take ignorant women by surprise. (It would seem, then, that that priestly rhetoric so valued by St Gregory and Hugh of Fouilly can have disastrous consequences for women when it is employed in their pursuit; many a maiden has had cause to regret a cleric's knowledge of

---

78 *Li Bestiaires*, ed. Segre, pp. 9–10; trans. Beer, p. 3.
79 Cf. p. 72 above.
80 *Li Bestiaires*, ed. Segre, pp. 133–5; trans. Beer, pp. 56–7.

how to suit style to auditor and occasion.) Moreover, the text continues, clerics are not the best men for women to associate with, the clear implication being that marrying them is not a prudent course of action. It ruins their careers for a start, since celibacy is necessary for promotion to the highest offices;[81] at least, that is how I understand the remark, 'Li clers em pert a estre pourveüs de sainte Eglise, ou il seroit canoinnes ou vesques' ['the cleric loses a prebend from our Holy Church where he could be canon or bishop . . .']. And the woman loses out too, since she could have married a knight who would have provided far better for her: 'li demoisele aroit .j. chevalier gentil home dont ele seroit a honneur et deportee plus que de chelui qui tel riqueche n'a mie' ['the maiden could have had a knightly gentleman who would give her more happiness and honour than the cleric, who has no comparable wealth'].

As became very evident in our discussion of the *Amphitrion* and *Babio*, male writers worried about whether they had been emasculated—metaphorically to be sure, though Abelard's fate was painfully literal—by their intellectual training and clerical status. Here, in the *Response*, it is noted that, however much of a problem their sexuality presented to clerics, for women its consequences could be equally, or even more, drastic. If this is not actually the voice of a woman, it is certainly a telling piece of ventriloquism. The female voice is, of course, markedly absent from the ending of the *Rose,* wherein Jean de Meun presents realized male desire which is triumphantly unhindered by any impediment, whether clerical or physical.

Comic climax and performance of masculinity

The comparisons which may be drawn between the Latin *comediae* summarized above, *Li Bestiaires d'amours,* and the final section of the *Rose* will serve to support my view that there is

---

[81] Clerical marriage had been tolerated (albeit with reluctance) until the eleventh century, at which point extreme legal measures had been applied. See Anne Llewellyn Barstow, *Married Priests and the Reforming Papacy: The Eleventh-Century Debates* (New York, 1982); also Dyan Elliott, 'The Priest's Wife: Female Erasure and the Gregorian Reform', in her *Fallen Bodies: Pollution, Sexuality, and Demonology in the Middle Ages* (Philadelphia, 1999), pp. 81–106.

nothing 'marginal' about Jean de Meun's terminal humour, although for some readers it may kill (or at least damage) any claims the text ultimately may have to moral authority. That is one of the reasons why I am reluctant to accept the view that the intended audience of the *Rose* was made up of those on the margins of society. For the poem's humour is, in my view, utterly mainstream. And it cannot be reduced to some kind of Bakhtinian 'safety valve' or, following Freud, to a control mechanism whereby people are jollied into acceptance of their lot. Such cultural-materialist terms of reference reduce and even trivialize the cultural values which appertain in communities that are directed by comprehensive belief systems. The laughter at issue here is that of those who fundamentally *believe*, who have no problem in accepting the tenets of the current culture but who nevertheless—indeed, I doubt if they would see any contradiction here—are aware of its paradoxes, tensions, and apparent absurdities (or what can be presented as such). Hence those 'goliardic' texts which were not, as was once supposed, the products of such marginal characters as wandering scholars and disaffected students, but rather the recreational activities of pillars of the establishment (or men who hoped to achieve such status). Hence the Latin *comediae* of the twelfth century. Hence the *Bestiaires d'amours*, written by a high-ranking churchman and eminent physician. And also the *Tractando cómo al ome es nescesario amar* of Alfonso de Madrigal, 'El Tostado' (*c.*1410–1455), who became bishop of Avila in 1445, a scholar renowned for both the learning and the exceptional length of his commentaries on biblical and secular texts—definitely not someone who could be accused of congenital frivolity.[82] And, to leap ahead even further in time, that rather tedious *fabliau* which was composed by Sir, and Saint, Thomas More.

In short, the humour we are investigating is present in texts written by individuals among whom many had enjoyed the best education that the medieval schools could provide. Within the

---

[82] This Ovidian *jeu d'esprit* deals with the inevitability of love and the impact it has on the lover, here represented by the I-*persona*. For discussion of this text see Alan Deyermond, *A Literary History of Spain: The Middle Ages* (London, 1971), p. 144; see further Ottavio di Camillo, *El humanismo castellano del siglo XV* (Valencia, 1976), pp. 115–16. On Alfonso's biblical exegesis, see Minnis, 'Savonarola and de Madrigal', pp. 163–80.

texts under discussion, highly respectful attitudes to poetic forms and rhetorical devices could coexist with mockeries of the follies of men and the alleged failings of women; the laughter here presupposed could encompass the most cynical of attitudes and be the intended response (it would seem) to the most scurrilous of jests. This, moreover, is a humour characteristic of a world without women, wherein the hardships of enforced celibacy are often relieved by elaborate sexual fantasies and sometimes express themselves through an interest in virility which is, in every sense, purely academic. Some of those who, to cite the standard symbolism, had made themselves eunuchs for the kingdom of heaven (cf. Matt. 19: 21), or who at least appreciated the force of that ideal, seem to have been haunted by the fear of physical castration and the consequent removal of that very male potency which their vocation prohibited them from exercising.

One of the problems about the *Rose*, of course, is that it appealed and was available (on account of its vernacular status) to an audience far wider than the highly privileged group presupposed by, say, the *De planctu naturae*. This audience comprised, along with the inevitable clerics,[83] high-ranking aristocrats (including women), people whose different estate meant that they pursued lifestyles very unlike those of the clerics. Most obviously, for them marriage was eminently possible, and often a good career move; within their lay culture sexuality was constructed somewhat differently. Jean de Montreuil evinces a measure of awareness of this when, in the context of arguing that the *finis* of the *Rose* is 'the propagation of the species' (cf. p. 24 above), he speculates that a certain detractor—presumably he has Chancellor Jean Gerson in mind—was led to think and speak as he did 'because of his religious vocation and his vows'. Or perhaps because, Jean adds nastily, he was the sort of man who is 'rendered useless for the propagation of the species', i.e. a eunuch. Jean de Montreuil seems to have been affected by the phallocentric discourse of Jean de Meun.[84] The implication

---

[83] And the clerics themselves were divided in their reactions to this incorrigibly plural poem; cf. Ch. 5 below.

[84] Moreover, he is echoing the type of abuse which Roscelin of Compiègne and Fulco of Deuil heaped on the castrated Abelard: see Irvine, 'Abelard and Remasculinization', pp. 91–4.

of his remarks seems to be that the doctrine of the *Rose* is aimed not at churchmen but rather at those who are able, because of their lay status and possession of the necessary equipment, to participate in the work of propagation, thereby following the example of Amant.[85] As we have seen, in the *Amphitrion* and *Babio* manliness is shown as being subverted, indeed even destroyed, by scholastic instruction, and the fate of Abelard was often seen as a particularly graphic illustration of loss of manhood through learning. In similar vein, Jean de Montreuil seems to be suggesting that Gerson's learning and ecclesiastical status rendered him incomprehending, and perhaps incapable, of man's natural work.

Jean de Meun's entire literary *œuvre* is, indeed, poised between two worlds; it included translations of Boethius, Vegetius, and the correspondence of Abelard and Heloise for an aristocratic audience (his rendering of Boethius being dedicated to King Philippe le Bel), as well as poems on moral and religious subjects, if the attributions can be believed. And so is the *œuvre* of Richard de Fournival. *De Vetula* circulated in both French and Latin versions, and though the *Bestiaires d'amours* is in French it is permeated with attitudes towards women and love which are redolent of the schoolroom, though certainly accessible to, and in some measure acceptable by, a sophisticated lay audience. It should be recalled that Richard was a licensed surgeon, and the son of a medical man, Roger de Fournival,

---

[85] But, to add to the complexity and paradox, possession of testicles could be deemed essential for entry into the Church of the Lord. In his *Historia calamitatum* Abelard speculates that 'God so abominated eunuchs that men who had their testicles cut off or bruised were forbidden as offensive and unclean to enter a congregation and in sacrifice animals of like character were utterly rejected'. In evidence he cites Lev. 22: 24 and Deut. 23: 1. See *The Story of Abelard's Adversities*, trans. Muckle, pp. 39–40. But Abelard is indulging in self-dramatizing rhetorical exaggeration; canon law clearly decreed that only men who had been guilty of *self*-mutilation (like Origen) were barred from ordination or from performing the duties of priesthood. The First Nicaean Council (of 325) set the standard: it unequivocally states that if any have been made eunuchs by barbarians, or by their masters, but otherwise are found worthy, they may be received into the number of the clergy. To his credit, Abelard himself admits that in the passage in question he is following the letter of the Old Law, 'which kills', i.e. quoting Old Testament doctrine which has been superseded by the new, life-giving Law of Christian revelation (of course, he is echoing 2 Cor. 3: 6). Furthermore, on becoming a monk Abelard appropriated discourses relating to the 'holy eunuch', one who has been spiritually castrated; see Clanchy, *Abelard*, pp. 223–7.

who was personal physician to King Philip Augustus. His
cosmopolitan cultural formation is very much in evidence in the
Consaus d'amours,[86] a work in which Richard professes to
advise a 'fair, gentle sister' as a 'good brother' who is obliged to
respond to her request that he should teach her the means of
undertaking love. It combines (albeit rather awkwardly) impeccable material culled from Cicero's *De amicitia* with milder
versions of some of Andreas Capellanus's radical ideas, ending
with a knightly adventure which is heavily indebted to the fifth
dialogue in Book 1 of *De amore*. The various discourses which
compete within this text, as well as the type of the competition
itself, are reminiscent of those which characterize the *Rose*. And
these works share a distinctive uncertainty about their target
audience, about which interpretative community they are being
aimed at. Their vernacular availability is at variance with the
Latinate exclusiveness which marks their learning and occasions
much of their laughter; the assumption of clerical superiority
coexists uneasily with an awareness of lay fashions and lifestyles.

Of course, what is entertaining to one person or one interpretative community may be improper or deeply offensive to
another, whereupon it may be criminalized and suppressed. And
it would be very naïve to minimize the differences in perception
and taste which existed between various clerical groups; one
such group could reject the texts which were accommodated by
another. A good example may be cited from the early fourteenth
century, when the lord chancellor of Oxford University, 'desiring . . . that each and all the scholars of the university and their
subordinates (*subditos*) should be adorned with morals',
decreed that 'every master regent in grammar and every other
public teacher of grammar' should avoid 'the reading and interpretation of the book of Ovid, *De arte amandi*, and *Pamphilus*,
and of any other book which might lure or provoke his scholars to what is forbidden'.[87] Yet these texts had, for several
generations, been used with confidence in the elementary education of boys and male adolescents.

---

[86] Ed. G. B. Speroni, 'Il "Consaus d'amours" di Richard de Fournival', *Medioevo
romanzo*, 1.2 (1924), 217–78.
[87] Quoted from a group of regulations dated between 1335 and 1344 by Edith
Rickert, *Chaucer's World*, ed. C. C. Olson and M. M. Crow (New York and
London, 1948), p. 134.

Then again, humour functions within definite cultural boundaries, may not travel very well, and often fails to improve with age. That is certainly true of the humour which surrounds the rape scene in the *Pamphilus* and the plucking of the rose in Jean de Meun's poem. However, I do not wish to deny the major contrasts between those two episodes, and cannot agree with those who describe Amant's forceful penetration of his virgin rose as a rape.[88] Surely what we are dealing with are different manifestations of sexual violence, different linguistic strategies which result in the depersonalization and objectification of woman. And that is where the basis of their similarities may be found. Neither text offers contact between male and female of a kind which is reciprocally emotional, mental, human. There is no inscription of shared pleasures (of the kind found in the much-ignored third book of Ovid's *Ars amatoria*), but rather the assault on a castle by one of love's soldiers who cunningly exploits his knowledge of an adversary who in the event acts true to type. Indeed 'Galatea' is little more than a site for various clichés concerning female weakness and male strength ('What little strength women have! How easily you overcome both my hands. . . . You'll be the victor in this fight—although I struggled!'). Inevitably, at the climax of such a narrative the self-absorbed male revels in his triumph and the woman acts as the vanquished or victim—or at best as one who, in the face of superior force, has acquiesced in surrender. Little wonder, then, that the laughter surrounding such escapades rings hollow nowadays. And that modern post-feminist audiences enforce their own prohibitions, albeit more subtly than the fourteenth-century lord chancellor of Oxford University mentioned above. Apparently we are dealing with a humour which threatens to kill the text, to be effectively terminal.

But there is another way to read the end of the *Rose*. It could be declared that *of course* we are dealing here with a ' "performance" érotique mâle vue du côte masculin exclusivement': that is precisely what Jean de Meun set out to show. At this point in

---

[88] See esp. Leslie Cahoon, 'Raping the Rose: Jean de Meun's Reading of Ovid's *Amores*', *Classical and Modern Literature*, 6 (1986), 261–85. Similarly, in her *Ravishing Maidens: Writing Rape in Medieval French Literature and Law* (Philadelphia, 1991), Kathryn Gravdal claims that 'The "seduction" of Rose, the courtly lady, is depicted blatantly as the rape of a virgin' (p. 68).

his text, fears of emasculation have been dispelled by fruitful *coitus*; the *signe d'estre malles* are unambiguous and in correct use. Any possible threat of deviant sexuality has long since receded, and heterosexual achievement sets the seal on normative maleness as Jean rewrites whilst reaffirming Alan of Lille's homophobic script. This argument may be clarified and furthered by bringing into play recent speculation concerning the vernacular readership of another text which highlights male sexual performance, the *Pamphilus*. Ann Schotter has contrasted the 'original twelfth-century audience' of this text, described as 'young, clerical, and male', for whom the 'poem was a school exercise' and who 'would most likely have been amused by the rape', with its 'later audience','extending through the fifteenth century and mixed in gender (because it read the poem in vernacular versions as well as in Latin)'. In her view, this later audience—or at least its female members—could have responded to what she sees as 'Galathea's strong voice', as giving expression to 'a real world social problem'. In my view, however, the crucial issue derives from the fact of the text's origin in a world 'where women do not belong', to borrow a phrase from Marjorie Curry Woods,[89] a world in which the tradition of sexual violence (including rape) has had a long and continuous presence.[90] It could be argued that a text like the *Pamphilus*, which in the all-male elementary schoolroom enabled boys and young men to 'learn about sexual violence as a method of defining their manhood and controlling their own lives',[91] is like the proverbial fish out of water in the wider context of vernacular reception and lay readership: wrenched from the social situation which gave it meaning, its role within the instruction of young men in the correct social codes of

[89] 'Rape and Pedagogical Rhetoric', p. 72.

[90] Moreover, the medieval classroom often witnessed scenes of actual violence, flogging being a common practice, as is noted by Walter J. Ong, 'Latin Language Study as a Renaissance Puberty Rite', in his *Rhetoric, Romance and Technology: Studies in the Interaction of Expression and Culture* (Ithaca, NY, 1971), pp. 124–6. Much of what Ong says about Renaissance Latin teaching holds good for the earlier period. 'The status of Latin', as taught in schools which were closed to women, 'encouraged in a special way the development of a puberty-rite setting and puberty-rite attitudes' (p. 119); literary models of 'normal' male behaviour (particularly of courage—one valued form of aggression) were used to guide a boy's maturation and socialization.   [91] Woods, 'Rape and Pedagogical Rhetoric', p. 73.

manhood is at the very least problematized, perhaps even thwarted. In other words, what we are left with is uneasy, decontextualized laughter, humour bereft of the original context within which it performed a useful pedagogic function.

Even more frequently than the *Pamphilus*, the minor poems of Ovid had been used as set texts in the classroom teaching of grammar. As already noted, commentaries on Ovid's *Ars amatoria* regularly stated that this text was written for the instruction of young men, and the concept of youth is vitally important in the French *L'Art d'amours*, which assures us that it was the hearts of the young that Ovid sought to ease. Moreover, Ovid wrote the *Ars amatoria* when he himself was an adolescent and a young man, and in so doing was prepared to reveal the fickleness (*legiereté*) of his youth.[92] Thus the *Ars amatoria* is put firmly in its place within the wider cultural scheme of things, its love doctrine viewed from a perspective which enables its limitations to be perceived. Likewise, in the *Rose* Amant's youth is noted at the outset, and its final scene can be read as an account of the young lover's first sexual experience as recalled from a position of emotional maturity. To recall the remark of Per Nykrog, the narrator regards 'ses débuts dans sa jeunesse timide avec une certaine distance ironique quoique affectueuse'.[93] Here, then, at the end of the *Rose* we are presented with a masculine rite of passage which furthers Amant's development from adolescent to mature man.[94]

Against this it could be argued that Amant's youth, while certainly a facet of his character, is hardly stressed at the end of the *Rose*; indeed, it is the woman's sexual inexperience rather than the man's to which attention is drawn (cf. p. 175 above). We are some distance away from the emphases of *L'Art d'amours*. And the *Rose*'s extensive treatment of male sexual anxieties and mores ranges far beyond the sphere of adolescence. For example,

---

[92] See above, pp. 57–8.

[93] It may also be recalled that Jean de Meun's arch-defender Pierre Col could argue that when he wrote the *Rose* the poet had left behind his youthful follies. This is substantiated with reference to Jean de Meun's own *Testament*, in which the poet admits that in his youth he made 'many works through vanity', these being 'various ballades, rondeaux and virelais that we do not have in writing'—which are not to be confused with that later, mature work, the *Rose*. See *Le Débat*, ed. Hicks, p. 95; trans. Baird and Kane, p. 98. Cf. p. 248 below.

[94] Here I recall the idiom of Ong's study, as cited in n. 90 above.

Dame Raison's declaration that '*whoever* lies with a woman ought to wish with all his might to continue his divine self' evidently applies to sexually active males in general, and Genius's exhortation that 'barons' should 'plough and restore' their 'lineage' has no age limit placed upon it (*Rose*, 4385 ff. and 19671–2). Moving on to the issue of reader response, surely it would be very difficult to offer the end of the *Rose* as a text designed to help young men learn 'about sexual violence as a method of defining their manhood and controlling their own lives', to appropriate Woods's superb remark about the *Pamphilus*. For a start, its readership was not confined to men— and that vociferous female reader Christine de Pizan would have ridiculed any suggestion that it taught men to put off violence as a childish thing. She tells the tale—maybe a rhetorical invention, but her fear is real enough—of how a man, after reading the *Rose* to his wife, 'puis fiert et frappe sus et dist: "Orde, telle come quelle il dist, voir que tu me fais tel tour. Ce bon sage homme maistre Jehan de Meung savoit bien que femmes savoient fere!" Et a chascun mot qu'il treuve a son propos il fiert ung coup ou deux du pié ou de la paume' ['would become violent and strike her and say: "These are the kinds of tricks you pull on me. This good, wise man Master Jean de Meun knew well what women were capable of!" And at every words he finds appropriate, he gives her a couple of kicks or slaps'].[95]

It may be concluded, then, that there are considerable difficulties in extending Woods's pedagogic rationalization of the schoolroom reading of rape narratives—a practice which she relates to the possible educational advantages of boys and young men being taught Ovid's amatory poetry—to cover the end of the *Rose*. If there is some sort of 'male maturation narrative' inherent in the genre of *comedia* which seems to have influenced Jean at that point, all one can say is that he has allowed its operation to be subverted by other forces. In any case, the notion that the *comediae* generally conform to the *Pamphilus* in such matters is quite problematic, for other examples of the genre support Woods's hypothesis far less well. The *Amphitrion* and *Babio* are different from the *Pamphilus* in many ways; it

---

[95] *Le Débat*, ed. Hicks, p. 139; trans. Baird and Kane, p. 136.

would be very difficult to claim that they taught inexperienced young men how to find and keep girls (in the best Ovidian manner).[96] More specifically, the *Pamphilus* tells how a girl of rank and wealth is won by a young man who has neither,[97] but this pattern of social as well as sexual aspiration is not present in either of those other two *comediae*. It may be added that, although beast lore was widely used in the elementary classroom (one thinks of the *Physiologus* and Aesop's fables), in his *Bestiaires d'amours* Richard de Fournival seems quite uninterested in the age of the lover.

We are on firmer ground, I believe, with the more general proposition, as presaged earlier in this chapter, that the end of the *Rose* has as a potential didactic function the illustration and advocacy of that heterosexual behaviour which is the cultural norm. This text is about what might be termed 'masculation', by which I mean the process of 'becoming male'.[98] Specifically, the *signe d'estre malles* signify the integrity and wholeness of true masculinity, which expresses and realizes itself in *coitus;* required social behaviour is affirmed through the performance of sexual normality.[99] Little wonder, then, that at the climax of Jean's text the female figure is shadowy and unrealized, as in the Latin *comediae*; the *rite de passage* is not hers but her male lover's, and vicariously that of the text's male readers. Given the medical belief that the female had to take pleasure in intercourse in order to produce seed, it could be inferred that the Rose enjoyed her sexual experience—but even if this inference were granted such feeling would be minute in comparison with Jean's

---

[96] As could be, and was, said of the *Pamphilus*; cf. Woods, 'Rape and Pedagogical Rhetoric', p. 70.   [97] As Woods notes: ibid. 70–1.

[98] For a recent major contribution to comprehension of this complicated phenomenon, see Cohen and Wheeler (eds.) *Becoming Male in the Middle Ages*. The collection includes three essays on Abelard's post-castration projection of his own masculinity, by Martin Irvine, Bonnie Wheeler and Yves Ferroul. According to Irvine, Abelard was concerned to remasculate himself 'with new imagined objects of wholeness', whereas in Wheeler's view Abelard, with Heloise's complicity, consistently represents himself as fully masculine. See further Clare A. Lees (ed.), *Medieval Masculinities: Regarding Men in the Middle Ages* (Minneapolis, 1994), and of course the foundational study by Eve Kosofsky Sedgwick, *Between Men: English Literature and Male Homosocial Desire* (New York, 1985).

[99] Amant is in no doubt of what Birria and Geta (in the *Amphitrion*) took some time to realize, that successful heterosexual intercourse is incumbent on 'being a man': cf. p. 180 above.

extensive and explicit (if oblique) account of male pleasure.[100] In the text's performance of masculinity the spotlight must fall exclusively on Amant, and the more passive and objectified the woman, the better that effect may be achieved. *A la conclusion tient tout.* The end is every tale's strength, and it is male strength which is the chosen subject of this ending.[101]

Here, then, is something which can be said to have survived the transition from school pedagogy. In the homosocial[102] world of the classroom in which Latin literacy was taught, heterosexual desire was, paradoxically enough, actively encouraged as a means of preparing boys and male adolescents for adulthood. Texts like the *Ars amatoria* and *Pamphilus* served this purpose well. Control of desire was also on the agenda, of course, an objective supposedly furthered by the *Remedia amoris*. Revealingly, in her *Epistre au dieu d'Amours* Christine de Pizan has the God condemn the teaching of this text in grammar school, since here Ovid maligns women, thereby giving clerics a means of warning their pupils against the female sex.[103] The central point here is emphasized wonderfully in George Sewell's eighteenth-century translation of Thomas Hoccleve's Middle English version of Christine's poem. 'These wicked Clerks', Sewell declares, teach boys

> To shun their [i.e. women's] Charms, and hate the Sex betimes;
> Of guilty Maids, and Lovers lost, enroll
> A canting, lying, lamentable Scroll.

---

[100] Cf. Peter of Spain, who tortuously argues that in the sex act male pleasure is more intense than female. Women may enjoy sex in more ways than men do, but the sum total of their pleasure is less. See Wack, *Lovesickness*, pp. 116–17.

[101] I am reading Amant's amatory apotheosis in a way very similar to Ralph Hexter's characterization of the 'Ovid' of *De Vetula* as a figure who is obsessed with his virility; cf. Hexter's account of this text's 'fiercely normalizing discourse' in 'Ovid's Body', p. 341. According to some *accessūs* Ovid witnessed the Emperor Augustus engaging in a homosexual act—this being one of the possible reasons for his exile. Such accounts no doubt contributed to Ovid's reputation as a champion of normative sexuality. Francis Petrarch was going against this grain when he complained about Ovid's 'female weakness of spirit'—but it should also be noted that the *Antiovidianus* takes the poet to task for his long complaints about his exile in the *Tristia*. Cf. Hexter, *Ovid and Medieval Schooling*, pp. 96–7; 'Ovid's Body', pp. 335, 342–3.					[102] On this concept see p. 205 below.

[103] *Poems of Cupid*, ed. Fenster and Erler, pp. 48–9.

Thus ev'ry Boy of some false Nymph can tell,
And curses Woman, as he learns to spell.

$$(252-6)^{104}$$

The clerks wanted their pupils to have 'normal' sexual feelings, yet remain chaste or continent.[105] Thus merely literary ladies (those feigned 'false Nymphs') performed a useful educational function, whereas real women presented a threat. Boys and adolescent males were being told that in some measure they should despise the very thing they were being encouraged to want, curse the mandatory channel for their desire. In 'the adult and mixed gender world of the vernacular' (to borrow another phrase from Woods)[106] such mixed signals became even more confusing. Here, then, is a clue to the puzzle of the end of the *Rose*. As in the case of the vernacular *Pamphilus*, the humour is unsure of its adherents and its targets alike. Lacking its original locus, it can hardly perform a higher ludic function in the service of an accepted pedagogic goal.

My emphasis on the *Rose's* concluding affirmation of its heteronormative agenda should not, however, be taken as denying the possibility that earlier parts of the narrative may hint at homoerotic possibilities. Critical interest in this question has focused on the male gender of Bel Acueil. In the most substantial analysis to date, Simon Gaunt has suggested that the text 'forces us to pay attention to the literal plot here, which has Amant courting another man, and it therefore generates conflict between the literal (homosexual) and the allegorical (heterosexual) plots'.[107] Such conflicts between literal and allegorical values were, to be sure, a common feature of late medieval allegoresis.[108] For example, in a standard medieval interpretation of the Orpheus story, literally Aristaeus is a rapist while allegorically he is virtue trying to join itself to (and elevate) concupiscence; in the biblical narrative of David and Bathsheba,

---

[104] *The Proclamation of Cupid*, in *Poems of Cupid*, ed. Fenster and Erler, p. 230.
[105] And those who thought of entering the priesthood were faced with the paradox (on a certain reading of Levi. 22: 24 and Deut. 23: 1) that possession of testicles was necessary even though their sexual use was forbidden. See n. 85 above.
[106] Woods, 'Rape and Pedagogical Rhetoric', p. 72.
[107] 'Bel Acueil and Improper Allegory', p. 69.
[108] Here 'allegory' is being used in a broad sense to encompass integumental writing, allegory of the kind found in the Bible, and indeed aspects of 'personification allegory' or prosopopoeia.

literally the lady's husband, Uriah, is a loyal and courageous warrior who is sent to his doom by his rival in love, while allegorically he signifies the devil or the Jews, standard enemies of the Christian church.[109] Hence it could be argued that Jean de Meun was engaged in a typical allegorical practice which provoked no particular anxiety. Against this, however, it may be noted that certain medieval thinkers did worry about the discrepancies between literal and allegorical significance,[110] and therefore it could be claimed that such difference was a source of daring indeterminacies for an ambitious poet. Indeed, as already noted, at one point Jean de Meun jocularly has Amant address Lady Raison as a well-bred girl who should not be talking dirty.[111] (Had Boethius sought the same effect, no doubt his I-*persona* in *De consolatione philosophiae* would have told Lady Philosophy that she should not be worrying her pretty little head about difficult matters like free will and predestination.) But this can hardly be regarded as daring indeterminacy. The provocation of subversive ambiguity in the sphere of sexual relations, in contrast, would probably have been regarded as a high-risk strategy.

Of course, it is perfectly possible to invoke Louis Althusser's dictum that often literature is 'overdetermined' and can textualize far more than the sum of its determinations. But if, on the other hand, emphasis is placed on the actual semantic array which is possible or plausible within a given culture, then certain checks and balances are inevitably put in place for interpretation of texts which were produced within that culture. We would not, I trust, wish to argue that the teaching/preaching accomplishments of Lady Nature (implicating her as a sort of priest or *papissa*) call in question the ubiquitous ecclesiastical prohibition of the ordination of women.[112] Or, by the same

---

[109] See Minnis and Scott, *Medieval Literary Theory*, pp. 207–8.
[110] Ibid. 208.   [111] Cf. Ch. 3 above, pp. 126–7.
[112] On the issues here raised see Alcuin Blamires, 'Women and Preaching in Medieval Orthodoxy, Heresy, and Saint's Lives', *Viator*, 26 (1995), 135–52; and A. J. Minnis, '*De impedimento sexus*: Women's Bodies and Medieval Impediments to Female Ordination', in Peter Biller and A. J. Minnis (eds.), *Medieval Theology and the Natural Body* (York, 1997), pp. 109–39. On the (utterly fictitious, in my view) *papissa* 'Pope Joan' see Valerie R. Hotchkiss, 'The Female Pope and the Sin of Male Disguise', in her *Clothes Make the Man: Female Cross Dressing in Medieval Europe* (New York, 1996), pp. 69–82. The case for Joan's historical existence has been made (eloquently but incredibly) by Peter Stanford, *The She-Pope: A Quest for the Truth behind the Mystery of Pope Joan* (London, 1998).

token, that the authority which Boethius afforded Lady Philosophy is a subtle challenge to that male hegemony which dominated the Christian church of his day. Prosopopoeiac gender can hardly be afforded significance which flies in the face of the cultural master discourses at work in a given medieval text. In the case of the *Rose*, I believe, the poem's master discourse of heteronormativity strives to keep any suggestion of sexual deviance in check; the *signe d'estre malles* demand to be read straight.[113]

However, it is, I think, perfectly possible to ground a homo*social* reading in parts of the *Rose*, including certain passages which define Amant's relationship with both Ami and Bel Acueil. As Eve Kosofsky Sedgwick has argued,[114] this term may usefully be applied to 'male bonding' of a kind which is characterized by fear, and indeed hatred, of homosexuality. In the *Rose* a homosocial bond certainly exists between Amant and Ami, and indeed can be claimed for aspects of the relationship between Amant and Bel Acueil; in both cases their mutual maleness is affirmed through the shared perception of the Rose as contrast, absent, other. Bel Acueil often acts out the role of friend, saying and doing things which would be appropriate behaviour for Ami. Amant declares that Ami 'mon avancement / voisist autresi bien con gié' ['desired my success as much as I did'] (3201–3). In similar vein, Bel Acueil is depicted as doing all he can to help Amant. For example, following Franchise's intervention he leads the lover (once more) into the enclosed garden and is described as taking pains to please him (3337–8). When Amant asks to be allowed to kiss the Rose, Bel Acueil addresses him as 'friend' ('Amis', 3377) but is reluctant to help. Then Venus appears, carrying her torch—which specifically is said to have warmed many a lady ('dont la flame / a eschaufee

---

[113] To be sure, this process was not universally successful. As Gaunt demonstrates (in his 'Bel Acueil and Improper Allegory'), some of the early scribes and illuminators did respond to the text's homoerotic suggestions, either by developing or suppressing them, though such reactions may be deemed the exception rather than the rule. If the *Rose*'s two most astringent critics, Christine de Pizan and Jean Gerson, had suspected anything of the kind, one can assume that they would have made it the object of vociferous attack. Here one may recall Gerson's 'terror of homosexuality', as B. P. McGuire has termed it (cf. below, Ch. 5, n. 135); the fact that he did not detect any homoerotic play in the poem is quite telling.

[114] In her highly influential monograph *Between Men* (cited in note 98 above).

mainte dame', 3407–8)[115]—and proceeds to win over Bel Acueil with her eloquence. To be sure, it is Bel Acueil who listens to Venus' recommendation of Amant's handsome mouth and sweet breath—hardly surprisingly, given that the Rose herself/itself is mute and incapable of response. (The objectification of the woman as flower caused considerable technical problems and stylistic difficulties for the *Rose* poets, here as elsewhere.)[116] And Bel Acueil certainly feels the warmth of that torch (3455–6) which only a few lines earlier had been seen as provoking desire in women only. Yet it is clearly the Rose which is kissed: 'un besier douz et savoré / pris de la rose erraument' ['I immediately took from the rose a sweet and delicious kiss'] (3460–1). It may be noted that in this same episode the 'female' Jalousie performs such male roles as ordering the construction of a castle to protect the Rose, garrisoning it, and capturing and imprisoning Bel Acueil. Consequently it may be more acceptable to hear Amant exclaim that Bel Acueil should keep his heart for him even though his body is imprisoned—an expression which, in any case, may be read as keeping well within the conventional parameters of *amicitia*, which often accommodated far more eroticized discourse than this.[117]

---

[115] In her translation Frances Horgan suggests that 'Venus appears here as the personification of feminine desire' (p. 338). See further Kay, 'Venus in the *Rose*', who argues that in the poem 'Venus is specifically identified ... with women's desire; she thus carries through the text the principle of sexual difference whose inauguration her birth represents' (p. 22). However, Kay goes on to argue that Venus can also destabilize 'the notion of sexual difference at the same time as she insinuates it'. 'She is made not only from a male [i.e. Saturn, in the fable of the birth of Venus] but from that which defines his maleness: his *virilia*. . . . What sense can we make of sexual difference if woman erases men's masculinity and then goes on to embody it herself?' (pp. 26–7).

[116] A point brought out well by Brownlee, 'Multiple Endings of the *Rose*', pp. 194–6, 207–8.

[117] See e.g. the discussion of carnal and spiritual kisses in book 2, ss. 21–7 of that primary source of Raison's theory of friendship, Aelred of Rievaulx's *De spirituali amicitia*. On Jean's use of Aelred, see L. J. Friedman, 'Jean de Meun and Ethelred of Rievaulx', *L'Esprit Createur*, 2 (1962), 135–41. As is well known, St Bernard and William of St Thierry drew shocking metaphors from the Song of Songs to express the strength of monastic friendship. For discussion see A. Fiske, *Friends and Friendship in the Monastic Tradition* (Cuernavaca, 1970). On late-medieval notions of friendship, particularly as influenced by books 8 and 9 of Aristotle's *Ethics*, see J. J. McEvoy, 'The Theory of Friendship in the Latin Middle Ages', in Julian Haseldine (ed.), *Friendship in Medieval Europe* (Stroud, 1999), pp. 3–44 (esp. pp. 13–15, 25–8).

For all these reasons, I believe that Amant, like 'Ovid' in the *De Vetula*, functions as 'a purposive and embodied erotic agent' of utterly conventional sexuality 'whereby men dominate women and gain their own subjectivity by that means'.[118] But, whatever the truth of this matter may be, we can, I hope, at least agree that the meaning of works like the *Rose*, the Latin *comediae*, and the above-mentioned productions of Richard de Fournival is highly elusive, and very much subject to interpretation by different textual communities both past and present. Little wonder, then, that a large part of the medieval reception of Jean de Meun's poem took the form of an attempt to prune the *Rose*, to gain control over it by singling out certain aspects of its significance. Various attempts at retrospective closure were made; in each case, however, what was being closed was somewhat at variance with what Jean had actually written (cf. pp. 258–60 below). However, the *Rose* itself (inasmuch as one can speak of it in the singular) obstinately resists closure, largely on account of its refusal to pursue any single self-authorizing strategy long enough for it to be determinate, or to invest heavily enough in any one genre.

And that resistance, that refusal, is in large measure abetted by Jean de Meun's terminal humour. Despite the precedent offered by 'the clerk Ovid'[119] as mock-*magister* of love, and the centrality of donnish humour to intellectual culture, laughter at—and in—love lacked exegesis.[120] Commentators could say of Ovid's *Ars amatoria*, 'in hoc opere ludicra tractat et iocosa', but that was as far as the inquiry went, despite the widely known Aristotelian definition of man as the only 'laughing animal', *homo ludens*.[121] The concept of an *auctor ludens*, like the related concept of an *auctor amans*,[122] failed to achieve full definition and rationalization. In medieval literary theory it

---

[118] Cf. Hexter, 'Ovid's Body', p. 343, who also describes this 'Ovid' as a 'Don Juan' figure.

[119] As John Gower terms him in *Confessio amantis*, i. 2274.

[120] Here of course I am leaving aside the issue of satiric wit and derision, since (as argued above) much of the humour in the *Rose* and other clerkly texts is not confined within such parameters.

[121] On which see esp. the classic study by Johan Huizinga, *Homo Ludens: A Study of the Play Element in Culture* (London, 1970).

[122] On the medieval problematics of being (or wishing to be) an *auctor* whilst actually being in love, see Minnis, 'Authors in Love'.

remained shadowy, risqué, suffering the suspicion of being a contradiction in terms. At the end of the *Rose* the poem's crisis of masculinity may basically have been resolved (however imperfectly), but other questions remain unanswered, perhaps unanswerable.

CHAPTER 5

Theorizing the Rose: *Crises of Textual Authority in the* Querelle de la Rose

During the period 1401–3 occurred the famous *querelle de la Rose*, in which Jean Gerson, august theologian and powerful chancellor of the University of Paris, and the 'proto-feminist' Christine de Pizan were ranged against three 'early humanists', the Col brothers, Pierre and Gontier, and Jean de Montreuil, provost of Lisle. The very same battles have been fought over again during the past forty years, Jean de Meun having found vigorous advocates in the persons of D.W. Robertson Jr. and John Fleming, who have followed their fifteenth-century counterparts in taking the line that the *Rose* functions as a rigorous *remedium amoris*, the voice of the author being the voice of reason—and specifically, of Jean's figure Raison.[1]

---

[1] Robertson, in his *Preface to Chaucer*, laments that an 'irate woman' and a 'zealous reformer' were 'not to be silenced by reason', and regards their views as essentially anti-humanistic (p. 364). Similarly, John Fleming declares that Christine de Pizan's 'part in the Quarrel has been rather inflated, one suspects, by modern feminists and should probably not be taken too seriously'. Like Robertson, he believes that in the history of criticism of the *Rose* the rot set in with Jean Gerson's misunderstanding: 'He was the first modern critic of the *Roman*, the first person to whom it must patiently be explained that Jean de Meun was a "true catholic, the most profound theologian of his day, versed in every science which the human kind can grasp" ' (*Allegory and Iconography*, p. 47; his quotation is from Gontier Col: see *Le Débat*, ed. Hicks, p. 9; cf. p. 1 above).The opponents of the *Rose* were, however, ably defended by J. L. Baird and J. R. Kane, '*La Querelle de la Rose*: In Defense of the Opponents', *French Review*, 48.2 (1974), 298–307. Douglas Kelly, in his *Medieval Imagination: Rhetoric and the Poetry of Courtly Love* (Madison, Wis., 1978), p. 262 n. 23, and Badel, *Rose au XIVe siècle*, pp. 411–82, offer more balanced assessments. 'There was a certain amount of bad rhetoric on both sides,' suggests Kelly, 'and ignorance and misunderstanding of what both Guillaume de Lorris and Jean de Meun intended.' The bibliography on Christine is vast, and expanding rapidly, important work having been done by, among others, Susan

The position of the attackers of the *Rose* has been supposed to mark 'a most decisive break with the traditions of medieval humanism': 'From this time forward humanists would find themselves frequently put on the defensive by the attacks of the righteous.'[2] This approach is, however, somewhat misleading, in that Jean's friends and foes alike drew on one and the same corpus of literary theory, the product of late medieval scholasticism, as found in the commentaries on classroom authorities. This theory is at the centre of both the *Rose* supporters' attempts to authorize the text and its attackers' vigorous efforts to refute that very claim. It is the aim of this chapter to explore that intellectual common ground, and hence to illuminate the significance of the various appropriations and adaptations of Latin critical discourse which occurred in the *querelle*. The standard medieval criticism of Ovid will figure largely in our inquiry, since it is evident that those who loved the *Rose* and those who loathed it could agree on one thing at least—Jean de Meun was a 'Medieval Ovid', for better or worse, as it were. However, Jean's best advocate, the eloquent Pierre Col, was not content to bracket his author with the ancient *magister amoris*: he endeavoured to go one better by invoking the precedent of biblical lovers, a daring—but certainly not unparalleled—move, which will involve us in a brief foray into scriptural exegesis. We shall begin with a discussion of the terms of engagement with which this battle of the books was fought, and then move on to consider the use of *persona* theory in the *querelle*, since this matter has received much attention in both the old and the new phases of the controversy, and is a major determinant of critical judgements regarding the success or failure of the opposing positions.

Croag Bell, Maureen Curnow, Sheila Delany, Nadia Margolis, Gianni Mombello, E. Jeffrey Richards, and Charity Willard. Their interests and objectives are, however, different from those of this chapter. Suffice it to say that I am in broad agreement with the views of Susan Schibanoff, 'Taking the Gold out of Egypt: The Art of Reading as a Woman', in E. Flynn and P. Schweikehart (eds.), *Gender and Reading* (Baltimore, 1986), pp. 83–106; Beatrice Gottlieb, 'The Problem of Feminism in the Fifteenth Century', in J. Kirshner and S. F. Wemple (eds.), *Women of the Medieval World* (Oxford, 1985), pp. 337–62; Maureen Quilligan, *The Allegory of Female Authority: Christine de Pizan's 'Cité des dames'* (Ithaca, NY, 1991); Kevin Brownlee, 'Discourses of the Self: Christine de Pizan and the *Romance of the Rose*', in Brownlee and Huot (eds.), *Rethinking the Rose*, pp. 234–61; and Brown-Grant, *Moral Defence* (see esp. her summation on p. 219).

2 Robertson, *Preface to Chaucer*, p. 364.

Debat gracieux, campus duelli? *The terms of engagement*

In an early letter in the *querelle de la Rose*, written to an unidentified church dignitary, Jean de Montreuil seems genuinely
puzzled about the rules of the game, which terms of engagement
are in play. He wonders if his addressee had argued 'in jest'
(*ioco protuleris*) about the *Rose*, and then appeals to male
knowingness about the licensed give-and-take of scholastic
disputatio: 'we are not so severe that we do not appreciate the
freedom of exchange permissible in debate (*disputando libertas*)
or do not know how to be indulgent toward exchange of
words'.[3] In another letter, apparently to the same correspondent, de Montreuil reiterates this point: 'we are . . . aware how
far the license of disputation (*disputandi licentia*) extends and
how often the early morning disputation contradicts the conclusions of the evening before'.[4] Quite extreme and outlandish
views could be tolerated in academic debate, providing that one
affirmed one's own (orthodox) point of view in the *determina-
tio* or *responsio*; furthermore, the same texts (*auctoritates*)
could be alleged in support of diametrically opposed positions,
and arguments could be adopted or rejected at will, depending
on the priority of proof on a given occasion. Generally speaking, the whole enterprise was conducted in an impersonal,
routinely professional manner (though on occasion individual
animus did perturb the role-playing). Little wonder, then, that
'the intelligentsia' sometimes regarded 'the rhetorical formulae
of misogyny as a game', in so far as it provided 'a suitable arena
in which to show off their literary paces'.[5] An excellent example is provided by the position-switching of Jean Le Fèvre. His
French translation (*c.*1371–2) of the extravagantly anti-feminist
Lamentationes of Matheolus seems to be the text which
Christine de Pizan famously castigated at the beginning of her
Livre de la Cité des dames, one of her most trenchant criticisms

---

[3] Letter 118 (*Quo magis*), in *Le Débat*, ed. Hicks, p. 30; trans. Baird and Kane,
p. 43.
[4] Letter *Etsi facundissimus*, in *Le Débat*, ed. Hicks, p. 38; trans. Baird and Kane,
pp. 44–5.
[5] Alcuin Blamires (ed.), *Woman Defamed and Woman Defended* (Oxford,
1992), p. 12.

being that it trivialized important matters, treated its subject frivolously ('en manière de trufferie').[6] This may mean that she regarded Le Fèvre as being more interested in showing off his debating skills (by learnedly treating a risqué and/or supposedly ridiculous subject) than in seeking out the truth about women. It is surely significant that, in his *Livre de Leesce,* Le Fèvre systematically refuted Matheolus' misogynistic arguments with the same enthusiasm and academic acumen which he had shown in presenting them.[7] Similarly, in the *Liber decem capitulorum* of Marbod of Rennes (*c.*1035–1123), a chapter on the destructive woman is followed by one on the good woman, and in two of its manuscripts the thirteenth-century *Blasme des Fames* is accompanied by the *Bien des Fames.*[8] Such texts seem to fall well within the remit of the regular *disputandi licentia.*

In marked contrast, there is a definite edge to much of the argument in the *querelle de la Rose.* Writing to Guillaume de Tignonville, Christine initially describes the quarrel as a 'debat gracieux et non haineux',[9] but goes on to call it a 'war (*guerre*)' undertaken 'against powerful and strong men'.[10] In similar vein, Gontier Col refers to the controversy as a 'field of battle (*campus duelli*)'.[11] Often the jibes and provocations seem to be all too personal, and the conventions of civility slip to reveal real anger. 'What so greatly irritates me is that they attack our master with insults,' complains Jean de Montreuil,[12] but he

---

[6] Cf. Blamires (ed.), *Woman Defamed,* p. 177. See further Renate Blumenfeld-Kosinski, 'Christine de Pizan and the Misogynistic Tradition', *Romanic Review,* 81 (1990), 279–92.

[7] On the relationship between these two works, see esp. Renate Blumenfeld-Kosinski, 'Jean Le Fèvre's *Livre de Leesce*: Praise or Blame of Women?', *Speculum,* 69 (1994), 705–25. As she notes, Le Fèvre's protestation that he had merely translated 'Ce que j'ay en latin trouvé' is highly reminiscent of Jean de Meun's apologetic argument at *Rose,* 15185–94. Jean de Meun is linked with Juvenal and Ovid as allies of 'Master Matheolus' (p. 721–2). More generally, see Karen Pratt, 'Analogy or logic; authority or experience? Rhetorical Strategies for and against Women', in Donald Maddox and Sara S. Maddox (eds.), *Literary Aspects of Courtly Culture: Selected Proceedings from the Seventh Triennial Congress of the International Courtly Literature Society* (Cambridge, 1994), pp. 57–66.

[8] Blamires, *Woman Defamed,* pp. 100–3; *Three Medieval Views of Women,* ed. and trans. G. K. Fiero, W. Pfeffer, and M. Allain (New Haven, Conn., 1989).

[9] *Le Débat,* ed. Hicks, p. 7. Baird and Kane rather loosely translate the phrase as 'good humoured debate' (p. 67).

[10] *Le Débat,* ed. Hicks, p. 8; trans. Baird and Kane, p. 68.

[11] *Le Débat,* ed. Hicks, p. 34; trans. Baird and Kane, p. 167.

[12] *Le Débat,* ed. Hicks, p. 32; trans. Baird and Kane, p. 166.

himself is adept at dishing them out, as when he describes Christine as sounding like the 'Greek whore (*meretrix*)' who 'dared to criticize the great philosopher Theophrastus'.[13] The ostensible point of the comparison is that Christine's intellectual powers are simply not up to the task she has taken on—but the misogynistic stereotyping is blatant, and recurs throughout the *querelle*.[14] Gontier Col calls her a 'femme passionnee' ['impassioned woman'] who has acted out of 'presompcion ou oultrecuidance' ['presumption or arrogance'];[15] maybe she was pushed into the affair by men who did not dare, or rather did not know how, to handle such a matter.[16] Even the term 'femme' becomes an insult to be hurled at Christine.[17] The sexual politics of the quarrel also extend to Jean Gerson—at one point Pierre Col goes so far as to question his manhood.[18] On such occasions *matiere de rire* is in short supply.[19]

By the same token, a model of debate which is elaborately fictionalized in the *Jugement du roy de Navarre* of Guillaume de Machaut, a poet in whose work the influence of the *Rose* is often writ large, is of limited applicability to the *querelle*. After a truly horrific account of the ravages of the plague, the fortunate narrator celebrates his survival by engaging in a debate on the nature of women—the pretext being that his earlier poem, the *Jugement du Roy de Behaigne*, presented the sex unfavourably—with a female figure named Bonneürte (meaning, and to some extent

[13] *Le Débat*, ed. Hicks, p. 42; trans. Baird and Kane, p. 153.

[14] Cf. the remark of Pierre Col who, in warning Christine that she has gone too far in deploying her talents against so great an author as Jean de Meun, compares her to the crow of the fable who sang too loudly and lost its supper (*Le Débat*, ed. Hicks, p. 100). As Brown-Grant says, this animal image 'recalls those frequently employed in misogynist texts to denigrate female speech' (*Moral Defence*, p. 22). In similar vein, Pierre advises Christine to 'keep your teeth to yourself!' (*Le Débat*, ed. Hicks, p. 100; trans. Baird and Kane, p. 103).

[15] *Le Débat*, ed. Hicks, p. 23; trans. Baird and Kane, p. 61.

[16] *Le Débat*, ed. Hicks, p. 10; trans. Baird and Kane, p. 58.

[17] Cf. Brown-Grant, *Moral Defence*, p. 22.

[18] See above, pp. 194–5.

[19] For this phrase see *Le Débat*, ed. Hicks, p. 20; trans. Baird and Kane, p. 54. Furthermore, I fail to see how Christine's part in the *querelle de la Rose* can be seen as a half-comic pose adopted for the occasion without serious intent, as is suggested by Fleming, *Allegory and Iconography*, p. 47. On the other hand, to talk of her 'usually sound, and almost always quite charming, arguments' is to miss the point by a (patronizing) mile; here I cite the introduction by Baird and Kane to their translation of the *querelle* documents, pp. 16–17.

personifying, 'Good Fortune' and 'Happiness'). The lady recognizes the Machaut construct as being knowledgeable about those sorts of merriment (*joileté*) 'which accord with morality (*honesté*)', and she sends her squire to bring him to her—after he has, however, prepared the poet for an amicable encounter. 'If you know anything about debating,' the I-*persona* is warned, 'you'll be good in this situation, for you'll have to play the advocate's role' (730–2).[20] The two male figures converse pleasantly, debating in these terms and with such game amusing themselves: 'De si fais mos nous debatiens, / Par gieu si nous en esbatiens' (735–6). When Bonneürte's interest is revealed, the narrator readily agrees to a disputation which he sees as providing joyful entertainment:

> . . . ce sera uns biaus mestiers
> D'oïr les raisons repeter
> Et les parties desputer
> Soutilment, par biaus argumens . . .
>   (1084–7)

> [. . . it will be a pleasant task
> To hear the arguments rehearsed
> And the parties dispute
> With subtlety, with pretty distinctions . . .]

For her part, the lady laughingly agrees to enter into the debate, 'however it might turn out' (1089–93). This is not to deny that serious issues are canvassed in the verses that follow, and I certainly do not want to compromise the subtleties of the *Navarre* by simplistically contrasting it with the *querelle de la Rose*. However, it seems fair to say that Machaut offers in abundance what is markedly absent from the *querelle*—'debat gracieux et non haineux'. In the *Navarre* the emphasis is on the 'biaus' nature of the discussion rather than on its weight. And the respectful final judgement (that women love longer and better than men) clearly indicates its distance from the level of seriousness which at its best the *querelle* can reach.

Gerson and Christine shared a vision of the good, Christian society, which had to be protected from such challenges to morality and respectability as those allegedly mounted by the

---

[20] *Judgment of the King of Navarre*, ed. and trans. Palmer, pp. 32–3.

Rose. But it would be quite wrong to regard their views as inter-changeable; these attackers had rather different interests and agendas.[21] Gerson writes very much as the learned Latin scholar, a trained theologian used to teasing out many *sensūs* and levels of meaning from biblical passages. It is quite ridicu-lous, he declared, to suggest that Jean de Meun 'wrote a great many good things, many of which are far above the general knowledge of all learned men and require, therefore, a ten-fold reading before they are understood'.[22] He seems genuinely angry at the implication that he has had difficulty in under-standing the *Rose*. Bonaventure's small book the *Itinerarium mentis in Deum*, which he read in a day, contains as much profound knowledge as the *Rose*, along with ten books like it, 'Yet you believe us to be too brutish and too dense to be able to understand this book of yours'. To Pierre Col's insulting sugges-tion that he should read the *Rose* again to understand it, he answers: 'Read, brother, and read again the fourth book of *De doctrina christiana*, for that work poses a great many more problems than your book in French (*in vulgari*).'[23]

Christine's education and cultural formation were, of course, very different from Gerson's. Her father, the court astrologer Tommaso da Pizzano, might have given his daughter as well as his sons a Latin education. This, however, is speculation, and the level of Christine's Latinity is a particularly vexed issue. In my view, the fact that she preferred to use vernacular translations/adaptations of Latin texts rather than the *originalia*—for example, the *Ovide moralisé* rather than the *Metamorphoses*—need not be taken as evidence of linguistic inadequacy. Having chosen to write in French, there were good practical reasons to follow models of learned and/or rhetorically

[21] Blanche H. Dow speaks of Christine's 'intellectual as well as temperamental' unanimity with Gerson; of 'a complete communion of ideas between them': *The Varying Attitude toward Women in French Literature of the Fifteenth Century: The Opening Years* (New York, 1936), p. 142. However, the position of D. Catherine Brown seems to be more accurate; she indicates the differences between the two opponents of the *Rose*, emphasizing that 'Gerson's attack . . . is much more that of the moralist than the feminist': *Pastor and Laity in the Theology of Jean Gerson* (Cambridge, 1987), pp. 224–5.
[22] *Responsio ad scripta cuiusdam*, in *Le Débat*, ed. Hicks, p. 166; trans. Baird and Kane, p. 147.
[23] *Responsio*, in *Le Débat*, ed Hicks, p. 174; trans. Baird and Kane, p. 151.

proficient vernacular discourse. (One may compare Chaucer's use of Jean de Meun's French Boethius in his own version of the *Consolatio philosophiae*.) Furthermore, her privileging of vernacular sources can be seen as a political act, a means of endorsing the value of the French productions. Christine's comment on Charles V's Latinity may reveal some of her own attitudes: 'although he understood Latin well, he wanted to have them [the translations] so that his heirs might be moved to virtue', and 'those who did not understand Latin would become knowledgeable' (*Livre du chemin de long estude*, 5022–6).[24] At the very least, Christine was able to read the Latin documents in the *querelle de la Rose*, draw on Thomas of Ireland's *Manipulus florum*, and translate the *Heures de contemplation* from Latin into French.[25] Most remarkable of all is the fact that she incorporated material into her *Avision* from Thomas Aquinas' commentary on Aristotle's *Metaphysics*.[26]

Whatever the level or extent of her learning, Christine seems to have decided that it was in her best interests to play it down (that being a major reason why modern scholarship has so little to go on). She presents herself as being neither learned nor schooled in subtle language, then goes on to declare that she 'will not hesitate to express' her 'opinion bluntly in the vernacular (*en gros vulgar l'oppinion de mon entente*)'.[27] She is no logician ('je ne suis logicienne'), she confesses to Pierre Col, making this at once an explanation and a justification for her direct treatment of the matter at hand: 'Without more ado, I will answer this bluntly (*sans passer oultre*)'.[28] Thus, Christine constructs herself as a straight-talking vernacular writer, who

[24] For discussion and bibliography, see Thelma Fenster, ' "Perdre son latin": Christine de Pizan and Vernacular Humanism', in Marilynn Desmond (ed.), *Christine de Pizan and the Categories of Difference* (Minneapolis, 1998), pp. 91–107 (esp. pp. 93–4).

[25] Ibid. 92–3.

[26] See Liliane Dulac and Christine Reno, 'L'Humanisme vers 1400, essai d'exploration à partir d'un cas marginal: Christine de Pizan, traductrice de Thomas d'Aquin', in Monique Ornato and Nicole Pons (eds.), *Pratiques de la culture écrite en France au XVe siècle: Actes du Colloque international du CNRS, Paris 16–18 mai 1992* (Louvain-la-Neuve, 1995), pp. 160–78.

[27] Letter *Reverence, honneur avec recommandacion*, in *Le Débat*, ed. Hicks, p. 12; trans. Baird and Kane, p. 47.

[28] Letter *Pour ce que entendement*, in *Le Débat*, ed. Hicks, p. 117; trans. Baird and Kane, p. 117.

cannot compete with the learned subtleties and stylistic adorn-
ments of the masters' language—the emphasis clearly falling on
the fact that what is being said is more important than how it is
being said. That, to be sure, was a formula commonly employed
by medieval preachers (and writers of preachers' handbooks),
who affirmed the importance of putting clear sense before elaborate rhetoric. But Christine has made the commonplace her
own—indeed, feminized it. For interconnected with it are artful
professions of womanly weakness, as when she tells the queen
of France that although she is weak to lead the attack against
such subtle masters (*soubtilz maistres*), her small wit (*entendement*) has chosen to employ itself in disputing (*a debatre*) with
those who attack and accuse women.[29] Her very womanliness
is a major weapon, medieval constructions of femininity being
deployed to good advantage.[30]

'De tant comme voirement suis femme, plus puis resmoing-
nier en ceste partie que cellui qui n'en a l'experience,' she firmly
tells Jean de Montreuil; 'because I am a woman I can speak
better in this matter than one who has not had the experience'.
In contrast, Jean de Meun could know nothing about the
married state *par experience*.[31] Such passages present Christine
as claiming the authority of experience. She responds from her
own particular subject-position as a woman, Pierre Col is
assured, and hence in this case can speak 'verité de certainne
science' ['the truth from certain knowledge'].[32] Belittling her
own literary efforts (she may perhaps have 'gathered some
lowly little flowers from the garden of delights'), and suggesting
that people were amazed by them not because of their greatness
but rather on account of their novelty value (i.e. the fact that a
woman could write in this way at all was marvellous), she
rejects any suggestion that she laid claim to any *auctorité* in her

[29] Letter *Tres haulte*, in *Le Débat*, ed. Hicks, p. 6; trans. Baird and Kane, p. 66.
[30] As Quilligan says, 'instead of confronting misogyny's essentialism head-on, she
redeploys it for her own purposes': *Allegory of Female Authority*, p. 45. See further
Brown-Grant, *Moral Defence*, pp. 17–28, and Brownlee's argument that Christine
was 'the first French literary figure who explicitly incorporated her identity as a
woman into her identity as an author': 'Discourses of the Self', p. 234.
[31] Letter *Reverence, honneur avec recommandacion*, in *Le Débat*, ed. Hicks, pp.
18–19; trans. Baird and Kane, pp. 52–3.
[32] Letter *Pour ce que entendement*, in *Le Débat*, ed. Hicks, p. 148; trans. Baird
and Kane, p. 143.

work.[33] Not pride but the desire to right a wrong, to refute those who ignorantly or maliciously wrote against the female sex, is her professed motivation (though it should be noted that this forms part of a larger discourse, which is driven by Christian ideals of public morality and social control). As a literary strategy, it is highly effective and artfully done. Male writers often apologized ostentatiously for their weak wit and inadequate rhetoric—that in itself being a recognizable rhetorical device. Christine cleverly appropriated and adapted those modesty topoi. Such artfulness need not lead into specious debate as to whether she was merely using the *querelle* to further her own ambitions as a professional writer.[34] She can hardly be criticized for stylistic practices and self-promoting behaviour (economic necessity being, on her own account, a major consideration) of kinds which generations of medievalists have deemed to be perfectly acceptable in the case of male writers.[35]

[33] *Le Débat*, ed. Hicks, pp. 148–9; trans. Baird and Kane, p. 143.

[34] As is suspected by e.g. Sheila Delany: 'we should not forget that it was she who first publicised the documents of what began as a private literary discussion, and that this publication, though not her first, effectively enhanced her career at court': 'Mothers to Think Back Through', p. 100. Delany's provocative article criticizes what is seen as Christine's sociopolitical and intellectual conservatism, prudish moralizing, and regressive advocacy of traditional feminine roles (cf. pp. 146–8 above). There have been several challenges to the view that Christine espoused attitudes which were 'already obsolete', and a questioning of what Delany regards as genuinely 'radical' politics and thought. See esp. Quilligan, *Allegory of Female Authority*, pp. 7–10, 260–74; Reno, 'History, Politics, and Christine Studies'; and Delany's response to Reno, 'History, Politics, and Christine Studies: A Polemical Reply', in Margaret Brabant (ed.), *Politics, Gender, and Genre: The Political Thought of Christine de Pizan* (Boulder, Colo., 1992), pp. 193–206. A somewhat different argument is pursued by David Hult, who suggests that 'Christine knowingly used the *querelle*, or even instigated it, in order to consolidate her position as a court author': 'Words and Deeds', p. 355.

[35] The possibility that a double standard may be operating in some modern scholarship concerning Christine should be considered. Generations of Chaucer critics have not sought to devalue the *Book of the Duchess* on the grounds that the poet wrote it opportunistically to further his career, even though that—it seems reasonable to assume—was a major motivation. (This poem praises the virtues of the dead Blanche of Lancaster, and celebrates the exemplary conduct of her husband, John of Gaunt, in both feeling her loss and bearing it like a man.) It should be added, however, that Delany is sceptical of the notion that Christine was obliged to make her living as a writer: she was far from destitute and had other prospects: e.g. she could have remarried, got herself to a nunnery (as she did later), or accepted the invitation of Henry IV of England 'to take up residence at the English court, where her son was companion to the young prince' (pp. 101–2). For a response to these arguments see Reno, 'History, Politics, and Christine Studies', p. 186 n. Whatever

In propria persona, in persona aliorum: *author* versus *character*

Rien ne change; toujours la même chose. Following in the footsteps of Jean de Montreuil and the Col brothers, D. W. Robertson claimed that Christine de Pizan fundamentally misunderstood the way in which Jean de Meun had deployed his *personae*. 'Her accusation against Raison', he declares, refers to a passage 'where the idea that it is better to deceive is attributed by Raison to lovers and certainly not advocated by Raison herself. La Vielle, Jalousie, and Genius all speak in character; no one of them represents the views of the author'.[36] Of Gerson he says: 'it is easy to see how a man who assumes that the *Roman* is an autobiography and who attributes the views of all *personae* to the author would be horrified by the poem'.[37] Similarly, John Fleming regards the 'psychomachic architectonics' of the poem as 'commonplace', and finds it 'difficult to explain why so few critics have grasped them'. The underlying 'critical principle here enunciated' is identified as

the very ancient one of literary decorum: the actions and speeches of fictional characters should consistently reflect their feigned natures. The obligation which this principle implies for the critic is that he must carefully distinguish between creature and creator, unless there is substantial reason to think that the two share a common point of view ... Yet the prevailing critical abuse of Jean's poem observes no such amenities, however elementary. The inanities of a befuddled lover, the lewd guffaws of an aging prostitute, the ludicrous self-exculpation of an evil friar, the ravings of a jealous husband—all this, and more, is passed off as the personal opinions of Jean de Meun. ... Even Gerson

other life-choices she may or may not have had, it seems curious that Christine's wish to function as a professional writer should be construed so negatively, almost as a failure to exploit the other opportunities and offers she had in her grasp. Turning to the charge of sycophancy which also has been levelled against Christine, suffice it to note that anything of the kind which may be found in her writings pales into insignificance when compared to the over-the-top idealizations of patrons who function as the judges and heroes of Guillaume de Machaut's *Jugement du Roy de Behaigne, Jugement du Roy de Navarre,* and *Fonteinne amoureuse.*

[36] Robertson, *Preface to Chaucer,* p. 361.
[37] Ibid. 363.

knew better, in theory, than to ascribe to a poet the postures of his purely fictional creations. Pierre Col, who shared Gerson's theory but, unlike the Chancellor, actually practised it, never forgot; and his reminder that the Lover in the *Roman* talks like a lover, the Jaloux like a jaloux, and so forth, is one with which all serious criticism of Jean's poem must begin, wherever it intends to end. [38]

In addressing the questions here raised it will be helpful to ask how this 'critical principle' developed, and in what forms it came to the Cols and Gersons of the late-medieval world.

Our point of departure is provided by the distinction between three styles of writing (the *characteres scripturae*), which goes back to the fourth-century commentary by Servius on Virgil's *Bucolics*. The style of a work can be called 'exegematic' when the author speaks in his own person; 'dramatic' when he speaks in the persons of others; and 'mixed' when both these styles are used.[39] This classification was applied to both secular and sacred writings. According to Isidore of Seville, in Virgil's *Georgics* only the poet speaks, while in tragedies and comedies, wherein the dramatic mode is employed, only the characters speak. In the *Aeneid*, he continues, Virgil speaks sometimes in his own person and sometimes through characters, this being a mixture of the narrative mode and of the dramatic mode.[40] Writing over two centuries later in his *De arte metrica*, Bede declares that 'In the dramatic or active type the characters (*personae*) are presented speaking without any intervention by the poet, as is the case with tragedies and fables', and he proceeds to identify the Song of Songs as having been written in this way.[41] In his Psalter commentary (*c*.1144–69) Gerhoh of Reichersberg says that in the Pentateuch, Moses speaks in his own person, in the Song of Songs, the introduced persons speak, while in the Apocalypse and in the *Consolatio philosophiae* the author speaks both in his own person and through others.[42] A twelfth-century Ovid commentator argues that in the *Heroides* Ovid employs the dramatic method because there characters are used, without 'an invocation, nor does he set out what his

[38] Fleming, *Allegory and Iconography*, p. 107.
[39] Servius, *In Vergilii carmina commentarii*, ed. G. Thilo and H. Hagen (Leipzig, 1881), iii.1.   [40] *Etymologiae*, viii.7.11, ed. Lindsay.
[41] Ed. H. Keil, *Grammatici Latini*, vii (Leipzig, 1880), p. 259.
[42] *PL* 191, 630–1.

subject is to be. If he were to do that he would be using the exegematic method.'[43]

Some scholars built on these commonplaces an interpretative method capable of distinguishing between types of literary responsibility and of placing the responsibility for the diverse statements made in a given work where it belonged, whether to a specific character or to the author speaking *in propria persona*. Boethius commentary is a major focus for such theory—as one would expect, given the way in which Boethius conveyed his philosophy on fate and free will through two major characters, the lamenting and limited Boethius *persona* (who is not to be confused with the author himself) and Dame Philosophy, in whose mouth Boethius put his own most profound insights. Writing in the late thirteenth century, William of Aragon explained that in this work two *personae* are feigned ('duplex persona confingitur . . .'), namely, the learned and the learner, or the sufferer along with the physician.[44] This account enjoyed a wide dissemination in the Romance world, since part of William's prologue to his commentary—wherein it is to be found—was translated and incorporated in the prologue to Jean de Meun's French translation of Boethius, and in its turn Jean's prologue was taken over by those responsible for the 'revised mixed version' of the *Consolatio* to serve as the preface to what turned out to be the most popular of all medieval translations of this work.[45] Similarly, in his widely influential commentary on the *Consolatio*, Nicholas Trevet distinguished between the *persona indigens*, the person in need of consolation, and the *persona afferens*, the person effecting that consolation. The first metre of the *Consolatio* is said to present the former, the sorrowing Boethius lamenting his misery in elegiac verses, whereas the first prose presents the latter, the figure of Dame Philosophy.[46]

---

[43] *Accessūs ad auctores*, ed. Huygens, p. 32. Cf. the discussion in Minnis, *Authorship*, pp. 22, 57–8.

[44] The Latin text of this prologue has been edited by R. Crespo, 'Il Prologo alla traduzione della *Consolatio philosophiae* di Jean de Meun e il commento di Guglielmo d'Aragonia', in W. den Boer et al. (eds.), *Romanitas et Christianitas: Studia I. H. Waszink oblata* (Amsterdam, 1973), pp. 55–70. Cf. Jean de Meun's version, as ed. Dedeck-Héry, 'Boethius's *De Consolatione* by Jean de Meun', pp. 101–1.

[45] Cf. Minnis, 'Medieval French and English Traditions', p. 314.

[46] Here once again I draw on the unpublished edition of Trevet's commentary by E. T. Silk.

What is especially interesting about these accounts is the recognition of the fictionality of the characters and their distance from the author himself.

This emerges even more clearly in the efforts of scriptural exegetes to preserve the reputations of inspired authors in the face of certain unacceptable or dubious statements which appear in their writings. In his highly popular commentary on Ecclesiastes (written 1254–7), St Bonaventure had asked whether, if its putative author Solomon was a wicked man, this work could be said to have any authority.[47] Drawing on a passage in St Gregory's *Dialogues*,[48] Bonaventure explains that here sometimes Solomon speaks in his own person and sometimes in the persons of others. When he speaks in the person of the foolish man, he does not approve of this foolishness but rather abhors it; however, when he speaks as a wise man his words are to be taken as directly conducive to good behaviour. Solomon's own views are made clear by the *sententia* which is clearly stated at the end of his work; this epilogue, it would seem, provides us with a measure with which to judge the ways in which doctrine is being communicated throughout the text.

Vernacular writers drew on these methods of assigning, devolving—or indeed avoiding—responsibility. In the Latin commentary which (it would seem) John Gower wrote to accompany his Middle English *Confessio amantis* the distance between the passions of the narrator and the wisdom of the author is emphasized. Gower is not speaking *in propria persona*, but rather is conveying the emotions of others, according to the key gloss:

Hic quasi in persona aliorum, quos amor alligat, fingens se auctor esse Amantem, varias eorum passiones variis huius libri distinccionibus per singula scribere proponit.

[Here as it were in the person of other people, who are held fast by love, the author, feigning himself to be a lover, proposes to write of their various passions one by one in the various distinctions of this book.][49]

---

[47] The relevant passage is translated in Minnis and Scott, *Medieval Literary Theory*, pp. 231–2.   [48] *Dialogi*, iv.4; PL 77, 321–5.
[49] *English Works*, ed. Macaulay, I.37.

And at the end of the *Confessio* (just as at the end of Ecclesiastes) the author reasserts himself in his proper role, leaving behind all the limited *personae* through whom he had spoken during its course. Amans gives way to the author-moralist John Gower; *amor*, now revealed in all its ephemerality and relativity, is bettered—at least according to the Latin gloss—by *caritas*.[50]

In the *querelle de la Rose*, the supporters of Jean de Meun sought to defend him by arguing that certain controversial statements in the *Rose* were made not by the writer himself but by *personae* of limited standing or indeed of reprehensible character. In his 1402 *Traité contre le Roman de la Rose*, Jean Gerson imagines someone making such a defence, which is recognized as taking its precedent from sacred Scripture, one of the crucial texts being the book of Ecclesiastes. What evil is there, such an advocate might say, if Jean de Meun, a man of great perception, learning, and fame, should have wished to compose a book that features characters (*personnaiges*) which speak according to their respective natures? After all, the prophet David, speaking in the person of a fool, said there is no God (Ps. 13: 1 and 52: 1), and wise Solomon composed the whole book of Ecclesiastes in such a manner. Why, then, cannot Jean de Meun be allowed to do likewise?

Et quel mal est ce, dit l'ung des plus avisés, quel mal est ce, je vous pry, se cest home de tel sens, de tel estude et de tel renon a volu composer ung livre de personnaiges ouquel il fait par grant maistrise chascun parler selond son droit et sa proprieté? Ne dit pas le prophete en la persone d'ung fol que Dieu n'est pas? Et le sage Salemon ne fist il en especial tout son livre *Ecclesiastes* en ceste maniere, par quoy on le sauve de cent et cent erreurs qui la sont en escript?

['And what evil is there,' said one defender more skilful than the others, 'What evil is there, I pray, if this man of such great perception and learning and fame should have wished to compose a book in which characters are introduced with great skill, each one speaking to his own law and nature? Did not the prophet say in the person of a fool, "There is no God"? And wise Solomon, did he not specifically compose the entire Ecclesiastes in such a manner?' And, therefore, he

---

[50] These few sentences do not do justice, of course, to the elaborate ending of the *Confessio amantis*. For further discussion see Minnis, '*De Vulgari Auctoritate*', pp. 56–63.

[i.e. Jean de Meun] is saved and defended from a hundred errors which are written in this book [i.e. the *Rose*].][51]

But, Gerson retorts, 'to a fool his own foolishness must be made manifest': the folly of the lover is not adequately revealed in the text. To say that the author does not himself speak but others who are there introduced is 'too slight a defence for so great a crime'. If someone were to call himself an enemy of the king of France and make war on him, this title would not save him from being punished as a traitor. If one were to write erroneous things against Christianity in the person of a heretic or Saracen, this would not excuse him. (Gerson proceeds to ask which is worse, for a Christian clerk to preach against the faith in the person of a Saracen, or for him to bring forth a real Saracen speaking or writing against the Faith. While the latter is not to be borne, the former is actually the worse, he answers, because the 'secret enemy' is more injurious than the open one.) If someone defames others by means of the characters which he introduces in his book, he is legally held to be wicked and deserving of punishment. In sum, the author is responsible for what his characters say; he cannot hide behind his *personae*.

What, then, of the argument that, since Holy Scripture presents Solomon and David as having been foolish lovers, Jean de Meun is perfectly justified in portraying Amant as such?[52] Gerson's retort is that the Bible uses these characters to reprove evil, in such a way that everyone might perceive 'le reproche du mal et l'aprobacion du bien', and most importantly, all those things are done 'sans excés de legiereté' ['without excessive frivolity']. Jean de Meun, by contrast, does not provide clear condemnation of immoral speeches in the relevant contexts:

Mais j'entens bien ce que vous murmurés ensemble: vous doctes, comme par avant l'ung de vous allega, que Salemon et David ont ainssy fait. C'est ycy trop grant outraige pour excuser ung fol amoureulx, accuser Dieu et ses sains et les mener a la querelle; mais ne se puet faire: je voulroie bien que ce Fol Amoureulx n'eust usé de ces personnaiges fors ainssy que la sainte Escripture en use, c'est assavoir en reprouvant le mal, et tellement que chascun eust apperceu le reproche du mal et l'aprobacion

---

[51] *Le Débat*, ed. Hicks, p. 64; trans. Baird and Kane, p. 74.
[52] This aspect of the *querelle* will be treated in more detail in the final section of the present chapter.

du bien, et—qui est le principal—que tout se fist sans excés de legiereté. Mais nennin voir. Tout semble estre dit en sa persone; tout semble estre vray come Euvangille,[53] en especial aux nices folz amoureulx auxquelz il parle; et, de quoy je me dueil plus—tout enflamme a luxure, meismement quant il la samble reprouver: neis les bien chastes, s'ilz le daingnoient estudier, lire ou escouter, en vaurroient pis.

[But I hear clearly what you are muttering together, what one of you previously alleged: namely, that Solomon and David did thus. This is too great an outrage, that some Foolish Lover may be excused by accusing God and his saints, by drawing them into accusation. Nay, this cannot be done. I would wish that every man might perceive that condemnation of evil and that approbation of good, and (what is most important) that all those things could have been done without excessive frivolity. But no. Everything seems to be said in his own person; everything seems as true as the Gospel, particularly to those foolish and vicious lovers to whom he speaks. And I regret to say, he incites the more quickly to lechery, even when he seems to reproach it. Truly, the chaste, if they should consider it worthy to give time and trouble to this book of his, to hear it, or to read it, for this reason they would be the worse in the future.][54]

To sum up these objections, Gerson clearly feels that in the *Rose* there is no clear distinction between *personae* and poet. It is not that he is unaware of the theoretical distinction between *auctor* and *persona*—but rather that in this particular case he believes that Jean de Meun, as author, does not sufficiently distance himself from his problematic *personae*. The result is moral confusion—or at least a failure to spell out the correct moral response or course of action which the occasion demands. To say that Gerson does not fully understand the medieval literary theory of *personae* would be simplistic and inaccurate, not to say patronizing. His criticism of Jean de Meun is on quite different grounds, i.e. that 'immoral speeches—without clear, unambiguous disapproval in the context—are to be condemned, whoever says them' (to borrow the clear formulation by Baird

---

[53] 'As true as the Gospels' is an obvious way of affirming the absolute truth of some proposition, and of course is used ironically here, to refer to the spurious 'truth' of the *Rose*. But there is probably more to it than that. The Evangelists were regarded as the first-hand witnesses for the life of Christ, so Gerson may have felt that Jean de Meun, in similar fashion, stands by and is responsible for what he says in the *Rose*, rather than having *personae* express views with which he is not in agreement.   [54] *Le Débat*, ed. Hicks, p. 74; trans. Baird and Kane, p. 81.

and Kane).[55] Clear condemnation is, of course, what happens in, for example, Ecclesiastes, as interpreted by Bonaventure—a reading of that text with which Gerson is obviously in general agreement. Gerson goes beyond this type of argument, however, when he remarks that Jean seems to say everything *in propria persona* and, even when he seems to reproach lechery, is actually inciting his readers to it; hence even the chaste could well be corrupted by the poem.

But Pierre Col, writing at the end of summer 1402 in defence of the *Rose*, pressed home the argument that it is a fully 'dramatic' work (in the sense defined above) and hence the opinions of the characters must not be confused with those of their creator—it is crucial to consider all problematic statements with reference to *l'endendement de l'aucteur* (cf. the *accessus* term *intentio auctoris*).[56] Ovid, in his *Ars amatoria*, may have spoken *in propria persona*, 'sans parler per personnaiges',[57] but that was certainly not Jean's method. 'Je . . . dy que maistre Jehan de Meung en son livre introduisy personnaiges, et fait chascun personnaige parler selonc qui luy appartient: c'est assavoir le Jaloux comme jaloux, la Vielle come la Vielle, et pareillement des autres' ['I say that Master Jean de Meun in his book introduced characters, and made each character speak according to what appertains to him, that is, the Jealous Man as a jealous man, the Old Woman as an old woman, and similarly with the others']. It is wrong-headed, he continues, to say that the writer thinks of women in the same way as the Jaloux does. Jean merely reports (*recite*) what a jealous man always says about women in general, in order to demonstrate and correct the very great irrationality and disordered passion which exist in people like him.

This concept of objective reporting in contradistinction to personal affirmation had, of course, been used by Jean de Meun himself in the *apologia* to the *Rose*. There, however, it concerned the repetition of what Jean's authors had said (about women), not what his *personae* had said. The text moves deftly from an echo of Romans 15: 4 ('all is for our doctrine', 15173)

---

[55] Baird and Kane, 'In Defence of the Opponents', p. 302.
[56] *Le Débat*, ed. Hicks, p. 99.
[57] Letter *Aprés ce que je oÿ parler*, in *Le Débat*, ed. Hicks, pp. 105, 100; trans. Baird and Kane, pp. 108, 103–4.

to a disavowal of personal responsibility for what he is merely
repeating from his sources, to a justification of his personal
additions with reference to the Horatian precept (cf. *Ars poetica,* 333–4) that poetry should offer profit and delight:

> D'autre part, dames honourables,
> s'il vos sample que je di fables,
> por manteür ne m'an tenez,
> mes aus aucteurs vos an prenez
> qui an leur livres ont escrites
> les paroles que g'en ai dites,
> et ceus avec que g'en dirai;
> ne ja de riens n'an mentirai,
> se li preudome n'en mentirent
> qui les anciens livres firent. . . .
> *Je n'i faz riens fors reciter,*
> se par mon geu, qui po vos coute,
> quelque parole n'i ajoute,
> si con font antr'eus li poete,
> quant chascuns la matire trete
> don il li plest a antremetre;
> car si con tesmoigne la letre,
> profiz et delectaction.
> c'est toute leur entencion.

(15185–212)

[Moreover, honourable ladies, if it seems to you that I am making
things up, do not call me a liar, but blame those authors who have written in their books what I have said, and those in whose company I will
speak. I shall tell no lie, unless the worthy men who wrote the ancient
books also lied. . . . *I merely repeat,* except for making a few additions
on my own account which costs you little. Poets do this among themselves, each one dealing with the subject that he wants to work on, for,
as the text tells us, their intention is solely to edify and to please.]

The logical distinction between *reportatio* and *assertio* had for
long been part and parcel of the system whereby medieval writers reconciled their apparently discordant authorities: in his *Sic
et non* prologue, Peter Abelard had warned that the views
expressed in an author's citations of other men's books should
not be attributed to the author himself.[58] This became a

---

[58] The relevant passage is translated in Minnis and Scott, *Medieval Literary
Theory,* pp. 90–2.

commonplace of scriptural exegesis. To take but one example among many, in his *Summa quaestionum ordinariarum* the Paris-trained theologian Henry of Ghent brings his discussion of the apparent fictions and falsehoods in Scripture to a close with the statement that 'whatever lies are found in Scripture, it does not proffer to us as being true by positively asserting (*asserendo*) their truth and commending them, but in reporting (*recitando*) them in the text solely for our instruction'.[59] Moreover, many of the great compilers of the late Middle Ages had declared that they were 'reporting' the opinions of the authors who were their sources rather than 'affirming' their own views.[60] Jean, and his defenders and attackers, appear to have followed such usage.

Worthy of special note is the fact that Pierre Col, on Jean's behalf, is disavowing authorial responsibility for statements made by the characters in the *Rose*, a use of the distinction which had been anticipated, around a decade earlier, by Geoffrey Chaucer's rejection of personal blame for what his Canterbury pilgrims had to say. I pray you, Chaucer's narrator asks the audience, not to regard as churlishness my plain speaking in telling the pilgrims' tales in their own words. For whoever repeats another man's tale must report (*reherce*) his every word as accurately as he can (*Canterbury Tales*, General Prologue, I (A) 725–33). Characters like the Miller and Reeve are certainly churls, and hence speak in a churlish manner—and herein lies Chaucer's defence of his inclusion of their tales.[61] He is obliged to 'reherse / Hir tales alle, be they bettre or werse', but he himself is not saying anything 'of yvel entente' (I(A) 3173–4).

The distinction between reporting and asserting forms the basis of Col's challenge (in the letter which he wrote at the end of the summer of 1402) to Gerson's argument about the enemy of the king of France and the Saracen not being able to avoid blame by appealing to their roles. Powerful counter-examples are brought forward.[62] If Sallust recites the conspiracy of Cataline against the republic of Rome, is he guilty for this? If Aristotle recites the opinions of the ancient philosophers which

---

[59] Ibid. 266.   [60] Cf. Minnis, *Authorship*, pp. 191–203.
[61] Cf. pp. 130–1 above.
[62] *Le Débat*, ed. Hicks, pp. 101–2; trans. Baird and Kane, p. 105.

contain philosophical errors, does this make him an advocate of errors? If Holy Scripture recites the abominable sins of Sodom and Gomorrah, does it exhort one to commit such sins?[63] Vices have to be declared in order to be denounced, as is common practice among preachers. Read Jean de Meun's own justification, Col urges his opponents, for there and only there does he speak 'as author' ('la seulement parle il come aucteur et la come aucteur dit'), as one who is personally responsible for what is said.[64] And what he says there—that nobody ought to despise a woman, that his intention was not to speak against the clergy, that his bawdy or foolish expressions are required by his subject-matter, that he writes under the correction of Holy Church—is unexceptionable.

But neither of those two formidable opponents of the *Rose*, Christine de Pizan and Jean Gerson, was impressed, and held to the view that 'truth and honour must be preserved in fictional characters', as Gerson put it.[65] The first of Christine's direct responses to the issue occurs in a letter to Jean de Montreuil, where she complains that many people attempt to excuse Jean de Meun by saying that 'c'est le Jaloux qui parle, et voirement fait ainsi comme Dieu parla par la bouche Jeremie' ['it is the Jealous Man who speaks and that in truth Meun does no more than God himself did when He spoke through the mouth of Jeremiah'].[66] Here her main point seems to be that, according to Jean's supporters, his strictures on women should be taken with the same seriousness as Jeremiah's social criticism; both discourses may be partial, but they stem from a higher source. Clearly, Christine is indignant that the *Rose* should be aggrandized by such a comparison with Scripture—or, in other words, that Jean de Meun's authority claim should be furthered by a comparison which, in her view, is utterly far-fetched and insupportable. Instead of exploring the technical distinction between *auctor* and *personae*, however, Christine concentrates on the poem's content, bringing out a glaring contradiction in the characters'

---

[63] On the theological tradition of analysis of the apparent fictions and falsehoods in Scripture, see Minnis and Scott, *Medieval Literary Theory*, pp. 209–11.

[64] *Le Débat*, ed. Hicks, pp. 110–11; trans. Baird and Kane, p. 113.

[65] Gerson, sermon *IVa Dominica Adventus: Poenitemini* (24 December 1402), in *Le Débat*, ed. Hicks, p. 182; trans. Baird and Kane, p. 183.

[66] *Le Débat*, ed. Hicks, p. 15; trans. Baird and Kane, p. 50.

view of women (as interpreted by Jean's defenders), namely that
men are ordered to flee what they should pursue and to pursue
what they should flee. Christine's second, and fuller, response
forms part of her later letter to Pierre Col.[67] Jean de Meun is
responsible for what his characters say: 'selonc le gieu que on
veult jouer il convient instrumens propres' ['the will of the
player manipulates such instruments to his own purpose']. (It
would seem that, on her, the 'I'm just the piano player' excuse
would not work.) Besides, Christine continues, de Meun is so
concerned to slander women that he has some of his *personae*
attack them even when such sentiments are not appropriate to
their supposed natures, i.e. go beyond the qualities which they
personify. Col's appeal to the Bible's 'reportage' of evils is
summarily dismissed on the grounds that in Holy Scripture,
whenever such matters are recounted, they are condemned
unequivocally, which is not done in the *Rose*.[68]

For his part, Gerson persisted in his belief that there was little
distinction between Jean's characters and Jean himself. Genius,
he declares, praises lechery, saying that it follows nature, 'and
afterward the author in his own person says the same thing even
more disgustingly in the end of the work'.[69] This, one may add,
is the exact opposite of what Solomon had done in
Ecclesiastes—for at the end of that work his own moral viewpoint was affirmed, as Bonaventure had explained (cf. p. 222
above). The material which has been offered above makes it
abundantly clear, I hope, that late medieval theologians were
thoroughly aware of the principle of literary decorum and well
used to practising it in their scriptural exegesis.[70] Gerson was at
least as adept as Pierre Col in putting this principle into practice; the difference consisted simply in the fact that in Gerson's

[67] *Pour ce que entendement*, in *Le Débat*, ed. Hicks, p. 132; trans. Baird and
Kane, p. 130.
[68] *Le Débat*, ed. Hicks, pp. 133–4; trans. Baird and Kane, p. 131.
[69] Gerson, sermon *Poenitemini V: La chasteté conjugale*, in *Le Débat*, ed. Hicks,
p. 184; trans. Baird and Kane, p. 168.
[70] This interpretative principle was bolstered by other exegetical ideas, including
the notion that knowledge of the 'circumstances of the letter' was essential for the
understanding of a given passage. See Chenu, *Thomas d'Aquin*, p. 121; and P. C.
Spicq, *Esquisse d'une histoire de l'exégèse latine au moyen âge* (Paris, 1944), pp.
250–1. Then there was the distinction between words considered in themselves (*de
vi vocis*) and words as they functioned within a passage (*de vi sermonis*), on which
see Minnis, ' "Authorial Intention" and "Literal Sense" ', pp. 27–9.

opinion the *Rose* could not be rescued by such means. This was
'too slight a defence for so great a crime'.[71] Therefore
hermeneutics of a type which had for generations been used to
affirm the authority of Latin texts both sacred and secular could
not, in the view of Gerson and Christine, be used as part of an
authority claim for the *Rose*. For them its authority remained
unproved, and utterly unprovable.[72]

The different positions are, then, fundamentally irreconcilable. And, as well as 'bad rhetoric on both sides'[73] there were
plenty of good arguments on both sides. It should be remem-
bered that Geoffrey Chaucer, that great advocate of the principle that *personae* should be allowed to speak according to their
different natures (the author being free of blame for what he
reported of their speech), at several points in his *œuvre* evinced
a certain scepticism concerning the efficacy of such a defence.
For example, his Nun's Priest brings together two versions of
the reporter's defence—that on the subject of women he is
merely repeating what his authors say, and that he is merely
repeating the words of his character Chaunticleer—in a context
which makes the whole business seem rather ludicrous:

> Rede auctours, where they trete of swich mateere,
> And what they seyn of wommen ye may heere.
> Thise been the cokkes wordes, and nat myne;
> I kan noon harm of no womman divyne.
>
> (VII.3263–6)

In particular, his attempt to put the blame for his own banter-
ing misogyny onto the cock is blatantly—and amusingly—
unfair, since Chaunticleer certainly did not utter the words for
which he is here made responsible. The implication would seem
to be that the buck stops with the Nun's Priest. Then there is the
infinitely more complex case of the Manciple's Tale, in which
Chaucer, *inter alia*, revisits the 'very ancient principle of decorum' as he had formulated it in the General Prologue.[74] This

---

[71] Gerson, *Traité*, in *Le Débat*, ed. Hicks, p. 72; trans. Baird and Kane, p. 80.

[72] On their assault on the authority of the *Rose* see esp. Brown-Grant, *Moral Defence*, pp. 30–43.

[73] Cf. Douglas Kelly's comment as cited in n. 1 above.

[74] See esp. the repetition of the *sententia* of 'the wise Plato' that 'the word moot nede accorde with the dede' (IX(H) 207–8; cf. General Prologue, I(A) 741–2).

tale features a reporter (albeit the reporter of an event—the adultery of Phoebus' wife—rather than of speech) who is severely punished by his impetuous master. The lot of a messenger is not a happy one; his claim of 'reporter status' will not always ensure his safety.

Similarly, no author can be confident of devolving all his moral responsibility to his *personae*; he may be brought to book by a reader who feels that his 'crime' far exceeds the bounds of such a 'defence'. And few of us seem altogether comfortable with the notion that the depiction of certain actions in a film, no matter how offensive or repugnant they may be, must be allowed to stand because they are carried out by fictional characters who do not express the personal views of the filmmakers. One of the claims made in the so-called 'Newson Report' of 1994 is that there is a new kind of violent and violence-inciting film in which 'the viewer is made to identify with the perpetrator of the [brutal] act, not the victim'.[75] But, generally speaking, current controversies ignore such specifics of characterization to concentrate instead on the issue of what *effects* a film in its totality may have on certain audiences.[76] Which is very much the intellectual position from which Christine de Pizan and Jean Gerson attacked the *Rose*. Their views on the fifteenth-century equivalent of media 'ill effects' are certainly not as unconsidered or quaint as some modern defenders of the *Rose* would have us believe.

Take their worries about the effect Jean's text might have on impressionable readers or hearers, for instance. An emphasis on

[75] Quoted by Martin Baker, 'The Newson Report: A Case Study in "Common Sense" ', in Martin Barker and Julian Petley (eds.), *Ill Effects: The Media/Violence Debate* (London and New York, 1997), p. 16. Elizabeth Newson's report on film violence followed in the wake of press attempts to attribute blame for the murder of the toddler James Bulger to the video of *Child's Play III* which, it was (falsely) alleged, the young perpetrators had watched. Trenchant criticisms of Newson's methods and conclusions are offered by several of the contributors to this collection.

[76] As is the case in the 1979 Williams Report, the outcome of a committee originally set up in 1977 by the Labour Government in Britain. However, in attempting to accommodate aesthetic considerations it gives some credence to the belief that if novels and films are pornographic they 'must be no good', and in part this failure results from inadequate characterization: 'Their participitants are not characters, but mere locations of sexual possibilities; there is no plot, no development, no beginning, middle or end . . .': Bernard Williams (ed.), *Obscenity and Film Censorship: An Abridgement of the Williams Report* (Cambridge, 1981), p. 106.

the possible impact of obscenity on susceptible people has also figured largely in twentieth-century British legislation. In the first half of the twentieth century the so-called 'Hicklin Test' appertained in England, the key issue being 'whether the tendency of the matter charged as obscenity is to deprave and corrupt those whose minds are open to such immoral influences and into whose hands a publication of its kind might fall'.[77] Similarly, the Obscene Publications Act of 1959 maintained that obscenity 'shall be considered relative to its effect on its likely readers'. In 1979 the Williams Committee defined obscenity as material which is 'offensive to reasonable people'—one may recall Christine's remark that 'people who do not delight in such carnality' rightly find the *Rose* offensive[78]—'by reason of the manner in which it portrays, deals with or relates to violence, cruelty or horror, or sexual, faecal or urinary functions, or genital organs'.[79] No direct legislative changes resulted from this committee's work, but since the mid-1970s the prosecution of the written word has been very rare indeed;[80] the agenda has shifted to visual imagery of a sexually explicit or supposedly depraved kind as found in films, home videos, and on the Internet.

It could be said that in all these situations the problem is, in

[77] The following account is indebted to Grace, *Testing Obscenity*, p. 5, 6, 15.

[78] Cf. p. 155 above. An excellent discussion of the belief in the 'reader's moral vulnerability' which Christine and Gerson shared is provided by Brown-Grant, *Moral Defence*, pp. 43–9. Gerson seems to have been very aware (though he does not spell this out) that the vernacularity of the *Rose* made it dangerously accessible to a wide, lay audience. On one occasion he complained to Pierre d'Ailly that Parisian theologians spent a lot of time on vain speculations which made them forget Holy Scripture, when they could have been writing little treatises which taught the people the essentials of the Christian religion: hence the many vernacular texts which he himself produced for the benefit of 'simples gens'. Cf. Gilbert Ouy, *Gerson bilingue: Les deux rédactions, latine et française, de quelques œuvres du chancelier parisien* (Paris, 1998), pp. xiii–xv.

[79] Williams, *Abridgement*, p. 124; cf. p. 122.

[80] The Williams Report itself recommended that 'neither suppression nor restriction should be applied to any publication which consists entirely of the written word (or, to put it rather more precisely, the offensive element in which consists of the written word)': ibid. p. x; cf. p. 102. The main justification offered is that 'to be offended by written material requires the activity of reading it', this being a voluntary activity—whereas 'immediate involuntary offensiveness' (i.e. involuntarily reception of offensive material) is what the report seeks to suppress and restrict. This seems to miss the point that going to the cinema to see a possibly offensive film, or hiring it from a video shop, could equally well be deemed voluntary activities.

essence, a rhetorical one—a matter of *who* is presenting the material in question and at *whom* it is aimed. (For instance: is the motivation acceptable, on whatever value system is being applied, and is the recipient a potential victim, a child for example, or a potentially consenting adult?) Here we are invoking those rules of rhetoric which emphasize the importance of considering 'who is speaking' and 'to whom he speaks'. These phrases echo Jean Gerson's stricture on Raison for having used sexually explicit language to a Foolish Lover, rather than to 'a wise and mature' man who would have been able to cope with it.[81] He suggests that a person of a 'melancholic, infirm and weak temperament' will be particularly susceptible. It is not unfair, I think, to juxtapose those remarks with the 1993 statement by the *Independent* columnist Bryan Appleyard that he 'would prefer [Quentin Tarantino's *Reservoir Dogs*] not to be seen by the criminal classes or the mentally unstable or by inadequately supervised children with little else in their lives'.[82] It may be difficult to approve of Gerson's conclusions, but at least the force (not to say the longevity) of his argument should be respected.

Jean de Meun as Medieval Ovidian

Behind Jean de Meun's controversial French text, its attackers believed, lay controversial Latin ones, particularly the *Ars amatoria*. They saw Jean as a modern Ovid not least because he was duplicating Ovid's great fault: he had written an 'art of love' which offended against public morality. Reading books which stimulate lust is particularly dangerous, declares Gerson in a sermon (preached on 17 December 1402); men who own them should be required by their confessors to tear them up—books like Ovid's, or Matheolus, or parts of the *Rose*.[83] In a later sermon (24 December 1402) he declares that, had he the

---

[81] *Traité*, in *Le Débat*, ed. Hicks, pp. 84–5; trans. Baird and Kane, p. 89.

[82] Quoted by Graham Murdock, 'Reservoirs of Dogma: An Archaeology of Popular Anxieties', in Barker and Petley (eds.), *Ill Effects*, p. 84. Murdock criticizes the way such thinking deflects attention from those major social problems in contemporary Britain which breed violence.

[83] *Le Débat*, ed. Hicks, p. 179; trans. Baird and Kane, p. 158.

only copy of the *Rose*, worth a thousand *livres*, he would burn it rather than have it published in its present form.[84]

In similar vein, Christine considered if the *Rose* has any *utilité*. 'I do not know how . . . to consider this book useful in any way,' she exclaims in a letter (written in the summer of 1401) to Jean de Montreuil: 'ne sçay considerer aucune utilité ou dit traictié. . . .'[85] Apparently she is using the term in the technical sense which the Latin form *utilitas* bears in the *accessūs ad auctores*, as designating the didactic effect and moral worth which one requires in an authoritative work of literature. More specifically, *utilitas* was one of the headings characteristic of the 'type C' academic prologue (as designated by R. W. Hunt), a prologue which, according to E. A. Quain, had its origin in late antique Greek commentaries on Aristotle's works.[86] Hence the medieval version of this paradigm, as one would expect, emphasized the philosophical credentials of a literary text, regularly identifying the 'part of philosophy' to which it pertained as ethics and describing its usefulness in behavioural and pedagogic terms (the emphasis often being placed on its claim to moral edification). For example, Arnulf of Orléans, commenting on Lucan, declared that the *Pharsalia* is very useful in that it reveals the horrors of civil wars, thereby warning men not to engage in them.[87] The *utilitas* of the Roman satirists was, as already noted, usually located in their harsh reprehension of vice and recommendation of virtue: the censures by Juvenal and Persius of 'poets writing to no purpose' (*poetas inutiliter scribentes*) won much approval.[88]

Other commentators picked up Horace's dictum that poets

---

[84] Sermon *IVa Dominica Adventus: Poenitemini*, in *Le Débat*, ed. Hicks, p. 182; trans. Baird and Kane, p. 164. Cf. Gerson's statement in his letter *Responsio ad scripta cuiusdam* (to Pierre Col, winter 1402–3), in *Le Débat*, ed. Hicks, p. 172; trans. Baird and Kane, p. 151.

[85] Letter *Reverence, honneur avec recommandacion*, in *Le Débat*, ed. Hicks, p. 20; trans. Baird and Kane, p. 54. Cf. the earlier formulation, 'To what purpose or to what profit (*a quel utilité ne a quoy prouffite*) is it that the hearers of this book have their ears assailed by so much sinfulness?': *Le Débat*, ed. Hicks, p. 15; trans. Baird and Kane, p. 49.

[86] Hunt, 'Introductions to the *Artes*', and Quain, '*Accessūs ad auctores*'.

[87] See Minnis and Scott, *Medieval Literary Theory*, p. 155.

[88] From an *accessus* printed in Cranz and Kristeller, *Catalogus*, i.192–3, 195, 198; iii.225–7.

aim to profit or delight ('aut prodesse volunt aut delectare poetae').[89] It could be exploited in praising those poets who managed to combine both functions, as in an *accessus* to the fables of Avianus, where the authorial intention is described as 'to delight us in the fables and to profit us in the correction of behaviour' while the *utilitas* is identified as 'delectatio poematis et correctio morum'; the work pertains to ethics, because it treats 'de correctione morum'.[90] Alternatively, poems could be categorized in terms of whether they offered profit, delight, or both, as in the 'Bernard Silvestris' commentary on Virgil, where Horace is cited in support of the view that 'Some poets write with a useful purpose in view, like the satirists, while others, such as the writers of comedies, write to give pleasure, and yet others, for example the historians, write to a useful end and to give pleasure'.[91] Occasionally in *accessūs ad satiricos* the Roman satirists are aggrandized at the expense of those who supposedly wrote to give pleasure only—and sometimes Ovid appears in that group. 'It should be known', declares a fifteenth-century *accessus* to Juvenal, 'that certain poets direct themselves towards usefulness alone, like Horace and this Juvenal; others to delight alone, like Ovid'.[92] Could Christine de Pizan have been influenced by such a comment? Certainly she seems to have in mind not only Horace's dictum but also its importance as a basis for categorizing different kinds of poet:

car oeuvre sans utilité et hors bien commun ou propre—poson que elle soit delictable, de grant labour et coust—ne fait a louer.

[For a work without usefulness, contributing nothing to the general or personal good (even though we concede it to be delightful, the fruit of great work and labour), in no way deserves praise.][93]

---

[89] For examples see *Accessūs ad auctores*, ed. Huygens, pp. 26, 45, 63, 84, 86, etc. Cf. *Ars poetica*, 333–4, which Jean de Meun himself had echoed at *Rose*, 15211 (quoted on p. 227 above).

[90] *Accessūs ad auctores*, ed. Huygens, p. 22. The series of *accessūs* here edited is found in full in Munich, Clm 19475 (twelfth century; Tegernsee), and in part in two other MSS, both dating from the end of the twelfth or the beginning of the thirteenth century.   [91] Minnis and Scott, *Medieval Literary Theory*, p. 152.

[92] Kristeller et al., *Catalogus*, i.192; cf. the citation and relevant discussion in A. J. Minnis, ' "Moral Gower" and Medieval Literary Theory', in A. J. Minnis (ed.), *Gower's 'Confessio amantis': Responses and Reassessments* (Cambridge, 1983), pp. 55–6.   [93] *Le Débat*, ed. Hicks p. 21; trans. Baird and Kane, p. 55.

This reinforces her earlier point that Jean should have been able to write a far better book, more profitable and of higher sentiment ('plus prouffitable et de sentement plus hault').

On rare occasions a scholiast will indicate the pleasure-giving function of Ovid's poetry, without any apparent wish to denigrate it thereby, as in an *accessus* to the *Amores* which Ralph Hexter has edited from Munich, Bayerische Staatsbibliothek Clm 631: 'Utilitas est delectio, uel apud Corinnam sui ipsius commendatio.'[94] But, as Hexter says, medieval Ovid critics normally 'paid little attention to' literary delight, concentrating instead on its didactic function.[95] This did not necessarily entail a specifically ethical reading,[96] but very frequently that was precisely what was emphasized, particularly in the introductions to Ovid's *Heroides*. Here one of the most common formulations of literary *utilitas* was that this poetry showed its audience both what to do and what to avoid. Having seen the advantages of lawful love and the disasters or disadvantages which result from unlawful and foolish love, the readers of the *Heroides* 'may reject and shun foolish love and adhere to lawful love'.

Finalis causa talis est, ut visa utilitate quae ex legitimo procedit et infortuniis quae ex stulto et illicito solent proseque, hunc utrumque fugiamus et soli casto adhereamus.

[The ultimate end of the work is that, having seen the utility gained from lawful love, and the misfortunes which arise from foolish and unlawful love, we may shun both of these and may adhere to chaste love.][97]

---

[94] Hexter, *Ovid and Medieval Schooling*, pp. 16 n., 103, 224. This particular item dates from the fourteenth century. Cf. the first *accessus to the Amores* edited by Huygens, in *Accessūs ad auctores*, p. 36: 'Intentio est delectare'.

[95] Hexter, *Ovid and Medieval Schooling*, p. 212.

[96] Ibid. 16–17, 25, 156–8, 213.

[97] *Accessūs ad auctores*, ed. Huygens, p. 30; trans. Minnis and Scott, *Medieval Literary Theory*, p. 21. In these early *accessūs* the term *finalis causa* is either used as a synonym for *utilitas* or as a term which helps to elaborate some aspect thereof. In the later 'Aristotelian Prologue', which came into vogue in the thirteenth century, *finalis causa* referred to the ultimate end or objective in writing; i.e. it came to cover material hitherto included under discussions of *intentio* and/or *utilitas*. See Hexter, *Ovid and Medieval Schooling*, pp. 46–7, 103, 111, 147, and Minnis, *Authorship*, p. 29; cf. *Accessūs ad auctores*, ed. Huygens, pp. 28, 30, 32, 33, 37.

The same ideas are reiterated in *accessus* after *accessus*, to such an extent that we may take this as the standard medieval view of the *Heroides*:

Utilitas vel finalis causa secundum intentiones diversificantur, vel illicitorum vel stultorum amorum cognitio vel quomodo aliquae per epistolas sollicitentur vel quomodo per effectus ipsius castitatis commodum consequamur. Vel finalis causa est ut per commendationem caste amantium ad castos amores non invitet vel ut visa utilitate quae ex legitimo amore procedit visisque infortuniis vel incommoditatibus quae ex illicito et stulto amore proveniunt, et stultum et illicitum repellamus et fugiamus et legitimo adhereamus.

[The usefulness or ultimate end of the book differs according to the various intentions, depending on whether the intention is the recognition of unchaste or foolish forms of love, or else to show how some women may be courted by letter, or how the results of living chastely may befit us. Alternatively, the ultimate end of the book is that by commending those who engage in chaste love, he may encourage us to chaste love. Or else, having seen the utility of lawful love and the disasters or disadvantages which result from unlawful and foolish love, we may reject and shun foolish love and adhere to lawful love.][98]

Christine anticipates Jean de Montreuil offering a similar defence of the *Rose*: 'Je sçay bien que sur ce en l'excusant vous me respondréz que le bien y est ennorté pour le faire et le mal pour l'eschiver' ['I know well that you will excuse it by replying to me that therein he enjoins man to do the good but to eschew the evil']. But this justification is unacceptable, she declares: there is no point in reminding human nature, 'qui de soy est encline a mal, n'a nul besoing que on lui ramentoive le pié dont elle cloche pour plus droit aler' ['which is naturally inclined to evil, that it limps on one foot, in the hope that it will then walk straighter'].[99] Why, Christine continues, should the good in this book be praised (for she is prepared to admit that it contains some good things), when one can find far more virtuous things, and more profitable to the decorous and moral life, in the works of certain philosophers and teachers of the Christian faith like Aristotle, Seneca, St Paul, and St Augustine? The fact that Christine offers this argument immediately after her protestation

---

[98] Ibid. 32; trans. Minnis and Scott, *Medieval Literary Theory*, p. 23.
[99] *Le Débat*, ed. Hicks, p. 22; trans. Baird and Kane, p. 55.

that the *Rose* lacks *utilité* strengthens the suggestion that throughout this entire excursus she had stock medieval Ovid criticism in mind, even though Ovid himself is not named here.

The connection between the *magister amoris* and Master Jean de Meun is, however, made quite explicit in Jean Gerson's reaction to these same critical ideas. In his 1402 treatise against the *Rose*, Gerson imagines a supporter of de Meun saying that, while there is some evil in the book it contains much more that is good, and so 'praingne chascun le bien et laisse le mal!' ['Let every man receive the good and reject the evil'].[100] Gerson retorts, are the evil things in the book thereby deleted? Indeed not—a hook does not injure the fish less if it is covered in bait; a sword dipped in honey does not cut less deeply. Furthermore, the good things contained in the book actually make it more dangerous. One should recall how Mohammed, in order to attract Christians more readily to his own law and to cover his own outrages, mixed in some Christian truths with his own impure errors. St Paul (1 Cor. 15: 33), Seneca and experience all teach that evil speaking and writings corrupt good morals.

This argument naturally leads Gerson to consider the salutary example of Ovid's exile.[101] The *Tristia* is cited as proof that he was exiled on account of his wretched *Ars amatoria*; even his refutation of its false teaching, the *Remedia amoris*, could not save the poet from this fate. This is standard *accessus* fare. In the introduction to the *Tristia* edited by Huygens, several opinions are given concerning the reason for Ovid's exile, one of which is that 'he had written a book, *On the Art of Love*, in which he had taught young men how to deceive and attract married women. This gave offence to the Romans, and it was for this reason that he is alleged to have been sent into exile'.[102] Similarly, in the extensive *vita Ovidii* found at the head of Giovanni del Virgilio's commentary on the *Metamorphoses*, the composition of the *Ars amatoria* is described as having incurred Augustus's wrath, 'and according to some, this is why [Ovid]

---

[100] *Le Débat*, ed. Hicks, p. 65; trans. Baird and Kane, p. 75.
[101] *Le Débat*, ed. Hicks, p. 76; trans. Baird and Kane, p. 83.
[102] *Accessūs ad auctores*, ed. Huygens, p. 36; trans. Minnis and Scott, *Medieval Literary Theory*, p. 27. On Ovid's exile, see further the extensive materials from Ovid commentary cited by Hexter, *Ovid and Medieval Schooling*, pp. 87–97, 136, 211, 213; cf. Hexter, 'Ovid's Body', pp. 334–6, 342.

was exiled from Rome, because he had taught unchaste [love]'.[103]
The *Remedia amoris* was commonly regarded as an attempt by
Ovid to make up for this great mistake. 'Afterwards he regretted
what he had done,' states the *accessus* to the *Remedia amoris*
edited by Huygens, 'and, being anxious to be reconciled with
those he had offended, he saw that the best way of achieving this
was to discover the antidote for the love which he had proffered
to them.'[104] According to Giovanni del Virgilio, the *Remedia* was
one of a series of books which he wrote in exile. The *Fasti* having
failed to mollify the emperor, 'Ovid wrote his fifth book, *Ovid on
the Remedy for Love*, so that he should remove the reason for his
having been sent into exile. But because he saw that this was of
no avail, he wrote his sixth book, *Ovid's Sorrows . . .* '.[105] Gerson
was of the opinion that Augustus was absolutely right—and that
his example could teach present-day rulers a thing or two. How
amazing it is, he declares, that a pagan and infidel judge (obviously a reference to Augustus) should condemn a book which
incites to foolish love, while among Christians such a work is
supported, praised, and defended![106]

Despite such outrage, the 'take the good and leave the evil'
defence of literature survived, and appeared in a variety of forms
and in many different contexts. In the preface to his English
'Moral Ovid' (1480), William Caxton quotes Romans 15: 4 ('All
that is written is written for our doctrine'), and explains that the
good is written to the end that example should be taken of those
who do well, and the evil to the end that we should abstain from
evil.[107] Caxton also applied this argument to a famous collection
of prose tales, Thomas Malory's *Morte Darthur*, which he
printed in 1485: 'Doo after the good and leve the evyl . . . al is
wryton for our doctrine. . . .'[108] The problem about this defence

---

[103] Trans. Minnis and Scott, *Medieval Literary Theory*, p. 362.
[104] *Accessūs ad auctores*, ed. Huygens, p. 34; trans. Minnis and Scott, *Medieval
Literary Theory*, p. 25.   [105] Ibid. 363.
[106] *Le Débat*, ed. Hicks, pp. 75–7; trans. Baird and Kane, pp. 82–4.
[107] *The Metamorphoses, translated by William Caxton, 1480* (New York, 1968),
i, unfol. Moreover, Rom. 15: 4 is echoed at the very beginning of the *Ovide moralisé*, a work which Christine certainly knew. See Minnis, *Authorship*, pp. 205–6.
[108] *Malory: Works*, ed. E. Vinaver, 2nd edn. (Oxford, 1971), p. xv. Cf. the similar
use of Rom. 15: 4 in the prologue to Caxton's 2nd edn. of *The Game and Playe of
the Chesse*, ed. W. J. B. Crotch, *The Prologues and Epilogues of William Caxton*,
EETS OS 176 (London, 1928), pp. 10–11.

is, of course, that it can be used to justify practically anything—
any genre, form or style; any text whatever, whether it be edifying, innocuous or offensive.[109] Christine and Gerson saw the
inherent weakness in its argument with clarity and total conviction. 'Good people,' pleads the latter in his sermon of 24
December 1402, 'take these books [i.e. Jean, Ovid, Matheolus]
away from your daughters and children! For they will take the
evil and leave the good' ('Car ilz prandront le mal et laisseront le
bien').[110]

If Jean de Meun's resemblance to Ovid could cut both ways,
so also could the notion that he had surpassed Ovid. For the
poem's opponents, the fact that the *Rose* was more comprehensive and thoroughgoing than the *Ars amatoria* made it all the
more dangerous. It is clear, declares Gerson in his *Traité contre
le Roman*, that this work 'soit pieur que celle d'Ovide' ['is worse
than that of Ovid'], because the *Rose* contains not only Ovid's
Ars amatoria but also other books 'qui ne sont point moins
deshonnestes et perilleux' ['which are not any the less dishonest
or dangerous'], books which are there 'translatés, assemblés et
tirés come a violance et sans propos' ['translated, brought
together, and drawn in by force and to no purpose']. Gerson
proceeds to argue that Jean de Meun had fewer scruples than his
Roman predecessor. Ovid clearly stated in the *Ars* that he is not
writing about good matrons or of ladies joined in marriage, nor
of those who could not be loved lawfully (cf. *Ars amatoria*,
i.31–4, ii.599–600). But the *Rose* is no respector of persons: 'Il
reprent toutes et blasme toutes, mesprise toutes, sans aucune
exepcion' ['it mocks all, blames all, despises all without any
exception'].[111]

But for the poem's supporters, the fact that Jean had
surpassed Ovid made his poem all the more praiseworthy, as
may be seen from Pierre Col's ingenious amplification of a
common defence of Ovid and its application to the *Rose* (written in the summer of 1402).[112] When Jean de Meun described
the way in which the Rose's castle was captured, he claimed this

[109] Cf. the discussion in Minnis, *Authorship*, pp. 204–8.
[110] *Le Débat*, ed. Hicks, p. 182; trans. Baird and Kane, p. 163.
[111] *Le Débat*, ed. Hicks, pp. 76–7; trans. Baird and Kane, pp. 83–4.
[112] *Le Débat*, ed. Hicks, pp. 104–5; trans. Baird and Kane, p. 108.

was done in order to forewarn its defenders—armed with this knowledge, they would be enabled to guard it better in the future. Moreover, because Jean had written in the vernacular ('en langaige commun a homes et fanmes, jeunes et vielz' ['in the common language of men and women, young and old']) he had made this knowledge widely available. By contrast, the 'fin' of the *Ars amatoria* was exclusively to teach men how to assault the castle; Pierre proceeds to make his anachronistic remark (as discussed on pp. 76–8 above) that, since Ovid had written in Latin, his work was unavailable to women who were unable to read it. Here *fin* is used in the technical sense carried by *finis* or *finalis causa* in the *accessūs*.[113] The crucial point being made is that the *finis* of the *Rose* far excels that of the *Ars amatoria*. Pierre may have been influenced by the standard view of another one of Ovid's poems, the *Remedia amoris*, to the effect that it reveals the stratagems of love, thereby forewarning and forearming people against them.[114] Though Pierre does not mention the later Ovid poem here, his assumption seems to be that the *Rose* is a bigger and better *remedium amoris* than the one provided by Jean's Roman predecessor.[115]

At this point in his letter Pierre Col changes tack, and argues that Ovid was unfairly maligned;[116] obviously he realizes that if this case is made convincingly he will be in a good position to defend the ancient poet's modern counterpart. To this end he accuses the Roman husbands who objected to the *Ars amatoria*, thereby causing Ovid's exile, as being excessively and unreasonably jealous. Little has changed, he continues, for nowadays it is said that the wife of the least jealous Italian husband is more strictly watched than the wife of the most jealous French one. The upshot of all this is that the national characteristics of the French equip them to take the *Rose* in the spirit in which it was meant, in contrast with the Romans, who were congenitally disposed to react violently against the *Ars amatoria*. Not that the exile of the poet did any lasting damage

---

[113] For uses of *finis* in twelfth-century *accessūs* and also in later commentaries, see the references on p. 174, n. 30.

[114] See e.g. the *accessus* edited by Huygens, *Accessūs ad auctores*, p. 34, and trans. Minnis and Scott, *Medieval Literary Theory*, p. 25.

[115] Cf. Col's subsequent argument, as described on p. 243 below.

[116] *Le Débat*, ed. Hicks, p. 105; trans. Baird and Kane, pp. 108–9.

to the poem's posterity, adds Pierre, for it endures, will endure, and has endured in all Christendom. Besides, Ovid recanted by writing the *Remedia amoris*. Viewed in the light of these facts—that the controversial book itself did not suffer (they would have served their interests better by burning it), and that the poet repented—the exiling of Ovid is seen to be unjustifiable by reason, and must have been motivated by enormously cruel jealousy.

What, then, of the argument that Jean drew on works other than the *Ars amatoria*? This made the work even more effective, Pierre declares; the more varied the forms of attack that he describes the better he teaches the defenders to guard the castle, 'et a celle fin le fist il' ['and it was for this purpose that he wrote it'].[117] As evidence of this enhanced effectiveness Pierre cites the case of a friend who borrowed his copy of the *Rose*: largely due to his reading of the poem, this man managed to disentangle himself from foolish love. The obvious implication is that the *Rose* is a powerful *remedium amoris*. To be more precise, Col is claiming that the *Rose* does something which generations of *accessūs* to the *Remedia amoris* had claimed for that book of Ovid's. It would seem, then, that some of the stock justifications of Ovid's poetry have been appropriated in the defence of the *Rose*.

But Christine de Pizan was not convinced. Pierre Col's claim that Jean was on the side of the defenders of the castle was, in her view, 'mervilleuse' ('incredible'). Master Jean, she retorted in a letter dated 2 October 1402, does nothing at all to help the defenders in closing up the gaps, for he does not speak to them at all and is not of their counsel; rather, he aids and abets the attackers in every form of assault.[118] If he were to suggest that the poet is simply recounting how the castle fell rather than recommending it, she warns Pierre Col, she would reply that a man who described an evil way of making counterfeit money would be teaching that method quite sufficiently. By introducing Ovid's *Ars amatoria*, she continues, Pierre has been caught in his own trap; it would have been better for his case if he had not introduced it. The only way he could have cited it to good

[117] *Le Débat*, ed. Hicks, pp. 105–6; trans. Baird and Kane, p. 109.
[118] *Le Débat*, ed. Hicks, pp. 136–7; trans. Baird and Kane, p. 134.

effect would have been to say that the *Ars*, wherein Ovid spoke of nothing but chastity, is the foundation and principle of the *Rose*, which is a mirror and exemplar of the good and chaste life—a proposition which is ridiculous. Christine's basic premiss here is that a bad work cannot be the foundation of a good one. Furthermore, she continues, when Pierre says that Jean de Meun included in his poem the work of many authors other than Ovid, by his own reasoning it is proved that the poet is speaking only to the attackers, just like Ovid, from whom he borrowed. Here her point seems to be that, by supporting Ovid's *Ars* with other similar writings, Jean is quite clearly supporting the attackers rather than the defenders: a proliferation of evil material does not make for a good *fin*. But Pierre has said that the more diverse the methods of attack which are revealed to the guards the better they are taught the art of defence. This is tantamount to saying that a man who attacks you and tries to kill you is merely showing you how to defend yourself!

Christine does not question Col's assumption that the *Ars amatoria* was written exclusively for a male audience. On the contrary, she is convinced that the Latin poem has nothing good to say to or about women; she is silent about its third book. Similarly, in her earlier *Epistre au dieu d'amours* (1399) Christine had declared roundly that Ovid was one of those clerics who 'were smitten even more than other men' (324); frustrated in his desire to have many women, he set about bad-mouthing the entire sex (321–3). Little wonder that men of his kind had mistresses and wives who played them false— 'What wonder's that?' (326–9). They ardently pursue women (not knowing those who are 'good, esteemed and prized'), no matter how much privation and suffering their passion may entail. And it was to show such men the art of tricking women that Ovid wrote the *Ars amatoria*.

> Et de ceulx parle Ovide en son traictié
> De *l'Art d'amours*, car pour la grant pitié
> Qu'il ot de ceulx compila il un livre
> Ou leur escript et enseigne a delivre
> Comment pourront les femmes decevoir
> Par faintises et leur amour avoir.
> (365–70)

[Now Ovid speaks of men like that in his
The Art of Love; the pity that he felt
For them encouraged him to write a book
In which he teaches them and openly
Elucidates the way to trick the girls
By means of subterfuge, and have their love.][119]

Far from teaching the *condicions* and ways of loving well, Christine declares, the *Ars* does quite the opposite.

This is very much of a piece with her 1402 letter to Pierre Col, to which we may now return.[120] Pierre gives further proof of having fallen into his own trap, Christine says, when he argues that Ovid was banished due to jealousy rather than reason. To refer to the poet's exile on account of the *Ars amatoria* is to make a dangerous admission; the Romans, who at that time governed their deeds with excellent judgement, had everything to fear from the dissemination of such a work. They wisely perceived 'la perverse doctrine, et le venin engoisseux apresté pour lancier es cuers des jeunes a les atraire a dissolucion et oiseuse et les engins tendus a decepvoir, prendre, soborner et sostraire la virginitey et chaasté de leurs filles et fames' ['the perverse and poisonous doctrine prepared in order to sow in the hearts of the young the desire for dissoluteness and idleness, as well as the traps readied to deceive, capture, suborn, and undermine the virginity and chastity of their daughters and wives']. One may recall the somewhat sensationalist comment found in an *accessus* to the *Amores*, to the effect that when Ovid wrote the *Ars amatoria* he had 'made adultresses of almost all the married women and maidens', which, not unnaturally, 'made the Romans hostile towards him'.[121] Christine is prepared to give the ancients more credit for having anticipated the danger in advance—and, indeed, for the relative leniency (or indulgence) of the punishment they meted out to the poet. The fact that they were acting rationally is emphasized by their attempt to suppress the book (there is no doubt that they burned it where they could find it, Christine says). But the root of a bad plant always survives.

---

[119] *Poems of Cupid*, ed. Fenster and Erler, pp. 48–53.
[120] *Le Débat*, ed. Hicks, pp. 137–9; trans. Baird and Kane, pp. 134–6.
[121] *Accessūs ad auctores*, ed. Huygens, p. 37; trans. Minnis and Scott, *Medieval Literary Theory*, p. 28.

The *Ars amatoria* is mistitled, she concludes this phase of her attack, for it contains nothing of real love. 'Ha! Livre mal nommé *L'Art d'amours!*' This book is badly named, 'for of love there is nothing. It could well be called the art of falsely and maliciously deceiving women.'[122] Here Christine is reiterating a point she had made more fully in the earlier *Epistre au dieu d'amours*:

> Si l'appella *Livre de l'Art d'amours,*
> Mais n'enseigne condicions ne mours
> De bien amer mais ainçois le contraire.
> Car homs qui veult selon ce livre faire
> N'amera ja, combien qu'il soit amez.
> Et pour cë est ki livres mau nommez,
> Car c'est *Livre d'Art de grant decevance,*
> Tel nom lui don, *et de faulce apparence!*
>
> (371–8)

> [And then he called the book *The Art of Love,*
> Although it doesn't teach the terms or ways
> Of loving well, but quite the opposite.
> The man who would behave as in that book
> Will never love, however he is loved.
> Because of that its title's misconceived,
> Its subject is *The Art of Great Deceit,*
> Of False Appearances—I dub it that!][123]

'*Titulus*' was one of the most important discussion-headings within the *accessus* repertoire, particularly because the title was regarded as the key to the work which followed it. Indeed, *titulus* was supposed to be derived from *titan*, the sun: just as the sun illuminates the world, so the book title illuminates the book.[124] In Christine's view, the title of Ovid's *Ars amatoria* failed to illuminate the true subject of this text. Regarded in the light of her trenchant response to Pierre Col's attempt to assign a good *fin* and *endendement* to Jean de Meun's poetry, it would seem that Christine is turning traditional *accessus* vocabulary against the scholars for whom its use would have been second

---

[122] Letter *Pour ce que entendement,* in *Le Débat,* ed. Hicks, pp. 138–9; trans. Baird and Kane, p. 135.

[123] *Poems of Cupid,* ed. Fenster and Erler, pp. 52–3. Cf. Baird and Kane, p. 36.

[124] Minnis, *Authorship,* p. 19.

nature. Taken together, her arguments and Jean Gerson's make it abundantly clear to defenders of the *Rose* both past and present that their case cannot uncontroversially be strengthened by recourse to discourses characteristic of the standard medieval criticism of Ovid. Indeed, both masters of love seem to stand or fall together; crises of authority have been provoked concerning the original *praeceptor* and his thirteenth-century disciple.

Beyond Ovid: the precedent of biblical lovers

Finally, we come to the most daring defence of the *Rose* to figure in the *querelle*. In the letter which he wrote at the end of the summer of 1402, Pierre Col went beyond all analogies with Ovid to appeal to the precedent of biblical lovers.[125] In his *Traité* Gerson had attacked the *Rose* on the grounds that the man who made it was a foolish lover ('fol amoureux'). Why then, Col retorts, does Lady Eloquence—a personification in Gerson's work which he insists on reading as a female figure— not first draw such conclusions against Solomon, David, and other foolish lovers, who lived long before Jean de Meun, whose books are part of Holy Scripture and whose words are part of 'the holy mystery of the Mass'? It was a *fol amoureux* who 'fist tuer Urie le bon chevalier par traïson, pour commettre adultere avec sa fame' ['caused Uriah the good knight to be killed by treachery in order to commit adultery with his wife']. It was a *fol amoureux* (i.e. Solomon) 'qui fist edifier temples aux ydoles pour l'amour de fames estranges' ['who caused the temples with the idols to be built for the love of strange women'].

Col proceeds to extol the advantages of knowing one's enemy by personal experience. Saints Peter and Paul were more firm in the faith after they had sinned, he declares; similarly, Jean de Meun, because he had been a foolish lover, was very firm in reason, for the more he knew by his own experience the folly which is in foolish love the more he was able to despise it and praise reason. When he wrote the *Rose* he was no longer a foolish lover, and had repented of having been one: 'quant il fist ce livre de la Rose il n'estoit plus fol amoureux, ains s'en repantoit

---

[125] *Le Débat*, ed. Hicks, p. 94; trans. Baird and Kane, pp. 97–8.

de l'avoit esté'.[126] This, Col continues, is manifest by the fact
that he speaks so well of reason, for a foolish lover would be
unable to do such a thing. The voice of Raison, it would seem,
is in large measure the voice of Jean de Meun—a point of view
which has recently been echoed by Robertson and Fleming.[127]

This ingenious appeal to the Bible echoes a long-running
controversy in scriptural exegesis, over how the sins of major
scriptural *auctores* could be reconciled with their undeniable
authority. Theologians had for generations attempted to cope
with the unpalatable historical facts that King David, saint and
supreme prophet, had committed adultery with Bathsheba and
engineered the situation in which her husband Uriah was killed,
and that King Solomon, the son of that mutual pair, had been
led astray by his excessive love of women, even to the extent of
worshipping strange gods.[128] Twelfth-century biblical commentators had allegorized David as Christ, Bathsheba as the church,
and Uriah as the devil. Their successors, some of whom seem to
have been worried by the obvious clash between the literal and
spiritual meanings here,[129] were willing to accept that David
and Solomon (and, in a very different capacity, St Paul) had
indeed sinned, but translated them into *exempla* of what to do

---

[126] Col supports this argument by citing Jean de Meun's own *Testament*, in which,
Col declares, Jean admits that in his youth he made 'many works through vanity',
these being 'various ballades, rondeaux and virelais that we do not have in writing'—a far cry from that later work, the *Rose* (*Le Débat*, ed. Hicks, p. 95; trans.
Baird and Kane, p. 98). It may be suggested that Jean de Meun, in his *Testament*
and indeed within the *Rose* itself, had engaged in Ovidian self-fashioning, presenting and interpreting his own writings in a way which his later supporters were to
adopt and amplify. Similarly, Giovanni Boccaccio 'constructed details of his own
"vita" in accordance with what he found in Ovid's', as has been demonstrated by
Robert Hollander, *Boccaccio's Two Venuses* (New York, 1977), pp. 112–16. He
concludes that Boccaccio 'is the "new Ovid" in that he thinks of himself as the
prime vernacular writer in the matter of love, but he wants simultaneously to keep
himself separate from Ovidian sentiments that are only carnal' (p. 116). On Chaucer
as a 'great medieval Ovid', see esp. Calabrese, *Chaucer's Ovidian Arts of Love*.

[127] Robertson argues that 'Raison speaks with the voice of Patristic authority,
Boethius and Cicero. She is, as it were, Lady Philosophy, who is described by
Guillaume as the Image of God. He who seeks Jean de Meun's opinions will find
them here, not in the discourses of the other characters who, with Ciceronian decorum, speak as their natures demand' (*Preface to Chaucer*, p. 199). Cf. Fleming, who
believes that Raison is 'associated in the poem with the *Sapientia Dei Patris* or
Christ': *Allegory and Iconography*, p. 107; see also pp. 132–5.

[128] For discussion and references see Minnis, *Authorship*, pp. 103–8.

[129] Cf. pp. 203–4 above.

and what to avoid. St Bonaventure, in the commentary on
Ecclesiastes which we have had cause to cite earlier, affirmed
that this work was written not by a sinner but by a penitent man
who regretted his sins.[130] Similarly, the English Dominican
Thomas Waleys, commenting on the Psalter in the early fourteenth century, described David and St Paul as having passed
through a state of sin: they were writing not as sinners but as
men who had once been sinners, and hence one can have confidence in what they wrote.[131] Arguments like this were obviously in Col's mind when he wrote the above passage. A writer's
amatory experience, then, does not necessarily invalidate his
work—providing that, like David or indeed like the exiled Ovid,
he has put his *amours* behind him.

But what if a writer does not leave his love behind? That is a
far more difficult proposition to defend. But Col, to his intellectual credit, tries to do just that in a later passage of this very
same letter.[132] He turns from past love to present and indeed
future love. Gerson had argued that Jean's character Raison
should have suited his teaching to his audience (thereby following the rules of rhetoric), remembering that he was speaking to
a Foolish Lover, who could easily be incited to carnality, rather
than to a layman, clerk, or theologian. Despite what Lady
Eloquence says, Col replies, being a clerk, philosopher, or
theologian is not irreconcilable with being a foolish lover—
witness the examples of David, Solomon, and others.

... semble par ses paroles [i.e. of 'dame Eloquance'] qu'estre clerc,
philozophe, ou theologien et fol amoureux ne se sueffrent pas ensemble, ains sont incompatibles. Hélas! il en va bien autrement, et est alé et
ira—dont c'est dommages—, come de David et Salemon et autres ...

[... it seems by her words that being a clerk, a philosopher, or a
theologian is not compatible with being a foolish lover, that they are
irreconcilable. Alas, it is, it has been, and it will forever be, far otherwise. Look at the examples of David, Solomon, and others.][133]

---

[130] Trans. Minnis and Scott, *Medieval Literary Theory*, pp. 232–3; cf. the discussion on pp. 207–9.
[131] *Postilla super primos xxxviii psalmos Davidicos Thomae Iorgii* (London,
1481), pp. 1–3.
[132] *Le Débat*, ed. Hicks, p. 97; trans. Baird and Kane, pp. 100–1.
[133] *Le Débat*, ed. Hicks, p. 97; trans. Baird and Kane, p. 100.

Indeed, he adds, some clerics even say that Solomon wrote the
Song of Songs on account of his love of Pharaoh's daughter.
('Scarcely a Catholic view,' Gerson was to declare in his
reply.[134]) One could bring forth, Col exclaims, more than a
thousand examples of people who were clerks and foolish lovers
at one and the same time. These roles are 'auxi bien ensemble'
['as compatible'] with one another as being at once 'clerc et
chevalereux' ['clerk and knight'], as were Pompey, Julius Caesar,
Scipio and Cicero.

Gerson's problem, Col continues, is that he believed everyone
to be like himself: because he was a clerk, philosopher, and
theologian without being a foolish lover, he thought that all
others were like him.[135] This is manifestly not the case.

[134] Le Débat, ed. Hicks, p. 168; trans. Baird and Kane, p. 149. In fact, some
commentators on the Song of Songs—including William of St Thierry, Philip of
Harvengt, and Honorius 'of Autun'—were willing to consider the possibility that
this work was occasioned by the king's marriage with Pharaoh's daughter. See
Minnis, Authorship, pp. 48, 238 n.

[135] Could it be that this is a deliberately provocative remark, given Gerson's
reputation (probably well established by the time of the querelle) as a theologian
with an exceptionally strong distrust of human emotions and affections? Johan
Huizinga views Gerson as 'the great dogmatic and moral censor of his time', a
theologian acutely aware of the 'dangers' even of 'spiritual love': The Waning of
the Middle Ages (London, 1924), pp. 174, 179. Cf. the comment in De distinc-
tione verarum revelationum a falsis (written in early 1402, at roughly the same
time as the Traité) that 'even though love begins from the spirit, it is to be greatly
feared that through its charms it gradually gives way and is consummated in the
flesh. ... For passion assaults even ironclad minds and tears away at their
strength. As Virgil says, a man burns up just in seeing a woman (Georgics, iii.
215)': Gerson, Early Works, trans. McGuire, p. 356. In an extraordinary passage
in the same work, Gerson seems to be describing his own experience in speaking
of 'a man' who 'took into the embrace of familiar friendship in the Lord a certain
virgin living the religious life. At first there was present no trace of carnal love',
but finally, 'through frequent contact, love slowly grew, but not wholly in the
Lord', and 'the man' came to realize that 'he was heading for great evil unless God
in his goodness had averted it' (pp. 357-8). B. P. McGuire believes that such fears
led Gerson to rule out the possibility of those sentimental and spiritual friendships
which had been acceptable to the Church for centuries: 'Jean Gerson and the End
of Spiritual Friendship: Dilemmas of Conscience', in Haseldine, Friendship in
Medieval Europe, pp. 229-50. See further McGuire's article 'Sexual Control and
Spiritual Growth in the Late Middle Ages: The Case of Jean Gerson', in Nancy
van Deusen (ed.), Tradition and Ecstasy: The Agony of the Fourteenth Century
(Ottawa, 1997), pp. 123-52, which includes an account of Gerson's short treatise
on the confession of masturbation (De confessione mollitiei). Gerson's fear of
masturbation is a symptom of his 'terror of homosexuality', according to
McGuire; he 'equivocates masturbation with homosexuality, for both are acts
"against the laws of nature" ' (p. 134). McGuire concludes that 'Gerson refused

Moreover, even if the great Gerson himself were, in the future, to become a foolish lover, this would not make him any the less a clerk—at least, in the early stages of this passion, the implication being that when it took proper hold it could well interfere with his proper functioning as a clerk, philosopher and theologian.

Et n'est il pas possible que il meismes, ou tamps a venir, soit fol amoureux? Par Dieu si est! Si n'en seroit il ja moins clerc, au moins au commansement de la fole amour.

[And is it not possible that even he in the future may be a foolish lover? By God, it is so; and he would not be any the less a clerk therefore, at least in the beginning of the foolish love.][136]

This vacillation is fascinating. On the one hand, Col does not want to set aside the argument that Jean wrote the *Rose* not as an actual lover but as a repentant one: 'when he made this book of the *Rose,* he was no longer a foolish lover, and had repented of being one' (cf. p. 247 above). On the other, he is tempted to brush it aside by claiming that even if Jean had written his poem while under the influence of foolish love, this would not have interfered with the text's clerkly, philosophical, and theological achievements.

Col does not explain what lies behind that last argument, but one may speculate that he had in mind the notion, which has its source in Aristotle, that certain kinds of moral short-coming do not impinge on one's intellectual ability. Knowledge (*scientia*) is not a moral virtue, declares Thomas of Chobham in his *Summa de arte praedicandi,* because, as Aristotle says, it does little or nothing to lead one to the virtues[137]—a reference to the seminal passage in Book 2 of the *Nicomachean Ethics,* 'Ad virtutes autem scire quidem parum

to subscribe to any expression of human love and union in a meeting between sexual desire and spiritual yearning. Instead he condemned the mingling of body and spirit as a nightmare he saw in the humanist, secular environment linked to the *Roman de la Rose*' (p. 151). The possibility of Gerson becoming a 'foolish lover' at any time in the future might have struck some of the readers of Col's letter as ridiculous, even hilarious.

[136] *Le Débat,* ed. Hicks, p. 97; trans. Baird and Kane, p. 101.
[137] *Summa,* ed. Morenzoni, pp. 61–3. This is identical with the anonymous discussion transcribed from Paris, Bibliothèque Nationale, MS Lat. 3108, by Jean Leclercq, 'Le Magistère du prédicateur au XIIIe siècle', *AHDLMA* 21 (1946), 105–47 (pp. 129–30).

aut nihil potest'.[138] To turn once again to Henry of Ghent's
Summa quaestionum ordinariarum, there the argument is
offered that someone can be said to be a teacher of theology
by dint of the knowledge which he possesses and his consequent intellectual ability to teach.[139] Once this condition is
established, Henry continues, it cannot be lost through
immoral behaviour. In this sense a sinner may be regarded as
a teacher of theology, for he is able to possess correct doctrine
just like the righteous man, and indeed he may be better
educated than the righteous man in terms of the technical
knowledge which he possesses. Arguments like these figured
largely in the debates over whether an immoral preacher can
and/or should be allowed to preach: indeed, the passages I
have cited above from Thomas of Chobham and Henry of
Ghent appear in *quaestiones* respectively entitled 'Whether to
preach in a state of mortal sin is itself a mortal sin or not' and
'Whether a sinner can be a teacher of theology'. The central
ideas involved had a long life, appearing in many different
guises.They may lie behind the challenging question posed by
Chaucer's Pardoner: can an immoral man tell a moral tale?[140]
Applying all this to Pierre Col's enigmatic and convoluted
statements, one may speculate that he is groping towards the
hypothesis that, since the sound doctrine and knowledge of a
well-educated cleric is not necessarily damaged by any vices to
which he may fall prey, the issue of whether or not Jean de
Meun was a foolish lover when he wrote the *Rose* is irrelevant
to our consideration of the intellectual content of what he has

[138] Quoted from Robert Grosseteste's version of the Latin text, as printed in *S.
Thomae Aquinatis in decem libros ethicorum Aristotelis ad Nicomachum expositio*,
ed. R. M. Spiazzi (Marietti, 1949), p. 11. For discussion of the implications of this
sententia, see A. J. Minnis, 'The *Accessus* Extended: Henry of Ghent on the
Transmission and Reception of Theology', in Mark D. Jordan and Kent Emery
(eds.), *Ad Litteram: Authoritative Texts and their Medieval Readers* (Notre Dame,
Ind., 1992), pp. 291–304.
[139] *Summae quaestionum ordinariarum ... Henrici a Gandavo* (in aedibus J.
Badii Ascensii, Paris, 1520; rpt. by the Franciscan Institute, Louvain and Paderborn,
1953), fos. 79ᵛ–81ʳ.
[140] For discussion see Minnis, 'Chaucer's Pardoner and the "Office of Preacher" ',
and my later article 'The Author's Two Bodies? Authority and Fallibility in Late-
Medieval Textual Theory', in P. R. Robinson and R. Zim (eds.), *Of the Making of
Books: Medieval Manuscripts, their Scribes and Readers. Essays presented to M. B.
Parkes* (Aldershot, 1997), pp. 259–79.

written.[141] It is hardly surprising that Col was reluctant to spell this out. He knew full well that it was far more difficult to reconcile the roles of clerk and lover than it was to reconcile the roles of clerk and knight.

Giovanni Boccaccio, it may be recalled, was even less keen to grasp this particular nettle. In his short treatise in praise of Dante, the *Trattatello* (first version *c.*1351–5), he agonized over whether Dante's persistent 'lust'—which found 'most ample space; and not just in his youthful years, but also in maturity'—devalued his writing.[142] Having shifted some of the blame onto the irresistible female sex (with the aid of ideas from Walter Map), and briefly referred to the power of love as demonstrated by classical mythology, Boccaccio then proceeds with a familiar argument about the sins of scriptural authors. 'David, even though he had many wives, only needed to see Bathsheba to forget, on her account, God, his kingdom, himself, and his integrity, becoming first an adulterer and then a murderer . . . And Solomon, to whose wisdom nobody, excepting the Son of God, has ever attained: did he not abandon Him who had made him wise and, to please a woman, kneel and adore Baalim?' In view of this evidence, Dante cannot be excused: but, given that he is in such distinguished company, his head need not hang 'so low as it would otherwise have done had he alone been at fault'.[143] The point is that Boccaccio could not blame the poet's

---

[141] There was, indeed, a possible medical justification for this view, to be found in the pseudo-Aristotelian *Problemata*, but Col seems unaware of it: see below, Ch. 6, n. 137.

[142] Trans. David Wallace in Minnis and Scott, *Medieval Literary Theory*, pp. 502–3.

[143] Similarly, in his *Decameron* (Fourth day, Introduction) Boccaccio had used the same sort of argument in defence of his own liking for women and wish to please them in his writing. Feminine beauty, he points out, was 'much admired' by 'Guido Cavalcanti and Dante Alighieri in their old age, and by Cino da Pistoia in his dotage'. Then Boccaccio moves from the moderns to the ancients. He could pursue his case still further by citing history books which are 'filled with examples from antiquity of outstanding men, who, in their declining years, strove with might and main to give pleasure to the ladies'. The point seems to be that if such distinguished men were still susceptible to female charm, then he, Boccaccio, can hardly be accused with utter severity. *Opere di Giovanni Boccaccio*, ed. C. Sergio (Milan, 1967), pp. 258–9; trans. G. H. McWilliam, *Boccaccio: The Decameron* (Harmondsworth, 1972), p. 329. Cf. the strategy adopted by John Gower, who at the end of his *Confessio amantis* has his narrator (now revealed to be a *senex amans*) take encouragement from his visionary encounter with a company of lovers,

sins on his youthfulness, in which age a man was physiologically
prone to sexual passion. To be of mature age and be in love was
much harder to defend (and to be an aged lover was to run the
risk of being regarded as utterly ridiculous—witness the many
medieval caricatures of the *senex amans*).[144]

It would seem, then, that to go beyond the terms of reference
of 'the Medieval Ovid' and look towards Scripture, as Col tried
to do in defending Jean de Meun, and as Dante most certainly
did in his *Comedy*, did not guarantee an escape from those
problems regularly encountered by those medieval Ovidians,
both critics and authors, who sought to appropriate that (rather
paradoxical) respectability enjoyed by the writer who was the
great expert not only on human love but also on its rejection.
Quite clearly, in medieval literary theory, *amor* sits uncomfort-
ably with *auctoritas*.[145] When such theory is pressed into the
moral defence of poetry which has human love as its central
subject, the problems and paradoxes are many and various.

*

This inquiry has demonstrated how, in the *querelle de la Rose*,
a common body of ideas from commentary tradition were
manipulated to serve two utterly opposed and irreconcilable
points of view. When the opponents of the *Rose* castigated it as
worthless, or when its supporters affirmed its great value, they
shared certain paradigms, and revealed themselves to be influenced by certain principles, which figure largely in medieval
commentary tradition, most relevantly in the *accessūs Ovidiani*.

---

particularly the group of old lovers which includes David, Solomon, Aristotle,
Virgil, and Ovid: 'I thoghte thanne how love is swete, / Which hath so wise men
reclamed, / And was miself the lasse aschamed' (viii.2720–2). This passage is
discussed in Minnis, '*De Vulgari Auctoritate*'. Christine de Pizan brought together
David, Solomon, and Ovid, in a more obviously negative context: they are examples
of men who could not be loyal 'even to the loveliest'; in the case of the first two,
'God grew enraged and punished their excess': *Epistre au dieu d'amours*, ll. 316–22,
in *Poems of Cupid*, ed. Fenster and Erler, pp. 48–9.

[144] Evrart de Conty explains that the old 'have forsaken the desires of sensuality
(*luxure*) and have reduced them to good measure', the reason being that since
sensual desires come from great and superabundant heat, the natural coldness of
aged people sharply reduces their capacity to experience such pleasure. *Eschez
amour. moral.*, ed. Guichard-Tesson and Roy, pp. 482–3.

[145] See further the discussion below, pp. 273–4.

Defenders and attackers alike turned to this corpus of criticism when they sought to theorize the *Rose*. Indeed, it may be no exaggeration to say that scholastic literary principles of the kinds illustrated above actually determined some of the parameters of the debate itself.

My assessment of the evidence would seem to indicate the speciousness of the argument that what separated Christine de Pizan and Jean Gerson from the *cognoscenti* who defended Jean de Meun was ignorance of, or lack of familiarity with, the textual issues involved. All the participants in the debate were fully aware of the terms of reference of the late medieval 'ethical poetic', to use Judson Allen's apposite term. Given Gerson's education, and the regularity with which many of the fundamental issues and relevant methods of textual analysis occurred in the standard scriptural exegesis of his day, this is hardly surprising. What, then, of Christine? Some modern defenders of the *Rose* have tried to devalue her contribution by implying she lacked the learning to cope with the niceties of literary debate.[146] But, as has been argued above, Christine was quite knowledgeable about many relevant aspects of medieval literary theory, including at least some of the standard criticism of Ovid. The depth of this knowledge, the extent of her education, must remain a matter of debate. But I have demonstrated, I hope, that she was sufficiently well versed in the relevant principles and theoretical discourses to engage with Jean de Montreuil and the Col brothers on their own terms, so to speak. Skilful exploitation of ideas is quite different in kind, and looks quite different, from semi-comprehension of them. In Christine's case, the skill implies the knowledge to at least some degree. At any rate, Jean Gerson was impressed by the acuity of his comrade-in-arms, whom he honoured with the accolade *virago*.[147] 'The very anxiety and ingenuity of your evasiveness shows that the woman had you hard pressed by the sharpness of her reasoning', he

---

[146] See e.g. Robertson, *Preface to Chaucer*, p. 21; cf. p. 85. *Au contraire*, see the discussion of Christine's learning, and comparison of her culture with that of the Col brothers, in Badel, *Rose au XIV siècle*, pp. 436–47.

[147] On the etymology of *virago*, 'manly woman', see Minnis, *Chaucer: Shorter Poems*, pp. 424–5. It has a special purchase as applied to Christine, given that she managed to assume the male prerogative of authorship. (In the passage here quoted, Gerson may be crediting her with mastery of male techniques of argumentation.)

taunts Pierre Col.[148] If the term *femme* had become an insult to be hurled at Christine (cf. p. 213 above), here *mulier* functions to increase the discomfiture of her opponents—the learned 'Secretary of the King our Lord' has been bested in argument by a woman!

Working together, Gerson and Christine challenged the 'single most authoritative clerkly figure in the medieval French literary canon'.[149] From the point of view of authorial self-fashioning, however, Christine had far more at stake than the eminent chancellor of the University of Paris. She struggled to expand 'the very terms of the clerkly discursive system in such a way as to authorize her own identity as clerkly speaking subject'.[150] In the process of disclaiming any *auctorité*, in maintaining that she was motivated not by pride but the desire to right the wrongs done to women in literature which men had monopolized,[151] Christine actually valorized her own literary activities. Out of the crises of textual authority which she and Gerson had precipitated concerning the poetry of their contemporary *magister amoris* and his Roman forebear, Christine forged an identity for herself as that rarest of creatures—a female authority.

---

[148] *Le Débat*, ed. Hicks, p. 168; trans. Baird and Kane, p. 148.
[149] As Kevin Brownlee has described Jean de Meun; 'Discourses of the Self', p. 259.
[150] To borrow another statement from Brownlee; ibid. 259.
[151] *Le Débat*, ed. Hicks, pp. 148–9; trans. Baird and Kane, p. 143; cf. pp. 217–18 above.

CHAPTER 6

Pruning the Rose: *Evrart de Conty* and European Vernacular Commentary

The supporters and opponents of Maistre Jehan de Meun in the *querelle de la Rose* were not the only medieval readers who could not agree on the poem's significance. Many scribes, scholars, and poets experienced similar dilemmas, and made their mark on the text in various ways. P.-Y. Badel has spoken of its 'double descent'.[1] On the one hand, the *Rose* strongly influenced poets of *fine amor*, such as Machaut, Froissart, and Deschamps, who produced many elegant *dits* of love and reason for the entertainment and edification of aristocratic patrons. On the other, it inspired monastic writers like Gilles li Muisis and Guillaume de Deguileville. Indeed, the latter went so far as to declare, at the beginning of his *Pèlerinage de la vie humaine*, that having 'read, studied, and looked closely at the beautiful *Romance of the Rose*' he was 'sure that this was what moved' him 'most to have the dream' on which his religious allegory is avowedly based.[2]

This phenomenon may be related to what Badel terms the 'discontinuous' or 'fragmentary' way in which the *Rose* apparently was read: different readers would focus on an array of specific things and be blind to others, skipping from one passage to another.[3] Moral *sententiae* were appreciated in defiance of larger textual contexts which threatened to problematize them;

---

[1] *Rose au XIVe siècle*, p. 94.

[2] *Guillaume de Deguileville, The Pilgrimage of Human Life*, trans. E. Clasby (New York, 1992), p. 3. However, he seems to have changed his opinion of the *Rose* by the time he revised his *Pèlerinage* in 1355; see Huot, *Rose and Its Readers*, pp. 225–38.

[3] See Badel, *Rose au XIVe siècle*, pp. 141–2, 499–501, and also the development of this idea in Dagenais, *Ethics of Reading*, pp. 150–1, 169, 210.

au contraire, titillating passages could be enjoyed without recourse to the ethical correctives on offer elsewhere. Substantiation for this theory may be found in abundance in manuscript rubrication, annotation, and decoration. Sylvia Huot's survey has revealed copies which cast the *Rose* as love-poetry and signal enjoyment of its erotic climax, while others gloss it as 'an exposition of the follies of youth, and stress the sacred content of Genius's discourse'.[4] Recognition of the text's 'sacred content', or at least sacred potential, achieved full expression in Jean Molinet's *Romant de la Rose moralise cler et net* (composed *c*.1482, printed in 1500), which rewrites the *Rose* as an explicit Christian allegory. Amant's pursuit of his beloved is interpreted as man's attempt to reach heavenly bliss, the God of Love being identified as 'nostre Seigneur'.[5] Such *integumenta* weigh very heavily; indeed, they smother the original text.

Moving back to the earlier years of the *Rose*'s reception, it is intriguing to find that the B-text group of manuscripts, whilst displaying considerable variation among themselves, commonly recast Jean de Meun's part of the poem in the spirit of Guillaume's, making it more of a courtly romance.[6] Raison's defence of plain speaking has been suppressed, and that word which Christine de Pizan found so offensive, *coilles*, has disappeared along with

---

[4] Huot, *Rose and Its Readers*, pp. 28–9.

[5] See Badel, *Rose au XIVe siècle*, p. 122; Huot, *Rose and Its Readers*, p. 315; and Rosemund Tuve, *Allegorical Imagery: Some Medieval Books and their Posterity* (Princeton, NJ, 1966), pp. 237–46. Molinet, *grand rhétoriqueur*, was also the author of an obscene mock-sermon, the *Sermon de Saint Billouart*, on which see Jacques E. Merceron, 'Obscenity and Hagiography in Three Anonymous *Sermons Joyeux* and in Jean Molinet's *Saint Billouart*', in Ziolkowski (ed.), *Obscenity*, pp. 332–44.

[6] This process continues in the second of the two Dutch translations of the *Rose*, the *Tweede Rose* (*c*.1290), by an anonymous Flemish author whose copy of the French poem was related to the B-family of manuscripts. Here the unrequited lover-poet-narrator enounters two blissfully happy lovers, Jolijs and Florentine, and, having heard the young nobleman's account of how he won his lady, asks him to provide instruction in matters of love. This serves as a new introduction for the version of the poem which follows; 'I hope that I will be able to learn from that what love and her ways are like, and how I should deal with them so that I can achieve happiness with her whom I love loyally.' Hence, 'the *Second Rose*'s story becomes a directly explanatory text for lovers to learn how to achieve happiness in love', with the rose itself symbolizing Florentine's virginity. Cf. Karin Lesnik-Oberstein, 'Some [Dutch] Adaptors and their Adaptations: *Le Roman de la Rose* and *Floire et Blaunchefleur*' (MA diss., University of Bristol, 1986), pp. 30–6, and D. E. Van der Poel, 'A Romance of a Rose and Florentine: The Flemish Adaptation of the *Romance of the Rose*', in Brownlee and Huot (eds.), *Rethinking the Rose*, pp. 304–15. For the first Dutch translation, see n. 8 below.

Jean's account of their owner, Saturn.[7] Far more extensive revision was carried out by the cleric Gui de Mori, who added substantial interpolations but also deleted thousands of lines. Announcing himself as the third *Rose* poet, he at least has the humility to predict that 'he will not be of such renown as Jean or Guillaume'.[8] De Mori insists on linking Amant with Jean, as in the remark, 'thus stands Master Jean de Meun, by whom is signified (*signifiés*) the lover . . .'.[9] More generally, he seems to want to tidy up the text, by relocating blocks of material and imposing 'a clearer, more linear structure'.[10] In Gui's version, the work's didacticism is affirmed and amplified by further recourse to such authoritative sources as Macrobius, Boethius, and Alan of Lille. The overall effect, however, is not one of disambiguation, since additional material is also provided on the art of love.[11] Yet Gui feels uncomfortable with some of the *Rose*'s sexual/textual discourse. Amant is allowed to experience sexual pleasure in the consummation of his love, and to impregnate his Rose, but the more graphic elements of this episode have gone, along with the Pygmalion episode and Amant's metaphorical language of scrip and stiff pilgrim staff. As in the B-text manuscripts, Saturn's infamous *coilles* have been removed together with the fable in which such dirty talk features. This *Rose*, declares de Mori in his prologue, will be 'more accessible and more enjoyable to listen to' than the original.[12] Sylvia Huot concludes:

[7] Huot, *Rose and Its Readers*, pp. 131, 132, 140.

[8] In similar vein, the first Dutch translator of the *Rose*, Heinric van Aken (from Brussels, writing *c.*1284?), displaces Guillaume de Lorris at the point where Jean de Meun names him, substituting hs own name and having the God of Love praise him as 'so courtly, and so mild'. Furthermore, in one of the manuscripts a mysterious 'Michiel' declares—in a manner obviously reminiscent of Jean's statement about his continuation of Guillaume's *Rose*—that he has finished this text which Heinric left incomplete. Cf. Lesnik-Oberstein, 'Some [Dutch] Adaptors', pp. 13–16, 20, 22. Her conclusion is that 'mainly by selective omission' the 'multifaceted original' is transformed 'into a one-dimensional text'; more specifically, the text reads as 'a didactic story' about human love which mainly brings out 'its sordid aspects' (pp. 58, 57).

[9] See David Hult, *Self-Fulfilling Prophecies: Readership and Authority in the First 'Roman de la Rose'* (Cambridge, 1986), pp. 49, 51. Hult offers a substantial discussion of de Mori's *Rose* (pp. 34–64). See also Badel, *Rose au XIVe siècle*, pp. 144–5, and Huot, *Rose and Its Readers*, pp. 85–129, 131–2, 136, 139, etc.

[10] Ibid. 89.   [11] Cf. ibid. 89.

[12] However, at the same point he affirms his respect for the text's existing *ententions* and *mataire*: see Hult, *Self-Fulfilling Prophecies*, p. 35.

Gui saw the *Rose* as containing both the art and the remedy of love, with the latter accomplished both through the exposition of acceptable alternatives—love of God, friendship, reasonable courtship, marriage and procreation—and through the revelation of the sordid side of erotic pursuit.[13]

She also compares Gui's reading of the *Rose* with that of Pierre Col, and sees him as anticipating some of the criticisms which Christine de Pizan and Jean Gerson were to make later. It may be added that Gui has brought the *Rose* much nearer to the moral economy of the *Eschez amoureux* poem and its commentary. To these texts we may now turn.

The poem is anonymous but seems to have been written between 1370 and 1380. Its author evinces considerable respect for both the *Rose* poets. Introducing his own depiction of the Garden of Delight, he declares that 'the best and most gracious' version was provided at the beginning of the 'joli Roumant de la Rose'; a few lines later he praises the person who completed (*parfit*) this 'bel roumant', creating a 'notable oeuvre' of subtle design and great mystery (*grant mistere*): 'never since has there been any more beautiful, more accomplished or more complete book on the subject'.[14] Furthermore, the *Eschez* poet pays the *Rose* the compliment of substantial imitation, the initial setting of the text's allegorical action being strongly reminiscent of the 'joli Roumant'. The narrator of the *Eschez amoureux* is presented as experiencing in his youth a springtime vision of the goddess Nature, who tells him about the two paths between which he must choose, the way of reason and the way of sensuality. Subsequently he meets Mercury and the goddesses Venus, Juno, and Pallas; in a re-enactment of the Judgment of Paris he declares his preference for Venus, who rewards him by setting him on the road to the Garden of Delight, where he will find a lover. On the way, however, he is upbraided by Diana for his choice, but her efforts are in vain. In the garden he meets Delight playing a game of chess with a beautiful lady. Each chess piece represents a quality, disposition, or activity associated with love,

[13] Huot, *Rose and Its Readers*, p. 93.
[14] *Eschez amoureux*, ed. Christine Kraft, *Die Liebesgarten-Allegorie der 'Echecs amoureux': Kritische Ausgabe und Kommentar* (Frankfurt a.M., 1977), pp. 94–5 (ll. 55–90); cf. Hult, *Self-Fulfilling Prophecies*, pp. 56–7.

there being one set for the man and a different set for the woman. Having been checkmated by the lady, the young man is instructed in the *ars amatoria* by the God of Love. Finding himself alone after all this, the narrator looks for the lady, anxious to engage her in a return match, but instead he meets the third goddess involved in the Judgment of Paris, Pallas, the goddess of Reason. She explains the conflict between the passionate life and the life of reason, and offers him the principles whereby he can pursue the good life. The *Eschez* poet proceeds to offer an abundance of doctrine drawn from such sources as Jacques de Cessoles' *Libellus de moribus hominum et de officiis nobilium super ludo scaccorum,* Giles of Rome's *De regimine principum,* and Pierre Bersuire's *Ovidius moralizatus.* In the fullest version of the text which survived into the twentieth century, it breaks off in the course of a discussion of such matters (a far cry from the *Rose*) as the proper conduct of marriage, child-rearing, domestic economy, and financial prudence.[15] The final part of the *Eschez amoureux* is lost— assuming, of course, that its author actually completed it. One can easily imagine it ending with florid affirmation of Christian salvation. To judge by what we have, however, the text's pedagogic objective was in clear view throughout. Indeed, it could be argued that the *frisson* of the *ars amatoria* is designed to entice the young aristocrat into the moral centre of the text, where unimpeachable doctrine holds sway.

In his commentary on the *Eschez amoureux* Evrart de Conty picks out some of the similarities between it and the *Rose.*[16]

---

[15] Here I follow the Dresden MS of the poem, as summarized by S. L. Galpin, 'Les Eschez amoureux: A Complete Synopsis with Unpublished Extracts', *Romanic Review,* 11 (1920), 283–307. Given the obliteration of this text during the Second World War, we are obliged to rely on the even more fragmentary text preserved in Venice, Biblioteca Nazionale Marciana, MS Fr. App. 23 (=267). See Kraft, *Die Liebesgarten-Allegorie,* pp. 19–26.

[16] In the discussion which follows, as previously in this book, I have drawn on the English translation of the *Eschez amoureux* commentary included in Joan Morton Jones's unpublished doctoral dissertation, 'The Chess of Love [Old French Text with Translation and Commentary]' (Ph.D. diss., University of Nebraska, 1968). However, particularly since this translation antedates the critical edition and is based on a single MS of Evrart's work, Paris, Bibliothèque Nationale, MS Fr. 9197, I have been obliged to make some changes. Moreover, as Reginald Hyatte has pointed out in a critique of Jones's judgements, BN MS Fr. 9197 is a faulty and highly individual copy: 'The Manuscripts of the Prose Commentary (Fifteenth Century) on *Les Echecs amoureux*', *Manuscripta,* 26 (1982), 25. This article, of

Discussing the *Eschez* poet's version of the Garden of Mirth
(which has Oyseuse[17] as its porter), Evrart remarks that this
was not 'faint[18] sanz cause raisonable' ['feigned without reasonable cause'] in either the *Rose* or the *Eschez*; that good 'reason'
is spelled out in his commentary, which, for example, interprets
the river which flows before the garden as the passage of time.[19]
The *Eschez* poet had been influenced by the series of images
which Guillaume's Amant saw on the wall of the love garden.
Evrart explains that these images signify to us various things
that by their proper nature are contrary to the life of love;
hence, 'au commencement du *Rommant de la Rose*' they are
'paintes et pourtraictes' ['painted and portrayed'] around and
outside the walls of the garden of Mirth or Love, whose people
voluntarily withdraw from these contrary things, for Love and
Mirth love only joy and delight. Therefore it is said that such
people are not worthy of entering the garden, as they symbolize
all types of sorrow. Evrart then returns to the *Eschez amoureux*:
'Et pour ce faint aussi l'acteur du livre dessusdit dont nous
parlons qu'il vit semblablement toutes les .x. ymages dessusdites, a l'aprochier du vergier dessusdit, pourtraictes au dehors'

course, was written before the discovery of the commentary's authorship by
Françoise Guichard-Tesson. Hyatte, in collaboration with Maryse Ponchard-
Hyatte, went on to produce an edition (from the 5 Bibliothèque Nationale manuscripts) of astronomical and musical extracts from Evrart's work: *L'Harmonie des
sphères: Encyclopédie d'astronomie et de musique extraite du commentaire sur 'Les
Echecs amoureux'* (New York, 1985). At least it can be said of BN MS Fr. 9197 that
it is stunningly illuminated, this being the work of 'the master of Antoine Rolin',
chancellor of Burgundy, for whom it was prepared between 1490 and 1495. A
facsimile of some of its pages has been published by Anne-Marie Legaré with the
collaboration of Françoise Guichard-Tesson and Bruno Roy, *Le Livre des echecs
amoureux* (Paris, 1991).

[17] An ambiguous term which can mean both idleness and leisure; cf. p. 53 above.
Ovid is quoted as saying that love has no power over one who flees Oyseuse: *Eschez
amour. moral.*, ed. Guichard-Tesson and Roy, p. 367.
[18] Meaning 'invents, imagines, makes up'; cf. the Latin verb *fingo*. Translated as
'feigned' throughout this chapter, to preserve the technical sense.
[19] *Eschez amour. moral.*, ed. Guichard-Tesson and Roy, p. 441. Evrart reiterates
the point later in his commentary: 'voult faindre ainsy l'acteur du *Rommant de la
Rose* que Oyseuse estoit portiere du vergier de Deduit et que elle ly ouvry la porte
et le mist ens premiere, at aussi fait l'acteur semblablement du livre rimé dessusdit
dont nous devons parler' ['the author of the *Romance of the Rose* wishes to feign
that Idleness/Leisure was the gate-keeper of the Garden of Mirth, and that she
opened the gate to him and first let him in. And so the author of the abovemen-
tioned rhymed book about which we should be speaking feigns the same thing'] (p.
516).

['And so, the author of this poem we are discussing also feigns that he, in the same way, saw all ten of the above-mentioned images, on the approach to the above-mentioned garden, portrayed outside'].[20] When he is condemning the type of love which pursues pleasure only, and hence is bestial and unreasonable, Evrart says 'c'est l'amour que Raison tant reprend ou *Rommant de la Rose*, et aussi fait Pallas ou livre rimé dessusdit dont nous parlons' ['this is the love that Raison so much reprehends in the *Romance of the Rose*, and so does Pallas in the aforesaid rhymed book of which we are speaking'].[21] Explaining the clothing of the God of Love, which is so diverse and changeable that the I-*persona* cannot tell what material it is made of or what colour it is, Evrart claims that this signifies to us the great changes of lovers' hearts, which are so often moved to so many opinions and thoughts, as Ovid says, that it is a marvel, and proceeds to quote the *Rose*'s account of love's contraries: 'Et c'est ce que Raison veult dire en la descripcion d'amours ou *Rommant de la Rose*, quant elle dit, sy come l'acteur faint, que "amours est paix hayneuse, amours est hayne amoureuse"' ['And this is what Raison means in the description of love in the *Romance of the Rose* when he says, as the author feigns, that "Love is hateful peace, Love is amorous hatred"; cf. *Rose*, 4263–4].[22] Furthermore, he assimilates Jean de Meun's definition of love to his own hierarchical schema of the different kinds of love (which constitutes a substantial elaboration of what the *Eschez* itself says).[23]

From all this, then, may it be inferred that Evrart regards the *Rose* as a *remedium amoris* which reveals the pains and dangers brought about by obsessive love, and expects the ending to be read as a tacit condemnation of Amant's folly? That would be to offer a highly reductive view of his hermeneutics; the situation is, in my view, rather more complicated. When considering the roses which are part of the traditional 'picture' of Venus, Evrart asserts that the red rose signifies unreasonable love,

---

[20] *Eschez amour. moral.*, ed. Guichard-Tesson and Roy, p. 511.
[21] Ibid. 549. Cf. p. 623, where Evrart argues that the love of those who are interested merely in delight 'is not properly love or appropriate in reasonable men, but is bestial love and baseness. And this is the love that Raison wishes to reprehend in the *Romance of the Rose*'.   [22] Ibid. 554.
[23] Ibid. 365–6; cf. below, pp. 306ff.

which mainly desires carnal delight.[24] But no attempt is made to apply this doctrine to the ending of the *Rose*—indeed, no comment at all is made about Jean de Meun's conclusion, and when Evrart speaks of the condemnation of carnal love in the *Rose* he consistently confines himself to citation of Raison's disquisition on the subject. Furthermore, Evrart's account of loyal love—of which he certainly approves—includes the statement that the lover should, as best he can, keep and accomplish all the commandments of Love, 'ainsy qu'ilz sont escrips ou *Rommant de la Rose* et es autres livres aussi d'amours. Le livre mesmez dont nous parlons en parle en briefs paroles assez souffisaument et par soutil maniere' ['as they are written in the *Romance of the Rose* and also in the other books of love. This very book we are discussing [i.e. the *Eschez amoureux*] speaks sufficiently enough about it in brief words and in a subtle manner'].[25] He also speaks approvingly of the *Rose*'s account of Courtesy and Bel Acueil (these being figures who reappear in the later poem).[26]

However, the point cannot be made strongly enough that

---

[24] *Eschez amour. moral.*, ed. Guichard-Tesson and Roy, p. 239.

[25] Ibid. 552. Cf. the later statement that loyal and excellent love cannot be for many, just for one person; 'Et pour ce fu il dit ou *Romant de la Rose* que le cuer qui "s'amour en pluseurs lieux depart, partout en a petite part" ' ['And that is why it is said in the *Romance of the Rose* that the heart that "divides its love between many places leaves a poor part of it everywhere" '; cf. *Rose*, 2233-4] (p. 678).

[26] See ibid. 516: 'faint aussi l'acteur du *Rommant de la Rose* que Bel Acueil est filz de Courtoisie' ['the author of the *Romance of the Rose* feigns that Fair Welcome is the son of Courtesy'], and Evrart defines this in the warmest of terms; 'ceulz qui sont gentilz et de noble courage sont courtoiz par nature' ['those who are well bred and of noble heart are courteous by nature']. He does not make the point that in this case Bel Acueil may be employed in a bad cause. Cf. pp. 517–18: 'Pour ce donc que courtoisie est en nostre humaine communicacion et en toute honnourable compaignie tres gracieuse chose et chose bien seans, et par especial entre les amoureux auxquielx elle est grandement proufitable, pour ce faint l'acteur dessusdit que Courtoisie vint au devant de ly, qui le recuit et acueilli moult debonnairement et ly habandonna plainement le vergier ou il estoit entrés pour ly dedens deduire et solacier tout a sa voulenté, maiz qu'il se gardast bien de faire y vilenie; et tout ce faint aussi pareillement l'acteur du *Rommant de la Rose*' ['Because, then, courtesy is, in our human communication and in all honourable company a very gracious and appropriate thing, and especially among lovers, to whom it is highly profitable, the above-mentioned author feigns that Courtesy came before him, received him, and welcomed him very graciously and made him openly free with the garden he had entered, to live and enjoy himself at his will, but that he should carefully keep himself from doing any baseness there. And the author of the *Romance of the Rose* feigns all this in the same way'].

Evrart is commenting on the *Eschez amoureux* and not on the *Rose*. Allusions to the earlier work (as viewed within the commentary as a whole) are few and far between. Evrart has his own chosen text to expound, his own vernacular mythography to construct. It is hardly surprising that, at those few points when he does make contact with the *Rose*, he should proclaim its consonance with the *Eschez*. This was, after all, an absolutely commonplace academic procedure in Latin commentaries; generally speaking, exegetes were very reluctant to point out marked disagreements between the texts they were expounding and between the statements of revered authorities. Evrart is treating the *Rose*, a prestigious vernacular text, in this respectful manner; this certainly does not mean that we should use the commentary on the *Eschez amoureux* as if it were a commentary on the *Rose*, as has tended to happen in some modern criticism.[27] The two poems are very different in style, scope, and didactic mode. Christine de Pizan could not have complained of the *Eschez amoureux* (as she did of the *Rose*) that, by failing to conclude 'in favour of the moral way of life',[28] it had not left the reader with clear ethical instruction. There is no reason to doubt that Evrart was aware of the extent to which the *Eschez amoureux* had deviated from the poem without which it could not have existed. His own intellectual gifts inspire confidence on that score. And he lived and worked in an exceptional intellectual environment, wherein vernacular hermeneutics were promoted on a grand scale.

My project in the present chapter, which seeks to relocate the *Eschez amoureux* and its commentary within the reception history of the *Rose*, is therefore twofold. On the one hand, Evrart's exegesis will be read as an attempted erasure of a substantial part of Jean de Meun's legacy as *magister amoris*. Jean's narrow concern with male performance of desire (female sexuality being fetishized into the vaginal rose, 'a single, detached, passive body part')[29] has been replaced with a more comprehensive vision of married love as a normative (within the

---

[27] The use which modern defenders of the *Rose* have made of the *Eschez amoureux* commentary has judiciously been criticized by Douglas Kelly, *Medieval Imagination*, pp. 107–8.

[28] *Le Débat*, ed. Hicks, p. 135; trans. Baird and Kane, p. 132.

[29] To borrow a phrase from Brownlee, 'Multiple Endings of the *Rose*', p. 208.

active life) choice which affords excellent opportunities for
socioeconomic success as well as the satisfaction of desire. On
the other hand, it will be read as an individual inscription of the
same literary-theoretical traditions which did so much to
overdetermine the *Rose* itself (as our discussion in the preceed-
ing chapters has, I hope, made sufficiently clear). The latter
inquiry will involve the relation of Evrart's *Eschez amoureux*
commentary to both its immediate and larger milieux—as a
product of the state-sponsored vernacular hermeneutics of the
age of Charles V, and as a major moment within the European
history of literary criticism.

State hermeneutics: Charles V's commentary-translations

The fact that we are in a position to investigate the immediate
milieu of the *Eschez amoureux* commentary is largely due to the
research of Françoise Guichard-Tesson, who identified its
author as Evrart de Conty, physician to Charles V and also to
Blanche of Navarre, widow of Philippe VI.[30] The main evidence
for this attribution consists of many correspondences between
the *Eschez amoureux* commentary and a known work of
Evrart's, the *Livre des problèmes d'Aristote*, a French rendering
of the pseudo-Aristotelian *Problemata* which Evrart presumably
regarded as an addition to the Aristotle translations undertaken
by Nicole Oresme at the king's command.[31] Moreover, as a
physician Evrart would have had a special interest in a treatise
which discusses, *inter alia*, the physical effects of and problems
concerning: sexual intercourse;[32] fatigue; lying down and

[30] For the proof of Evrart's authorship see F. Guichard-Tesson, 'Evrart de Conty,
auteur de la *Glose des Echecs amoureux*', *Le Moyen français*, 8–9 (1981), 111–48;
also *Eschez amour. moral.*, ed. Guichard-Tesson and Roy, pp. liii–liv.

[31] On this work, of which we have an autograph MS of some 500 folios, see esp.
F. Guichard-Tesson, 'Le Métier de traducteur et de commentateur au XIVe siècle
d'après Evrart de Conty', *Le Moyen français*, 24–5 (1990), 131–67. However, it was
not completed in the lifetime of Charles V, as Guichard-Tesson notes (p. 133). There
is good reason to believe that the *Livre des problèmes* pre-dates the *Eschez amoureux*
commentary: cf. *Eschez amour. moral.*, ed. Guichard-Tesson and Roy, p. liv.

[32] For example: why does sexual excess cause the eyesight to deteriorate, why do
men grow hair when they begin to be capable of intercourse, why are bare feet bad
for sexual desire, why do young males hate the women with whom they have their
first sexual experiences, why are men who frequently ride more inclined to lust, why

adopting various postures; chills and shivering; bruises and scars; hairiness and baldness; pleasant and unpleasant smells; the different temperaments (with a special interest being taken in *melancholia*); studiousness (including reading as a help or hindrance to sleep); the various shrubs, plants, breads, and fruits; salt water and hot water; breath, air, and wind; continence and incontinence; the eyes, ears, nostrils, mouth, and teeth; and the complexion.[33] Evrart's authorship of the *Eschez amoureux* commentary is confirmed by an acrostic in the verses with which the work ends, together with the interest in medical matters which runs throughout.[34] For instance, he speaks of the melancholy that is caused 'by loving excessively *par amours,* which malady is called in medicine *amor hereos*',[35] discusses at some length the physical conditions appertaining to the various ages of man,[36] and even offers an anecdote of how, 'in Amiens in my youth', a very rich lady was reduced to such a melancholy that whenever she was offered anything to drink, whether wine or water, it always seemed to her that the cup was full of spiders.[37]

It would appear, then, that Evrart de Conty was a member of the distinguished group of scholarly translators who furthered the pedagogic and political ambitions of Charles V. The king commissioned 'over thirty translations of authoritative classical and medieval works as part of a conscious policy to legitimate

is *coitus* so very pleasant, why do some men enjoy sex when they play an active part and some when they do not, and why do the melancholic have such strong sexual urges? Pseudo-Aristotle also touches, very obliquely, on the perplexing issue of why some men feel homosexual desire; the commentator Peter of Abano's 'inarticulate' and 'evasive' response has been discussed by Joan Cadden, 'Sciences/Silences: The Natures and Languages of "Sodomy" in Peter of Abano's *Problemata* Commentary', in K. Lochrie, P. McCracken, and J. A. Schultz (eds.), *Constructing Medieval Sexuality* (Minneapolis, 1997), pp. 40–57.

[33] For an edition and modern English translation of the original Greek, see *Aristotle: Problems, Books I-XXI,* ed. W. S. Hett (Cambridge, Mass., 1936), and *Aristotle: Problems, Books XXII–XXXVIII and Rhetorica ad Alexandrum,* ed. W. S. Hett and H. Rackham (Cambridge, Mass., 1937). Modern scholarly opinion is unanimous in denying Aristotle's authorship; however, he does seem to have written a book of *Problems,* of which parts were incorporated into the extant work— the text of which is corrupt, badly organized and repetitive.

[34] And indeed, the influence of the *Problemata* is obvious; a full comparison of the two works in respect of their medical lore is a major desideratum.

[35] *Eschez amour. moral.,* ed. Guichard-Tesson and Roy, p. 191; cf. p. 544.
[36] Ibid. 473–95.   [37] Ibid. 200.

the new Valois dynasty',[38] including the *De proprietatibus rerum* of Bartholomaeus Anglicus (by Jean Corbechon; 1372), Valerius Maximus (a translation of the first four books, by Simon de Hesdin, is extant; 1375), Augustine's *De civitate Dei*, portions of the Bible (by Raoul de Presles, between 1371 and 1375), Giles of Rome's *De regimine principum* (by Jean Golein; 1379),[39] and of course the Aristotle translations of Nicole Oresme, who provided scrupulous renderings of the *Politics*, *Nicomachean Ethics*, and *On the Heavens* (*De caelo*) along with the pseudo-Aristotelian *Economics*.[40] *Le Livre des problèmes d'Aristote* was Evrart de Conty's contribution. Charles's regal predecessors, including his father, had promoted the translation of works deemed to serve the public good, but his patronage was on a far more lavish and ambitious scale—and evinced considerable belief in the future success of the French language. Whereas thirteenth-century Parisian grammarians had remarked that 'universal grammar' governed French as much as

---

[38] C. R. Sherman, *Imaging Aristotle: Verbal and Visual Representation in Fourteenth-Century France* (Berkeley, Calif., 1995), p. 6. See further C. R. Sherman, 'Les Thèmes humanistes dans le programme de traduction de Charles V: Compilation des textes et illustrations', in Monique Ornato and Nicole Pons (eds.), *Pratiques de la culture écrite en France au XVe siècle: Actes du colloque international du CNRS, Paris, 16–18 Mai 1992* (Louvrain-la-Neuve, 1995), pp. 527–37. A (partly inaccurate) list of the works commissioned by Charles V is provided in Christine de Pizan's adulatory *Livre des fais et bonnes meurs du sage roy Charles V*, ed. S. Solente (Paris, 1936), ii. 42–5. On the development of 'royal propaganda' in this period, see Gilbert Ouy, 'Humanism and Nationalism in France at the Turn of the Fifteenth Century', in B. P. McGuire (ed.), *The Birth of Identities: Denmark and Europe in the Middle Ages* (Copenhagen, 1996), p. 110. Albeit with some reluctance, Ouy accepts that 'for a long period, neither in France nor anywhere else in Europe could humanism disengage from nationalism', which 'might actually be considered one of the very factors of its emergence' (p. 122).

[39] An earlier translation had been produced by Henri de Gauchy in 1282, at the request of King Philip III. See the edn. by S. P. Molenaer, *Li Livres du gouvernement des rois: A Thirteenth-Century French Version of Egidio Colonna's Treatise* (New York, 1899). Yet another translation—not to be confused with the versions of Henri de Gauchy and Jean Golein—has a substantial commentary attached to it, which makes considerable use of the Bible and Thomas Aquinas. This anonymous French text and gloss seems to have been prepared for Guillaume de Beles Voies, a bourgeois of Orléans. See Charles F. Briggs, *Giles of Rome's 'De regimine principum': Reading and Writing Politics at Court and University, c.1275–c.1525* (Cambridge, 1999), p. 76.

[40] On Oresme's milieu and works see Sherman, *Imaging Aristotle*, pp. 6–33; also *Maistre Nicole Oresme: Le Livre de politiques d'Aristote*, ed. A. D. Menut (Philadelphia, 1970), pp. 5–33.

Greek, Hebrew, or Latin, and cursorily held out the prospect of
scholarly study of the linguistic features of French (cf. pp. 121–2
above), Oresme *cum suis* subscribed to a vision of French as the
'top vernacular' whose time was coming. In the introduction to
his *Livre de ethiques d'Aristote* Oresme comments that 'Latin is
at present (*a present*) a more perfect and a more copious
language (*plus parfait et plus habondant*) than French',[41] the
clear implication being that this state of affairs need not
continue. He goes on to speak of French as being the 'younger
language'; hence it is difficult to translate into it a 'a science'
such as ethics which 'is inherently difficult'. But others will
come after him and improve on his efforts—after all, the nobility of the French language and the intelligence of its speakers
match well the nobility of this science: 'Please God, through my
effort this noble science will be better understood and turned by
others in the future into clearer and more perfect French. And
surely, the rendering into French of such works about the arts
and sciences is a highly profitable labor; for French is a noble
language, used by people of great intelligence, ability and
prudence.'[42] Similarly, Raoul de Presles had no doubt that what
was good for French and the French was good for the whole of
Christendom: King Charles, he declares, has 'wished that this
book [i.e. *De civitate Dei*] should be translated from Latin into
French (*françois*) for the profit and utility (*utilité*) of your kingdom, of your people, and of all Christianity'.[43]

Within this programme, translation and commentary were
intertwined. *Translatio* was, after all, seen as a type of *expositio*.

[41] This is why, he continues, one cannot 'translate "properly" (*proprement*) all
the Latin into French': e.g. in Latin *homo* means both man and woman, but no
single French word has this meaning.
[42] *Le Livre de ethiques d'Aristote*, ed. A. D. Menut (New York, 1940), p. 100;
cf. *Le Livre de politiques*, ed. Menut, p. 27.
[43] From the introduction to his translation of *De civitate Dei*; quoted by
Françoise Autrand, *Charles V: Le sage* (Paris, 1994), p. 724. On the notions of the
unique position of the French king, *rex Christianissimus*, and the special devotion
of his kingdom to the true faith, see Joseph R. Strayer, 'France: The Holy Land, the
Chosen People and the Most Christian King', in *Action and Conviction in Early
Modern Europe: Essays in Memory of E. H. Harbison* (Princeton, NJ, 1969), pp.
3–16. Gilbert Ouy believes that 'for a long period, neither in France nor anywhere
else in Europe could humanism disengage from nationalism', which 'might actually
be considered one of the very factors of its emergence': 'Humanism and Nationalism
in France', p. 122.

'Translation (*translatio*) is the exposition of meaning through another language (*expositio sententiae per aliam linguam*)', claims Hugutio of Pisa in the *Magnae derivationes* which he compiled between 1197 and 1201.[44] Such discourse is echoed by Jean de Meun in the preface to his Boethius translation, when he remarks that if he had 'expounded (*expons*) the Latin by the French word for word, the book would have been too obscure for laymen' and clerks of moderate learning would not easily have understood the Latin from the French.[45] As already noted, Jean drew on two commentaries on the *Consolatio philosophiae*, by William of Conches (for the text) and William of Aragon (for the prologue), in producing his *Livres de confort*. Nicole Oresme's use of academic commentary in particular and Latin scholarship in general was far more thorough; hence A. D. Menut can refer to his *Livre de ethiques*, *Livre de politiques*, *Livre de yconomiques*, and *Livre du ciel et du monde* as 'commentated translations' of Aristotle's works.[46] It is 'difficult to determine' what Oresme has taken from Latin commentaries and what he has provided himself,[47] though some sources are evident—apparently, for his *Livre de politiques* he consulted the *Politics* commentaries of Albert the Great and Walter Burley, along with the *De potestate regia et papali* of John of Paris and the highly controversial *Defensor pacis* of Marsilius of Padua.[48] There is little evidence of 'dumbing down' to suit the supposedly

[44] *Magnae derivationes*, s.v. *glossa*, in Oxford, Bodleian Library, MS Bodley 376, fo. 84^r. This statement was repeated in the *Catholicon* (1286) of John of Genoa, which is heavily dependent on the *Magnae derivationes*: *Catholicon*, s.v. *glossa* (Venice, 1483), unfol. When defining *interpres*, John explains that 'an interpreter is in between two languages when he translates or expounds one language through another'. Such comments reflect common grammatical teaching, as may be illustrated from an anonymous twelfth-century gloss on Priscian: '*interpretatio* [here meaning 'translation'] is the exposition (*expositio*) of one language by another', as when the Greek *anthropos* is rendered in Latin as *homo*. Quoted by Richard Hunt, 'The Lost Preface to the *Liber derivationum* of Osbern of Gloucester', in Hunt, *Collected Papers*, p. 156. Cf. the *Summa super Priscianum* of Petrus Helias, which describes *interpretatio* as 'translatio de una loquela in aliam' (ibid. 155). See further Copeland, *Rhetoric, Hermeneutics*, pp. 88–91.

[45] *Li Livres de confort*, ed. Dédeck-Héry, p. 168.

[46] *Le Livre de politiques*, ed. Menut, p. 20.

[47] Cf. Peter Dembowski, 'Scientific Translation and Translators' Glossing in Four Medieval French Translations', in Jeanette Beer (ed.), *Translation Theory and Practice in the Middle Ages* (Kalamazoo, Mich., 1997), p. 126.

[48] *Le Livre de politiques*, ed. Menut, pp. 26–7.

lesser capacities of his wider audience; Oresme's vernacular scholarship carries on the business of Latin commentary—as when, for example, he criticizes the views of Albert the Great in his *Livre de politiques*.[49] And he was acutely aware of the procedures and status of commentary itself.[50] Manuscripts of Oresme's Aristotle translations attempt, in various ways, to distinguish between text and gloss, and we need not doubt that this reflects the translator's own wishes.[51] The care with which he annotated his translations is evident by the extent to which he sought to improve on them. Copies of the *Livre de politiques* and the *Livre de yconomiques* indicate an ongoing process of revision of the commentary; we have no fewer than three redactions of the *Politiques* in eighteen manuscripts, wherein the text remains largely the same but the gloss is changed substantially.[52]

In preparing his translation of *De civitate Dei*, Raoul de Presles consulted the commentaries on that text by Nicholas Trevet and Thomas Waleys.[53] For his part, Evrart de Conty equipped his rendering of the *Problemata* (the text used being Bartholomew of Messina's Latin version) with extensive vernacular glosses, which draw substantially on the Latin commentary by Peter of Abano.[54] The very first lines of this work highlight

[49] One may compare Evrart de Conty's criticisms, in his *Livres des problèmes*, of Peter of Abano: Guichard-Tesson, 'Le Métier de traducteur', pp. 163–5.

[50] Oresme was, of course, the author of a substantial corpus of Latin commentary. See esp. his (recently recovered) scholarship on the *De anima*, ed. Benoît Patar, *Nicolai Oresme expositio et quaestiones in Aristotelis de Anima* (Louvain, 1995). Patar regards Oresme as a disciple of Jean Buridan's. See further *The Quaestiones de Spera of Nicholas Oresme*, ed. G. Droppers (Madison, Wis., 1966).

[51] Dembowski, 'Scientific Translation and Translators' Glossing', pp. 125–6.

[52] *Le Livre de politiques*, ed. Menut, p. 20. The care lavished on the *Politiques* no doubt reflects Oresme's view that of all the 'sciences mundaines' politics is 'la tres principal et la plus digne et la plus profitable'. He claims that Aristotle's treatise on the subject is 'plus accepté et en plus grande auctorité'; it teaches of laws which are natural, universal, and perpetual, and to which all particular, local and temporary laws are subjected (p. 44).

[53] C. C. Willard, 'Raoul de Presles's Translation of Saint Augustine's *De civitate Dei*', in Jeanette Beer (ed.), *Medieval Translators and their Craft* (Kalamazoo, Mich., 1989), p. 331. Willard notes (p. 336) Raoul's interest in the problem of authentic book-division in Augustine's text, which had been discussed by Trevet and Waleys; cf. Minnis, *Authorship*, p. 154.

[54] Cf. *Eschez amour. moral.*, ed. Guichard-Tesson and Roy, p. liii; Guichard-Tesson, 'Le Métier de traducteur. As yet there is no full study of Evrart's *Livre des problèmes*; the article by P. M. Gathercole, 'Medieval Science: Evrart de Conty', *Romance Notes*, 6 (1965), 175–81, is perfunctory and outdated. Book 11 of the

Evrart's awareness of the crucial connection between translation and commentary: 'Ce livre des Probleumes a present empris a *translater* ou *exposer* aucunement en françois. . . .'[55] When Evrart came to comment on the *Eschez amoureux* he expended no less erudition, afforded the French text no less respect, though obviously his sources were quite different. They include all the above-mentioned sources of the anonymous poem itself with many more besides—with the *Roman de la Rose* occupying a specially privileged (though certainly not determining) position. Two distinguished Latin commentaries are drawn on, Macrobius on Cicero's *Somnium Scipionis* and Remigius of Auxerre on Martianus Capella, the assumption being that it is quite proper to display such materials, and pursue such an exegetical method, in expounding the *Eschez amoureux*.[56] Here the move has easily been made from translating existing academic commentary on an authoritative Latin work, the *Problemata,* to providing academic-style commentary on a work written originally in the vernacular.[57] In order to appreciate better the significance of this move, we must place Evrart's efforts within the larger milieu of European vernacular commentary.

Quasi comento: *Latin traditions, vernacular texts*

Throughout late medieval Europe, vernacular works of an original nature (though in many instances still dependent on Latin

original work was second only to Boethius's *De musica* as the 'fullest source for ancient musical theory known to the middle ages': cf. Charles Burnett, 'Hearing and Music in Book XI of Pietro d'Abano's *Expositio Problematum Aristotelis*', in Nancy van Deusen (ed.), *Tradition and Ecstasy: The Agony of the Fourteenth Century* (Ottawa, 1997), p. 153. A comparison of the music theory in Evrart's translation-commentary on the *Problemata* (which is far from a compliant reiteration of Abano's exposition) and his discussion of music in the *Eschez amoureux* commentary would be particularly fruitful. On the abundance of medical lore in 'Aristotle's' text and Abano's commentary, see n. 32 above.

[55] Quoted by Guichard-Tesson, 'Le Métier de traducteur', p. 132. In the autograph MS of *Le Livre des problèmes* the French text of each and every problem is organized into *texte* and *glose*.

[56] On Evrart's use of Macrobius see below. Remigius is named twice, and on another occasion cited as the 'expositeur de Marcien': *Eschez amour. moral.*, ed. Guichard-Tesson and Roy, pp. 79, 94, 258.

[57] A similar development occurred in late medieval Castile, as has been described by Julian Weiss, *The Poet's Art: Literary Theory in Castile, c.1400–60* (Oxford, 1990), p. 121; cf. p. 297 below.

models) were beginning to demand attention of a kind which previously had been afforded only to the established *auctores*. Academic commentary became a precedent and source for 'modern' commentary (i.e. commentary on authors who were *moderni*), including 'self-commentary' or 'autoexegesis'. Innovative scholars set about the business of producing commentaries on 'new' texts, texts written by their contemporaries and even by themselves.

Some of these appropriations of method and matter were more daring than others. Of special interest are the commentaries on texts which contain an erotic element. Here our investigation takes us to fourteenth-century Italy, where the most sophisticated traditions of 'modern' commentary and 'self-commentary' are to be found. Much of the credit must go to Dante Alighieri, one of the most innovative of medieval literary theorists. His confidence as self-commentator provided a powerful precedent for lesser mortals; the commentaries on the *Divine Comedy* constitute the single most important corpus of contemporary criticism on any medieval writer. In his first attempt at 'autoexegesis', the *Vita nuova*, Dante employed the scholastic technique of 'exposition by division' (*divisio textus*).[58] However, the later *Convivio* manifests a more thorough appropriation of the principles and terminology of academic literary theory; Dante rightly calls it 'quasi comento', a kind of commentary in the technical sense of the term.[59] It has a formal commentary-prologue (featuring Aristotelian notions of causality and science) and employs traditional exegetical techniques,[60] particularly the practice of what was sometimes termed 'reverent interpretation'—hermeneutics of a kind which revealed the text in the best possible light, eliminating any apparent discrepancies between it and works of the highest authority, and generally highlighting and/or amplifying its impeccable doctrine.[61] Hence, at the outset Dante is anxious to

---

[58] On Dante's appropriation and adaptation of this technique, see esp. Thomas C. Stillinger, *The Song of Troilus: Lyric Authority in the Medieval Book* (Philadelphia, 1992), pp. 44–117.

[59] *Il Convivio*, i.3, ed. Bruna Cordati (Turin, 1968), p. 13.

[60] Cf. Minnis and Scott, *Medieval Literary Theory*, pp. 377–8.

[61] On 'reverent interpretation', see Chenu, *Thomas d'Aquin*, p. 122; Minnis, *Authorship*, pp. 43, 56; Weiss, *The Poet's Art*, p. 132.

display his credentials. The reader of these *canzoni* may have formed the impression that he had pursued a great passion of love, he admits. But in fact virtue was the 'moving cause' (*movente cagione*; cf. such *accessus* terms as *causa movens ad scribendum* and *causa efficiens*), as, he promises, the subsequent expositions will make clear.[62] Any potential threat to the authority of the text or the good character of its author is destroyed by the sheer weight of the learning which Dante deploys at great length, and on occasion by allegorical exposition. Quite clearly, one aspect of Dante's ambition was to be regarded as a vernacular *auctor*, to have his works enter the canon. In the *Convivio* he is seeking the validation which academic exegesis could bring to his art.[63]

Following in his master's footsteps, Giovanni Boccaccio (1313–75), who in the last years of his life was to comment on Dante, equipped his own *Teseida* (1339–41?) with a commentary.[64] Indeed, as is generally recognized, Boccaccio's statement of his intention in writing the *Teseida* (which occurs in its envoy) alludes to Dante's account in *De vulgari eloquentia* of the gravest subjects for poetry. From the time when 'the Muses began to walk naked in the sight of men' (i.e. since poetry began to be written in the vernacular, as Boccaccio's gloss explains), 'there have already been those who have employed them in fine style for moral discourse—and others have enlisted them in the service of love'. But Boccaccio's poem 'may be seen as the first ever to have had them celebrate the performance of martial feats in the vulgar tongue'.[65] To equip this vernacular epic with glosses of the kind regularly found in manuscripts of the

---

[62] *Il Convivio*, i.2, ed. Cordati, p. 12. On the *accessus* vocabulary here cited, see p. 48 above.

[63] See esp. the important articles by Albert Russell Ascoli, 'The Vowels of Authority (Dante's *Convivio* IV, vi, 3–4)', in K. Brownlee and W. Stephens (eds.), *Discourses of Authority in Medieval and Renaissance Literature* (Hanover, NH, 1989), pp. 23–46, and 'The Unfinished Author: Dante's Rhetoric of Authority in *Convivio* and *De vulgari eloquentia*', in Rachel Jacoff (ed.), *The Cambridge Companion to Dante* (Cambridge, 1993), pp. 45–66.

[64] The *Teseida*'s text and gloss, both written in Boccaccio's own hand, are found in Florence, Biblioteca Medicea Laurenziana, MS Acq. e Doni 325. In the following discussion I have used the edition by Mario Marti in vol. iv of his ed., *Giovanni Boccaccio: Opere minore in volgare* (Milan, 1969–72).

[65] *Teseida*, xii, st. 84; trans. N. R. Havely, *Chaucer's Boccaccio* (Cambridge, 1980), p. 151.

auctores, including the Latin epic poets, is an obvious corollary to this ambition—the Muses may be walking naked, but certainly they are walking tall.

Much later, in his *Genealogia deorum gentilium*, Boccaccio was to complain that while other kinds of text (legal, philosophical, scriptural, etc.) have their commentaries, 'poetry alone is without such honour. Few—very few—are they with whom it has dwelt continuously'.[66] Given the amount of medieval exegesis of Latin poetry, this must be taken as rhetorical exaggeration (although the scale of commentary on poetry was indeed relatively small), and Boccaccio was well aware of previous attempts to remedy the deficiency—the influence of *De vulgari eloquentia* on the poetics of the *Teseida* is profound, and in the *chiose* on its seventh book Boccaccio cites Dino del Garbo's (Latin) commentary on *Donna mi prega*, the *canzone d'amore* of Guido Cavalcanti (*c*.1259–1300).[67] (Indeed, we owe the survival of Dino's commentary to Boccaccio's copy, made by his own hand.) Hence it seems reasonable to assume that, in the *chiose* on *Il Teseida*, Boccaccio saw himself as writing within a tradition of vernacular hermeneutics. His autoexegesis brings traditional mythographic material to bear on the new fiction (which, however, he grandly presents as a Greek tale with no Latin translation).[68] He seems to have believed that the *Teseida* merited an apparatus of the kind which accompanied its great Latin counterparts, the *Thebaid* and *Aeneid*, in manuscript, an apparatus designed to dispose the discerning reader in favour of the poem and underline for his benefit the superlative literary criteria in accordance with which it should be judged and esteemed.[69]

---

[66] *Genealogia* xv.6; trans. Charles Osgood, *Boccaccio on Poetry. Being the Preface and the Fourteenth and Fifteenth Books of Boccaccio's 'Genealogia Deorum Gentilium'* (Indianapolis, 1956), p. 117.

[67] There are two modern editions of Dino's commentary: Otto Bird, 'The *Canzone d'Amore* of Guido Cavalcanti according to the Commentary of Dino del Garbo', *MS* 2 (1940), 150–203, and 3 (1941), 117–60; and G. Favati, 'La glossa latina di Dino del Garbo a *Donna me prega* del Cavalcanti', *Annuali del Scuola Normale Superiore di Pisa*, 2nd ser., 21.1–2 (1952), 70–103.

[68] *Teseida*, i, st.2; ed. Marti, ii, 257.

[69] Cf. the quite explicit manner in which the sixteenth-century commentaries on Ludovico Ariosto's *Orlando Furioso* sought to establish that this work 'either descended from or was the modern equivalent of the canonical epics of antiquity': Daniel Javitch, *Proclaiming a Classic: The Canonization of 'Orlando Furioso'*

What, then, of that 'tiresome and minimal' repetition of details in Boccaccio's glosses, which led Robert Hollander to suspect that he was 'pulling our collective leg'?[70] What is certain is that the medieval glossators on Ovid, Boethius, and the rest, who said exactly the same kind of thing, did not have that particular motive. Boccaccio's *chiose* must be compared with the standard and popular late medieval commentaries in terms of their techniques and strategies, not (as has misleadingly been done) with Lactantius Placidus' gloss to Statius' *Thebaid* which he admired, and came to possess, but which seems to have had little if any influence on his autoexegesis.[71] There is, however, one point at which the monolithic 'reverent interpretation' of the commentary seems to break down, where its writer goes so far as to claim that he, too, is made subject by carnal love. The poem has been describing the anguish which Arcita and Palemone suffer in love. This is how Love treats his servants; whoever has been captured by him is well aware of these facts

(Princeton, NJ, 1991), p. 4. Javitch argues that this was 'the first modern work of European poetry whose canonical eligibility became an issue of extensive debate'; in his view this contestation illustrates 'more general truths about canon formation, the primary one being that the aristocratic attributes of texts that become canonical—and what is the canon if not an aristocracy of texts?—are not inborn but are conferred upon them' (pp. 8–9). No such debate characterizes the early reception of the *Teseida*, but its *chiose* can, I believe, be regarded as a tactically performative act on Boccaccio's part, intended to implicate the prospect of its authorization. However, despite Boccaccio's efforts, and those of a few other glossators of the *Teseida*, it was the *Orlando Furioso* which came, so to speak, to 'fill the need for a modern equivalent of the canonical epics of antiquity', though there was a prolonged debate about whether the poem was generically an epic or a romance, Ariosto being taken to task by 'militant neoclassicists', as Javitch calls them, who condemned his work for failing to conform to the conventions of ancient poetics as codified in Aristotle's *Poetics* (pp. 12, 14, 17–20, etc.).

[70] 'The Validity of Boccaccio's Self-Exegesis in his *Teseida*', *Medievalia et humanistica*, n.s. 8 (1977), 163–83.

[71] The beginning of his work on the *Teseida* is marked by a letter to an anonymous friend in which he complains that he has been having difficulty in reading Statius' *Thebaid* 'without guidance or glosses', and expresses his wish (later realized) to have a copy of the commentary by Lactantius Placidus. See David Anderson, *Before 'The Knight's Tale': Imitation of Classical Epic in Boccaccio's 'Teseida'* (Philadelphia, 1988), p. 39. Modern scholarship has failed to find any marked dependence on Lactantius in Boccaccio's self-commentary on the *Teseida* or indeed in the poem itself; cf. Hollander, 'Validity of Boccaccio's Self-Exegesis', pp. 167–8; and Susan Noakes, *Timely Reading: Between Exegesis and Interpretation* (Ithaca, NY, 1988), p. 89. See further Anderson's discussion of two mid-fifteenth-century commentaries on the *Teseida*: *Before 'The Knight's Tale'*, pp. 18–21, 33–4.

(*Teseida*, III. 35, 5–8). 'Che sono io,' declares the gloss; 'I am that person.' Hollander asks: 'is this "Boccaccio" speaking, or the supposed anonymous scholar who lives in his margins?' He prefers the latter view ('not least because the passage [i.e. the gloss] is more amusing seen in this way'), and declares that the commentator, as much as the author, is being presented as one of Love's subjects, even though he should know better. But surely that enigmatic little gloss, 'Che sono io', should not be given more weight than it can bear. We could regard it as a minor lapse—quite forgivable given the scale of the *Teseida*'s text and gloss. Alternatively, we may discover here a poet who is experimenting with two different methods of self-construction and for the most part has managed (to his credit) to confine one method to the text and the other to the gloss. In the *proemio* the stilnuovist poetic is operating, reiterating the principle (beloved of the troubadours and the authors of the *dits amoureux*) that commitment to love is necessary for the composition of love poetry. In the commentary the learned antecedents and aspirations of the poem are highlighted, with the implication that the writer himself, as opposed to his *persona*, can hardly be serious about an emotion which scholastic doctrine has so unequivocally revealed as being dangerous and destructive. But at one point Boccaccio-as-commentator makes contact with Boccaccio-as-lover: that 'Che sono io' declares that he is not feigning, that he really meant what he said in the *proemio* to the *Teseida*, where the hope is expressed that his 'most noble lady' will recognize his love and 'abandon the disdain' she has been showing him.[72] The gloss 'Che sono io' and the *proemio* speak with one voice, for the one and only time. Elsewhere the voices are clearly different, in the interests of self-authorization. Like Dante, Boccaccio has self-consciously appropriated techniques of exposition which traditionally were used in interpreting 'ancient' and Latin authoritative texts, to indicate and announce the literary authority of an Italian work. Functioning together, the *Teseida*'s text and gloss make the case that epic poetry may be composed in 'the illustrious vernacular'.

---

[72] Trans. Havely, *Chaucer's Boccaccio*, p. 105. See further the excellent discussion of 'Che sono io' in Stillinger, *The Song of Troilus*, pp. 3–12. He regards it as 'deliberately indeterminate', mimicking 'the gesture of an author stepping forth from behind his text' yet preserving 'an impenetrable anonymity' (p. 6).

The efforts of Dante and Boccaccio at self-commentary are overshadowed, however, in quantity if not in quality, by the Latin commentary which Francesco da Barberino, lawyer and episcopal notary, wrote to accompany his Italian *Documenti d'Amore* (apparently produced during the period 1309–13).[73] Here Barberino set out to do for 'the laws of love' what Justinian and Gratian had done for Roman law and canon law respectively, i.e. the collection and harmonization of diverse and discordant documents.[74] His overall purpose, he says, is to expound the text diligently with regard to divine love and spiritual intention (*intentio*).[75] Certain people who looked at the text condemned it, saying he had exclusively considered carnal love, and therefore he decided to weave and place (*texere ac locare*) these present glosses around both the Latin and the vernacular texts, in order to indicate the motivation and result (*motus et actus*) of his own purpose.[76] There follows a discussion of the *Documenti d'Amore* under four of the standard *accessus* headings (*intentio, materia, utilitas* and *cui parti philosophie subponatur*), to which a fifth, *modus agendi*, is added later.[77] Barberino's declared ambition is to teach the form of love, providing documents whereby the vices may be known

---

[73] During the period 1309–13 Barberino was in Provence, where he substantially composed the *Documenti*, though at least part of the Latin commentary thereon seems to have been completed after his return to Italy. Here I follow the argument of Antoine Thomas, *Francesco da Barberino: Littérature provençale en Italie au moyen âge* (Paris, 1883), p. 68. It is best to regard the *Documenti* as a tripartite work, consisting of the Italian poem, its literal Latin translation, and the Latin commentary. Barberino himself seems to have been responsible for the layout of the two earliest extant MSS, wherein two columns of Italian verse are bracketed with two columns of the Latin translation, which in turn are surrounded by the Latin glosses. Illustrations and explanatory diagrams play a major part of this *mise-en-page*: see Daniela Goldin, 'Testo e immagine nei *Documenti d'Amore* di Francesco da Barberino', *Quaderni d'italianistica*, 1 (1980), 125–38; also the cogent account in Elizabeth Sears, *The Ages of Man: Medieval Interpretations of the Life Cycle* (Princeton, NJ, 1986), pp. 104–7.

[74] Cf. the fuller discussion in A. J. Minnis, '*Amor* and *Auctoritas* in the Self-Commentary of Dante and Francesco da Barberino', *Poetica* [Tokyo], 32 (1990), 25–42.

[75] *I documenti d'amore di Francesco da Barberino*, ed. Francesco Egidi (Rome, 1905–27), i.3–5.

[76] Given the general agreement between text and gloss, it is difficult to understand Barberino's worries—this protestation may be largely rhetorical, designed to emphasize the tripartite work's ethical purpose.

[77] *Documenti*, ed. Egidi, i.5–6.

for what they are and thence eschewed, and the virtues may be loved. This is the moral principle which underlies his attempts at reconciling authorities which are very different in status and in kind, love being regarded in its most universal aspect.

Throughout the commentary philosophers and theologians (for example, Aristotle, Augustine, Jerome, John Chrysostom, St Bernard, Hugh and Richard of St Victor) rub shoulders with not only the poets of antiquity but also those of the writer's own time, including a formidable array of Provençal poets, several of whom are unknown apart from Barberino's citations. (Richard de Fournival's attempt to yoke together heterogeneous authorities on love in his *Consaus d'Amours*[78] pales into insignificance next to Barberino's massive effort to bring out the *concordantia discordantium canonum*.) There is no sense of distance between Barberino's text and gloss, but rather total collusion and cross-reference, the 'reverent interpretation' of the exegesis being demanded by the vernacular poem. Indeed, on occasion the text is nothing more than the pretext for what is said in the didactic gloss, as when Barberino's Italian verse openly and unapologetically directs us to the commentary for full accounts of subjects on which the text is touching very briefly. Here no distance remains between the poet's I-*persona* and 'the supposed anonymous scholar who lives in his margins'. Text collapses into gloss, the moralizing agenda of the latter taking over the former.[79] This process contributes to an erasure, or at least a

---

[78] Cf. pp. 73–4 above.

[79] As Thomas says, the text cannot do without the commentary any more than the commentary can do without the text. He goes on to compare Barberino's entire edifice to a house with three floors or levels. Those who cannot understand Latin cannot get beyond the first stage, having to be content with the vernacular language and with the miniatures which illustrate it. Knowledgeable people, with an understanding of Latin, can stop at this first stage if they wish, but they have privileged access to the second level, where they will find a far richer apartment, an exclusive area where they do not have to rub shoulders with those inferiors from the first level: here Thomas is referring to those who can follow the Latin translation. Finally, the élite enjoy a princely dwelling on the third and top level, as well as free access to the floors underneath. They are 'les vrais propriétaires'; the whole building was designed for their benefit. Their level was not simply added on after the rest of the building had been constructed; it was rather part of the original plan, indeed its most important part, for the lower stages were destined to render possible the access to the top stage. Cf. *Francesco da Barberino*, pp. 59–60. Here, then, is a case in which, one might say, the text is serving the gloss rather than (as per normal) the other way around.

marked diminution, of the subversive element of medieval Ovidianism.

By contrast, in the commentaries on texts which do retain something of that subversive element, the interpretative distance between text and gloss is often marked.[80] Thus, Boccaccio's *chiose* to his *Teseida* amplify the negative aspects of the text's depiction of the passions which Arcita and Palamon feel for the same woman, Emilia.[81] A similar disjunction sometimes exists between the French *Eschez amoureux* and John Gower's English *Confessio amantis* and the commentaries which seek to bring out their moral significance. The latter poem was produced, in its three versions, in the 1390s; all these versions were equipped with a Latin commentary, which seems to have been the work of the poet himself.[82] The former appears to be the first large-scale exegesis of any original work in French, and hence merits full consideration with reference to the genre to which it largely belongs, that of the medieval commentary.

Here I use the word 'largely' advisedly, in view of the debate on how the French work should be characterized and what title should be assigned to it. For P.-Y. Badel, it is essentially a commentary—and a commentary of great significance, being 'le premier commentaire en français d'une poème en français'.[83] But, he notes, the commentator does not often make 'appréciations synthétiques' or 'une vue d'ensemble' of the poem he is expounding. Rather,

Le commentaire résume en quelques lignes un épisode du livre rimé, puis il passe à son explication. Les points d'attache de l'exégèse sont les noms propres mentionnés par le livre: avant tout, noms des dieux et héros de la mythologie antique; subsidiairement, noms des abstractions personnifées comme Fortune, Nature. La méthode est, dans son

[80] This distance is of course a fundamental and necessary feature of Latin commentary tradition, involving techniques which, when appropriated in 'modern' commentary, were no doubt thought through and self-consciously applied. In marked contrast are the interventionist strategies of the *Rose*'s revisers, who wrote their poetic selves into the poem and added new first-person narrative (cf. the discussion at the beginning of this chapter).
[81] Particularly in the extended gloss on book vii, st. 50 (on the two Venuses); *Teseida*, ed. Marti, ii, 713–29.
[82] In contrast, Chaucer does not seem to have produced any self-commentary. At least, none of the glosses which occasionally appear in manuscripts of his poetry can confidently be attributed to him.   [83] Badel, *Rose au XIVe siècle*, p. 291.

principe, celle du grammairien qui suit l'ordre du texte à expliquer; mais le commentateur a une telle passion pour la mythologie que le grammairien est parfois victime en lui du mythographe qui expose selon un plan systématique ses connaissances.[84]

This is absolutely fair comment. In particular the *Eschez amoureux* commentary does not provide that precise *divisio textus* which, as noted above, Dante had inherited from Latin commentary tradition; neither does it adopt the practice of using *lemmata*, i.e. short quotations from the text under consideration, to mark the stages of its exposition. Yet it should be emphasized that in their commentaries on the Latin *poetae* many grammarians, or others who elaborated on the grammarian's basic model of commentary, often moved far from 'the letter' of their texts. Neither was this phenomenon limited to commentaries on Latin authors. In Dante's autoexegesis of three of his vernacular *canzoni* (in the *Convivio*), the actual texts are regularly left behind as the work threatens to turn into a learned treatise on some point or other to which the poetry has merely alluded. That having been said, Evrart's interest in the moral significance of mythology is certainly considerable, and on many occasions one feels that one is reading a mythography rather than *explication de texte*. The work's editors, Françoise Guichard-Tesson and Bruno Roy, focus on other features which, in their view, take the work beyond the normal run of commentaries: 'Elle est en effet non seulement un commentaire, mais aussi une "suite" du poème des *Eschez amoureux* . . ., une explication . . ., en plus d'être une mise au clair . . ., et même une "réécriture" . . .'.[85] In an itinerary of books belonging to Philippe le Bon mention is made of *Le Livre des eschez amoureux moralisez*, this (now lost) copy having been earlier than any of the six manuscripts which have survived. And that is the title which Guichard-Tesson and Roy adopt. One could follow Badel's lead and argue that, in essence, the features here singled out are in fact endemic to the commentary tradition. But their unusual scale and extent in the present work must freely be admitted.

On balance, then, there is ample justification for referring to

---

[84] Ibid. 295.
[85] *Eschez amour. moral.*, ed. Guichard-Tesson and Roy, p. xi.

it either as the *Livre des eschez amoureux moralisez* or as 'The
Commentary on the *Eschez amoureux*', the latter designation
being understood as indicating the basic genre to which the
work belongs, in its critical vocabulary and procedure of
following 'l'ordre du texte à expliquer', though the individual
talent which Evrart has brought to bear on commentary tradition must be recognized and respected. Here we will concentrate
on his debt to a specific early medieval commentary (indeed,
one of the most important of all), Macrobius' exposition of the
Somnium Scipionis, and to the type of late medieval commentary with which the work's intellectual challenge and pedagogic
approach have most in common, the *accessūs Ovidiani*.

Speaking par figure et fabuleusement: *Evrart de Conty's theory of poetic fiction*

Evrart was concerned to expound a theory of poetic fiction
within which he could locate the *Eschez amoureux*, comparing
its method (albeit cursorily) with that employed in its great
predecessor and very inspiration, the *Roman de la Rose*. At the
outset he declares that his author, following the precedent of the
ancient poets, wishes to offer profit and delight (a variation on
the Horatian dictum; *Ars poetica*, 333–4). This dictum was
often applied in late medieval *accessūs* to classical poets, as for
example in the prologue to the 'Bernard Silvester' commentary
on the *Aeneid*: 'the verbal ornament and the beauty of the style'
give pleasure, while Virgil's *exempla* impart 'the knowledge of
how to act properly'.[86] The *generalis intentio* of the *Heroides*,
declares an anonymous scholiast, 'is to give pleasure, and to
give profitable advice to all his readers'.[87]

Evrart's own emphasis is decidedly on the profit or *utilitas*, as
is indicated by his version of a conventional apology for poetry:

... l'entente principal de l'acteur dessusdit et la fin de son livre, c'est
de tendre a vertu et a bonne oeuvre, et de fouir tout mal et toute fole
oyseuse.

---

[86] Minnis and Scott, *Medieval Literary Theory*, p. 152.
[87] Ibid. 23.

[. . . the principal intention [cf. the Latin *intentio*] of the author in question and the end [cf. *finis*] of his book, is to lead to virtue and good works and to flee from all evil and all foolish idleness.][88]

The parallel with the *accessūs Ovidiani* is obvious. 'Follow the good and flee the evil' is a principle commonly expressed therein (cf. pp. 237–41 above). The *intentio* of the *Heroides* was supposed to have been the castigation of 'men and women who are held fast in the grip of foolish and unlawful love. . . . It pertains to ethics, which inculcates good morality and eradicates evil behaviour'.[89] Or, according to one of several views given by another anonymous scholiast, Ovid's *intentio* 'in this book [the *Heroides*] is to encourage the pursuit of virtue and to reject vice'. Its ultimate end (*finalis causa*) may be described as follows: 'having seen the advantages (*utilitas*) of lawful love and the disasters or disadvantages which result from unlawful and foolish love, we may reject and shun foolish love and adhere to lawful love. It pertains to ethics, since it teaches us about lawful love'.[90]

That view is certainly shared by Evrart, and therefore he was anxious to put some distance between the poem's author and the *personae* deployed in the text, including the *persona* of the amorous young man who plays the chess of love with his lady.[91] Thus Evrart explains that the author feigns being in bed one morning, thinking very intently about the beauty of the season, the song of the birds who surrounded him, and about several other pleasures and new marvels that he was considering in his heart, and was dwelling more on his pleasure than he ever before had been in the habit of doing. Then it seemed to him that he saw a lady called Nature, who appeared before him and came to instruct and scold him for laziness and for spending too much time in bed.[92] Evrart then explains that many of the things that are said in the poem's narrative are not to be taken according to the literal meaning of the words (*a la lectre*). Rather, they may be feigned in a manner which is perfectly

---

[88] *Eschez amour. moral.*, ed. Guichard-Tesson and Roy, p. 3.

[89] Minnis and Scott, *Medieval Literary Theory*, p. 20.

[90] Ibid. 23. Cf. Ch. 5 above, where the influence of such theory on aspects of the *querelle de la Rose* is proposed.

[91] On *persona* theory, see the discussion in Ch. 5 above.

[92] *Eschez amour. moral.*, ed. Guichard-Tesson and Roy, p. 22.

reasonable, and may contain some hidden truth, which, God willing, he hopes to explain.

... nous devons savoir premierement ... que l'aucteur de la rime dessusdite faint et dit moult de choses qui ne sont pas a entendre a la lectre, ja soit ce que elles soient raisonablement faintes, et qu'il y ait aucune verité soubz la lettre et la fiction secretement mucie, sy come il apperra se Dieu loysir me donne de declarier la chose.

[. . . we should know first of all that the author of this poem . . . makes up and says things that are not to be taken literally, although they may be feigned in a reasonable manner, and that there may be some truth secretly hidden beneath the letter and the fiction, as will appear if God permits us to make the matter known.][93]

Because of this, Evrart continues, the poet feigns and introduces several characters (*personnes*; cf. Latin *personae*), each of whom speaks in his turn as is appropriate to his nature, in the 'manner of feigning' (*la maniere qu'il est faint*) used in the *Rose*. And no doubt one can sometimes feign and speak figuratively and in fable in a way which is beneficial and to a good end: 'Sanz faille, on peut bien faindre aucunesfoiz et parler par figure et fabuleusement . . .'. Similarly, in the Latin commentary on his English *Confessio amantis*, John Gower takes pains to distinguish between the moral *auctor* identified by the scholar who lives in his manuscript margins and the love-obsessed characters who inhabit the vernacular text: 'Here as it were in the person of other people (*quasi in persona aliorum*), who are held fast by love, the author, feigning himself to be a lover (*fingens se auctor esse amantem*), proposes to write of their various passions one by one in the various distinctions of this book.'[94] In both cases, then, a clear distinction is made between what the author 'makes up' or 'feigns' and what he really may believe, what lies behind the immediately obvious meaning of his statements. True, in the course of his commentary on the *Eschez amoureux* Evart refers to its author and I-*persona* as one and the same figure. But this may be deemed an economy of reference, a useful shorthand.

Here, then, are no allegorical secrets to unveil, all that is required being an understanding of how the fictional first-person narrator operates. Secrets aplenty—in the sense of literal (usually

---

[93] *Eschez amour. moral.*, ed. Guichard-Tesson and Roy, p. 22.
[94] *English Works*, ed. Macaulay, i.37.

astrological), natural and moral interpretations—will be revealed when Evrart explains the *fabulae poetarum* as they appear in his text. Enthusing later about 'l'entencion des anciens poetes', Evrart claims that they frequently wished to speak, in their 'fabuleuses paroles', of history or of some secret thing pertaining to the sky or to the facts of Nature. 'And they well mingled (*entremellent*) these three together at one time,' he continues, as in the case of the fable of Saturn.[95] Pagan mythology constitutes a wonderful treasure trove, which Evrart can be confident of divine approval in making known, since 'there is no good thing imaginable to a reasonable man that the ancient poets, who were wise and great philosophers, have not meant to express by various gods and goddesses—neither maintaining nor believing that they were real deities(!)'.[96]

But let us return to Evrart's preliminary disquisition on poetic fiction. The structure of his explanation of 'the three ways in which fiction may reasonably be employed' may be summarized as follows:

1. In order to speak more safely and securely (*parler plus seurement*). This can be done by three methods:
   i. by having a resuscitated corpse speak;
   ii. by using 'the manner of a dream';
   iii. by using 'imaginary vision'.
2. In order to speak more secretly (*parler plus secretement*).
3. In order to speak more subtly, pleasantly and delightfully (*parler plus subtilement, plaisaument et delectablement*).

The first way in which fiction may reasonably be employed is in order to speak more safely and securely.[97] In certain situations people are not prepared to accept plain speaking (*parler plainnement*), Evrart explains, especially when the subject is difficult and very obscure to the human understanding, or when it is problematic in some way. The alternative is to be silent—as was Aristotle, who, because he did not like to dissimulate (*faindre*), simply stopped speaking when he came to hard places and difficult subjects. The discussion then moves into an account of three methods whereby one may feign (*manieres de*

---

[95] *Eschez amour. moral.*, ed. Guichard-Tesson and Roy, p. 76.
[96] Ibid. 63.   [97] Ibid. 23.

faindre) in order to speak more securely and blamelessly. The
first is by adopting the device of having a resuscitated corpse
speak. Plato, unlike Aristotle, did employ fiction, as when he
used the myth of Er. When he wished to treat of the soul's state
after death, he feigned how a knight who had been killed in
battle returned to settle this matter. This method, however, did
not appeal to the people, who felt that he should have spoken
openly on the subject. And this reaction of the ignorant explains
why, as Macrobius explains, Cicero did not follow Plato's
example. Instead he employed the second method of feigning,
i.e. in his *Somnium Scipionis*. By using 'the manner of a dream'
(*maniere de songe*) he sought to avoid all unreasonable objections (cf. Macrobius, *In somn. Scip.*, I.i.1–2).[98] Cicero therefore
feigned that King Scipio saw his ancestor Scipio the African, and
with him his father, in a dream, and that 'those two told him of
great wonders and secret things of the heaven and of the earth',
and of other matters concerning his situation and person. In
particular, they confirmed that those who sustain, defend, and
govern the country well by reason and justice are finally translated to the heavens, and that this is their right and proper
dwelling-place, where they live forever in great beatitude. Those
who, on the contrary, fail in these duties are left below on the
earth. And this, declares Evrart, spelling out the message for his
Christian audience, is 'ce que nous voulons dire quant nous
disons que les bons et les justes aprés la mort s'en vont en
paradiz, et les malvaiz au contraire en enfer' ['what we mean
when we say that the good and just go to paradise after death
and the bad, on the contrary, go to hell'].[99] He also notes that
the dream form sometimes excuses 'la personne qui parle
aucunesfoiz de moult de choses qui seroient tenues pour mal
dites' ['the person who speaks of many things that would be
considered badly said'] if they were taken 'estre avenues ou
vrayes a la lectre' ['as actually having happened or being literally true']. For the dreamer can always excuse himself on the
grounds that he himself cannot be held responsible for what he
dreamed about, answering that 'ainsi ly sembloit il en son
dormant, et que on s'en prengne au songe' ['it seemed that way

to him while he slept and that it was imposed on him in a dream'].[100]

The *Rose* is briefly compared to the *Somnium Scipionis* in that here too the dream form is employed: 'Et ainsi fu pour ce par avanture faiz ly *Rommans de la Rose*' ['And thus perhaps it was done in the *Roman de la Rose*']. There is, unfortunately, no ensuing discussion. One may recall, however, how Guillaume de Lorris, at the very beginning of the *Rose* (ll. 1–20), had sought to validate his own dream by appealing to Macrobius, 'qui ne tint pas songes a lobes' ['who did not take dreams as trifles']; his argument that a dream may signify 'des biens as genz et des anuiz' ['the good and evil that come to men'] certainly matches Cicero's poem. At no point, however, does the *Rose* actually use the defence that one cannot help what one dreams. Indeed, Jean de Meun takes rather a rationalist view of the problem, mentioning Scipio in the course of an account of how certain men through an excess of contemplation cause 'the objects of their meditations to appear in their thoughts', and 'truly believe that they see them clearly and objectively. But these are merely *trufle et mançonge*, lies and deceits' (18357–70; cf. p. 7 above). Given the *Rose*'s reticence about defining its own literary-theoretical basis, Evrart's wish to offer a theory of poetic fiction which will—however tentatively—encompass it along with the *Eschez amoureux* is all the more remarkable.

The third 'manner of feigning' is, by using 'imaginary vision' (*ymaginaire vision*).[101] This method, Evrart explains, was employed by Boethius in *De consolatione philosophiae*. When he wished to speak of the great misery into which Fortune had cast him, he feigned Philosophy coming to him to offer consolation. 'And he did this to avoid all presumption (*pour eviter toute presumpcion*)', presumably meaning that by using the figure of Philosophy he avoided setting himself up as a great authority on fate and divine providence.

It was this third method, of imaginary vision, which the author of the *Eschez amoureux* uses, his commentator continues. For the poet wishes to imagine that this vision of Nature and the things that later ensued were neither in a dream nor in *vision reele* of the literal type seen by corporeal eyes. 'Ainz fut

<hr>

[100] Ibid. 23.   [101] Ibid. 24.

tant seulement ymaginee telle'—'thus it (i.e. his vision) was only an imagined thing'. This apparent definition of *ymaginaire vision* as 'something made up'—indeed, a kind of 'feigning'—is rather intriguing, given the history of the Latin term *visio imaginaria* within discussions of the various types of vision. For, according to the Augustinian theory of the *tria genere visionum* (as transmitted for example, by the standard preface to the Apocalypse in the 'Paris Bible'), the *visio spiritualis seu imaginaria* occurs when someone, whether awake or asleep, sees images of things by which other things are signified, examples including Pharaoh's type of dreaming and Moses' vision of the burning bush.[102] In other words (than Evrart's), this type corresponds to what Macrobius describes as the enigmatic dream, the *oraculum* (*In somn. Scip.*, I.iii.10). On whatever account, the involuntary nature of the experience in question is obvious; we are far removed from the notion of 'something made up'. Therefore, Evrart seems to be offering what is, in fact, a personal redefinition of a quite common technical term. He concludes this phase of his discussion by remarking that there are other ways, apart from these three, in which one can feign in order to speak more securely and blamelessly, but he does not specify what they are.

The second way in which fiction may reasonably be employed is: in order to speak more secretly (*plus secretement*). Here the commentator defends deliberate obscurity on the grounds that on occasion meaning should be withheld from the unworthy. The subtle and wise philosophers sometimes do not wish to speak so plainly of certain things that one can understand them at first sight without study and without pain, explains Evrart. And so, they 'coeuvrent et celent la sentence, affin que ceulx les puissent tant seulement entendre qui en sont dignes' ['cover and close up the meaning to the end that only those who are worthy of understanding it can comprehend it']. These remarks may have been influenced by that crucial passage in Macrobius' commentary on the *Somnium Scipionis*, though Evrart himself does not cite it, where it is said that philosophers purposefully make use of fabulous narratives when 'they realize

---

[102] Cf. Minnis, 'Langland's Ymaginatif', pp. 92–4. The *locus classicus* is Augustine, *De Genesi ad litteram*, xii.

that a frank, open exposition of herself is distasteful to Nature'
(I.ii.17–18).[103] As noted in Chapter 2 above, such doctrine
underlay the twelfth-century practice of integumental discourse,
coterie language which was caviar to the general. But the
vernacular writer displays no interest in such matters; instead he
cites the scriptural warning against casting pearls before swine
(Matt. 7: 6), and notes that the Song of Songs and the
Apocalypse afford good examples of such appropriate obscurity.[104] Moreover, alchemists commonly use this method, and
sometimes astronomers, and prophets who wish to speak of
future events. And in this manner some speak of their loves,
Evrart continues, thereby bringing his doctrine to bear on the
text he is expounding.

A defence of obscurity is highly appropriate in a commentary
on a poem which is itself obscure in so many respects, most
notably in its depiction of the chess pieces. Each of these bears
a symbol; for example, the lady's pieces bear the images of the
crescent moon, rose, lamb, rainbow, ring, serpent, panther, and
eaglet. It takes little effort to deduce that the rose is a symbol of
beauty, but the crescent moon is hardly an obvious symbol of
youth, the rainbow of gentle appearance, or the panther of
goodness. Yet these abstract qualities are not actually identified
at any point in the poem: the images move around the chess
board, enigmatic and unexplained, even though the audience
needs to comprehend their significance in order to follow the
narrative. The requisite explanations, it would seem, were
meant to be found in a gloss rather than in the text. In the
Venice manuscript of the *Eschez amoureux*, the only one now
legible,[105] a diagram of the chess board is provided, with all the
pieces duly named, their symbolic meaning thereby being made
manifest; moreover, explanatory glosses (in Latin) are provided
in the margins of this manuscript. Could the Latin glosses on the
Eschez amoureux have been a self-commentary, provided by the

---

[103] Trans. Stahl, pp. 86–7.
[104] On scriptural obscurity, see the famous passage in Augustine, *De doctrina
christiana*, ii.6, which discusses the Song of Songs; see further the relevant ideas of
Pseudo-Dionysius the Areopagite, summarized in Minnis and Scott, *Medieval
Literary Theory*, pp. 172–3. Both positive and negative understandings of *obscuri-
tas* are described in Jan M. Ziolkowski's admirable study, 'Theories of Obscurity in
the Latin Tradition', *Mediaevalia*, 19 (1996 [for 1993]), 101–70.
[105] Cf. n. 15 above.

anonymous poet himself as a guide to the significance of his own poem? On this matter Evrart, whose knowledge of the information in this textual apparatus is obvious, is silent; neither does he speculate about the identity of the *Eschez*-poet. But this seems a reasonable assumption, given the amount of privileged information which the Latin glosses contain.

En passant, it should be noted that one of the two extant manuscripts of John Lydgate's Middle English translation (*c.*1410) of the first part of the *Eschez amoureux*, namely Oxford, Bodleian Library, MS Fairfax 16, contains a redaction of those same Latin glosses.[106] This may be taken as evidence that someone—perhaps the English author himself—wanted the translation to share the *mise-en-page* of its original. Moreover, it would seem that Lydgate had drawn on the Latin explication in producing his version of the story of *Reson and Sensuallyte*. There is one fascinating piece of external evidence for this hypothesis.[107] In the Fairfax manuscript, alongside these English verses—

> Thorient, which ys so bryght
> And casteth forth so clere a lyght,
> Betokeneth in especiall
> Thinges that be celestiall
> And thinges, as I kan diffyne,
> That be verrely dyvyne.[108]

—is positioned a gloss which identifies them as 'the words of the expositor in Latin and the translator in English' ('Verba expositoris in latino et translatoris in anglico'). This seems to refer back to the previous Latin gloss: 'a consideratione celestium et eternorum et leuiter transeundo per ista terrena semper redit et finaliter se conuertit ad eterna . . .'. That is to say, *here* are the Latin words of the expositor which Lydgate has Englished in the

---

[106] Lydgate's poem breaks off shortly after beginning its account of the fourth pawn on the chessboard. The last Latin gloss in MS Fairfax 16 concerns the third pawn; cf. the gloss beginning 'Tertius est Doulz Penser . . .' as published in *Eschez amoureux*, ed. Kraft, *Die Liebesgarten-Allegorie*, p. 239.

[107] This has been confirmed by my own comparison—conducted as far as the fragmentary nature of both the Venice copy of the French poem and of Lydgate's translation has allowed—of *Reson and Sensuallyte* with the text and gloss of the *Eschez amoureux* as edited by Christine Kraft.

[108] Lydgate, *Reason and Sensuality*, ed. E. Sieper, EETS, ES 84 (London, 1901), p. 18.

lines quoted above: and the glossator of *Reson and Sensuallyte* wants to draw attention to that fact. Unfortunately, a comparison of these glosses with those on the *Eschez amoureux* itself is not possible because the Venice manuscript lacks the entire first part of the original poem. Given the loss of the Dresden text of the *Eschez*, Lydgate's translation of that part, together with the Fairfax 16 version of the Latin glosses which originally had sought to mitigate its obscurity, constitutes the best witness we have to a major section of the French poem's narrative.

However, in considering the occasional obscurity of the *Eschez amoureux* it is important not to lose sight of the vital fact that the amount and type of 'secrecy' in the French poem is rather different from that found in either the Song of Songs or the Apocalypse. Evrart's category is very broad—it can even include lovers' secret speech—and hence it brings together strange bedfellows. More positively, it could be suggested that here—as elsewhere—he is elevating his French text by associating it with ancient texts of great authority. To change the discourse, neither the *Eschez*-poet nor Evrart de Conty was interested in perpetuating élitist *integumenta*. Their chosen mission, given that the Muses were now walking naked in the vernacular (to recall Boccaccio's phrase), was rather to remove the fabulous veils for the benefit of a larger—and, in particular, a lay—audience, thereby following in the footsteps of those ancient poets who had conveyed an abundance of philosophical doctrine through the figures of the pagan gods and goddesses, deities that they believed in only as educational aids. In his *Problemata* translation Evrart had remarked, somewhat loftily, that here Aristotle had not written 'aus enfans ne aus ignorans' but addressed his words 'aus anciens et aus sages' who were skilled in 'plusieurs parties de philozophie'; hence he had expressed himself briefly and in a highly sententious manner— the result being an obscure text.[109] But the *Eschez amoureux* is a very different proposition. Its obscurity is of a different kind, the removal and resolution of which is constitutive of an educational programme for aristocratic layfolk, rather than a secret code which may be understood only by 'anciens' and 'sages'.

That, however, is inference. Evrart does not consider the

---

[109] Guichard-Tesson, 'Le Métier de traducteur', p. 137.

implications of his account of justifiable literary obscurity for
the interpretation of the *Eschez amoureux* itself. Instead he
proceeds to describe the third way in which fiction may be
defended; namely, in order to speak more subtly, pleasantly, and
delightfully.[110] Once again we may detect the unacknowledged
influence of Macrobius (cf. *In Somn. Scip.*, I.ii.8). Things which
are subtly presented, Evrart claims, cause us to marvel and
consequently to feel pleasure, 'for marvellous things are by
nature delightful', as Aristotle says. The reference is unclear;
maybe Evrart had in mind the beginning of the *Metaphysics*
(I.2; 982^b12–21), or perhaps even Averroes' version (as translated by Hermann the German) of Aristotle's statement that
man instinctively takes delight in skilled representation.[111] The
continued influence of Macrobius, however, is confirmed when
Evrart goes on to say that this is why people delight in the fables
of Aesop (cf. *In Somn. Scip.*, I.ii.9) and, he adds, of Renard the
Fox, and indeed in amorous writings:[112] they take pleasure in
'The Amorous Catch', i.e. Jean Acart de Hesdin's *La Prise
amoureuse* (completed in 1332),[113] 'and in many other treatises
of love, because of the subtle and reasonable way of speaking
beneath which a pleasant and delightful meaning is enclosed—
and, very often, a *moralité* of great profit'. All these three
reasons, Evart concludes, may lie behind the fictions employed
in the *Eschez amoureux*.

At the end of the commentary, the large fictional element in
the poem is emphasized; the early definition of 'imaginary
vision' as 'something made up' is tacitly affirmed.[114] Evrart is
concerned to warn us that what the text says should not be

---

[110] *Eschez amour. moral.*, ed. Guichard-Tesson and Roy, pp. 24–5.

[111] See Minnis and Scott, *Medieval Literary Theory*, p. 293. However, the limited
circulation of Hermann's translation should be noted.

[112] This is, in a way, an updating of Macrobius, who had spoken of 'the narratives
replete with imaginary doings of lovers in which Petronius Arbiter so freely indulged
and with which Apuleius, astonishingly, sometimes amused himself': *In somn. Scip.*,
I.ii.8; trans. Stahl, p. 84.

[113] In Acart's poem *prise* designates the 'catch' or 'prey', the animal killed at the
successful end of a hunt. According to Jean's somewhat ghoulish allegory the lover
is the catch, who in Love's hunt is captured, killed, and divided into three parts as
if he were an animal. His blood is sucked by hunting dogs named Pleasure, Will,
Thought and Hope, and so forth. Thus the poet images the narrator's total aban-
donment to love. For a useful account of this poem see Thiébaux, *Stag of Love*, pp.
145–6, 153–61.

[114] *Eschez amour. moral.*, ed. Guichard-Tesson and Roy, pp. 764–6.

taken as a simple record of the writer's own experience. In the first instance, the defence of feigning as appropriate obscurity is canvassed. Thus, the author of whom we are speaking wishes to show secretly by the game of chess how in his youth he was taken and moved ('esmeuz et esprins') by the love of a young girl. But this soon gives way to the argument that what he says about having mated 'ne doit pas estre ainsy, a la verité, entendu en maniere qu'il feust ainsy d'amours afolez ne seurprins' ['should not be understood in such a way as to mean that truly he was maddened and overcome by love']. Rather, we are assured, 'il le faint ainsi pour prendre occasion de mieulx parler d'amour et plus plaisamment et plus bel, car ainsi est ceste matiere a moult de gens plaisant et agreable, si comme il fu dit au commencement de ce livre present' ['he feigns this, to take the occasion for speaking of love better, more pleasantly, and more beautifully. For thus the matter is made more pleasant and agreeable to many people, as it was said at the beginning of the present book [i.e. the commentary]']. The commentator is quite consistent, therefore, in his desire to sunder the author from his *persona*.

The moral note is then struck, as Evrart moves from *delectatio* to *utilitas* in a way which puts the pleasure principle in context. This feigning was also done, he declares, to show better the error and deception that exist in mad, pleasurable love ('l'erreur et la decepcion qui est en la fole amour delictable') and the great, innumerable dangers in which those who excessively indulge in it place themselves.

Car c'est la principal entencion de l'acteur dessusdit et la fin de son livre, que de reprendre et blasmer leur folie comme chose a raison contraire, si comme il peut apparoir clerement par le procés de son livre rimé.

[It is the principal intention of the above-mentioned author and the end of his book to reprehend and blame their folly as a thing contrary to reason, as can clearly appear by the procedure of his rhymed book.]

We are back in the world of the *accessūs Ovidiani*. Ovid's *Heroides*, declares a representative scholiast, 'pertains to ethics, because he is teaching good morality and eradicating evil behaviour. The ultimate end (*finalis causa*) is that, having seen the

advantage (*utilitas*) gained from lawful love, and the misfortunes which arise from foolish and unlawful love, we may shun
both of these and adhere to chaste love.'[115] Clearly, according
to its commentator the *Eschez amoureux* also pertains to ethics.
Fole amour is against reason, his argument continues; the fact
that the author presents himself (*faint*) as having been mated in
the garden of mirth in the left corner of the chessboard is highly
significant, for the left signifies sensuality and the right, reason.
And the poet's recognition of this, Evrart claims, is obvious
from the final part of his poem.

There the God of Love believes (incorrectly, as it turns out)
that he has won the young man; he feels great joy and presents
him with the commandments of love. The direct source of this
part of the poem, though Evrart does not say so here, is Ovid's
Ars amatoria. Apparently, though the commentary does not put
it in so many words, this should be understood as the victory of
unreason. This victory is, of course, only temporary; the *ars* is
followed by a *remedium amoris*. Pallas ('c'est a dire sapience, ou
prudence, ou raison') is given the last word. She comes, Evrart
explains, 'finally to reprove and blame his folly and to show
him primarily how the life of pleasure that Venus and Love and
Delight and Idleness teach [people] to follow is a deceptive and
perilous life', inimical to reason and even contrary to nature.
Then he offers a rapid summary of what is in fact a major part
of the poem.

Et lui dist dame Pallas et moustra moult d'enseignemens beaulx et
moult de belles choses prouffitables a meurs et a honneste vie et qui
seroient belles a declairier, maiz pour certaine cause je m'en tairay
atant quant a present. Amen.[116]

That last phrase is not wholly clear. Joan Morton Jones translates as follows: 'And there the lady Pallas told and showed him
many beautiful lessons and fine things profitable to ethics and
to honest life, and which it would be good to explain. But for
certain reasons I shall be quiet at this for the moment.
Amen.'[117] On the other hand, Guichard-Tesson and Roy believe
that here Evrart is declaring that his task is now finished: the

[115] Cf. p. 237 above.
[116] *Eschez amour. moral.*, ed. Guichard-Tesson and Roy, pp. 765–6.
[117] Jones, 'The Chess of Love', p. 1294.

'cause' of his work having been made 'certaine', rendered understandable, he can stop at the present time: 'il déclare en effet qu'il n'entreprendra pas de le *declairier*, car son propos est terminé'.[118] This explanation is eminently plausible, for really there is little of substance left for Evrart to say. His silence is appropriate because the text, by its explicit didacticism, has at this point rendered the gloss redundant.

Traditionally, the *accessūs* to the *Remedia amoris* explain that, in order to make amends for the offensive *Ars amatoria*, on account of which he had been exiled, Ovid 'set out to write this book [the *Remedia*] in which he advises both young men and girls trapped in the snares of love as to how they may arm themselves against unlawful love'.[119] The art of love and its remedy therefore go together; the one follows, and indeed presupposes, the other within the sequence established by the *vitae Ovidii*. That sequence became a narrative sequence in the works of certain medieval Ovidians (cf. pp. 42–4), a good example being afforded by the *De amore* of Andreas Capellanus, which offers a 'retraction' in its final book. The *Eschez amoureux* poet may be regarded as having followed that sequence also, the *remedium* component being substantially amplified with an abundance of material on the good active life. When the rules of the *ars amatoria* govern the text, the commentator has as his task the provision of erudite doctrine and moral guidance; when the *remedium* follows, as predictably as night follows day, the commentator's job is finished. Having helped his author over the earlier hurdles, Evrart can take his leave of him in the final stretch, wherein the young are offered explicit instruction in the ethical, economic, and political virtues, 'according to the spirit and the letter of the *De regimine principum* of Giles of Rome'.[120]

We may recall Francesco da Barberino's remark that, in order to ward off the condemnation of those who felt that the text of his *Documenti d'amore* had exclusively considered carnal love, he had woven Latin glosses around both its Latin and Italian versions, in order to spell out the moral motivation of the

---

[118] *Eschez amour. moral.*, ed. Guichard-Tesson and Roy, p. lviii.
[119] Minnis and Scott, *Medieval Literary Theory*, p. 25.
[120] As Guichard-Tesson and Roy put it; *Eschez amour. moral.*, p. lviii.

enterprise (cf. p. 278 above). Evrart has done for the *Eschez amoureux* what Barberino did for his own *Documenti*. But once the poem itself becomes reverent there is no longer any need for 'reverent interpretation'. Henceforth the reader does not need to be assured that the *Eschez* pertains to ethics.

From academe to lay audience: the chequered reception of vernacular commentary

It is often difficult to make confident assertions about the reception of late-medieval commentaries, both in Latin and *in vulgari*, on vernacular texts. The commentaries on the classical poets, or indeed on the biblical poets, had a definite social context, being produced and consumed within academic milieux. Masters would 'read' (i.e. comment on) their prescribed texts in lectures which formed part of the pupils' training as grammarians, theologians, or lawyers; the pupils would as a matter of course go on to produce similar lectures, perpetuating the wisdom of their masters and making their own contributions. When literary theory and the practice of commentary move beyond the confines of the schools, the interpretative communities become less circumscribed, more varied, and harder to determine.

Patronage, of course, had a crucial role. Charles V's commissions were quite outstanding, and, as already noted, his translators often provided vernacular commentary to elucidate their work. A similar pattern of patronage involving both text and gloss may be found in late medieval Castilian literary culture.[121] Enrique de Villena (1384–1434) made a complete translation of Virgil's *Aeneid* and produced a vernacular commentary on its first three books (which survives in a single manuscript, Madrid, Biblioteca Nacional, MS 10111). Villena prefaces his commentary with an epistle to Juan de Aragón, who had

---

[121] Here I draw on information provided by Ronald G. Keightley, who has published studies on Spanish translations of *De consolatione philosophiae* and the Eusebius commentary of Alfonso de Madrigal; see esp. his article, 'Alfonso de Madrigal and the *Cronici canones* of Eusebius', *Journal of Medieval and Renaissance Studies*, 7 (1977), 225–48. I am also indebted to the indispensable monograph on Castilian literary theory by Julian Weiss, *The Poet's Art*.

commissioned it soon after ascending the throne of Navarre. It seems clear that Villena had intended to cover the entire poem; the reasons for its incompletion are unclear. Villena's translation of the *Rhetorica ad Herennium* has been lost, but a version of his translation of Dante's *Comedy* has survived, fitted around a glossed copy (the glosses being in Latin and Castilian) of the original Italian text. This manuscript was owned by his friend Íñigo López de Mendoza, first marquis of Santillana (1398–1458); indeed, many of the Castilian glosses are in Santillana's own hand. Alfonso de Madrigal's (incomplete) Castilian commentary on Jerome's Latin version of Eusebius' *Chronici canones* was an offshoot of the translation of this work which, in 1449–50, he had made for Santillana.The marquis also possessed translations of two Latin commentaries on Dante, an anonymous translation of Pietro Alighieri's commentary, and, commissioned from his physician, Martín González de Lucena, a translation of parts of Benvenuto da Imola's commentary. Furthermore, his library included a Spanish translation of Pierre Bersuire's *Ovidius moralizatus* and, almost certainly, the *Biblia de Osuna* (a Spanish *Bible moralisé*), along with the Spanish translation of Old Testament prophetic and wisdom literature (Madrid, Biblioteca Nacional, MS 10288), two Latin Bibles, and a concordance of the Latin text. Accompanying them was a full translation of portions of Nicholas of Lyre's *Postilla* on the Old Testament, which was made by the Franciscan Alfonso de Algezira at the behest of Alfonso de Guzmàn, son of the first Count of Niebla; the bulk of the work was carried out between 1420 and 1422.

From the 'first wave' of commentaries (as Julian Weiss describes it), which was 'inspired by translations' of authoritative Latin works, 'the practice of textual annotation [in the vernacular] spread to contemporary Castilian literature'.[122] Here once again Santillana played an important part. The version of his *Proverbios* which had been dedicated (in 1439) to King Juan II of Castile and his son Prince Enrique was equipped with a self-commentary (consisting of historical glosses). Pero Díaz de Toledo considerably amplified this commentary, and in the 1460s wrote glosses for a poem by Santillana's nephew,

[122] Ibid. 121.

Gómez Manrique.[123] Juan II and Álvaro de Luna were patrons of Juan de Mena (1411–56), who provided a commentary for his own poem *La coronación*.[124]

The cultural situation of the Italian city-states was markedly different. Dante's innovative autoexegesis would have been perfectly comprehensible in the circles of *litterati* for whom he was writing; highly educated men who were *inter alia* well versed in commentary on both secular and sacred authors would have at once appreciated his erudition and grasped the polemical implications of his chosen form. The same can be said of the text and gloss of Francesco da Barberino's *Documenti d'amore*. With regard to these works we should perhaps envisage a context of private reading. But, thanks to Dante's subsequent stature, series of public lectures on his masterpiece could be, and sometimes were, funded. The Florentine civic authorities sponsored Boccaccio's lectures on the *Comedy* which commenced on 23 October 1373, in the church of Santo Stefano di Badia. One member of Boccaccio's audience, Benvenuto da Imola, was inspired to organize and deliver another series of Dante lectures, at Bologna in 1375.[125]

However, no such context for the delivery of literary lectures existed in the England of John Gower's day. There has been considerable debate about the extent and significance of the literary patronage dispensed by King Richard and his familiars, and this is not the place to open up those questions again. Suffice it to identify myself as one of those who believe it to have been more substantial than has sometimes been claimed.[126] But it can only seem small in comparison with the cases I have been citing from Italy, France, and Spain. (Moreover, all the blame cannot be laid at the door of Richard II, for Lancastrian literary patronage marks only a modest increase. Even more important for the present argument is the fact that in fifteenth-century England there was no major attempt to promote vernacular hermeneutics, a point to which we will return.) However, if we set about looking in Ricardian

---

[123] Weiss, *The Poet's Art*, p. 129.   [124] Ibid. 133–4.
[125] Cf. David Wallace's account in Minnis and Scott, *Medieval Literary Theory*, pp. 456–8.
[126] See my discussion in *Chaucer: Shorter Poems*, pp. 11–35.

England for translations of those texts which were deemed to be
fit for kings and princes, we are led to the Gloucestershire
magnate Sir Thomas Berkeley (1352–1417), and his daughter
Elizabeth Berkeley (d. 1422), who married Richard de
Beauchamp, earl of Warwick.[127] It was for Thomas Berkeley
that John Trevisa produced English translations of *De proprietatibus rerum* and *De regimine principum* along with Ralph
Higden's 'universal history', the *Polychronicon*. To the last of
these works are prefixed two remarkable original prefaces on
translation, which raise at least some of the issues also discussed
by Charles V's translators. An anonymous translation of
Vegetius (maybe by one William Clifton) followed in 1408, after
Trevisa's death. The Boethius translation of John Walton (1410)
was almost certainly made for Elizabeth Berkeley.[128] Recent
research would seem to suggest that, in addition to translating
the text, Walton translated extracts from Trevet's Boethius
commentary as well, for Elizabeth's edification.[129]

As the closest English counterparts of the French kings and
princes, then, we can do no better than nominate the Berkeley
family, with full (perhaps also with somewhat embarrassed)
recognition that their patronage was on a far more modest scale.
The London-based John Gower was not of their circle, but he had
sufficient financial means to pursue his own interests—and that
included the production of a long English poem, together with
sporadic Latin glosses, following an unspecific request from his
monarch.[130] In the case of the *Confessio amantis* it is reasonable

---

[127] On the family's literary patronage see esp. Ralph Hanna, 'Sir Thomas Berkeley
and His Patronage', *Speculum*, 64 (1989), 878–916. See further his article, 'The
Difficulty of Ricardian Prose Translation: The Case of the Lollards', *Modern
Language Quarterly*, 51 (1990), 319–40. Honourable mention should also be made
of John of Gaunt's patronage of two Anglo-Latin writers, Richard Maidstone and
Walter of Peterborough. The latter produced for Gaunt a Christian allegorization of
Ovid's *Metamorphoses*, which has been lost. See George Rigg, *A History of Anglo-
Latin Literature, 1066–1422* (Cambridge, 1992), pp. 276–8, 285–6.

[128] Cf. Minnis, 'Medieval French and English Traditions', pp. 343–7, 350–1,
where it is demonstrated that, in addition to Chaucer's *Boece*, Walton used Trevet's
Boethius commentary in preparing his translation.

[129] One MS of Walton's Boethius, Copenhagen, Køngelige Bibliotek, Thott 304 fol,
contains Middle English glosses translated from Trevet's commentary; this manuscript was the basis of the first printed edition (1525) of Walton's work, which also
has a version of the commentary. See Brian Donaghey and Irma Taavitsainen,
'Walton's Boethius: From Manuscript to Print', *English Studies*, 80 (1999), 398–407.

[130] Cf. Minnis, *Chaucer: Shorter Poems*, p. 19.

to envisage a context of private reading, or of performance to small audiences of the noble and/or the wealthy. The better educated the reader of this composite text the more 'academic' and profoundly moral an understanding he can gain of the poem, enjoying access to the didactic classicism of the (often quite elaborate and sometimes cryptic) Latin verses which are interspersed throughout the English text and, more readily, to the blunt moral statements of the simpler Latin prose glosses. Such an educated reader would have had some experience, at the very least, of exegetical lectures on literature as part of his grammar school training, and hence would have been in a position to understand the nature and function of Gower's glosses. Moreover, one can imagine a person of that calibre reading aloud a section of the *Confessio* to a group of aristocrats, and either before, during or after the reading conveying such material from the Latin apparatus as he thought fit, in accordance with the taste and mood of the audience.

Gower's English text is, however, quite comprehensible without any gloss, whereas this is certainly not true of parts of the *Eschez amoureux* poem: as has been noted above, the significance of the chess pieces is not described in the work itself and requires explication of the type which is found in the Latin glosses of the Venice manuscript. Guichard-Tesson and Roy conceive of a social situation involving a reader-teacher and his 'pupil', with a chess board and pieces being used as a visual aid:

On en conclut que l'auteur a conçu le poème non pas comme un texte autosuffisant, mais plutôt comme partie d'un ensemble simultanément textuel-oral-gestuel. La métaphore des échecs lui aura suggéré une création originale, qu'on appellerait volontiers *multi-media*, dans notre jargon. Cette constatation est importante pour la compréhension des *Eschez amoureux*. En tant que texte, le poème est incomplet parce qu'il nécessite non seulement un échiquier sur lequel se jouera en temps réel une véritable partie d'échecs, mais aussi un dialogue entre le précepteur et son élève.[131]

Their characterization of the *Eschez amoureux* poem as 'texte-guide' designed to occasion the 'initiation érotique, éthique et scientifique' of a young nobleman applies equally well to Gower's *Confessio amantis*, which, like the *Eschez amoureux*,

---

[131] *Eschez amour. moral.*, ed. Guichard-Tesson and Roy, p. lxii.

owes much to the *de regimine principum* tradition.[132] A similar appeal and reception may be conjectured for Evrart de Conty's full-scale vernacular commentary on the *Eschez amoureux*; the scope and ambition of this work is quite comprehensible within the sophisticated milieu of the court of Charles V (though it was actually completed after the king's death). All three works teach Aristotelian practical philosophy and offer much ethical 'lore' as well as amatory 'lust' (i.e. pleasure; here I am echoing Gower's statement that his poem provides 'Somewhat of lust, somewhat of lore': Prologus, 19). They seem designed to edify and entertain an aristocratic audience, though it should be noted that, as far as we know, Gower did not move easily and frequently in court circles, whereas Evrart de Conty, as king's physician, most certainly did.

It may also be suggested that the movement of commentary beyond the academic confines of the schools had, at least in some instances, an effect on its very substance and style. Freed from classroom constraints and requirements commentary could become more demanding in content, more elaborate in form. An excellent example of this is afforded by the exceptional scholarship of the English Dominican Nicholas Trevet, who often wrote for, and sometimes at the specific request of, learned prelates, who demanded fare far more subtle than the staple diet of schoolboys.[133] Trevet's commentaries on, for example, the tragedies of Seneca were certainly not intended for delivery to a class of young pupils at the very beginning of their careers, and it is significant that when the English grammar-master William Wheteley (*fl.*1309–16) wished to use Trevet's richly learned commentary on the *De consolatione philosophiae* of Boethius in his classroom he had to simplify it considerably.[134] Moreover, commentary became less of a 'dependent' genre, i.e. less dependent on the text it was explicating, and

[132] On this aspect of Gower's poem, see esp. Elizabeth Porter, 'Gower's Ethical Microcosm and Political Macrocosm', in Minnis (ed.), *Gower's Confessio Amantis*, pp. 135–62.

[133] Cf. Minnis and Scott, *Medieval Literary Theory*, pp. 316, 324–5, 340–3. See further Smalley, *English Friars and Antiquity*, pp. 58–65, and Minnis, 'Medieval French and English Traditions', pp. 314–51.

[134] On Wheteley see esp. H. F. Sebastian, 'William Wheteley's Commentary on the Pseudo-Boethius' tractate *De disciplina scolarium* and Medieval Grammar School Education' (Ph.D. diss., Columbia University, 1970).

began to reconstruct itself as treatise literature. This could occur even within the world of academe, as happened with the theological commentaries on the *Sentences* of Peter Lombard, which in the fourteenth century often took little notice of the Lombard himself. Within 'new' commentary on vernacular texts this development is also marked, as in the cases of Dante's *Convivio* and Evrart de Conty's *Livre des eschez amoureux moralisés* (as its editors, Guichard-Tesson and Roy, prefer to call it).

That having been said, it should also be noted that much 'new' commentary retained one major feature of the classroom glosses which were its ancestors: the values of the text were not necessarily the same as those of its accompanying gloss. And this could be true even if one and the same author wrote both text and gloss. A good example is afforded by Dante's exegesis of the first *canzone* which features in the *Convivio*, the *Voi che'ntendendo*. Here the compassionate *donna gentile* who, according to the *Vita nuova*, had comforted him for a time after the death of Beatrice is allegorized as Lady Philosophy (Dante's discussion being influenced, as he himself intimates, by the female personification created by Boethius).[135] The consolation involved was, allegedly, the consolation of philosophy rather than of a brief love affair. In similar vein, between the text of the *Eschez amoureux* and Evrart's commentary thereon there exists, as we have suggested above, an interpretative distance until the poem becomes blatantly and unequivocally moral, at which point the commentator's task is done; the conceptual gap closes, and ultimate consonance and agreement of purpose are achieved.

In his *Convivio* Dante was determined to be as learned as possible, to put on conspicuous display his mastery of that learning which featured in the most comprehensive of scholastic commentaries. But other vernacular commentators disclose an awareness that they are addressing audiences rather different in nature from the usual consumers of scholastic hermeneutics. We have already noted how the anonymous translator-glossator of *L'Art d'amours* secularizes his scholia in line with the interests of a new public.[136] This process is more

---

[135] *Convivio*, ii.12; ed. Cordati, p. 82.
[136] Cf. Ch. 1 above, pp. 61–2.

advanced and thoroughgoing in the *Eschez amoureux* commentary.[137] Particularly intriguing is the progress Evrart made towards a 'secular' mythography. For instance, selective use is made of Bersuire's *Ovidius moralizatus* (a work which Bersuire himself sought to justify in terms of its usefulness to preachers), with the allegorical material which refers to prelates or prelatical theology being systematically reduced.[138] The use of biblical quotations which is a major feature of Bersuire's work is severely curtailed; such reference is at once occasional and vague. Characteristically, Bersuire's interpretation of the satyrs who run to and fro around Diana as 'prelates ... who should, out of feelings of deep affection' serve the Virgin Mary with

[137] In this regard, the stimulus of Evrart's medical learning seems to have been profound, exercising an influence far more extensive than the specific ideas which appear in the *Eschez amoureux* commentary can possibly quantify. (Cf. what was said in Ch. 1 about the significance of medical discourse in *L'Art d'amours*, and the therapeutic advantages of sex according to Constantine the African.) In the *Problemata* Evrart read e.g. of the beneficial physical effects of lust and the 'fact' that the emission of semen benefits the body through the expulsion of waste products (phlegm and bile), that sexual intercourse is naturally pleasant because of the sensation produced by the escape of vaporous moisture (this being quite independent of any pleasure induced by the thought that another living creature may be generated), and of how men of melancholic temperament have a strong inclination towards *coitus*. Following such instruction in morally neutral diagnosis and the rationale of natural causality, the theological taxonomy of fornication and mortal sin can hardly have looked the same. 'Aristotle' had even asserted that 'all men who have become outstanding in philosophy, statesmanship, poetry or the arts are melancholic'—and then proceeded to reiterate the view that 'the melancholic are usually lustful' (*Problems*, bk. 30; trans. Hett, pp. 155, 159. Cf. p. 163: 'those with whom [bile] is excessive and hot become mad, clever or amorous and easily moved to passion and desire'). It requires little inference to produce the proposition that the cleverest men have the strongest sex drives. Pierre Col would have found such information advantageous in his assertion to Jean Gerson that it is perfectly possible for a man to be both a great cleric and 'a foolish lover'.

[138] See F. Guichard-Tesson, 'La *Glose des Echecs amoureux*: Un savoir à tendance laïque: comment l'interpreter?', *Fifteenth-Century Studies*, 10 (1984), 229–60. However, it is often difficult to determine exactly which mythographer Evrart is using at a given point, because he is drawing on sources in addition to Bersuire. For one clear example of a case in which Bersuire is being drastically abbreviated, see Evrart's portrait of Mars: *Eschez amour. moral.*, ed. Guichard-Tesson and Roy, p. 83; cf. *Reductorium morale, lib. XV: Ovidius moralizatus, cap. 1: De formis figurisque deorum, Textus e codice Brux., Bibl. Reg. 863–9 critice editus*, ed. J. Engels (Utrecht, 1966), pp. 15–16. On the other hand, Evrart's interpretation of the birth of Venus, wherein the sea in which Saturn's genitals are thrown is understood as the belly of man, which ebbs and flows like the sea, clearly recalls Fulgentius (*Mith.* ii. 1), as does his general association of Saturn with the production of abundant fruits and vegetables and their consumption (cf. further *Mith.* i. 2): *Eschez amour. moral.*, ed. Guichard-Tesson and Roy, pp. 65–76.

devotion (an excursus which culminates in a quotation from the Song of Songs)[139] is not to be found in Evrart's 'picture' of that goddess. Instead Evrart offers an astronomical/astrological interpretation, including an explanation of Diana's influence on the development of the child in the womb (again and again Evrart returns to the subject of pregnancy), proceeding to a brief historical interpretation and an account of her association with virginity.

The most striking feature of the 'tendance laïque' of the *Eschez amoureux* commentary is, however, its regular affirmation of the values and virtues of marriage, this being related to a general resistance to the misogyny which features in many of Evrart's sources. This tendency was, of course, already quite marked in the *Eschez amoureux* poem. For example, in a passage which draws heavily on the *Remedia amoris* the *Eschez* poet responds to Ovid's statement that no woman can be trusted with a counter-argument for trust and respect of good women, declaring that if a lady is worthy of love then she is worthy of marriage.[140] Evrart goes much further, as I now hope to show.[141] Elaborating on the Fulgentian interpretation of the Judgment of Paris, he interprets the *troiz manieres de vies* represented by the three goddesses as the *contemplative*, the *active*, and the *voluptueuse*, in a fashion which, whilst not calling in question the ultimate supremacy of the *vie contemplative*, nevertheless takes a very positive view of the *vie active*. Contemplatives are 'angelic' or 'demigods' and better than men. However, 'ceulz qui vivent en compaignie humaine en enssivant

[139] See the quotation of this passage in Ch. 2 above, p. 115.

[140] See the discussion by Hyatte, 'The *Remedia amoris* in Old French Didactic Poetry', pp. 48–9. Cf. the recommendation of marriage in Guiart's Ovid translation, discussed in Ch. 1 above.

[141] Cf. the significant but less thoroughgoing affirmation of marriage in Nicole Oresme's *Livre de yconomiques*. Here the family is defined as the basic economic unit, and a wife—who is not to be treated as a servant—is seen as essential to its right functioning. Emphasis is placed on the companionate aspect of marriage, and Oresme evinces confidence that 'two young people' can love each other in a manner which involves both joy and reasonableness. Such a relationship is described as a 'friendship' which 'comprises at once the good of usefulness, the good of pleasure, and the good of double enjoyment—that is, both the carnal and the virtuous or the sensual and the intellectual pleasures'. For discussion see Sherman, *Imaging Aristotle*, pp. 286–91, 297–301, who believes that, 'although the context of the discussion is consistently patriarchal, Oresme makes a genuine contribution to humane concepts of the marriage relationship' (pp. 290–1).

le chemin de vertu et de raison sont homes proprement, et
homes proprement doivent estre appellés, car ceste vie active,
. . . par raison ordenee, est droite vie propre et naturele a home'
['those who live in human society by following the path of
virtue and reason are properly men, and should properly be
called men, for the active life . . ., ordered by reason, is the life
which is right, proper and natural to man'].[142] Here the influence of Aristotle (perhaps as interpreted in Giles of Rome's *De
regimine principium*) is evident,[143] as it is in the subsequent
statement that mankind does not like to live a solitary life, but
wants to live 'en compaignie . . . et en communication' by
nature and because it is necessary to the continuation of our
human species, marriages being appropriate to the active life.[144]
Evrart reassures his readers he is not claiming that, since the
active life is more proper and suitable to man insofar as he is
man, it is therefore the best life. Rather, one could say that,
while in absolute terms gold is worth more than iron, in a battle
an iron sword is worth more than a gold one.[145] It would seem
that Evrart is writing for those engaged in the battles of the
active life, for whom 'iron' values and mores—marriage
included—are of more use than the higher virtues of the
contemplative life.

Later in his commentary Evrart explains the purpose of
Venus, or human desire, with reference to Nature's wish to
ensure the survival of the species. A special kind of love exists
between man and woman, which is 'sur toutes naturele et
merveilleuse, dont il avient souvent que ly hons entre mil en eslit
une seule qu'il aime et qu'il desire sy singulierement que on ne
en pourroit separacion faire, ne il n'en voulroit nulle autre
souhaidier' ['above all else natural and marvellous, by which it

---

[142] *Eschez amour. moral.*, ed. Guichard-Tesson and Roy, p. 350.
[143] Cf. Margaret J. Ehrhart, *The Judgement of the Trojan Prince Paris in Medieval
Literature* (Philadelphia, 1987), who describes this is a major departure from the
Fulgentian model. 'For Fulgentius, the active life was almost as reprehensible as the
voluptuous', whereas in the *Eschez amoureux* commentary 'the active life is the
virtuous life of man in society, as it was for Aristotle and medieval thinkers influenced by him' (p. 114). Ehrhart goes on to discuss the commentary's use of
Aristotle's preference for 'moderate wealth'.
[144] *Eschez amour. moral.*, ed. Guichard-Tesson and Roy, p. 353. By contrast,
Evrart continues, the voluptuous life is mad (*fole*) and unreasonable, more suited to
beasts than to men (p. 354).
[145] *Eschez amour. moral.*, ed. Guichard-Tesson and Roy, p. 356.

often happens that from a thousand women a man chooses a single one, whom he loves and desires so singularly that no separation can be made and he would not wish to desire any other'].[146] Unfortunately, this special pleasure in one single woman can induce melancholy, and therefore Raison, in the *Rose*, defines love as a mental illness, and the wise philosophers agree.[147] When Evrart returns to expand on this discussion, however, it is the positive aspects of *amour delitable* which are to the fore, with its best possible end being marriage. Venus's daughter Hymen can be understood as representing all kinds of harmony, especially that which exists between a man and a woman who 'franchement et sans riens refuser s'entreacordent ensamble' ['freely, without refusing anything, reciprocally accord with each other']. She

segnefie la delectacion qui est en mariage, ou les personnes sont par l'ordenance de la loy licitement conjointes, et ceste delectacion, sy come ilz dient, est la plus grant des autres et la mains amellee de tristece, pour ce que on y peut mielx, plus franchement et plus licitement, toutes les delectacions acomplir dessusdites.[148]

[signifies the delight that is in marriage, where the people are by the ordinance of the law legally joined together, and this delight, as they say, is the greatest of them all and the least intermingled with sorrow, because [in marriage] one can accomplish better, more freely and more legally all the above-mentioned pleasures.]

A la lectre et a la verité, Venus signifies concupiscence, a natural inclination which moves us to carnal pleasure, and this is twofold: an 'inclinacion . . . general et premiere' which generally impels us all and a 'concupiscence especial' which we sometimes feel toward a particular person. This 'double amour' may simply be called 'amour' or 'amour par amours'.[149] But Evrart stresses the importance of 'concupiscence especial' or 'amour especial' since it presupposes reason to some extent; it determines a man to love one woman above all others, otherwise he would take mistresses at will and indifferently, which love would not be honourable or proper, but would be better suited to the love of beasts rather than of human beings.[150]

[146] *Eschez amour. moral.*, ed. Guichard-Tesson and Roy, p. 365.
[147] Ibid. 366.   [148] Ibid. 537.
[149] Ibid. 538–9.   [150] Ibid. 541.

Then, at last, Evrart offers us a full definition of love. First he draws on the *De amore* of Andreas Capellanus, who is referred to as 'an ancient wise man' (*un saiges anciens*): 'Love is a passion, i.e. an affection, which is engendered in the heart of a person by seeing and regarding a person of the opposite sex . . .'.[151] Jean de Meun's Raison is then quoted as offering a more succinct ('en briefs paroles') version of this same doctrine: love is a mental illness (*maladie de pensee*) 'afflicting two persons of opposite sex'.[152] Evrart proceeds to elaborate this with medical lore, quoting Avicenna on the perils of melancholy which is induced by thinking too intensely about one's desires, particularly when they are unrequited.[153] A declaration that love, properly understood, cannot exist between two people of the same sex is followed by a brief excursus on how, in the time of King Arthur, 'valiant knights loved ladies *par amours* very honourably and chastely', and had to prove their worth by deeds of arms.[154] Furthermore, such love must be freely given and the lovers must be free to give it. A problem therefore arises when the lovers get married, because then their freedom is replaced with legal obligation:

Et pour ce, des sy tost que un amant voit que l'autre le veult maistrier et soubzmetre, il ly anuie et desplait grandement, ne l'amour depuis ja ne sera sy certaine que devant ne sy ferme. Pour ce voit on souvent es mariages sourdre grans tençons et grans noises, mesmement entre ceulx qui devant par amours se entreamoient, car quant elle perçoit que cely qui par devant la souloit appeller dame et amie veult maintenant que elle le serve et obeisse a ly, ceste dansse nouvelle sur toutes autres ly est abhominable, car s'est contre la loy d'amours, come dit est. Et a la verité, ceste amour est de trop autre maniere que n'est l'amour qui est en mariage, ou les personnes sont l'une a l'autre obligies. . . . Et pour ce que c'est impossible que telle union vraie puist estre en lieu trouvee ou il a haussaige ne maistrie, pour ce convient il en amours que les personnes, quant au regard d'amours, soient equaulx et franches. Et

---

[151] Cf. Andreas Capellanus, *On Love*, ed. and trans. Walsh, pp. 32–3.
[152] Cf. Introduction, pp. 9–10 above.
[153] *Eschez amour. moral.*, ed. Guichard-Tesson and Roy, p. 544.
[154] Ibid. 545. Evrart had mentioned Arthurian *amour* a little earlier (p. 540), in explaining that, while *amour par amours* depends on the sense of touch, there is another kind of love which depends on the sense of sight—the sight of the beloved affording sufficient pleasure. And this love, continues Evrart, existed long ago in the time of King Arthur.

pour ce dit un sages ancien que 'amours et seignourie ne s'acordent pas bien ne ne soit pas ensamble convenables'.[155]

[And so, as soon as one lover sees that the other wishes to master and subjugate him, he is upset and greatly displeased, and from then on the love will never be so certain or so secure. Therefore one often sees great tensions and major quarrels surge up in marriage between those who were in love *par amours* beforehand, for when she perceives that the other, who had earlier been accustomed to call her 'lady' and 'mistress', now wishes that she should serve and obey him, this new dance is above all others abominable to her, for it is against the law of love, as was said. And truly, this love [i.e. love *par amours*] is of an extremely different kind from the love which is in marriage, wherein the people are obligated to each other. . . . And on account of this it is impossible that such a true union could be found in a place where there is arrogance or mastery, because in love it is appropriate that the two people are equal and free, as far as love is concerned. And therefore an ancient wise man says that love and lordship do not accord well and are not suitable together.]

This is the most controversial statement on love and marriage to be found in the *Eschez amoureux* commentary, and was clearly written under the influence of Andreas Capellanus, here once again cited as 'un sages ancien'. Andreas had audaciously quoted the countess of Champagne as affirming 'unambiguously that love cannot extend its sway over a married couple. Lovers bestow all they have on each other freely, and without the compulsion of any consideration of necessity, whereas married partners are forced to comply with each other's desires as an obligation, and under no circumstances to refuse their persons to each other'.[156] But Evrart is apparently uncomfortable with this, and certainly not content to let the matter rest with the declaration of a division between *amours* and *seignourie*. Immediately he goes on to state that the engendering

---

[155] *Eschez amour. moral.*, ed. Guichard-Tesson and Roy, p. 546.
[156] *On Love*, ed. Walsh, pp. 156–7. Cf. pp. 146–7, where it is argued that 'marital affection' should not be allowed 'to appropriate the name of love', emphasis being placed on the fact that 'Love is nothing other than an uncontrolled desire to obtain the sensual gratification of a stealthy and secret embrace', which cannot take place between married couples, 'since they are acknowledged to possess each other'. Those stealthy embraces are absent from Evrart's account, which is interested in presenting marriage as a state in which desire can indeed be controlled with reason and honour.

of one's kind is the *fin principal* of marriage, and all reasonable lovers should intend this end.

Delitable amour is then divided into three types. The first is that kind in which the lovers are interested mainly in the pleasure which it brings, and unconcerned with propagation; hence they do not love each other 'with sufficient or reasonable love'. This is all too common in the world, laments Evrart.[157] Therefore, 'the wise Philosopher', speaking of marriage, says that a man of 'saine pensee' ['healthy thought'] should direct his study and intent to the engendering of children 'en femme precieuse et bonne' ['in a wife who is precious and good'].[158] The third kind of love (which owes much to Andreas's account of *purus amor*)[159] is described as the type wherein lovers wish to live honestly and chastely. The delight which results from seeing each other and talking together, when place, time, and reason permit, is enough for them. Although Evrart does not say so, this seems to be identifiable with the love which existed in the days of King Arthur, as described previously. Evrart follows Andreas once again in his suggestion that it is permissible in this kind of love for the partners to embrace and kiss each other sometimes.

The second kind of love is of particular interest to us because Evrart seems to regard it as the happy mean between the two extremes of the other kinds of love. In this case lovers love their *amies* primarily because of the good they see in them, such as beauty, simplicity, and the other pleasing graces; for such lovers sensual delight is a secondary consideration. 'Une fame honnourable ne peut plus grant don faire ne plus grant amistié moustrer a son ami que de ly toute habandonner, s'amour et son cuer et son corps, sans ly riens refuser' ['An honourable woman cannot give a greater gift or demonstrate greater amity or friendship to her lover than to abandon everything to him, her love and her heart and her body, without refusing him anything'].[160] In return the lover should equally give his heart, body, and love, and certainly should love her more loyally than

---

[157] With this one may compare Francesco da Barberino's condemnation of illicit love which cannot be defined as, or said to be, love at all; in the common parlance of the upright it is known as 'madness' or 'frenzy' (*rabies*). Cf. Minnis, 'Amor and Auctoritas', p. 38.

[158] *Eschez amour. moral.*, ed. Guichard-Tesson and Roy, p. 547.

[159] *On Love*, ed. Walsh, pp. 180–1.

[160] *Eschez amour. moral.*, ed. Guichard-Tesson and Roy, p. 548.

before. This second kind of love, concludes Evrart, is more reasonable because it resembles true friendship (*amisté*), where virtue lies and loyalty is preserved.

> ... et pour ce convient il raison et mesure garder en maintenir amours. Et briefment, c'est l'amour qui est et qui doit estre en mariage, combien que elle puist moult bien estre entre personnes franches qui par amours s'entreaiment. Et de ceste amour voulons nous quant a present parler, et l'autre amour laissier qui en mariage a son lieu.

> [Therefore it is necessary to preserve reason and moderation in maintaining love. In brief, this is the love that is and which should be in marriage, however much it could much better exist between free people who love each other *par amours*. And it is about this love that we wish to speak at present, and to leave aside the love which has its place in marriage.]

Thus Evrart reacts against his source text, Andreas' affirmation of the superiority of love between couples who can bestow it freely. Obviously, Evrart's own inclination is to affirm the superiority of marriage.

Evrart rounds off this excursus with the claim that the first kind of love (the pleasure-obsessed, bestial kind) is the type which Raison reproved in the *Rose*,[161] and the cautious remark that, for the moment, he does not wish to praise or blame these *troiz amours*. Thus he formally suspends his judgement, though his own preferences have been clear enough. They emerge, once again, later in the commentary when Aristotle's authority is enlisted for an affirmation of the benefits which the *estat de mariage* brings:

> 'Ly hons de bon afaire doit desirer que sa femme soit bonne ey y doit metre painne', sy come Aristote dit, 'car c'est celle qu'il a a sa vie esleue pour estre sa compaigne et pour fin sy notable que pour le fait de generacion, car plus divine chose ne plus digne ne peut estre, en l'estat de mariage, que lignie engendrer en fame honeste et bonne', sy come il dit, car 'par engendrer son samblable acquiert estre ly hons immortel et divin'.[162]

---

[161] *Eschez amour. moral.*, ed. Guichard-Tesson and Roy, p. 549.

[162] Ibid. 583. This comment occurs in the context of Evrart's explication of the *Eschez* poet's rewriting of the *Rose*'s account of how Jealousy imprisoned Bel Acueil. Andreas had said that true love cannot exist without Jealousy. Evrart tacitly rejects that proposition with the *exemplum* of how the jealous Vulcan only made

['A respectable man should desire a good wife, and should take pains to see that he has one', as Aristotle says, 'for she is the one he has chosen for life to be his companion and for so important an end as the act of generation, for there cannot be a more divine or worthy thing in the estate of marriage than to engender descendants in an honest and good wife', as he says, for 'by engendering his kind a man becomes immortal and divine'.]

This attitude is maintained with remarkable consistency throughout the commentary on the *Eschez amoureux*; it is wholly consonant with Evrart's educational ambitions. The young aristocrats who are his target audience are advised to love honourably, avoiding excesses of carnal delight which cause damage to both body and soul.[163] Hence Evrart's recourse to the moralized *fabulae poetarum*, for nothing imaginable to a reasonable man escaped the ancient poet-philosophers when they spoke through the various gods and goddesses;[164] assigning to them *descripcions et figures diverses* according to 'les proprietés de leur natures' ['the properties of their natures'], in a manner similar to the way 'nous faisons les ymages des sains' ['we [Christians] make images of saints'].[165] *Bonne doctrine* and *bele parole* can often be received from the *sages anciens*, 'qui les jonez adrescent et enforment, et qui leur moustrent les chemins et les voyes qui sont a tenir raisonables' ['who address and inform the young to show them the reasonable roads and paths that are to be taken'].[166] But Evrart was troubled by the doctrine of one 'ancient sage', the author we know as Andreas Capellanus. As far as he was concerned, joining the ranks of the *magistri amoris* entailed mastership of the values and virtues of married love. Evrart remained convinced that what the young

matters worse by revealing the adultery of his wife, Venus, with Mars. It would seem that Vulcan treated Venus badly, and so Evrart offers advice on how to treat a wife well. The husband should encourage her towards goodness and virtue as much as he can by reason, and through *doctrine amiable* and fine words, and he himself should show her a good example to follow: for, as is often said, the good man often makes the woman good, whereas the bad man misleads her. The man should be careful that he is never maddened by love to such an extent that he becomes unreasonably jealous. For the more the woman sees herself exhorted to behave chastely, the more she will be tempted to do the opposite, unless she is restrained by her own good nature.

[163] Ibid. 439.   [164] Ibid. 63; cf. p. 285 above.
[165] Ibid. 65.   [166] Ibid. 358.

need to know is that 'great love' can exist between man and woman, and marriage is the best state in which it may flourish. Here is a reasonable road and path to which his secular readers and hearers must be directed.

Translatio studii, translatio auctoritatis?

A love-song which acts as a fly-catcher for priests and pedants looks very suspicious; and accordingly, on examination, it proves to be a poem beside the purpose of poetry, filled with metaphysical jargon, and perhaps the very worst of Guido's productions. Its having been written by a man whose life and works include so much that is impulsive and real, is easily accounted for by scholastic pride in those early days of learning.[167]

Thus said the leading Pre-Raphaelite Dante Gabriel Rossetti of Guido Cavalcanti's *Donna mi prega*, in the light of a medieval commentary on the poem which has falsely been attributed to Giles of Rome.[168] Rossetti concludes that therefore the poem is 'of little true interest', and excludes it from his collection of translations of works by Dante, his circle, and his predecessors (first published in 1861). This attitude totally fails to comprehend Guido's literary ambitions and the cultural situation in which he and his commentators were writing. A love-song which did not conform to the interpretative priorities and standards which had been established by 'priests and pedants' could not hope to attain the approval of the cultural establishment, and it was that approval which many of the most self-aware and theoretically articulate vernacular poets, along with their 'new' commentators, were seeking. In the traditional value-laden strategies of Latin commentary they found a means of bestowing value on vernacular literature.

The self-commentaries of Dante and Boccaccio appear to have this ambition. Evrart de Conty is perhaps more diffident, but he definitely has a high opinion of the French poem he is discussing. It is said to follow in the footsteps of the ancients by

[167] *Dante Gabriel Rossetti: The Early Italian Poets*, ed. Sally Purcell (London, 1981), p. 137.
[168] Discussed by J. E. Shaw, *Guido Cavalcanti's Theory of Love: The 'Canzone d'Amore' and Other Related Problems* (Toronto, 1949), pp. 149–59.

offering *delectatio* and *utilitas*, and its 'manner of feigning' is unblushingly compared with that used by the esteemed Boethius in his *Consolatio philosophiae* (since both works employ *ymaginaire vision*). Furthermore, in respect of its obscurity it may be compared to scriptural visionary works, the Song of Songs and the Apocalypse. Moreover, Evrart, like Boccaccio in his *chiose* on the *Teseida*, does have some sense of vernacular literary history, and they also seem to share a sense of involvement in the creation of a corpus of vernacular hermeneutics. Evrart refers to the *Esopet*, the *Renart*, and Acart's *Prise amoureuse*. He recognizes the *Rose* as the major model for the *Eschez amoureux*, and feels free to compare the dream form of the earlier French poem with that of the august *Somnium Scipionis*, and (more generally) to draw on Macrobius' commentary for his own theory of poetic fiction.

These manifestations of cultural exchange are utterly comprehensible within the context of that exceptional optimism concerning the future of vernacular literature which marks the age of Charles V. French was seen as 'the new Latin', as for instance in Nicole Oresme's assertion, 'thus in those times for the Romans, Greek was in relation to Latin what Latin is for us in relation to French. And at that time the students in Rome and elsewhere were introduced to Greek, and the sciences were usually presented in Greek; while the common mother language (*langage commun et maternel*) in that country was Latin.'[169] The mother language of his own country being French, Oresme can conclude 'that the project of our good King Charles, who has good and outstanding books translated into French, is to be commended'. Oresme is, in effect, proclaiming a *translatio studii*, the transition of scholarship from Rome to France, from Latin to French. Citing Cicero's *Academica*, he asserts that 'matters which are weighty and of great authority (*grant auctorité*) are delightful and agreeable to people when written in the language of their country'. Aristotle's *Politics*, a work previously translated from Greek into Latin, has now been rendered into French, at the king's command.[170] Christine de Pizan,

---

[169] *Le Livre de ethiques*, ed. Menut, p. 100; cf. *Le Livre de politiques*, ed. Menut, p. 27.
[170] Ibid. 44. The Cicero quotation also appears in the preface to Oresme's *Livre de ethiques*.

enthusing about Charles V's translation programme, declares that 'it was a noble and perfect action' to have had such works 'translated from Latin into French to attract the hearts of the French people to high morals by good example'.[171] She proceeds to develop the *translatio studii* theme, making the point that France has taken possession of a heritage which in days of yore had passed from Greece to Rome. For his part, Evrart de Conty saw the technical difficulties he had in rendering the *Problemata* into French as not peculiar to vernacular translation but rather as replicating those experienced by the ancient scholars who had translated this work from its original Greek into Latin. In other words, these difficulties were endemic to the *translatio studii*, no matter which languages were involved and how prestigious some of them may have been.[172] Once again, French has been placed in the position once enjoyed by Latin—and, far from having to kowtow to the older language, the vernacular seems ready to supplant it.[173]

The contrast with the situation in England is remarkable. There the *translatio studii* had, so to speak, been tainted by the Lollard heretics, at least in the eyes of the establishment. In the Oxford translation debate of *c.*1401 scholars had debated whether knowledge of God should hierarchically proceed from the Latinate clergy to the laity, whether layfolk could cope with a text so stylistically difficult as the Bible, and whether the

---

[171] *Chemin de long estude*; quoted by Sherman, *Imaging Aristotle*, p. 7; see also p. 9.

[172] According to Evrart, the obscurity of the *Problemata* may be explained, at least in part, by the fact that it is a translation from Greek, which has a different linguistic structure: because of the 'diversité des langaiges' one may be unable to find in the target language 'mots proprement' which correspond to the words and 'maniere de parler' of the original. Evrart also remarks that the *Problemata* is a badly organized text, perhaps due to the shortcomings of its translators, who were excessively literal in their renderings of the Greek into Latin, 'mettant mot par mot' rather than bringing out the *sentence*. Evrart assures his own readers that he himself has sought to 'ensuivre la sentence', 'car qui vouldroit le texte ensuivre et mettre mot pour mot, ce seroit chose mal seant en la langue françoise'. He is eager to ensure that this (very difficult) work may be understood by his lay and vernacular-reading audience. Cf. the quotations from *Le Livre des problèmes* printed by Guichard-Tesson, 'Le Métier de traducteur', pp. 137–46.

[173] Furthermore, Evrart seems to have cared greatly about the kind of French he wrote in the *Problemata* translation: hence his restoration of grammatical features which had fallen into disuse approximately a century previously. As Gilbert Ouy says, this linguistic reform did not survive its author: *Gerson bilingue*, p. xiv.

barbarous English language was capable of serving as a vehicle for the communication of divine truth.[174] When issues of social control impinged on the consciousness of the church authorities, however, the situation acquired a new urgency. They 'came to see that the vernacular lay at the root of the trouble', 'that the substitution [of English for Latin] threw open to all the possibility of discussing the subtleties of the Eucharist, of clerical claims, of civil dominion, and so on'.[175] Archbishop Arundel's *Constitutions* of 1409 banned the translation of biblical passages into English—and this applied not only to the 'Lollard Bible' in whatever version, in part or entire, but also to extracts from the Holy Scriptures included in vernacular books and treatises, and indeed those vernacular books and treatises themselves.[176] Inevitably, this inhibited the development not only of what Nicholas Watson has called 'vernacular theology' but also of 'vernacular commentary tradition' in general.[177]

All English writings, no matter how much or how little theology they contained, no matter how unimpeachable their orthodoxy may have been, inevitably fell under suspicion. When Bishop Reginald Pecock set out to produce a body of orthodox doctrine in English to counteract the Wycliffite corpus, he met with strong opposition and finally with condemnation.

[174] See Anne Hudson, 'The Debate on Bible Translation, Oxford 1401', in her *Lollards and Their Books* (London, 1985), pp. 67–84.
[175] Anne Hudson, 'Lollardy: The English Heresy?' in *Lollards and Their Books*, p. 145.
[176] Cf. ibid.; and Nicholas Watson, 'Censorship and Cultural Change in Late Medieval England: Vernacular Theology, The Oxford Translation Debate and Arundel's *Constitutions* of 1409', *Speculum*, 70 (1996), 822–64. This point is given more force by the fact that most Middle English biblical exegesis produced in the late fourteenth and early fifteenth centuries was of Wycliffite origin (including the 'Glossed Gospels' and the prefatory material included in the various versions of the Lollard Bible, particularly its 'General Prologue').
[177] On Lollard biblical scholarship, see Anne Hudson, *The Premature Reformation: Wycliffite Texts and Lollard History* (Oxford, 1988), pp. 228–77. More generally, see David Lawton, 'Englishing the Bible', in David Wallace (ed.), *The Cambridge History of Medieval English Literature* (Cambridge, 1999), pp. 454–82. There was, of course, *some* orthodox 'commentated translation' of biblical texts, including an anonymous Apocalypse translation with commentary, Richard Rolle's Prose Psalter (which reveals the influence of Peter Lombard's Psalter commentary), and a glossed Prose Psalter—not to be confused with Rolle's—which is derived from a (lost) French original. On the last of these works, see R. C. St-Jacques, 'The *Middle English Glossed Prose Psalter* and Its French Source', in Beer (ed.), *Medieval Translators and Their Craft*, pp. 135–54.

Admittedly, some of the bishop's radically rationalist views hardly helped his case, yet his (thwarted) ambitions for a lay educational programme bear comparison with those of Charles V (as constructed by his appreciative translators) and Enrique de Villena.[178] Such a culture of repression, involving both church and state, of theological and philosophical thinking and writing *in vulgari* was inimical to the emergence in England of a tradition of vernacular textual commentary. Little wonder, then, that there is no mythographic treatise on the *Parliament of Fowls* of the type produced by Evrart de Conty, or a *querelle* over *Troilus and Criseyde*, despite Chaucer's attempt to provoke one in the prologue to his *Legend of Good Women*. The impact of that extraordinary instance of Italian self-commentary and self-promotion, Dante's *Convivio*, on Middle English Literature was as the source for quite traditional (though perhaps ne'er so well expressed) doctrine on true nobility, as featured in the Wife of Bath's Tale, rather than as the model for autoexegesis by Chaucer or any of his English contemporaries or successors. We have only Gower's sporadic Latin glosses on his *Confessio amantis* to set alongside the autoexegesis of such Castilian writers as Santillana, Juan de Mena, Pedro de Portugal, Diego de Valera, and Gómez Manrique.[179] And modern scholars of Middle English literature would give much for an English counterpart to the massive *Cancionero da Barrantes* (1479–82), which contains works by three of the greatest Spanish poets of the fifteenth century, Santillana, Mena, and Pérez de Guzmán, accompanied by extensive commentary in Castilian and Latin.[180] In sum, the contrast between England in this period and the situation in other European countries at roughly the same time is marked, and most telling.

But we should be aware of the dangers of exaggerating and decontextualizing the significance of vernacular hermeneutics. It would be näive to take every instance of 'modern' commentary as a vote of confidence in the stature and future of literature *in vulgari*. If Antoine Thomas is right, ultimately the *Documenti d'amore* was designed for the benefit of élite Latin readers, who

---

[178] On Villena's belief that the wise man had a social commitment to disseminate his knowledge widely, see Weiss, *The Poet's Art*, pp. 82–3, 91.

[179] Ibid. 133–4.   [180] Cf. ibid. 122.

are 'les vrais propriétaires' of its tripartite architectonics.[181] The
vernacular Seneca commentary of Alonso de Cartagena
(1384–1456), bishop of Burgos, reveals his worries about the
spread of lay literacy; he became increasingly intolerant—in
marked contrast with the views of Enrique de Villena—of the
prospect of pagan literature forming part of an educational
programme for the nobility.[182] Furthermore, the cultural impact
of even the most substantial cases of vernacular hermeneutics
may be questioned. Charles V's enthusiasm for a Francocentric
translatio studii did not survive his death; the disastrous reign of
his son saw the dispersal of the royal library and a diminution
of literary patronage.[183] True, Evrart de Conty produced his
commentary on the *Eschez amoureux* in the reign of Charles VI,
but the impetus for this monument of vernacular commentary
clearly came from the intellectual aspirations of the age of
Charles V. Then there is the curious case of Enrique de Villena.
His Castilian *Aeneid* commentary seems to have attracted little
attention in its own day, and was never printed. There are
several possible reasons for this, one of the most likely being the
writer's own dubious reputation: having been accused of
sorcery, after his death King Juan II of Castile ordered his
library to be burnt (which goes some way towards explaining
why so much of Villena's work has not survived).[184] In the
case of the Dante commentaries we should not imagine a
smooth transition from medieval to Renaissance, with an early
flowering of criticism on vernacular poetry anticipating a spring
full of burgeoning varieties of vernacular poetry and prose.
Dante was vociferously criticized by humanists who believed
that he should have written in Latin; furthermore, it is important to recognize the outrage provoked by some of the poet's
political and religious views, along with the rancour of families
whose ancestors he had placed in Hell.[185] The fourteenth

[181] See n. 79 above.   [182] Cf. Weiss, *The Poet's Art*, pp. 82–3.
[183] Indeed, according to Gilbert Ouy, the *translatio studii* theme had been affirmed
at a time which actually saw a loss of French influence 'and the decline of the
University of Paris': 'Humanism and Nationalism in France', p. 110.
[184] Cf. Weiss, *The Poet's Art*, p. 106.
[185] See Deborah Parker, *Commentary and Ideology: Dante in the Renaissance*
(Durham, NC, 1993), pp. 31–3; cf. p. 145. This elegant study concentrates on the
Dante scholarship of Cristoforo Landino, Trifone Gabriele, and Bernardino
Daniello.

century was the peak period for production of Dante commentary. We have one early fifteenth-century offering, by the Franciscan John of Serraville (completed in 1416). Then there is a major gap until 1481, when Cristoforo Landino produced his heavily allegorizing commentary.[186] He was followed by three sixteenth-century commentators, Alessandro Vellutello (1544), Bernardino Daniello (1568), and Lodovico Castelvetro (1570).[187] These are rather slim pickings, in contrast with the scholarship on classical poetry fostered in Italy at that time.[188]

This is not, of course, to undermine or undervalue the significance of such vernacular commentary traditions as we do possess; I am merely seeking to point out their relative fragility in the face of a Latin culture which was to dominate for a long time to come. We may speak of how the fourteenth century saw a *translatio auctoritatis* (the term being coined on the model of *translatio studii*) as textual authority moved from Latin into certain European vernaculars,[189] or of a 'displacement' of authority as translations and adaptations of Latin texts came to occupy the prestigious space hitherto reserved for the original works.[190] But such terminology should be applied to individual

---

[186] On the great success of Landino's commentary, see ibid. 89–97.

[187] See Robert Hollander, 'Dante and His Commentators', in Rachel Jacoff (ed.), *The Cambridge Companion to Dante* (Cambridge, 1993), pp. 226–36 (esp. p. 229).

[188] It should be noted, however, that the decline in Dante's critical fortunes coincided with the rise of Petrarch's. Ten major commentaries on the latter's works were published between 1476 and 1582, on which see William J. Kennedy, *Authorizing Petrarch* (Ithaca and London, 1994), esp. pp. 25–81. (Despite its title, this generally admirable study has little to say about either medieval or Renaissance notions of textual authority.) In contrast with the controversy aroused by Dante, which certainly narrowed the *Comedy*'s readership, Petrarch enjoyed a whole series of quite different receptions—Florentine, Paduan, Milanese, Venetian (cf. Kennedy, pp. 37–8). However, Petrarch commentary was put in the shade by the extraordinary body of sixteenth-century exposition of Ariosto's *Orlando Furioso*, which 'quickly became the most widely read work of modern Italian poetry in the sixteenth century' and even joined the *syllabi* of Venetian schools—the only vernacular text to win such approval. See Javitch, *Proclaiming a Classic*, esp. pp. 9, 15, 21–48, and Paul F. Grendler, *Schooling in Renaissance Italy* (Baltimore, 1989), p. 298.

[189] As in Minnis, *Authorship*, p. xiii.

[190] As in Copeland, *Rhetoric, Hermeneutics*; see e.g. pp. 7, 129, 149, 150, 179, 222, 223, and 229. On the importance of issues of accessibility as opposed to those relating to prestige (including competitiveness with, and displacement of, Latin), see the discussion of 'The Notion of Vernacular Theory' in Jocelyn Wogan-Browne, Nicholas Watson, Andrew Taylor, and Ruth Evans (eds.), *The Idea of the Vernacular: An Anthology of Middle English Literary Theory, 1280–1520* (University Park, Penn., 1999), pp. 314–30.

literary enterprises, to specific acts of appropriation, rather than being totalized into some supposedly seismic shift within literary history. In the later Middle Ages, as far as vernacular poetics is concerned we are dealing with a 'Premature Renaissance'.[191] That great cultivator of the rose garden, Evrart de Conty, played a major role in its grand narrative.

---

[191] Here I happily acknowledge the influence of the title of Anne Hudson's *magnum opus, The Premature Reformation* (cf. n. 177 above).

Bibliography

Note: Items listed in the Abbreviations are not included in the Bibliography.

ABELARD, PETER, *Historia calamitatum,* trans. J. T. Muckle, *The Story of Abelard's Adversities* (Toronto, 1964).

ALAN OF LILLE, *De fide catholica,* in *PL* 210, 306–430.

—— *Anticlaudianus,* trans. J. J. Sheridan (Toronto, 1973).

—— *De planctu naturae,* ed. N. M. Häring, *Studi medievali,* 3rd ser., 19.2 (1978), 797–879. *Plaint of Nature,* translation and commentary by J. J. Sheridan (Toronto, 1980).

ALEXANDER DE VILLA DEI, *The 'Ecclesiale' of Alexander of Villa Dei,* ed. L. R. Lind (Lawrence, Kan., 1958).

ALLEN, JUDSON B., *The Friar as Critic* (Nashville, 1971).

—— *The Ethical Poetic of the Later Middle Ages* (Toronto, 1982).

ALLEN, PETER L., *The Art of Love: Amatory Fiction from Ovid to the 'Romance of the Rose'* (Philadelphia, 1992).

D'ALVERNY, M.-T., *Alain de Lille: Textes inédits* (Paris, 1965).

ANDERSON, DAVID, *Before 'The Knight's Tale': Imitation of Classical Epic in Boccaccio's 'Teseida'* (Philadelphia, 1988).

ANDREAS CAPELLANUS, *De amore (On Love),* ed. and trans. P. G. Walsh (London, 1982).

AQUINAS, THOMAS, *Opera* (Parma, 1852–72).

—— *In decem libros ethicorum Aristotelis ad Nicomachum expositio,* ed. R. M. Spiazzi (Marietti, 1949).

—— *Summa Theologiae,* Blackfriars edn. (London, 1964–81).

ARDEN, HEATHER M., *The Romance of the Rose,* Twayne World Authors Series 791 (Boston, 1987).

ARISTOTLE (Pseudo-), *Problems, Books I–XXI,* ed. W. S. Hett (Cambridge, Mass., 1936), and *Problems, Books XXII–XXXVIII and Rhetorica ad Alexandrum,* ed. W. S. Hett and H. Rackham (Cambridge, Mass., 1937).

ARNOLD OF VILLANOVA, *De coitu* (Basel, 1585).

L'Art d'amours: Traduction et commentaire de l'Ars amatoria' d'Ovid, ed. Bruno Roy (Leiden, 1974). Trans. Lawrence B. Blonquist, Garland Library of Medieval Literature, Ser. A, vol. 32 (New York, 1987).

ARTHUR, ROSS G., *Medieval Sign Theory and 'Sir Gawain and the Green Knight'* (Toronto, 1987).

ASCOLI, ALBERT RUSSELL, 'The Vowels of Authority (Dante's *Convivio* IV, vi, 3–4)', in K. Brownlee and W. Stephens (eds.), *Discourses of Authority in Medieval and Renaissance Literature* (Hanover, NH, 1989), pp. 23–46.

—— 'The Unfinished Author: Dante's Rhetoric of Authority in *Convivio* and *De vulgari eloquentia*', in Rachel Jacoff (ed.), *The Cambridge Companion to Dante* (Cambridge, 1993), pp. 45–66.

AUGUSTINE, ST, *The City of God against the Pagans*, ed. and trans. R. W. Dyson (Cambridge, 1998).

AUTRAND, FRANÇOISE, *Charles V: Le sage* (Paris, 1994).

BAIG, BONNIE P., 'Vision and Visualization: Optics and Light Metaphysics in the Imagery and Poetic Form of Twelfth- and Thirteenth-Century Secular Allegory, with Special Reference to the *Roman de la Rose*' (Ph.D. diss., University of California, Berkeley, 1982).

BAIRD, J. L., and KANE, J. R., '*La Querelle de la Rose*: In Defense of the Opponents', *French Review*, 48.2 (1974), 298–307.

BAIRD, LORRAYNE Y., 'O.E.D. Cock 20: The Limits of Lexicography of Slang', *Maledicta*, 5 (1981), 213–25.

—— 'Priapus Gallinaceus: The Role of the Cock in Fertility and Eroticism in Classical Antiquity and the Middle Ages', *Studies in Iconography*, 7 (1981/2), 81–111.

—— 'Christus Gallinaceus: A Chaucerian Enigma; or the Cock as Symbol of Christ in the Middle Ages', *Studies in Iconography*, 9 (1983), 19–30.

BALDWIN, JOHN W., *The Language of Sex: Five Voices from Northern France around 1200* (Chicago, 1994).

BARAŃSKI, Z. G., and BOYDE, PATRICK (eds.) *The 'Fiore' in Context: Dante, France, Tuscany* (Notre Dame, Ind., 1997).

BARKER, MARTIN, 'The Newson Report: A Case Study in "Common Sense" ', in Barker and Petley, *Ill Effects*, pp. 12–31.

—— and PETLEY, JULIAN (eds.), *Ill Effects: The Media/Violence Debate* (London, 1997).

BARNETT, ROBERT JOHN, JR., 'An Anonymous Medieval Commentary on Juvenal' (Ph.D. diss., University of North Carolina at Chapel Hill, 1964).

BARSTOW, ANNE LLEWELLYN, *Married Priests and the Reforming Papacy: The Eleventh-Century Debates*, Texts and Studies in Religion 12 (New York, 1982).

BARTHES, ROLAND, *The Rustle of Language*, trans. Richard Howard (Oxford, 1986).

BARTHOLOMAEUS ANGLICUS, *De proprietatibus rerum* (Frankfurt, 1601; repr. Frankfurt a.M. 1964), pp. 534–5. Trans. John Trevisa, *On the Properties of Things*, ed. M. C. Seymour et al. (Oxford, 1975).

BASWELL, CHRISTOPHER, 'The Medieval Allegorization of the *Aeneid*: MS Cambridge, Peterhouse 158', *Traditio*, 41 (1985), 181–237.

—— *Virgil in Medieval England: Figuring the 'Aeneid' from the Twelfth Century to Chaucer* (Cambridge, 1995).

BATE, KEITH, review of F. Bertini (ed.), *Le commedie latine*, *Latomus*, 35 (1976), 163–4.

BEDE, *De arte metrica*, in H. Keil (ed.), *Grammatici Latini*, vii (Leipzig, 1880).

BENTON, JOHN F., *Self and Society in Medieval France: The Memoirs of Abbot Guibert of Nogent* (New York, 1970).

BERNARD OF CLUNY, *De contemptu mundi*, ed. Ronald E. Pepin, Medieval Texts and Studies 8 (East Lansing, Mich., 1991).

'BERNARD SILVESTER', *Commentary on the First Six Books of the 'Aeneid' of Virgil*, ed. J. W. Jones and E. F. Jones (Lincoln, Neb., 1977). Trans. Earl G. Schreiber and Thomas E. Maresca (Lincoln, Neb., 1979).

—— *Commentary on Martianus Capella's 'De nuptiis Philologiae et Mercurii'*, ed. H. J. Westra (Toronto, 1986).

BERSUIRE, PIERRE, *Reductorium morale, lib. XV: Ovidius moralizatus, cap. 1: De formis figurisque deorum, Textus e codice Brux., Bibl. Reg. 863–9 critice editus*, ed. J. Engels, Werkmateriaal 3 (Utrecht, 1966).

BILLER, P. P. A., 'Birth Control in the West in the Thirteenth and Early Fourteenth Centuries', *Past and Present*, 94 (1982), 3–26.

BIRD, OTTO, 'The *Canzone d'Amore* of Guido Cavalcanti according to the Commentary of Dino del Garbo', *MS* 2 (1940), 150–203, and 3 (1941), 117–60.

BLAMIRES, ALCUIN (ed.), *Woman Defamed and Woman Defended* (Oxford, 1992).

—— 'Women and Preaching in Medieval Orthodoxy, Heresy, and Saint's Lives', *Viator*, 26 (1995), 135–52

—— *The Case for Women in Medieval Culture* (Oxford, 1997).

BLOCH, HOWARD, *Etymologies and Genealogies: A Literary Anthropology of the French Middle Ages* (Chicago, 1983).

—— 'Modest Maids and Modified Nouns: Obscenity in the *Fabliaux*', in Ziolkowski (ed.), *Obscenity*, pp. 292–307.

BLUMENFELD-KOSINSKI, RENATE, 'Christine de Pizan and the Misogynistic Tradition', *Romanic Review*, 81 (1990), 279–92.

—— 'Jean Le Fèvre's *Livre de Leesce*: Praise or Blame of Women?', *Speculum*, 69 (1994), 707–25.

BOCCACCIO, GIOVANNI, *Genealogia deorum gentilium*. Trans. Charles Osgood, *Boccaccio on Poetry: Being the Preface and the Fourteenth and Fifteenth Books of Boccaccio's 'Genealogia Deorum Gentilium'* (Indianapolis, 1956).

—— *Opere*, ed. C. Sergio (Milan, 1967).

—— *Opere minore in volgare*, ed. Mario Marti (Milan, 1969–72).

—— *The Decameron*, trans. G. H. McWilliam (Harmondsworth, 1972).

BOETHIUS, *The Theological Tractates and 'The Consolation of Philosophy'*, ed. H. F. Stewart, E. K. Rand, and S. J. Tester (Cambridge, Mass., 1973).

BOETHIUS OF DACIA, *On the Supreme Good, On the Eternity of the World, On Dreams*, trans. John F. Wippel, Medieval Sources in Translation 30 (Toronto, 1987).

BOLGAR, R. R. (ed.) *Classical Influences on European Culture, A.D. 500–1500* (Cambridge, 1971).

BRIGGS, CHARLES F., *Giles of Rome's 'De regimine principum': Reading and Writing Politics at Court and University, c.1275–c.1525* (Cambridge, 1999).

BRISTOW, JOSEPH, *Sexuality* (London, 1997).

BROWN, D. CATHERINE, *Pastor and Laity in the Theology of Jean Gerson* (Cambridge, 1987).

BROWNLEE, KEVIN, 'Discourses of the Self: Christine de Pizan and the *Romance of the Rose*', in Brownlee and Huot (eds.), *Rethinking the Rose*, pp. 234–61.

—— 'Pygmalion, Mimesis, and the Multiple Endings of the *Roman de la Rose*', *Yale French Studies*, 95 (1999), 193–211.

BROWNLEE, MARINA SCORDILIS, *The Status of the Reading Subject in the 'Libro de Buen Amor'* (Chapel Hill, NC, 1985).

BURIDAN, JEAN, *Questiones elencorum*, ed. R. Van der Lecq and H. A. G. Braakhuis (Nijmegen, 1994).

BURIDANT, CLAUDE, 'Jean de Meun et Jean de Vignay; traducteurs de l'*Epitoma rei militaris* de Végèce: Contribution à l'histoire de la traduction au moyen âge', in *Études de langue et de littérature française offertes à André Lanly* (Nancy, 1980), pp. 51–69.

BURKE, JAMES F., 'The *Libro de buen amor* and the Medieval Meditative Sermon Tradition', *La Coronica*, 9 (1980–1), 122–7.

BURNETT, CHARLES, 'Hearing and Music in Book XI of Pietro d'Abano's *Expositio Problematum Aristotelis*', in van Deusen (ed.), *Tradition and Ecstasy*, pp. 153–90.

BURROW, JOHN, *Medieval Writers and Their Work: Middle English Literature and Its Background 1100–1500* (Oxford, 1982).

—— *The Ages of Man: A Study in Medieval Writing and Thought* (Oxford, 1986).

BURSILL-HALL, G. L., *Speculative Grammars of the Middle Ages* (The Hague, 1971).

CADDEN, JOAN, *Meanings of Sex Difference in the Middle Ages: Medicine, Science, and Culture* (Cambridge, 1993).

CADDEN, JOAN, 'Sciences/Silences: The Natures and Languages of "Sodomy" in Peter of Abano's *Problemata* Commentary', in Lochrie et al. (eds.), *Constructing Medieval Sexuality*, pp. 40–57.

CAHOON, LESLIE, 'Raping the Rose: Jean de Meun's Reading of Ovid's *Amores*', *Classical and Modern Literature*, 6 (1986), 261–85.

CALABRESE, MICHAEL A., *Chaucer's Ovidian Arts of Love* (Gainesville, Fla., 1994).

CAMILLE, MICHAEL, 'Manuscript Illumination and the Art of Copulation', in Lochrie et al. (eds.), *Constructing Medieval Sexuality*, pp. 58–90.

CAMILLO, OTTAVIO DI, *El humanismo castellano del siglo XV* (Valencia, 1976).

CASAGRANDE, C., and VECCHIO, S., *Les Péchés de la langue: Discipline et éthique de la parole dans la culture médiévale*, trans. P. Baillet (Paris, 1991).

CAXTON, WILLIAM, *Prologues and Epilogues*, ed. W. J. B. Crotch, EETS OS 176 (London, 1928).

—— *Caxton's Aesop*, ed. R. T. Lenaghan (Cambridge, Mass., 1967).

—— *The Metamorphoses, translated by William Caxton, 1480* (New York, 1968).

CHAPMAN, JANET A., 'Juan Ruiz's "Learned Sermon" ', in Gybbon-Monypenny (ed.), '*Libro de buen amor*' *Studies*, pp. 29–51.

CHAUCER, GEOFFREY, *The Riverside Chaucer*, ed. Larry D. Benson et al. (Oxford, 1988).

CHENU, M.-D., 'Auctor, actor, autor', *Bulletin du Cange*, 4 (1927), 81–6.

—— *Introduction à l'étude de Saint Thomas d'Aquin*, 2nd edn. (Montreal, 1954).

—— '*Involucrum*: Le mythe selon les théologiens médiévaux', *AHDLMA* 22 (1955), 75–9.

CHRISTINE DE PIZAN, *Livre des fais et bonnes meurs du sage roy Charles V*, ed. S. Solente (Paris, 1936).

—— *Poems of Cupid, God of Love. Christine de Pizan's 'Epistre au dieu d'Amours' and 'Dit de la Rose'; Thomas Hoccleve's 'The Letter of Cupid'*, ed. T. S. Fenster and M. C. Erler (Leiden, 1990).

—— *The Book of the Body Politic*, trans. Kate Langdon Forhan (Cambridge, 1994).

—— *The Book of the City of Ladies*, trans. Rosalind Brown-Grant (Harmondsworth, 1999).

CLANCHY, M. T., *Abelard: A Medieval Life* (Oxford, 1997).

Clef d'amours, La: Texte critique avec introduction, appendice et glossaire, ed. A. Doutrepont, Bibliotheca Normannica 5 (Halle, 1890); repr. in A. M. Finoli, *Artes amandi, da Maître Elie ad Andrea Capellano* (Milan, 1969), pp. 123–228.

COHEN, JEFFREY J., and WHEELER, BONNIE (eds.), *Becoming Male in the Middle Ages* (New York, 1997).

COMBES, A., *Jean de Montreuil et le chancelier Gerson*, Études de philosophique médiévale 33 (Paris, 1942).

'*Comédie' latine en France au XIIe siècle, La*, ed. G. Cohen (Paris, 1931).

COOKE, JOHN D., 'Euhemerism: A Medieval Interpretation of Classical Paganism', *Speculum*, 2 (1927), 396–410.

COPELAND, RITA, 'Rhetoric and the Politics of the Literal Sense in Medieval Literary Theory: Aquinas, Wyclif, and the Lollards', in Piero Boitani and Anna Torti (eds.), *Interpretation: Medieval and Modern* (Cambridge, 1993), pp. 1–23.

COULSON, FRANK T., 'New Manuscript Evidence for Sources of the *Accessus* of Arnoul d'Orléans to the *Metamorphoses* of Ovid', *Manuscripta*, 30 (1986), 103–7.

—— 'The "Vulgate" Commentary on Ovid's *Metamorphoses*', *Mediaevalia*, 13 (1987), 29–61.

—— and MOLYVIATI-TOPTIS, U., 'Vaticanus latinus 2877: A Hitherto Unedited Allegorization of Ovid's *Metamorphoses*', *Journal of Medieval Latin*, 2 (1992), 134–202.

COURTENAY, W. J., 'Force of Words and Figures of Speech: The Crisis over *Virtus Sermonis* in the Fourteenth Century', *Franciscan Studies*, 44 (1984), 107–22.

COVILLE, A., *Gontier et Pierre Col et l'humanisme en France au temps de Charles VI* (Paris, 1934).

CRANZ, F. EDWARD, and KRISTELLER, P. O. (eds.), *Catalogus translationum et commentariorum*, iii (Washington, DC, 1976).

CRAUN, EDWIN D., *Lies, Slander and Obscenity in Medieval English Literature: Pastoral Rhetoric and the Deviant Speaker* (Cambridge, 1997).

CRESPO, R., 'Il Prologo alla traduzione della *Consolatio philosophiae* di Jean de Meun e il commento di Guglielmo d'Aragonia', in W. den Boer et al. (eds.), *Romanitas et Christianitas: Studia I. H. Waszink oblata* (Amsterdam, 1973), pp. 55–70.

DAGENAIS, JOHN, 'A Further Source for the Literary Ideas in Juan Ruiz's Prologue', *Journal of Hispanic Studies*, 11 (1986), 23–52.

—— *The Ethics of Reading in Manuscript Culture: Glossing the 'Libro de buen amor'* (Princeton, NJ, 1994).

DALY, THOMAS J., 'The Dialectical Crisis of the Thirteenth Century and Its Reflection in Richard de Fournival' (Ph.D. diss., Tufts University, 1975).

DANTE ALIGHIERI, *Il Convivio*, ed. Bruna Cordati (Turin, 1968).

DELANY, SHEILA, ' "Mothers to Think Back Through": Who Are They?

The Ambiguous Example of Christine de Pizan', repr. in Delany, *Medieval Literary Politics: Shapes of Ideology* (Manchester, 1990), pp. 88–103

—— 'History, Politics, and Christine Studies: A Polemical Reply', in Margaret Brabant (ed.), *Politics, Gender, and Genre: The Political Thought of Christine de Pizan* (Boulder, Colo., 1992), pp. 193–206.

DE LEY, MARGO Y. C., 'The Prologue in Castilian Literature between 1200 and 1400' (Ph.D. diss., University of Illinois, Urbana-Champaign, 1976).

DEMATS, PAULE, *Fabula: Trois études de mythographie antique et médiévale*, Publications romanes et françaises 122 (Geneva, 1973).

DEMBOWSKI, PETER, 'Scientific Translation and Translators' Glossing in Four Medieval French Translations', in Jeanette Beer (ed.), *Translation Theory and Practice in the Middle Ages* (Kalamazoo, Mich., 1997), pp. 113–34.

DENOMY, A. J., 'The *De amore* of Andreas Capellanus and the Condemnation of 1277', *MS* 8 (1946), 107–49.

DE RIJK, L. M., *Logica modernorum: A Contribution to the History of Early Terminist Logic* (Assen, 1962–7).

—— *Through Language to Reality: Studies in Medieval Semantics and Metaphysics*, ed. E. P. Bos (Northampton, 1989).

DEUSEN, NANCY VAN (ed.), *Tradition and Ecstasy: The Agony of the Fourteenth Century* (Ottawa, 1997).

DEYERMOND, A. D., 'Some Aspects of Parody in the *Libro de buen amor*', in Gybbon-Monypenny (ed.), '*Libro de buen amor*' *Studies*, pp. 53–78.

—— *A Literary History of Spain: The Middle Ages* (London, 1971).

DONAGHEY, BRIAN, AND TAAVITSAINEN, IRMA, 'Walton's Boethius: From Manuscript to Print', *English Studies*, 80 (1999), 398–407.

DOW, BLANCHE H., *The Varying Attitude toward Women in French Literature of the Fifteenth Century: The Opening Years* (New York, 1936).

DRONKE, PETER, *Fabula: Explorations into the Uses of Myth in Medieval Platonism* (Leiden, 1974).

—— 'A Note on *Pamphilus*', *Journal of the Warburg and Courtauld Institutes*, 42 (1979), 225–30.

—— 'Bernardo Silvestre', in *Enciclopedia Virgiliana*, ed. F. della Corte (Rome, 1984–91).

—— *Intellectuals and Poets in Medieval Europe* (Rome, 1992).

—— 'Andreas Capellanus', *Journal of Medieval Latin*, 4 (1994), 51–63.

DULAC, LILIANE, and RENO, CHRISTINE, 'L'Humanisme vers 1400, essai d'exploration à partir d'un cas marginal: Christine de Pizan, traductrice de Thomas d'Aquin', in Ornato and Pons (eds.), *Pratiques de la culture écrite en France au XVe siècle*, pp. 160–78.

DUNDES, ALAN, 'Gallus as Phallus: A Psychoanalytic Cross-Cultural Consideration of the Cock-Fight as Fowl Play', in Dundes (ed.), *The Cockfight: A Casebook* (Madison, 1994), pp. 241–82.

DUTTON, P., 'The Uncovering of the *Glosae super Platonem* of Bernard of Chartres', *MS* 46 (1984), 192–221.

DUVAL, JOHN, *Fabliaux Fair and Foul* (Binghamton, NY, 1992).

EBERLE, PATRICIA, 'The Lovers' Glass: Nature's Discourse on Optics and the Optical Design of the *Romance of the Rose*', *University of Toronto Quarterly*, 46 (1977), 241–61.

EDWARDS, M. C. E., 'A Study of Six Characters in Chaucer's *Legend of Good Women* with reference to Medieval Scholia on Ovid's *Heroides*' (B.Litt. diss., University of Oxford, 1970).

EHRHART, MARGARET J., *The Judgement of the Trojan Prince Paris in Medieval Literature* (Philadelphia, 1987).

ELIE, *Überarbeitung der ältesten französische Bearbeitung der Ars amatoria des Ovids*, ed. H. Kühne and E. Stengel (Marburg, 1886). Repr. in A. M. Finoli, *Artes amandi, da Maître Elie ad Andrea Capellano* (Milan, 1969), pp. 1–30.

ELLIOTT, A. G., '*Accessūs ad auctores*: Twelfth-Century Introductions to Ovid', *Allegorica*, 5.1 (1980), 6–48.

—— *Seven Medieval Latin Comedies* (New York, 1984).

ELLIOTT, DYAN, 'The Priest's Wife: Female Erasure and the Gregorian Reform', in *Fallen Bodies: Pollution, Sexuality, and Demonology in the Middle Ages* (Philadelphia, 1999).

Eschez Amoureux, ed. Christine Kraft, *Die Liebesgarten-Allegorie der 'Echecs amoureux': Kritische Ausgabe und Kommentar* (Frankfurt a.M., 1977).

EVANS, GILLIAN, *The Language and Logic of the Bible: The Earlier Middle Ages* (Cambridge, 1984).

FAVATI, G., 'La glossa latina di Dino del Garbo a *Donna me prega* del Cavalcanti', *Annuali della Scuola Normale Superiore di Pisa*, 2nd ser., 21.1–2 (1952), 70–103.

FENSTER, THELMA, ' "Perdre son latin": Christine de Pizan and Vernacular Humanism', in Marilynn Desmond (ed.), *Christine de Pizan and the Categories of Difference* (Minneapolis, 1998), pp. 91–107.

FERROUL, YVES, 'Abelard's Blissful Castration', in Cohen and Wheeler (eds.), *Becoming Male in the Middle Ages*, pp. 129–49.

FINOLI, A. M., *Artes amandi, da Maître Elie ad Andrea Capellano* (Milan, 1969).

FISKE, A., *Friends and Friendship in the Monastic Tradition* (Cuernavaca, 1970).

FLEMING, JOHN V., *The 'Roman de la Rose': A Study in Allegory and Iconography* (Princeton, NJ, 1969).

—— *Reason and the Lover* (Princeton, NJ, 1984).

—— 'Jean de Meun and the Ancient Poets', in Brownlee and Huot (eds.), *Rethinking the Rose*, pp. 81–100.

FOUCAULT, MICHEL, 'What Is an Author?', in *Language, Counter-Memory, Practice*, ed. and trans. D. F. Bouchard and S. Simon (Ithaca, NY, 1977), pp. 113–38.

FRAIOLI, D., 'Against the Authenticity of the *Historia calamitatum*', in *Fälschungen im Mittelalter V*, MGH, Schriften, Bd. 32, v (Hanover, 1988), pp. 167–200.

FRANCESCO DA BARBERINO, *I documenti d'amore di Francesco da Barberino*, ed. Francesco Egidi (Rome, 1905–27).

FREDBORG, K. M., 'Universal Grammar according to some Twelfth-Century Grammarians', in *Studies in Medieval Linguistic Thought Dedicated to G. L. Bursill-Hall*, ed. K. Koerner, H.-J. Niederehe, and R. H. Robins (Amsterdam, 1980), pp. 69–84.

FRIEDMAN, L. J., 'Jean de Meun and Ethelred of Rievaulx', *L'Esprit Createur*, 2 (1962), 135–41.

FULGENTIUS, *Mitologiae*, ed. R. Helm, *Fulgentii opera* (Leipzig, 1898).

—— *Mitologiarum libri tres*. Trans. Leslie George Whitbread, *Fulgentius the Mythographer* (Columbus, Oh., 1971).

GALPIN, S. L., *'Les Eschez amoureux*: A Complete Synopsis with Unpublished Extracts', *Romanic Review*, 11 (1920), 283–307.

GATHERCOLE, P. M., 'Medieval Science: Evrart de Conty', *Romance Notes*, 6 (1965), 175–81.

GAUNT, SIMON, *Gender and Genre in Medieval French Literature* (Cambridge, 1995).

—— 'Bel Acueil and the Improper Allegory of the *Romance of the Rose*', *New Medieval Literatures*, 2 (1998), 65–93.

GERHOH OF REICHERSBERG, *Commentarium in psalmos*, PL 191, 619–1814.

GERSON, JEAN, *Early Works*, trans. and introd. Brian Patrick McGuire (New York, 1998).

GILES OF ROME, *De potestate*. Trans. J. A. Watt, *On Royal and Papal Power* (Toronto, 1971).

GINSBERG, WARREN, *'Ovidius ethicus*? Ovid and the Medieval Commentary Tradition', in J. J. Paxson and C. A. Gravlee (eds.), *Desiring Discourse: The Literature of Love, Ovid through Chaucer* (Selinsgrove, Pa., 1998), pp. 62–86.

GOLDIN, DANIELA, 'Testo e immagine nei *Documenti d'Amore* di

Francesco da Barberino', *Quaderni d'italianistica*, 1 (1980), 125–38.

GOTTLIEB, BEATRICE, 'The Problem of Feminism in the Fifteenth Century', in J. Kirshner and S. F. Wemple (eds.), *Women of the Medieval World* (Oxford, 1985), pp. 337–62.

GOWER, JOHN, *The English Works*, ed. G. C. Macaulay, EETS, ES 81 and 82 (London, 1900).

GRACE, SHARON, *Testing Obscenity: An International Comparison of Laws and Controls relating to Obscene Material*, Home Office Research Study 157 (London, 1996).

GRAVDAL, KATHRYN, *Ravishing Maidens: Writing Rape in Medieval French Literature and Law* (Philadelphia, 1991).

GREEN, OTIS H., *Spain and the Western Tradition* (Madison, 1968).

GREENFIELD, C. C., *Humanist and Scholastic Poetics, 1250–1500* (London, 1981).

GREGORY THE GREAT, *Dialogi*, PL 77, 149–430.

GRENDLER, PAUL F., *Schooling in Renaissance Italy* (Baltimore, 1989).

GUIART, 'L'Art d'Amour de Guiart', ed. Louis Karl, *Zeitschrift für romanische Philologie*, 44 (1924), 66–79, 181–7.

GUICHARD-TESSON, F., 'Evrart de Conty, auteur de la *Glose des Échecs amoureux*', *Le Moyen français*, 8–9 (1981), 111–48.

——— 'La *Glose des Echecs amoureux*: Un savoir à tendance laïque: comment l'interpreter?', *Fifteenth-Century Studies*, 10 (1984), 229–60.

——— 'Le Métier de traducteur et de commentateur au XIVe siècle d'après Evrart de Conty', *Le Moyen français*, 24–5 (1990), 131–67.

——— and ROY, BRUNO, *Le livre des Échecs amoureux* (Paris, 1991).

GUILLAUME DE DEGUILEVILLE, *The Pilgrimage of Human Life*, trans. E. Clasby (New York, 1992).

GUILLAUME DE MACHAUT, *Le Jugement du Roy de Behaigne* and *Remede de Fortune*, ed. and trans. James I. Wimsatt and William W. Kibler (Athens, Ga., 1988).

——— *The Judgment of the King of Navarre*, ed. and trans. R. Burton Palmer (New York, 1988).

——— *The Fountain of Love (La Fonteinne amoureuse) and Two Other Love Vision Poems*, ed. and trans. R. Burton Palmer (New York, 1993).

GYBBON-MONYPENNY, G. B., 'Autobiography in the *Libro de buen amor* in the Light of Some Literary Comparisons', *BHS* 34 (1957), 63–78.

——— (ed.), '*Libro de buen amor*' *Studies* (London, 1970).

HANNA, RALPH, 'Sir Thomas Berkeley and His Patronage', *Speculum*, 64 (1989), 878–916.

—— 'The Difficulty of Ricardian Prose Translation: The Case of the Lollards', *Modern Language Quarterly*, 51 (1990), 319–40.

HÄRING, N. M., 'Thierry of Chartres and Dominicus Gundissalinus', *MS* 26 (1964), 271–86.

HASELDINE, JULIAN (ed.), *Friendship in Medieval Europe* (Stroud, 1999).

HAVELY, N. R. (trans.), *Chaucer's Boccaccio* (Cambridge, 1980).

—— 'Muses and Blacksmiths: Italian Trecento Poetics and the Reception of Dante in *The House of Fame*', in A. J. Minnis, C. C. Morse, and T. Turville-Petre (eds.), *Essays on Ricardian Literature in Honour of J. A. Burrow* (Oxford, 1997), pp. 61–81.

HENRI DE GAUCHY, *Li Livres du gouvernement des rois: A Thirteenth-Century French Version of Egidio Colonna's Treatise*, ed. S. P. Molenaer (New York, 1899).

HENRY OF GHENT, *Summae quaestionum ordinariarum . . . Henrici a Gandavo* (in aedibus J. Badii Ascensii, Paris, 1520; repr. by the Franciscan Institute, Louvain, 1953).

—— *Summa in tres partes praecipuas digesta* (Ferrara, 1646).

HENRYSON, ROBERT, *Poems*, ed. Denton Fox (Oxford, 1981).

HEXTER, RALPH, 'Medieval Articulations of Ovid's *Metamorphoses*: From Lactantian Segmentation to Arnulfian Allegory', *Mediaevalia*, 13 (1987), 63–82.

—— 'The *Allegari* of Pierre Bersuire: Interpretation and the *Reductorium Morale*', *Allegorica*, 10 (1989), 51–84.

—— 'Ovid's Body', in James I. Porter (ed.), *Constructions of the Classical Body* (Ann Arbor, Mich., 1999), pp. 327–54.

HILL, THOMAS D., 'Narcissus, Pygmalion, and the Castration of Saturn: Two Mythographical Themes in the *Roman de la Rose*', *Studies in Philology*, 71 (1974), 404–26.

HISSETTE, R., *Enquête sur les 219 articles condamnés à Paris le 7 Mars 1277*, Philosophes médiévaux 22 (Louvain, 1977).

HOLLANDER, ROBERT, *Boccaccio's Two Venuses* (New York, 1977).

—— 'The Validity of Boccaccio's Self-Exegesis in his *Teseida*', *Medievalia et Humanistica*, n.s. 8 (1977), 163–83.

—— 'Dante and His Commentators', in Rachel Jacoff (ed.), *The Cambridge Companion to Dante* (Cambridge, 1993), pp. 226–36.

HOLLIS, A. S., 'The *Ars amatoria* and *Remedia amoris*', in J. W. Binns (ed.), *Ovid* (London, 1973), pp. 84–115.

HOTCHKISS, VALERIE R., *Clothes Make the Man: Female Cross Dressing in Medieval Europe* (New York, 1996).

HUDSON, ANNE, *Lollards and Their Books* (London, 1985).

—— 'The Debate on Bible Translation, Oxford 1401', in *Lollards and Their Books*, pp. 67–84.

—— 'Lollardy: The English Heresy?', in *Lollards and Their Books*, pp. 141–63.

—— *The Premature Reformation: Wycliffite Texts and Lollard History* (Oxford, 1988).

HUGH OF FOUILLY, *Aviarium*, ed. and trans. W. B. Clark (Binghamton, NY, 1992).

HUGUTIO OF PISA, *Magnae derivationes*, in Oxford, Bodleian Library, MS Bodley 376.

HUIZINGA, JOHAN, *The Waning of the Middle Ages* (London, 1924).

—— *Homo Ludens: A Study of the Play Element in Culture* (London, 1970).

HULT, DAVID, *Self-Fulfilling Prophecies: Readership and Authority in the First 'Roman de la Rose'* (Cambridge, 1986).

—— 'Jean de Meun's Continuation of *Le Roman de la Rose*', in Denis Hollier et al., *A New History of French Literature* (Cambridge, Mass., 1989), pp. 97–103.

—— 'Language and Dismemberment: Abelard, Origen, and the *Romance of the Rose*', in Brownlee and Huot (eds.), *Rethinking the Rose*, pp. 101–30.

—— 'Words and Deeds: Jean de Meun's *Romance of the Rose* and the Hermeneutics of Censorship', *New Literary History*, 28 (1997), 345–66.

HUNT, R. W., 'The Introductions to the *Artes* in the Twelfth Century', in *Studia medievalia in honorem R. M. Martin, O.P.* (Bruges, 1948), pp. 85–115.

—— *The History of Grammar in the Middle Ages: Collected Papers*, ed. G. L. Bursill-Hall, Amsterdam Studies in the Theory and History of Linguistic Science, ser. 3, vol. v (Amsterdam, 1980).

—— 'The Lost Preface to the *Liber derivationum* of Osbern of Gloucester', in *The History of Grammar in the Middle Ages*, pp. 151–66.

HUNTER, IAN, SAUNDERS, DAVID, and WILLIAMSON, DUGALD, *On Pornography: Literature, Sexuality and Obscenity Law* (Basingstoke, 1993).

HYATTE, REGINALD L., 'The *Remedia amoris* of Ovid in Old French Didactic Poetry' (Ph.D. diss., University of Pennsylvania, 1971).

—— 'The Manuscripts of the Prose Commentary (Fifteenth Century) on *Les Echecs Amoureux*', *Manuscripta*, 26 (1982), 24–30.

—— and PONCHARD-HYATTE, MARYSE, *L'Harmonie des sphères: Encyclopédie d'astronomie et de musique extraite du commentaire sur 'Les Echecs amoureux'* (New York, 1985).

INEICHEN, GUSTAV, 'Le Discours linguistique de Jean de Meun', *Romanistiche Zeitschrift für Literaturgeschichte*, 2 (1978), 245–53.

IRVINE, MARTIN, 'Abelard and Remasculinization', in Cohen and Wheeler (eds.), *Becoming Male in the Middle Ages*, pp. 87–106.

ISIDORE OF SEVILLE, *Etymologiae*, ed. W. M. Lindsay (Oxford, 1911).

JACQUART, DANIELLE, and THOMASSET, CLAUDE, 'L'amour "héroïque" à travers le traité d'Arnaud de Villeneuve', in *La Folie et le corps*, ed. Jean Céard (Paris, 1985), pp. 143–58.

JACQUES D'AMIENS, *'L'Art d'amors' und 'Li Remedes d'amors'*, ed. Gustav Körting (Leipzig, 1868; repr. Geneva, 1976).

—— *L'Art d'amours van Jakes d'Amiens*, ed. D. Talsma (Leiden, 1925), repr. in A. M. Finoli, *Artes amandi, da Maître Elie ad Andrea Capellano* (Milan, 1969), pp. 31–121.

JAUSS, H. R., 'La Transformation de la forme allégorique entre 1180 et 1240: d'Alain de Lille à Guillaume de Lorris', in *L'Humanisme médiévale dans les littératures romanes*, Centre de Philologie et de Littératures Romanes de l'Université de Strasbourg, Actes et colloques 3 (Paris, 1964), pp. 107–46.

JAVITCH, DANIEL, *Proclaiming a Classic: The Canonization of 'Orlando Furioso'* (Princeton, NJ, 1991).

JEAN DE MEUN, *L'art de chevalerie: Traduction du 'De re militari' de Vegèce par Jean de Meun*, ed. Ulysse Robert, SATF (Paris, 1897).

—— *Li Livres de confort de philosophie*, ed. V. L. Dedeck-Héry, *MS* 14 (1952), 165–275.

—— *Le lettere di Abelardo ed Eloisa nella traduzione di Jean de Meun*, ed. Fabrizio Beggiato, Studi, testi e manuali, Istituto di filologia romanza dell'Università di Roma 5 (Modena, 1977).

—— *Le testament maistre Jehan de Meun: un caso letterario*, ed. Silvia Buzzetti Gallarati (Turin, 1989).

—— *La vie et les epistres Pierres Abaelart et Heloys sa fame: traduction du XIIIe siècle attribuée a Jean de Meun*, ed. Eric Hicks, Nouvelle bibliothèque du moyen âge 16 (Paris, 1991).

JEAN LE DANOIS, *Summa grammatica*, ed. Alfred Otto, Corpus philosophorum danicorum medii aevi (Copenhagen, 1955).

JEAUNEAU, EDOUARD, 'L'Usage de la notion d'*integumentum* à travers les gloses de Guillaume de Conches', in *Lectio philosophorum: Recherches sur l'école de Chartres* (Amsterdam, 1973), pp. 127–92.

—— 'Berkeley, University of California, Bancroft Library MS 2', *MS* 50 (1988), 438–56.

JENARO-MACLENNAN, LUIS, 'Los presupuestos intelectuales del prologo al *Libro de buen amor*', *Annuario de estudios medievales*, 9 (1974–9 [=1980]), 151–86.

JOHN OF GARLAND, *Morale scolarium*, ed. and trans. Louis Paetow,

Bibliography 333

Memoirs of the University of California, 4. 2 (Berkeley, Calif., 1927), pp. 65–273.
—— *Integumenta Ovidii: Poemetto inedito del secolo XIII*, ed. F. Ghisalberti (Messina, 1933).
—— *Parisiana Poetria*, ed. and trans. Traugott Lawler (New Haven, Conn., 1974).
JOHN OF GENOA, *Catholicon* (Venice, 1483).
JOHN OF PARIS, *De potestate*, ed. Jean Leclercq in *Jean de Paris et l'ecclésiologie du XIIIe siècle* (Paris, 1942); trans. J. A. Watt, *On Royal and Papal Power* (Toronto, 1971).
JOLIVET, J., *Arts du langage et théologie chez Abelard* (Paris, 1969; 2nd edn., 1982).
JONES, JOAN MORTON, '*The Chess of Love* [Old French Text with Translation and Commentary]' (Ph.D. diss., University of Nebraska, 1968).
JONES, JULIAN W., 'The So-Called Silvestris Commentary on the *Aeneid* and Two Other Interpretations', *Speculum*, 64 (1989), 838–48.
JORDAN, MARK D., *The Invention of Sodomy in Christian Theology* (Chicago, 1997).
JUVENAL, ed. and trans. G. G. Ramsay, *Juvenal and Persius*, rev. edn. (Cambridge, Mass., 1940). Also trans. William Gifford, *Juvenal, Satires, with the Satires of Persius* (London, 1992).
KARNEIN, ALFRED, '*Amor est Passio*: A Definition of Courtly Love?', in *Court and Poet: Selected Proceedings of the Third Congress of the International Courtly Literature Society*, ed. G. S. Burgess (Liverpool, 1980), pp. 215–21.
—— *De amore in volkssprachlicher Literatur, Untersuchungen zur Andreas-Capellanus-Rezeption in Mittelalter und Renaissance*, Germanisch-Romanische Monatsschrift, Beiheft 4 (Heidelberg, 1985).
KARRAS, RUTH MAZO, '*Leccherous Songys*: Medieval Sexuality in Word and Deed', in Ziolkowski (ed.), *Obscenity*, pp. 233–45.
KAY, SARAH, 'Women's Body of Knowledge: Epistemology and Misogyny in the *Romance of the Rose*', in Sarah Kay and Miri Rubin (eds.), *Framing Medieval Bodies* (Manchester, 1994), pp. 211–35.
—— *The Romance of the Rose*, Critical Guides to French Texts, 110 (London, 1995).
—— 'Venus in the *Roman de la Rose*', *Exemplaria*, 9.1 (1997), 7–37.
KEIGHTLEY, RONALD G., 'Alfonso de Madrigal and the *Cronici canones* of Eusebius', *Journal of Medieval and Renaissance Studies*, 7 (1977), 225–48.
KELLY, DOUGLAS, *Medieval Imagination: Rhetoric and the Poetry of Courtly Love* (Madison, Wis., 1978).

KELLY, DOUGLAS, *Internal Difference and Meanings in the 'Roman de la Rose'* (Madison, 1995).

KELLY, H. A., *Love and Marriage in the Age of Chaucer* (Ithaca, NY, 1975).

—— *Ideas and Forms of Tragedy from Aristotle to the Middle Ages* (Cambridge, 1993).

KENNEDY, WILLIAM J., *Authorizing Petrarch* (Ithaca, NY, 1994).

KINDERMANN, U., *Satyra: Die Theorie der Satire in Mittellateinischen: Vorstudie zu einer Gattungsgeschichte* (Nuremberg, 1978).

KINKADE, R. P., '*Intellectum tibi dabo* . . .: The Function of Free Will in the *Libro de Buen Amor*', *BHS* 47 (1970), 296-315.

KRETZMANN, N., KENNY, A., and PINBORG, J. (eds.), *The Cambridge History of Later Medieval Philosophy* (Cambridge, 1982).

KREUGER, ROBERTA L., *Women Readers and the Ideology of Gender in Old French Verse Romance* (Cambridge, 1993).

KÜHLHORN, G., *Das Verhältnis der 'Art d'amours' von Jacques d'Amiens zu Ovids 'Ars amatoria'* (Leipzig, 1908).

KVAM, K. E., SCHEARING, L. S., and ZIEGLER, V. H. (eds.), *Eve and Adam: Jewish, Christian and Muslim Readings on Genesis and Gender* (Bloomington, 1999).

LAMBERT OF AUXERRE, *Logica (Summa Lamberti)*, ed. Franco Alessio, Pubblicazioni della Facoltà di Lettere e Filosofia dell'Università di Milano (Florence, 1971).

LAWTON, DAVID, 'Englishing the Bible', in David Wallace (ed.), *The Cambridge History of Medieval English Literature* (Cambridge, 1999), pp. 454–82.

LECLERCQ, JEAN, *Jean de Paris et l'ecclésiologie du XIIIe siècle* (Paris, 1942).

—— 'Le Magistère du prédicateur au XIIIe siècle', *AHDLMA* 21 (1946), 105–47.

—— *Monks and Love in Twelfth-Century France* (Oxford, 1979).

LECOY, FELIX, *Recherches sur le 'Libro de buen amor' de Juan Ruiz* (Paris, 1938).

LEES, CLARE A. (ed.), *Medieval Masculinities: Regarding Men in the Middle Ages* (Minneapolis, 1994).

LEGARÉ, ANNE-MARIE, with FRANÇOISE GUICHARD-TESSON and BRUNO ROY, *Le Livre des echecs amoureux* (Paris, 1991).

LESNIK-OBERSTEIN, KARIN, 'Some [Dutch] Adaptors and Their Adaptations: *Le Roman de la Rose* and *Floire et Blaunchefleur* (MA diss., University of Bristol, 1986).

LEWRY, ORMUND, 'The Problem of Authorship', in Jan Pinborg, O. Lewry, K. M. Fredborg, et al., 'The Commentary on *Priscianus maior* ascribed to Robert Kilwardby', *Cahiers de l'Institut du Moyen-Âge Grec et Latin*, 15 (1975), pp. 12–17+.

LIDA DE MALKIEL, MARIA ROSA, *Two Spanish Masterpieces: The 'Book of Good Love' and the 'Celestina'* (Urbana, Ill., 1961).

LOCHRIE, K., MCCRACKEN, P., and SCHULTZ, J. A. (eds.), *Constructing Medieval Sexuality* (Minneapolis, 1997).

LOOZE, LAURENCE DE, *Pseudo-Autobiography in the Fourteenth Century* (Gainesville, Fla., 1997).

LOUIS, RENÉ, *Le Roman de la Rose: Essai d'interprétation de l'allégorisme érotique* (Paris, 1974).

LUSIGNAN, SERGE, *Parler vulgairement: Les intellectuels et la langue française au XIIIe et XIVe siècles* (Paris, 1987).

LYDGATE, JOHN, *Reason and Sensuality*, ed. E. Sieper, EETS, ES 84 (London, 1901).

MACROBIUS, *In somnium Scipionis*, trans. W. H. Stahl (New York, 1952; repr. 1990).

MALORY, THOMAS, *Works*, ed. E. Vinaver, 2nd edn. (Oxford, 1971).

MANIERÙ, ALFONSO, 'The Philosophy of Language', in *History of Lingustics*, ii: *Classical and Medieval Linguistics*, ed. Giulio Lepschy (London, 1994), pp. 272–315.

MAP, WALTER, *De Nugis curialium: Courtiers' Trifles*, ed. and trans. M. R. James, rev. C. N. L. Brooke and R. A. B. Mynors (Oxford, 1983).

MATTHEW OF VENDÔME, *Ars versificatoria*, in *Mathei Vindocinensis opera*, ed. F. Munari (Rome 1977–88), iii. Trans. Roger P. Parr (Milwaukee, Wis., 1981).

MCCRACKEN, H. N., 'Vegetius in English: Notes on the Early Translations', in *Anniversary Papers by Colleagues and Pupils of G. L. Kittredge* (Boston, 1913), pp. 398–403.

MCEVOY, J. J., 'The Theory of Friendship in the Latin Middle Ages', in Haseldine (ed.), *Friendship in Medieval Europe*, pp. 3–44.

MCGUIRE, B. P., 'Sexual Control and Spiritual Growth in the Late Middle Ages: The Case of Jean Gerson', in van Deusen (ed.), *Tradition and Ecstasy*, pp. 123–52.

—— 'Jean Gerson and the End of Spiritual Friendship: Dilemmas of Conscience', in Haseldine (ed.), *Friendship in Medieval Europe*, 229–50.

MCLAREN, ANGUS, *A History of Contraception, from Antiquity to the Present Day* (Oxford, 1990).

Medieval English Lyrics, ed. R. T. Davies (London, 1963).

MEHTONEN, PÄIVI, *Old Concepts and New Poetics: Historia, Argumentum, and Fabula in the Twelfth- and Early Thirteenth-Century Latin Poetics of Fiction*, Finnish Society of Sciences and Letters, Commentationes Humanarum Litterarum 108 (Helsinki, 1996).

MERCERON, JACQUES E., 'Obscenity and Hagiography in Three

Anonymous *Sermons Joyeux* and in Jean Molinet's *Saint Billouart*, in Ziolkowski (ed.), *Obscenity*, pp. 332–44.

MEWS, CONSTANT J., *The Lost Love Letters of Heloise and Abelard* (Basingstoke, 1999).

MILLER, PAUL S., 'The Mediaeval Literary Theory of Satire and Its Relevance to the Works of Gower, Langland and Chaucer' (Ph.D. diss., Queen's University of Belfast, 1982).

—— 'John Gower, Satiric Poet', in A. J. Minnis (ed.), *Gower's 'Confessio Amantis': Responses and Reassessments* (Cambridge, 1983), pp. 79–105.

MILLETT, BELLA, and WOGAN-BROWNE, JOCELYN, *Medieval English Prose for Women* (Oxford, 1990).

MINNIS, ALASTAIR J., ' "Authorial Intention" and "Literal Sense" in the Exegetical Theories of Richard FitzRalph and John Wyclif', *Proceedings of the Royal Irish Academy*, 75, section C, no. 1 (Dublin, 1975).

—— 'Aspects of the Medieval French and English Traditions of the *De consolatione philosophiae*', in M. T. Gibson (ed.), *Boethius: His Life, Thought and Influence* (Oxford, 1981), pp. 312–61.

—— 'Langland's Ymaginatif and Late-Medieval Theories of Imagination', *Comparative Criticism*, 3 (1981), 71–103.

—— *Chaucer and Pagan Antiquity* (Cambridge, 1982).

—— ' "Moral Gower" and Medieval Literary Theory', in A. J. Minnis (ed.), *Gower's 'Confessio amantis': Responses and Reassessments* (Cambridge, 1983), pp. 50–78.

—— 'Chaucer's Pardoner and the "Office of Preacher" ', in P. Boitani and A. Torti (eds.), *Intellectuals and Writers in Fourteenth-Century Europe* (Tübingen, 1986), pp. 88–119.

—— '*Amor* and *Auctoritas* in the Self-Commentary of Dante and Francesco da Barberino', *Poetica* (Tokyo), 32 (1990), 25–42.

—— '*De vulgari auctoritate*: Chaucer, Gower and the Men of Great Authority', in R. F. Yeager (ed.), *Chaucer and Gower: Difference, Mutuality, Exchange*, English Literary Studies, Monograph Series 51 (University of Victoria, 1991), pp. 36–74.

—— 'The *Accessus* Extended: Henry of Ghent on the Transmission and Reception of Theology', in Mark D. Jordan and Kent Emery (eds.), *Ad Litteram: Authoritative Texts and Their Medieval Readers* (Notre Dame, Ind., 1992), pp. 275–326.

—— 'Authors in Love: The Self-Exegesis of Medieval Love Poets', in C. Morse, P. Doob, and M. C. Woods (eds.), *The Uses of Manuscripts in Literary Studies: Essays in Honor of Judson B. Allen* (Kalamazoo, Mich., 1992), pp. 161–91.

—— (ed.), *Chaucer's 'Boece' and the Medieval Tradition of Boethius* (Cambridge, 1993).

—— 'Fifteenth Century Versions of Literalism: Girolamo Savonarola and Alfonso de Madrigal', in *Neue Richtungen in der hoch- und spätmittelalterlichen Bibelexegese*, Schriften des Historischen Kollegs Kolloquien 32, ed. Robert Lerner (Munich, 1996), pp. 163–80.

—— '*De impedimento sexus*: Women's Bodies and Medieval Impediments to Female Ordination', in Peter Biller and A. J. Minnis (eds.), *Medieval Theology and the Natural Body*, York Studies in Medieval Theology 1 (York, 1997), pp. 109–39.

—— 'The Author's Two Bodies? Authority and Fallibility in Late-Medieval Textual Theory', in P. R. Robinson and R. Zim (eds.), *Of the Making of Books: Medieval Manuscripts, Their Scribes and Readers. Essays presented to M. B. Parkes* (Aldershot, 1997), pp. 259–79.

—— 'Material Swords and Literal Lights: The Status of Allegory in William of Ockham's *Breviloquium* on Papal Power' (forthcoming).

—— and MACHAN, T. W., 'The *Boece* as Late-Medieval Translation', in Minnis (ed.), *Chaucer's 'Boece'*, pp. 167–88.

—— and NAUTA, LODI, '*More Platonico loquitur*: What Nicholas Trevet Really Did to William of Conches', in Minnis (ed.), *Chaucer's 'Boece'*, pp. 1–33.

MONSON, DON A., 'Andreas Capellanus and the Problem of Irony', *Speculum*, 63 (1988), 539–72.

MORAN, J. A. HOEPPNER, 'Literature and the Medieval Historian', *Medieval Perspectives*, 10 (1995), 49–66.

MURDOCK, GRAHAM, 'Reservoirs of Dogma: An Archaeology of Popular Anxieties', in Barker and Petley (eds.), *Ill Effects*, pp. 67–86.

MUSCATINE, CHARLES, 'The Fabliaux, Courtly Culture, and the (Re)Invention of Vulgarity', in Ziolkowski (ed.), *Obscenity*, pp. 281–92.

MYLES, ROBERT, *Chaucerian Realism* (Cambridge, 1994).

NAUTA, LODI, 'The Scholastic Context of the Boethius Commentary by Nicholas Trevet', in J. F. M. Hoenen and Lodi Nauta (eds.), *Boethius in the Late Middle Ages: Latin and Vernacular Traditions of the 'Consolatio philosophiae'* (Leiden, 1997), pp. 41–67.

NEPAULSINGH, COLBERT, 'The Rhetorical Structure of the Prologues to the *Libro de buen amor* and the *Celestina*', BHS 51 (1974), 325–34.

NEWMAN, BARBARA, *From Virile Woman to WomanChrist: Studies in Medieval Religion and Literature* (Philadelphia, 1995).

NOAKES, SUSAN, *Timely Reading: Between Exegesis and Interpretation* (Ithaca, NY, 1988).

NOLAN, BARBARA, *Chaucer and the Tradition of the 'Roman Antique'* (Cambridge, 1991).

NYKROG, PER, *L'amour et la Rose: Le grand dessein de Jean de Meun,* Harvard Studies in Romance Languages 41 (Cambridge, Mass., 1986).

—— 'Obscene or Not Obscene: Lady Reason, Jean de Meun, and the Fisherman from Pont-sur-Seine', in Ziolkowski (ed.), *Obscenity,* pp. 319–31.

OLSON, BIRGER MUNK, 'Ovide au moyen âge (du IXe au XIIe siècle)', in G. Cavallo (ed.), *Le Strade del testo* (Bari, 1987).

—— *I classici nel canone scolastico altomedievale* (Spoleto, 1991).

ONG, WALTER J., *Rhetoric, Romance and Technology: Studies in the Interaction of Expression and Culture* (Ithaca, NY, 1971).

ORESME, NICOLE, *Le Livre de ethiques d'Aristote,* ed. A. D. Menut (New York, 1940).

—— *Quaestiones de Spera,* ed. G. Droppers (Madison, 1966).

—— *Le Livre de politiques d'Aristote,* ed. A. D. Menut, Transactions of the American Philosophical Society, n.s. 60, pt. 6 (Philadelphia, 1970).

—— *Expositio et quaestiones in Aristotelis de Anima,* ed. Benoît Patar, Philosophes médiévaux, 32 (Louvain, 1995).

ORNATO, MONIQUE, and PONS, NICOLE (eds.) *Pratiques de la culture écrite en France au XVe siècle: Actes du colloque international du CNRS, Paris 16–18 mai 1992,* FIDEM, Textes et études du moyen âge 2 (Louvain-la-Neuve, 1995).

OSGOOD, CHARLES G., *Boccaccio on Poetry, being the Preface and the Fourteenth and Fifteenth Books of Boccaccio's 'Genealogia deorum gentilium'* (Princeton, NJ, 1956).

OUY, GILBERT, 'Humanism and Nationalism in France at the Turn of the Fifteenth Century', in B. P. McGuire (ed.), *The Birth of Identities: Denmark and Europe in the Middle Ages* (Copenhagen, 1996), pp. 107–25.

—— *Gerson bilingue: Les deux rédactions, latine et française, de quelques œuvres du chancelier parisien* (Paris, 1998).

OVID, *Metamorphoses.* Trans. Mary M. Innes (Harmondsworth, 1955).

—— *The Art of Love and Other Poems,* ed. with an English translation by J. H. Mozley (Cambridge, Mass., 1969).

OVID, Pseudo-, *'De Vetula': Untersuchungen und Text,* ed. Paul Klopsch (Leiden, 1967).

—— *De Vetula: Text, Introduction and Notes,* ed. Dorothy M. Robathan (Amsterdam, 1968).

Owl and the Nightingale, The, ed. E. G. Stanley (Manchester, rev. edn. 1970).

PARIS, G., 'Chrétien Legouais et autres traducteurs et imitateurs d'Ovide au moyen âge', *Histoire littéraire de la France*, 29 (1885), 489–97.

PARKER, DEBORAH, *Commentary and Ideology: Dante in the Renaissance* (Durham, NC, 1993).

PARKES, MALCOLM, *Pause and Effect: An Introduction to the History of Punctuation in the West* (Berkeley, 1993).

PELEN, MARC M., *Latin Poetic Irony in the 'Roman de la Rose'* (Liverpool, 1987).

—— 'The Manciple's "Cosyn" to the "Dede" ', *Chaucer Review*, 25 (1991), 343–54.

—— 'Murder and Immortality in Fragment VI(C) of the *Canterbury Tales*: Chaucer's Transformation of Theme and Image from the *Roman de la Rose*', *Chaucer Review*, 29 (1994), 1–25.

PETER OF SPAIN, *'Tractatus', called afterwards 'Summulae Logicales'*, ed. L. M. de Rijk (Assen, 1972). Trans. Francis P. Dinneen, *Language in Dispute: An English Translation of Peter of Spain's 'Tractatus'* (Amsterdam, 1990).

PETRUS, ALFONSI, *Disciplina clericalis*, ed. Eberhard Hermes with an English translation by P. R. Quarrie (London, 1977). Trans. J. R. Jones and J. E. Keller, *The Scholar's Guide* (Toronto, 1969).

PLATO, *Timaeus*, trans. H. D. P. Lee (Harmondsworth, 1965).

POIRION, DANIEL, 'Les Mots et les choses selon Jean de Meun', *Information littéraire*, 26 (1974), 7–11.

—— 'De la signification selon Jean de Meun', in L. Brind'Amour and E. Vance (eds.), *Archéologie du signe*, Papers in Mediaeval Studies 3 (Toronto, 1983), pp. 167–85.

PORTER, ELIZABETH, 'Gower's Ethical Microcosm and Political Macrocosm', in A. J. Minnis (ed.), *Gower's 'Confessio Amantis': Responses and Reassessments* (Cambridge, 1983), pp. 135–62.

POTANSKY, PETER, *Der Streit um den Rosenroman*, Münchener Romanistische Arbeiten 33 (Munich, 1972).

PRATT, KAREN, 'Analogy or Logic; Authority or Experience? Rhetorical Strategies For and Against Women', in Donald Maddox and Sara S. Maddox (eds.), *Literary Aspects of Courtly Culture: Selected Proceedings from the Seventh Triennial Congress of the International Courtly Literature Society* (Cambridge, 1994), pp. 57–66.

PRZYCHOCKI, G., 'Accessus Ovidiani', *Rozprawy Akademii Umiejetnosci*, wydzial filologiczny, Ser. 3, vol. iv (1911), pp. 65–126.

QUAIN, E. A., 'The Medieval *Accessus ad auctores*', *Traditio*, 3 (1945), 228–42.

QUILLIGAN, MAUREEN, *The Allegory of Female Authority: Christine de Pizan's 'Cité des dames'* (Ithaca, NY, 1991).

340   Bibliography

QUINTILIAN, *Institutio oratoria*, ed. H. E. Butler (Cambridge, Mass., 1920–2).

RABY, F. J. E., *A History of Secular Latin Poetry in the Middle Ages* (Oxford, 1934).

—— 'Nuda Natura and Twelfth-Century Cosmology', *Speculum*, 43 (1968), 73–8.

RALPH OF LONGCHAMPS, *In Anticlaudianum Alani commentum*, ed. Jan Sulowski (Wrocław, 1972).

RENO, CHRISTINE, 'Christine de Pizan: "At Best a Contradictory Figure?" ', in Margaret Brabant (ed.), *Politics, Gender, and Genre: The Political Thought of Christine de Pizan* (Boulder, Colo., 1992), pp. 171–91.

REYNOLDS, SUZANNE, *Medieval Reading: Grammar, Rhetoric and the Classical Text* (Cambridge, 1996).

RICHARD DE FOURNIVAL, *Li Bestiaires d'amours* and *Li Response du bestiaire*, ed. Cesare Segre (Milan, 1957). Trans. Jeanette Beer, *Master Richard's Bestiary of Love and Response* (Berkeley, Calif., 1986).

—— *Li Consaus d'amours*, ed. G. B. Speroni, *Medioevo romanzo*, 1.2 (1974), 217–78.

RICHARDS, EARL JEFFREY, 'Christine de Pizan and Sacred History', in M. Zimmermann and D. De Rentiis, *The City of Scholars: New Approaches to Christine de Pizan* (Berlin, 1994), pp. 15–30.

RICKERT, EDITH, *Chaucer's World*, ed. C. C. Olson and M. M. Crow (New York, 1948).

RICO, FRANCISCO, 'Sobre el origen de la autobiografía en el *Libro de buen amor*', *Anuario de Estudios Medievales*, 4 (1967), 301–25.

RIGG, GEORGE, *A History of Anglo-Latin Literature, 1066–1422* (Cambridge, 1992).

ROBATHAN, DOROTHY M., 'Introduction to the Pseudo-Ovidian *De Vetula*', *Transactions and Proceedings of the American Philological Association*, 88 (1957), 197–207.

—— and CRANZ, F. EDWARD (with KRISTELLER, P. O., and BISCHOFF, B.), 'A. Persius Flaccus', in F. Edward Cranz and P. O. Kristeller (eds.), *Catalogus translationum et commentariorum*, iii (Washington, DC, 1976), pp. 201–312.

ROBERTSON, D. W., *A Preface to Chaucer: Studies in Medieval Perspectives* (Princeton, NJ, 1962).

ROSSETTI, DANTE GABRIEL, *The Early Italian Poets*, ed. Sally Purcell (London, 1981).

ROY, BRUNO, 'Arnulf of Orléans and the Latin "Comedy" ', *Speculum*, 49 (1974), 258–66.

RUIZ, JUAN, *The Book of True Love: A Bilingual Edition*, ed. and trans.

Saralyn R. Daly and Anthony N. Zahareas (University Park, Penn., 1978).

ST-JACQUES, R. C., 'The Middle English Glossed Prose Psalter and Its French Source', in Jeanette Beer (ed.), *Medieval Translators and Their Craft* (Kalamazoo, Mich., 1989), pp. 135–54.

SALLUST, ed. J. C. Rolfe (Cambridge, Mass., 1971).

SANFORD, E. M., 'Juvenalis, Decimus Junius', in F. E. Cranz and P. O. Kristeller (eds.), *Catalogus translationum et commentariorum*, i (Washington, DC, 1960), pp. 175–238.

SCHIBANOFF, SUSAN, 'Taking the Gold Out of Egypt: The Art of Reading as a Woman', in E. Flynn and P. Schweikehart (eds.), *Gender and Reading* (Baltimore, 1986), pp. 83–106.

SCHMITZ, G., *The Fall of Women in Early English Narrative Verse* (Cambridge, 1990).

SEARS, ELIZABETH, *The Ages of Man: Medieval Interpretations of the Life Cycle* (Princeton, NJ, 1986).

SEBASTIAN, H. F., 'William Wheteley's Commentary on the Pseudo-Boethius' tractate *De disciplina scolarium* and Medieval Grammar School Education' (Ph.D. diss., Columbia University, 1970).

SEDGWICK, EVE KOSOFSKY, *Between Men: English Literature and Male Homosocial Desire* (New York, 1985).

SEIDENSPINNER-NÚÑEZ, D., *The Allegory of Good Love: Parodic Perspectivism in the 'Libro de buen amor'* (Berkeley, Calif., 1981).

SERVIUS, *In Vergilii carmina commentarii*, ed. G. Thilo and H. Hagen (Leipzig, 1881–7).

SHAW, J. E., *Guido Cavalcanti's Theory of Love: The 'Canzone d'Amore' and Other Related Problems* (Toronto, 1949).

SHERMAN, C. R., *Imaging Aristotle: Verbal and Visual Representation in Fourteenth-Century France* (Berkeley, Calif., 1995).

—— 'Les Thèmes humanistes dans le programme de traduction de Charles V: Compilation des textes et illustrations', in Ornato and Pons (eds.), *Pratiques de la culture écrite en France au XVe siècle*, pp. 527–37.

SHOONER, HUGUES-V., 'Les *Bursarii Ovidianorum* de Guillaume d'Orléans', *MS* 43 (1981), 405–24.

SHRADER, C. R., 'The Ownership and Distribution of Manuscripts of the *De re militari* of Flavius Vegetius Renatus before 1300' (Ph.D. diss., Columbia University, 1976).

SILVESTRE, H., 'Réflexions sur la thèse de F. J. Benton relative au dossier "Abélard-Héloïse" ', *Recherches de théologie ancienne et médiévale*, 44 (1977), 215–16.

SIMONE, FRANCO, *The French Renaissance: Medieval Traditions and*

Italian Influence in Shaping the Renaissance in France, trans. H. Gaston Hall (London, 1969).

SMALLEY, BERYL, *English Friars and Antiquity in the Early Fourteenth Century* (Oxford, 1960).

—— 'Peter Comestor on the Gospels and his Sources', *RTAM* 46 (1979), 84–129.

SMITS, E. R., 'New Evidence for the Authorship of the First Six Books of Virgil's *Aeneid* Commonly Attributed to Bernardus Silvestris?', in M. Gosman and J. Van Os (eds.), *Sed Nove: Mélanges de civilisation médiévale dédiés à Willem Noomen* (Groningen, 1984), pp. 239–46.

SOLTERER, HELEN, *The Master and Minerva: Disputing Women in French Medieval Culture* (Berkeley, Calif., 1995).

SPERONI, G. B., 'Il "Consaus d'amours" di Richard de Fournival', *Medioevo romanzo*, 1.2 (1924), 217–78.

SPICQ, P. C., *Esquisse d'une histoire de l'exégèse latine au moyen âge*, Bibliothèque thomiste 26 (Paris, 1944).

STANFORD, PETER, *The She-Pope: A Quest for the Truth behind the Mystery of Pope Joan* (London, 1998).

STILLINGER, THOMAS C., *The Song of Troilus: Lyric Authority in the Medieval Book* (Philadelphia, 1992).

STOCK, BRIAN, *Myth and Science in the Twelfth Century* (Princeton, NJ, 1972).

STRAYER, JOSEPH R., 'France: The Holy Land, the Chosen People and the Most Christian King', in *Action and Conviction in Early Modern Europe: Essays in Memory of E. H. Harbison* (Princeton, NJ, 1969), pp. 3–16.

STRECKER, KARL (ed.), *Moralisch-Satirische Gedichte Walters von Chatillon* (Heidelberg, 1929).

STROSSEN, NADINE, *Defending Pornography: Free Speech, Sex, and the Fight for Women's Rights* (London, 1995).

SWIGGERS, P., 'Les Premières Grammaires des vernaculaires gallo-romans face à la tradition latine: stratégies d'adaptation et de transformation', *L'Héritage des grammairiens latins de l'antiquité aux lumières* (Paris, 1988), pp. 259–69.

SZITTYA, PENN, *The Antifraternal Tradition in Medieval Literature* (Princeton, NJ, 1986).

TAYLOR, P. B., 'Chaucer's *Cosyn to the Dede*', *Speculum*, 57 (1982), 315–27.

THIÉBAUX, MARCELLE, *The Stag of Love: The Chase in Medieval Literature* (Ithaca, NY, 1974).

THOMAS, ANTOINE, *Francesco da Barberino: Littérature provençale en Italie au moyen âge* (Paris, 1883).

THOMAS OF CHOBHAM, *Summa confessorum*, ed. F. Broomfield, Analecta Mediaevalia Namurcensia (Louvain, 1968).
—— *Summa de arte praedicandi*, ed. F. Morenzoni, CCCM 82 (Turnhout, 1988).
THOMSON, IAN, and PERRAUD, LOUIS (eds.) *Ten Latin Schooltexts of the Later Middle Ages: Translated Selections* (Lewiston, NY, 1990).
Three Latin Comedies, ed. Keith Bate, Toronto Medieval Latin Texts 6 (Toronto, 1976).
Three Medieval Views of Women, ed. and trans. G. K. Fiero, W. Pfeffer, and M. Allain (New Haven, Conn., 1989).
TOLAN, JOHN, *Petrus Alfonsi and His Medieval Readers* (Gainesville, Fla., 1993).
TREVET, NICHOLAS, commentary on Boethius, *De consolatione philosophiae*, ed. E. T. Silk (unpub.).
TUVE, ROSEMUND, *Allegorical Imagery: Some Mediaeval Books and Their Posterity* (Princeton, NJ, 1966).
ULLMAN, PIERRE L., 'Juan Ruiz's Prologue', *MLN* 82 (1967), 149–70.
VANCE, EUGENE, *Mervelous Signals: Poetics and Sign Theory in the Middle Ages* (Lincoln, Neb., 1986).
VAN DER POEL, D. E., 'A Romance of a Rose and Florentine: The Flemish Adaptation of the *Romance of the Rose*', in Brownlee and Huot (eds.), *Rethinking the Rose*, pp. 304–15.
VASVÁRI, LOUISE O., 'Fowl Play in My Lady's Chamber', in Ziolkowski (ed.), *Obscenity*, pp. 108–35.
VINEIS, E., 'Linguistics and Grammar', in *History of Lingustics* ii: *Classical and Medieval Linguistics* ed. Giulio Lepschy (London, 1994), pp. 136–272.
WACK, MARY FRANCES, *Lovesickness in the Middle Ages: The 'Viaticum' and Its Commentaries* (Philadelphia, 1990).
WAILES, STEPHEN L., 'Role-Playing in Medieval *Comediae* and Fabliaux', *Neuphilogische Mitteilungen*, 75 (1974), 640–9.
—— 'Why Did Jesus Use Parables? The Medieval Discussion', *Medievalia et humanistica*, 13 (1985), 43–64.
WALEYS, THOMAS, *Postilla super primos xxviii psalmos Davidicos Thomae Iorgii* (London, 1481).
WATSON, NICHOLAS, 'Censorship and Cultural Change in Late Medieval England: Vernacular Theology, The Oxford Translation Debate and Arundel's *Constitutions* of 1409', *Speculum*, 70 (1996), 822–64.
WEISS, JULIAN, *The Poet's Art: Literary Theory in Castile, c.1400–60*, Medium Ævum Monographs, n.s. 14 (Oxford, 1990).
WESTRA, H. J., review of *Guillaume de Conches: Glosae in Iuvenalem*, ed. Bradford Wilson, *Mittellateinisches Jarbuch*, 18 (1983), 368–9.

WETHERBEE, WINTHROP, 'The Literal and the Allegorical: Jean de Meun and the "De Planctu Naturae" ', *MS* 33 (1971), 264–91.

—— *Platonism and Poetry in the Twelfth Century* (Princeton, NJ, 1972).

WHITE, T. H., *The Book of Beasts, Being a Translation from a Latin Bestiary of the Twelfth Century* (London, 1954).

WILLARD, C. C., 'Raoul de Presles's Translation of Saint Augustine's *De civitate Dei*', in Jeanette Beer (ed.), *Medieval Translators and their Craft* (Kalamazoo, Mich., 1989), pp. 329–46.

WILLIAM OF CONCHES, *Glosae in Iuvenalem*, ed. Bradford Wilson, Textes philosophiques du moyen âge 18 (Paris, 1980).

—— *Glosae super Boetium*, ed. Lodi Nauta, CCCM 158 (Turnhout, 1999).

WILLIAM OF OCKHAM, *De sacramento altaris*, ed. and trans. T. B. Birch, Lutheran Literary Board (Iowa, 1930).

WILLIAM OF SHERWOOD, *Introduction to Logic*, trans. Norman Kretzmann (Minneapolis, 1966).

WILLIAMS, BERNARD (ed.), *Obscenity and Film Censorship: An Abridgement of the Williams Report* (Cambridge, 1981).

WIPPEL, JOHN F., 'The Condemnations of 1270 and 1277 at Paris', *Journal of Medieval and Renaissance Studies*, 7 (1977), 169–201.

WOGAN-BROWNE, JOCELYN, WATSON, NICHOLAS, TAYLOR, ANDREW, and EVANS, RUTH (eds.), *The Idea of the Vernacular: An Anthology of Middle English Literary Theory, 1280–1520* (University Park, Penn., 1999).

WOODS, MARJORIE CURRY, 'Rape and the Pedagogical Rhetoric of Sexual Violence', in Rita Copeland (ed.), *Criticism and Dissent in the Middle Ages* (Cambridge, 1996), pp. 56–86.

YEATS, W. B., 'A Coat', in *The Collected Poems of W. B. Yeats* (London, 1965).

ZAHAREAS, ANTHONY N., *The Art of Juan Ruiz* (Madrid, 1965).

ZEEMAN, NICOLETTE, 'The Schools Give a License to Poets', in Rita Copeland (ed.), *Criticism and Dissent in the Middle Ages* (Cambridge, 1996), pp. 151–80.

ZIOLKOWSKI, JAN, *Alan of Lille's Grammar of Sex: The Meaning of Grammar to a Twelfth-Century Intellectual* (Cambridge, Mass., 1985).

—— 'Theories of Obscurity in the Latin Tradition', *Mediaevalia*, 19 (1996 [for 1993]), 101–70.

—— 'Obscenity in the Latin Grammatical and Rhetorical Tradition', in Ziolkowski (ed.), *Obscenity*, pp. 41–59.

—— 'The Obscenities of Old Women: Vetularity and Vernacularity', in Ziolkowski (ed.), *Obscenity*, pp. 73–89.

Index

Abelard, Peter 3–4, 102 n., 120,
  132 n., 142, 144, 145, 167 n., 171,
  172–3, 181, 182, 195, 201, 227
Acart, Jean, de Hesdin 73 n., 232, 313
accessūs 13, 21, 24, 28, 39, 48, 50,
  65 n., 71, 92, 93, 94, 167, 226, 235,
  236, 237 n., 242 n., 246, 274;
  accessūs Ovidiani 12 n., 13, 36, 38,
  42, 44, 49, 55 n., 64 n., 67–8, 77,
  202 n., 238, 240, 243, 245, 254,
  282, 283, 293 243, 245, 254, 282,
  283, 293, 295
Adam and Eve 75–6, 151
Adonis 104, 105
Aelred of Rievaulx 3–4, 206 n.
Aesop 188, 201, 292
ages of man, the 56–8
Alan of Lille 3, 20, 35 n., 51, 85–6,
  107, 109, 118, 138 n., 198, 259;
  Anticlaudianus 20, 21, 83–4;
  De planctu naturae 21, 22, 24, 84,
  86, 100 n., 107, 125–7, 149, 166,
  170, 174–5, 177, 194
Alberic of London 17
Albert the Great 270, 271
Alchema 179–80
Alexander of Villa Dei 138 n.
Alfonso de Algezira 297
Alfonso de Guzmàn 297
Alfonso de Madrigal 193, 297
Alhazen 5
allegory and allegoresis 15, 16 n., 26,
  82–4, 85, 87, 89–90, 108, 113,
  114–16, 120, 132–3, 140, 203–4,
  248, 274, 284
Allen, Judson B. 11, 115 n., 138 n., 255
Allen, Peter L. 39 n.
Alonso de Cartagena 317
Althusser, Louis 204
Amant (figure in the Rose) 8, 17 n.,
  20, 21, 23, 86, 88, 89 n., 90 n., 101,
  103, 105, 107, 108, 113, 126–7,
  136–7, 145, 146, 148, 150, 155,
  156, 165, 173–8, 182, 185, 195,
  197, 199, 201 n., 202, 203, 205,
  206, 207, 224, 258, 259, 262, 263

Ami (figure in the Rose) 21, 96, 99,
  101, 102, 108, 172, 182, 205
amicitia 206
Amphitrion 179–82, 192, 195, 200,
  201 n.
Anderson, David 276 n.
Andreas Capellanus 4, 9–10, 31, 40,
  196, 295, 307, 308, 311
Antiovidianus 28 n., 202 n.
Appleyard, Bryan 234 n.
Aquinas, Thomas 132, 135, 216,
  268 n.
Ardent, Raoul 148 n.
argumentum 19 n.
Aristaeus 203
Ariosto, Ludovico 275–6 n.
Aristotle 5–6, 7, 43, 56 n., 63, 72, 74,
  156 n., 207, 216, 228–9, 235, 238,
  251–2, 254 n., 258, 267, 268, 270,
  271, 273, 279, 285, 286, 292, 301,
  305, 310, 311, 313; pseudo-
  Aristotle, Economics 268; pseudo-
  Aristotle, Problemata 253 n., 271,
  303 n.
'Aristotelian Prologue' 48, 50, 63, 64,
  114, 191, 237 n.
Arnold of Villanova 173
Arnulf of Orléans 20, 36–7, 77, 83,
  104, 107, 138, 166, 235
L'Art de'amours 12, 13, 44–62, 74,
  77–8, 80, 199, 302, 303 n.
Arthur, King 307, 309
Arthur, Ross G. 141 n.
Ascoli, Albert Russell 274 n.
Athis and Prophilias 45
Augustine, St. 132–3, 139, 143 n.,
  151 n., 215, 238, 268, 269, 271,
  279, 288, 289
Augustus, Roman emperor 12 n., 37,
  61, 202 n., 239, 240
authority 15, 26, 27, 28, 31–2, 58, 63,
  69, 81, 111–12, 131, 138, 164, 193,
  207–8, 211, 217–18, 231, 237,
  247–8, 254–6, 265, 267–8, 273–5,
  277, 291, 318
Averroes 292

Avianus 236
Avicenna 54 n., 307

Babio 180–2, 192, 195, 200
Bacon, Roger 5, 71 n.
Badel, P.-Y. 8 n., 25, 257, 280
Baird, Lorrayne Y. 187 n., 188 n.
Bakhtin, M. 193
Baldwin, John W. 62 n., 80
Barnett, Robert J. 93 n.
Barthes, Roland 164
Bartholomaeus Anglicus 100–1 n., 188, 268, 299
Bartholomew of Messina 271
Baswell, Christopher 82 n., 83 n., 115
Bede 220
Beer, Jeanette 73, 186
Bel Acueil (figure in the *Rose*) 22, 23, 203, 205–6, 264, 310 n.
Benvenuto da Imola 297, 298
Berkeley, Lord Thomas 299
Berkeley, Elizabeth 299
Bernard of Chartres 82, 83,
Bernard of Clairvaux 28 n., 206 n., 279
Bernard of Cluny 94–6, 97, 100 n.
Bernard Silvester 82; *Aeneid* commentary attributed to 15, 16 n., 83, 169, 236, 282; Martianus Capella commentary attributed to 15–16, 18, 19
Bersuire, Pierre 17, 21, 64 n., 115, 116 n., 138 n., 261, 297, 303
Bible moralisé 114
Biblia de Osuna 297
Biller, P. P. A. 175 n.
Birria 180, 201 n.
Bischoff, Bernard 98 n.
Blamires, Alcuin 29 n., 76 n.
Blanchandin 45–6
Blanche of Navarre 266
Bloch, Howard 87 n., 142 n., 143 n., 156–7
Blonquist, Lawrence B. 44 n.
Blumenfeld-Kosinski, Renate 212 n.
Boccaccio, Giovanni 32, 116, 118, 248 n., 255–6, 274–8, 280, 291, 298, 312, 313
Boethius: *Consolatio philosophiae* 3, 5, 45, 60, 61, 85, 104, 120, 120, 124, 126, 129–30, 132, 133, 136 n., 195, 204, 205, 216, 220, 221, 248 n., 259, 270, 276, 296 n., 299,

301, 302, 313; *De musica* 272 n., 287
Boethius of Dacia 6–7
Bonaventure, St 215, 222, 226, 230, 249
Bouvet, Honoré 2, 27
Bradwardine, Thomas 71 n.
Brown, D. Catherine 215 n.
Brown-Grant, R. 149 n., 213 n., 231 n., 233 n.,
Brownlee, Kevin 177 n., 206 n., 217 n., 256 n., 265 n.
Buridan, Jean 271 n.
Burley, Walter 71 n., 270
Burrow, John A. 56, 85 n.
Bursill-Hall, G. L. 5 n.

Cacus 104–5
Cadden, Joan 177–8 n., 267 n.
Calabrese, Michael A. 28 n., 248 n.
Calcidius 124
Camille, Michael 175 n.
Cancionero da Barrantes 316
Castelvetro, Lodovico 318
castration 30, 88, 90 n., 110, 122, 167–73, 181, 182, 185–7, 194–5, 197, 303 n.
causa efficiens 64, 69, 274
causae scribendi 48, 49
Cavalcanti, Guido 32, 71 n., 253 n., 275, 312
Caxton, William 240
Chapman, J. A. 65
Charles V, king of France 28, 31, 32, 57, 216, 266–72, 296, 299, 301, 314, 316, 317
Charles VI, king of France 317
Chaucer, Geoffrey 22, 119–20, 127 n., 128–32, 137, 140, 160–2, 163, 164, 165, 188, 218 n., 228, 231, 248 n., 252, 280 n., 316
Chenu, M.-D. 131 n.
Chrétien de Troyes 43
Christine de Pizan 1, 2, 3–4 n., 25, 27, 28–30, 76, 81, 88 n., 90 n., 95, 113 n., 123 n., 138, 146–58, 165, 167, 200, 205 n., 209, 211–19, 229–32, 233 n., 235–6, 238, 240 n., 241, 243–6, 255–6, 229–30, 232, 233, 254 n., 255, 260, 265, 268 n., 313–14; *Cité des dames* 29–30, 139, 211; *Epistre au dieu d'amours* 28–9, 202–3, 244–5, 246

Chrysostom, St John 172, 279
Cicero 74, 196, 248 n., 272, 286–7,
    313; *De inventione* 50–1; *Somnium
    Scipionis*, see Macrobius
Cino del Pistoia 253 n.
Clanchy, Michael 172–3
Clef d'amors 40 n.
Col, Gontier 1, 3, 4 n., 26, 33, 172,
    209, 212, 213, 219
Col, Pierre 1 n., 26, 27, 30, 76–8,
    111–12, 149, 152–4, 199, 209, 210,
    213, 215, 219, 220, 226, 228–9,
    230–1, 241–56, 260
comedy 24, 65, 90 n., 104, 159, 165,
    169, 178–85, 193, 200–1, 207–8
Confort d'amour 39, 40, 41–2
Conrad of Hirsau 91
Constantine the African 53, 54, 173,
    303 n.
Copeland, Rita 139–40, 318 n.
Corbechon, Jean 268
Coulson, Frank T. 36 n., 45 n., 83 n.
Courtenay, W. J. 134 n.
Coville, A. 1 n.
Croecus 180
Croesus 5, 165 n.
Cupid 110

Dagenais, John 64–5 n., 71 n., 257 n.
Daly, Thomas J. 14 n.
Daniello, Bernardino 318
Dante Alighieri 16 n., 32, 33, 72,
    113, 116–17, 253, 273–4, 277,
    278, 281, 297, 298, 302, 312, 316,
    317, 318
David 203, 223, 247, 248, 249, 254 n.
Delany, Sheila 146–7 n., 218–9 n.
De Madrigal, Alfonso 138 n.
De Rijk, L. M. 143 n.
Demats, Paule 115 n.
Des cinq vegiles 43–4
Deschamps, E. 257
Deyermond, A. D. 66 n.
Diana 115, 260, 303–4
Diego de Valera 316
Dino del Garbo 32, 275
Dionysius the Areopagite, pseudo-
    289 n.
Dipsas 127 n., 182–3
dits amoureux 60 n., 61, 257, 277
divisio textus 64 n., 273, 281
Dow, Blanche H. 215 n.
dream-vision 5–8, 59–60, 257, 285–8

Dronke, Peter 9, 82 n., 83 n., 171 n.,
    172 n., 181 n., 182
Drouart la Vache 10
Dundes, Alan 188 n., 189 n.
Dworkin, A. 147 n.

Egidius 55 n.
Elie, Master 78
Enrique de Villena 32, 296–7, 316,
    317
Eschez amoureux (anon. poem) 30,
    32–3, 40 n., 157, 260–1, 265, 280,
    282, 290, 291, 292, 294, 295,
    300–1, 302, 304
Eschez amoureux commentary, see
    Evrart de Conty
ethice supponitur (*accessus* term) 11,
    20, 38, 70–1
Eurydice 166
Eusebius 297
Evans, Gillian 141
Evrart de Conty 10 n., 21 n., 30–1,
    32, 33, 54 n., 56 n., 71 n., 73 n.,
    90 n., 106–7 n., 123 n., 157, 254 n.,
    257, 261–319; *Livre de problèmes*
    266–7, 268, 271–2, 291, 314
exempla 19 n., 108, 120, 165, 249,
    282, 310 n.
extrinsic prologue 13 n., 51, 63, 66,
    72, 189–90

fable (*fabula*), theory of 8, 17–18, 19,
    20, 21, 25, 82–3, 88, 105, 115,
    135–6, 166, 168–9, 188, 220, 236,
    282–96, 311
Faus Semblant 2–3,
Fernando de Rojas 65 n.
Ferroul, Yves 172, 173
Fet des Romains, Li 45
finalis causa 38, 50, 237 n., 238, 283,
    293
fine amor 40, 41–2, 47, 53, 60, 75,
    79, 157, 185, 257
finis 24, 37 n., 52, 165, 174, 194,
    242, 244
Fiore (anon. Italian sonnet sequence)
    33 n.
Fleming, John V. 17, 21, 85–6, 108,
    109, 111, 123 n., 146, 147 n.,
    177 n., 178, 209, 213 n., 219–20,
    248
Fodius 180–1

Fortune 5
Foucault, M. 32, 147 n.
Francesco da Barberino 278–80, 295–6, 298, 309 n.
Froissart, Jean 57, 59–60, 257
Fulco 77
Fulgentius 17, 18 n., 304

Galatea 177 n., 182–4, 197
Gaunt, Simon 22–3, 26, 156 n., 203, 205 n.
Gawain and the Green Knight, Sir 157
Geoffrey of Vinsauf 19 n.
Genius (figure in the *Rose*) 5, 86, 108–13, 166–71, 174, 200, 219, 219, 258
Gerald of Wales 3–4
Gerard of Berry 54, 55
Gerard of Borgo San Donnino 2
Gerhoh of Reichersberg 220
Gerson, Jean 2, 15, 23–4, 25, 26, 27, 30 n., 34, 102 n., 111 n., 113 n., 148 n., 151, 152 n., 165, 174, 194, 195, 209, 213, 214–15, 219, 220, 223–6, 228, 229–32, 233 n., 234, 235 n., 239, 241, 247, 249–51, 255, 260
Geta 179–82, 201 n.
Giles of Rome 261, 268, 295, 299, 305, 312
Gilles li Muisis 257
Ginsberg, Warren 38 n.
Giovanni del Virgilio 63–4, 69, 115, 239–40
Giovannino of Mantua 116 n.
Golein, Jean 268
Gómez Manrique 316
Gower, John 11, 222–3, 253 n., 280, 284, 298, 299, 300–1, 316
Gratian 278
Gravdal, Kathryn 197 n.
Gregory the Great 187 n., 190, 191, 222
Grosseteste, Robert 5, 252 n.
Gui de Mori 107 n., 112, 259, 260
Guiart 12, 39, 40 n., 42–4, 68 n., 70, 304 n.
Guibert de Nogent 28 n.
Guichard-Tesson, Françoise 266, 281, 294–5, 300, 302
Guillaume de Beles Voies 268 n.
Guillaume de Deguileville 257
Guillaume de Lorris 6, 8, 17, 80, 105,

108, 176, 177 n., 258, 259, 262, 287
Guillaume de Machaut 59, 60–1, 79 n., 157, 213–14, 219 n., 257
Guillaume de Tignonville 212
Gybbon-Monypenny, G. B. 65

Hanna, Ralph 299 n.
Hawley, F. F. 189 n.
Heinric van Aken 259 n.
Helias, Peter 121 n.
Heloise 3–4, 171, 172, 181, 195, 201 n.
Henri d'Andeli 156
Henri de Gauchy 268 n.
Henry of Ghent 133–4, 135, 228, 252
Henryson, Robert 188
Hercules 104–5
Hermann the German 292
'heroic love' 53, 54, 58, 267
Hexter, Ralph J. 36 n., 45 n., 48 n., 49, 115 n., 138 n., 175 n., 202 n., 237
'Hicklin Test' 233
Higden, Ralph 299
Hill, Thomas D. 107 n., 176–7
historia 19–20
Hoccleve, Thomas 29, 202
Holcot, Robert 71 n.
Hollander, Robert 248 n., 276–7, 318 n.
Hollis, A. S. 39 n.
homosexuality 22–3, 112 n., 167, 170, 174, 203–6, 267 n.
homosociability 23, 205
Horace 45, 74, 90, 93 n., 98, 227, 235–6, 282
Horgan, Frances 206 n.
Houwen, Luuk 187 n.
Hugh of Fouilly 187 n., 190
Hugutio of Pisa 270
Huizinga, Johan 207 n., 250 n.
Hult, David 1–2, 90 n., 123 n., 127 n., 147 n., 148 n., 169, 218 n., 259 n.
Hunt, R. W. 13 n., 37 n., 50, 235, 270 n.
Huot, Sylvia 107 n., 111–12 n., 258, 259–60
Huygens, R. B. C. 37, 38, 49, 240
Hyatte, Reginald L. 40 n., 261–2 n.

idleness, see leisure
impositio 22, 142–3, 144, 154

Íñigo López de Mendoza, first Marquis of Santillana 297, 316
institutio 22, 144–5, 151, 153, 154
integumentum 15–18, 21, 26, 82–4, 86, 87, 88, 89, 90, 91, 96, 105, 108, 113, 117, 120, 128 n., 132, 135–6, 137, 139, 145, 146, 164, 258, 291
intentio 37, 38, 49, 50, 67, 68, 95, 96, 113, 116, 226, 229, 237 n., 278, 282–3, 285
intrinsic prologue 51, 63, 66
ironia 93–4
Irvine, Martin 201 n.
Isidore of Seville 185
Isolde 176

Jacques d'Amiens 12, 39–41, 47, 53, 78, 79
Jacques de Cessoles 261
Jauss, H. R. 85, 86,
Javitch, Daniel 275–6 n.
Jean de Meun: cultural milieu 2–9; dating of his *Rose* 2 n.; *Livres de confort de philosophie* 3, 85, 104 n., 124, 130, 133, 195, 216, 221, 270; *Testament* 4 n., 199 n., 248 n.
Jean de Montreuil 24, 25, 26–7, 92, 98, 148, 155, 174, 194, 195, 209, 211, 212–13, 217, 219, 229, 235, 238, 255
Jean le Danois 121
Jeauneau, E. 83 n.
Jenaro-Maclennan, L. 65
Jerome 99, 102, 187 n., 279, 297
'Johannitius' 56 n.
John of Garland 16 n., 19, 36, 74, 94, 97
John of Gaunt 299 n.
John of Genoa 270 n.
John of Paris 132–3, 139, 270
John of Serraville 318
Jones, Joan Morton 261 n., 294
Jones, Julian W. 83 n.
Juan de Aragón 296–7
Juan de Mena 298, 316
Juno 16
Jupiter 88, 89, 109, 122, 168 n., 179, 181
Justinian 278
Juvenal 3, 21, 25, 87, 90, 91, 92, 93 n., 94, 95 n., 96, 97 n., 98, 99, 100, 101, 102, 103, 125

Karnein, Alfred 9, 10
Karras, Ruth Mazo 148 n.
Kay, Sarah 26, 168 n., 206 n.
Keightley, Ronald G. 296 n.
Kelly, Douglas 10 n., 25–6, 123 n., 150 n., 165, 209 n.
Kelly, H. A. 165 n.
Kennedy, William J. 318 n.
Kilwardby, Robert, and pseudo-Kilwardby 121, 143–4
Kinkade, R. P. 65
Klopsch, Paul 71 n.
Körting, Gustav 40
Kraft, Christine 290

Lactantius Placidus 276
Lambert of Auxerre 120, 143
Landino, Cristoforo 318
Laurent de Premierfait 113
Le Fèvre, Jean 14, 30 n., 167 n., 168 n., 211–12
Leclercq, Jean 28 n.
leisure 52, 53, 54 n., 59, 262, 294
Lilith 75 n.
Looze, Laurence de 65 n.
Louis, René 176
Lucan 20, 235
Luscignan, Serge 121 n., 122 n.
Lydgate, John 137, 290–1

McGuire, B. P. 205 n., 250–1 n.
Mackinnon, Catharine 147 n., 149 n.
Macrobius, commentary on Cicero's *Somnium Scipionis* 8, 31, 82, 91, 117, 259, 272, 282, 286, 287, 288, 292, 313
Malory, Thomas 240–1
Manfred, King of Naples and Sicily 5, 165 n.
Manierù, Alfonso 121 n.
Map, Walter 94, 95 n., 100–1, 102, 253
Marbod of Rennes 212
Marie de Champagne 9
marriage 30, 31, 43, 68, 171, 192, 241, 245, 260, 261, 304, 308–12
Marsilius of Padua 270
Martianus Capella 3, 15–16, 18, 19, 169 n., 272
Martín González de Lucena 297
materia 37 n., 38, 49, 95
Matheolus 211–12, 234, 241
matiere de rire 25, 213

Matthew of Vendôme 91
Medea 165 n.
Mehtonen, Päivi 19 n.
melancholy 54, 60–1, 234, 267,
    303 n., 306
Menut, A. D. 270
Mercury 16, 179, 260
Mews, Constant J. 172 n.
Miller, Paul 91, 93 n., 94 n., 98 n.
Minnis, A. J. 48 n., 59 n., 60 n., 61 n.,
    87 n., 97 n., 105 n., 132 n., 136 n.,
    164 n., 207 n., 255 n., 318 n.
modus agendi 37 n., 92, 140, 278
Molinet, Jean 258
Moran, J. A. Hoeppner 22
More, St Thomas 193
Moss, Ann 45 n.
Muscatine, Charles 156–7
Mussato, Albertino 116
Myles, Robert 129 n., 132 n., 143 n.

Narcissus 105, 106, 107, 110
Nature (allegorical figure) 5, 7, 84–5,
    91, 109, 110, 111 n., 117–18, 125,
    126, 127, 170, 171, 174, 204, 260,
    280, 283, 287, 289, 305
Nauta, Lodi 105 n., 136 n.
Nepaulsingh, Colbert 65
Nero 5, 165 n.
Newman, Barbara 172 n.
Newson, Elizabeth 232 n.
Nicholas of Lyre 132, 138, 297
Noakes, Susan 276 n.
Nolan, Barbara 12 n.
Nykrog, Per 176, 178, 199

obscenity 1, 5, 21–2, 23–4, 25, 26,
    88–90, 119, 122–3, 124, 156;
    obscenus 91–2
Oenone 38, 165 n.
Ong, Walter 198 n., 199 n.
Oresme, Nicole 266, 269–71, 304 n.
Origen 168 n., 195 n.
Orpheus 16, 117 n., 165–9, 203
Ouy, Gilbert 268 n., 269 n., 314 n.,
    317 n.
Ovid 3, 5 n., 10–14, 27, 28–30, 34,
    35–81, 92, 102, 103, 105, 107–8,
    120, 167, 175 n., 178, 182, 183,
    184, 191, 193, 196, 199, 201, 207,
    210, 234–5, 237–47, 249, 254, 255,
    263, 276, 280, 295; exile 11, 13,
    30, 61, 202 n., 239–40, 239–40,

242–3, 249; WORKS: Amores 12,
    235; Ars amatoria 11, 12 n., 25 n.,
    37, 39, 40, 41, 42–3, 44, 46, 49,
    53 n., 55, 56, 57, 67, 69, 77, 78,
    79–80, 87, 102, 103, 157, 182, 183,
    184, 197, 199, 202, 207, 226, 234,
    239, 241, 242, 243–6, 294, 295;
    Fasti 240; Heroides 12, 38, 43 n.,
    67, 68, 69, 165 n., 220–1, 237–8,
    282, 283, 293–4; Metamorphoses
    11, 12, 35, 36, 37, 63–4, 69, 83,
    110 n., 101, 103, 104, 115, 138,
    166, 182, 215, 239; Remedia amoris
    11, 29, 36, 37, 40, 43, 53 n., 55, 58,
    67, 70, 77, 79, 102, 182, 202, 240,
    242, 243, 295, 304; Tristia 239
Ovide moralisé 90 n., 115, 123 n.,
    215, 240 n.

Pallas 16, 30, 260, 263, 294
Pamphilus 24, 65, 182–4, 196, 197,
    198–9, 200–1, 202, 203
Paris (mythological figure) 16, 56 n.,
    261, 304
Parker, Deborah 317 n.
Parkes, Malcolm 114 n.
pars philosophiae 37 n., 278
passio (mental suffering) 9–10, 54 n.,
    307
Patar, Benoît 271 n.
Pecham, John 5
Pecock, Reginald 315
Pedro de Portugal 316
Pelen, Marc M. 120 n., 178
Penelope 38
Pepin, Ronald E. 95 n., 97 n.
Pérez de Guzmán 316
Pero Díaz de Toledo 297–8
Persius 18, 21, 90, 93 n., 94 n.,
    100 n., 125
persona-theory 3, 20, 27, 59, 109,
    128, 191, 193, 210, 219–26,
    229–32, 283–4
Peter Lombard 302, 315 n.
Peter of Abano 267 n., 271, 272 n.
Peter of Blois 74
Peter of Spain 55 n., 56 n., 79 n., 120,
    141 n., 145, 173, 202 n.
Peter the Venerable 95 n.
Petrarch, Francis 33, 202 n., 318 n.
Petrus Alfonsi 187–8
Phedra 38
Philip of Harvengt 250 n.

Philippe le Bel, king of France 3, 44, 133, 139, 195
Phyllida/Phyllis 38, 165 n.
Physiologus 201
Pierre d'Ailly 233 n.
Pietro Alighieri 71 n., 297
Plato 6, 16, 86, 119, 124, 129, 132, 135, 136 n., 142 n., 231, 286; *Timaeus* 16, 83 n., 124, 128
Plautus 189
Pliny 189
Poirion, Daniel 136 n., 168 n.
Pratt, Karen 212 n.
Priorat, Jean 4 n.
Priscian 51, 143, 270
Proteus 26,
Ptolemy 5, 57
Pygmalion 105, 106–7, 176–7, 259

Quain, E. A. 65 n., 235
querelle de la Rose 28, 76, 98, 112, 146, 148, 172, 209–56, 257
Quilligan, Maureen 217 n.
Quintilian 155–6

Rabanus Maurus 185 n.
Raby, F. J. E. 117 n., 118
Raison (figure in the *Rose*) 9–10, 21, 86, 87–8, 89 n., 90 n., 92, 99, 107, 108, 112, 122–3, 126–8, 130, 136–7, 139, 140–1, 142, 144–6, 152–4, 168 n., 170, 171, 177, 200, 206, 209, 219, 234, 248, 258, 263, 307, 310; (in Machaut) 59
Ralph of Longchamps 20,
Raoul de Presles 268, 269, 271
Remigius of Auxerre 93 n., 272
Renart, Jean 156
Reno, Christine 147–8, 218 n.
Response di Bestiaire, Li 74–6, 81, 191, 192
Reynolds, Suzanne 92, 113
Rhetorica ad Herennium 51
Richard II, king of England 298–9
Richard de Fournival 13–14, 62, 71–6, 184–5, 195, 207; *Bestiaires d'amours* 14, 72–6, 179, 184–92, 201; *Consaus d'amours* 72, 73–4, 185, 196, 279
Richards, Earl Jeffrey 139
Rico, Francisco 65 n.
Ridevall, John 17
Robathan, D. 71 n.
Robert de Sommercote 14

Robertson, D. W. 17, 21, 146, 147 n., 178, 209, 219, 248
Roger de Fournival 71, 195–6
Rolin, Antoine 262 n.
Rolle, Richard 315 n.
Roscelin of Compiègne 172 n., 194 n.
Rossetti, Dante Gabriel 312
Roy, Bruno 41 n., 44 n., 50, 78, 79, 294, 300, 302
Ruiz, Juan 13, 64–71

Sallust 123–4, 128, 131, 228
satire 15, 18–21, 25, 26–7, 90–103, 114, 164; *satirici officium* 25 n., 26, 92
Saturn 16 n., 88, 89, 90 n., 99, 110, 122, 168–9, 206 n., 259, 285, 303 n.
Savonarola, Girolamo 116
Scholia Pseudoacronis on Horace 98
Schotter, Ann 198
Scipio Africanus (the younger) 7, 8
Sedgwick, Eve Kosofsky 201 n., 205
Seneca 5, 165 n., 238, 239, 317
sensus litteralis and literalism 19, 20, 85–7, 89–90, 105–6, 114, 135, 136, 140, 203, 204, 283–5, 286, 306
sermon-prologue 62, 63–4, 71
Servius 17, 220
Sewell, George 29, 202–3
Sherman, C. R. 304 n.
Silk, E. T. 129 n., 221 n.
Simon de Hesdin 268
Smalley, Beryl 63, 138 n.
Socrates 181–1
Solterer, Helen 167 n., 186
Solomon 222, 223, 247, 248, 249–50, 253, 254 n.
speculative grammar 5
Statius 275, 276
Stillinger, Thomas C. 273 n., 277 n.
Strossen, Nadine 147 n.

Tarrant, R. J. 45 n.
Taylor, P. B. 129 n.
Tempier, Stephen, Bishop of Paris 8–9
Terence 3, 169 n., 178
Theophrastus 99, 213
Thierry of Chartres 50–1
Thomas, Antoine 278 n., 316–17
Thomas of Chobham 134
Thomas of Ireland 216
titulus 37 n., 49, 246
tragedy 19, 20, 165, 220

Trevet, Nicholas 129–30, 135–6, 299, 301
Trevisa, John 299
Tristran 176
Tweede Rose 258 n.

Ullman, P. L. 65
Ulysses 19 n.
utilitas 24, 28, 37, 50, 68, 92, 235, 236, 237, 238–9, 278, 282, 283, 293, 294, 313

Valerius Maximus 268
Vance, Eugene 143 n.
Vasvàri, Louise O. 188 n.
Vatican Mythographers, the 17
Vegetius 3–4, 299
Vellutello, Alessandro 318
Venus 16, 18, 23, 30, 56 n., 80, 88, 104, 105, 108, 169, 182, 183, 205, 206, 260, 280, 294, 305, 306, 311 n.
Vetula, De 14, 30 n., 58–9, 70, 71, 127 n., 175 n., 184–5, 195, 202 n., 207
Villon, François 123 n.
Vincent of Beauvais 121 n.
Vineis, E. 144 n.
Viola 180, 182
Virgil: *Aeneid* 16, 17, 32, 74, 83, 92, 104, 120, 220, 236, 250 n., 254 n., 275, 282, 296, 317
Vielle, La (figure in the *Rose*) 21, 23, 86, 96, 108, 127 n., 165 n., 183, 219, 226
Vincent of Beauvais 84–5
Vital of Blois 179–80
Vulcan 310–1 n.

'Vulgate' commentary on Ovid's *Metamorphoses* 36–7, 83 n., 166–7
Wack, Mary 54, 56 n.
Wailes, Stephen L. 181 n.
Waleys, Thomas 249, 271
Wallace, David 298 n.
Walter of Châtillon 94, 96
Walton, John 299
Watson, Nicholas 315
Watt, J. A. 133 n.
Weiss, Julian 272 n., 296 n., 297
Wetherbee, Winthrop 86
Wheeler, Bonnie 201 n.
Wheteley, William 301
Willard, C. C. 271 n.
William of Aragon 105, 221, 270
William of Conches 51, 82, 92, 96, 98, 100 n., 104–5, 117 n., 121, 136 n., 168, 169, 270
William of Ockham 132, 134–5, 139 n.
William of Orléans 36, 38, 49
William of Saint-Amour 2–3
William of Saint-Thierry 28 n., 206 n., 250 n.
William of Sherwood 120, 141 n.
Williams, Bernard 232 n., 233
Woods, Marjorie Curry 198, 200, 203
Wyclif, John 137–8, 315 n.
Yeats, W. B. 118
youth 48, 55–61, 199, 245, 253, 258
Zahareas, Anthony N. 66 n.
Zeeman, Nicolette 17 n., 142 n.
Ziolkowski, Jan. M. 127 n., 152 n., 156 n., 289 n.